A GRAMMAR

OF

Present-Day English

SECOND EDITION

R. W. Pence
DEPAUW UNIVERSITY

D. W. Emery
UNIVERSITY OF WASHINGTON

THE MACMILLAN COMPANY, NEW YORK
COLLIER-MACMILLAN LIMITED, LONDON

Library of Congress catalog card number: 63-7476

The Macmillan Company, New York
Collier-Macmillan Canada, Ltd., Toronto, Ontario

Printed in the United States of America

PREFACE to the Second Edition

In the preparation of the second edition of A *Grammar of Present-Day English* the authors have kept in mind the fact that the approach to English language study expressed in the preface to the original edition has filled the needs of thousands of users. The new edition, therefore, offers no really radical changes. The purpose of the book is still the same: to give an orderly presentation of how words behave when they are put together to make present-day English sentences. As with the original edition, it attempts no historical or comparative grammar. Similarly, the scope of the book precludes treatments of phonology and dialectology, exclusions which in no way are intended to minimize the great importance of these areas of linguistic study.

Although the larger units of the second edition follow the organizational pattern of the original, some rearrangements of parts have been made within the chapters. These changes have been designed, in the main, to reduce the number of subheadings and classifications. Although no essential material has been deleted, the ordering of the parts within some of the chapters has been tightened in the hope that the efficiency and manageability of the book as a teaching text will be enhanced.

Discussions of matters of usage, in both editions of A *Grammar of Present-Day English*, are limited to the common morphological and syntactic items which bring up problems of word choice for many a writer of English. In the new edition some usage problems have been restated to reflect, insofar as it is possible, the present-day practices followed by writers of serious English.

These revisions follow the helpful suggestions made by many college teachers who have used the book with their students. At the same time, the authors have not forgotten how heavily users of the original edition have relied on it for reference purposes. They have studied every change very carefully to make certain that this important and proven function of the book will not be lessened.

R. W. P.
D. W. E.

A decade or so ago it was the educational fad to maintain that the formal study of English grammar had little or no place in the curricula of our public school system. But today we are beginning to see the error of our ways. In throwing out the bathwater of some bad practices in the teaching of grammar we found that unwittingly we had thrown out the baby too. The result of this folly is that today we have a large group of young people who have not the slightest notion of any systematic understanding of the workings of their Mother Tongue. But even more alarming is the fact that we also have a large number of teachers who, growing up during the heyday of the mistaken notion, are themselves ill equipped to do much about restoring such a study to its rightful place in our educational system.

Fortunately, many of our colleges and universities, and especially our teachers' colleges, are trying to remedy the difficulty by installing courses in formal English grammar.[1] Present-day students need a book that will be so explicit that it may seem very elementary to him who chances to be well trained in grammar. They need a book so complete that it may serve as a reference book after it has filled its original function as a classroom text. The present volume attempts to meet just such needs.

During the period when the study of grammar almost ceased to exist in elementary schools and high schools, many fallacious notions were evolved to justify its banishment. Hence, it may be worth while to point out, first, what grammar does not pretend to accomplish and then, second, what a systematic study of the subject actually is and what values it may have.

First, grammar is *not* a set of rules thought up by and imposed by some invisible godlike creature. It is not a listing of the possible ways in which the unwary may blunder when he opens his mouth or takes pencil in hand. It is not something with which the erudite try to frighten the less informed. Grammar is merely the record of how words behave when they are put together to make sentences.

Second, a knowledge of grammar does *not* in itself guarantee that even the serious-minded student will thereby become a master of correct English. One can know all about grammar and still make stupid blunders, just as one may know nothing of the technique of the subject and

---

[1] And such courses are certainly being enthusiastically welcomed by our teachers of foreign languages.

yet never make a mistake. Indeed, a *formal* study of grammar would certainly be an inefficient means by which to learn how to avoid errors.

Third, a knowledge of grammar does *not* insure that one's composition will be effective, though such a knowledge will give its possessor reliable means by which he may attain an effectiveness in the use of language that might very well otherwise be denied him.

Finally, the study of grammar is *not* an end in itself. It can be an indispensable means to an enriched knowledge of the English language and of its infinite variety of resources that one may make use of as he tries to transmit a thought.

Let us now note briefly what grammar is and what values it may have for the average intelligent person.

Formal grammar is merely a *systematic* study of how words work in sentences. Instead of being a mass of important and unimportant facts about language, as some people seem to think, formal grammar is merely an *orderly* presentation of what goes on when sentences are formed— that is, a presentation that has the same logical relation of its parts that one demands when he studies any other subject of human interest— chemistry or political science, for instance. We all know from experience that we can grasp ideas much more readily when they have been organized according to some logical pattern than we can when they are thrust at us without any organization.

When through an orderly account one has learned how words work in sentences, he no longer has to depend on any rule in a given situation. His knowledge will provide him the means by which he may exercise his judgment as to what is good, what is better, what is best. He is in a position to choose among a wide range of locutions the one that represents his thought most accurately and most effectively. Hence, he will have a far larger number of linguistic resources at his disposal than he who has no such systematized knowledge. His knowledge of grammar can help him criticize and evaluate sentences already formed and to fashion more effective sentences when he sets out to compose them. In other words, through such a study he can hope eventually to emancipate himself from slavery to this or to any other book. For he will have discovered that grammar does not create sentences; it merely attempts to guide him as he makes them.

Finally, it is reasonable to hope that the study of formal grammar can have a cultural value. For surely any intelligent person ought to have an overwhelming curiosity as to the whys and wherefores of that which he uses every day of his life more often than he uses any other one thing—namely, his Mother Tongue.

Of a number of things which could be cited that brought the study of grammar into disrepute, one would be the vast confusion, utterly needless confusion, that arose from the multiplying of names for basic grammatical constructions. It seemed that every writer of a treatise on grammar felt that, in order to justify the publication of his new book, he must invent an entirely new set of names for old, old constructions. (See pp. 20 ff. for a list of some of the commoner variations in nomenclature.) No wonder the average student gave up the whole subject in despair. The present volume has used the names that are likely to be most familiar to the ordinary user.

There is nothing very revolutionary about this book. It is designed to be as practical as its subject will permit. It concerns itself with neither the theory nor the history of grammar and grammatical constructions. There are already excellent books on such aspects, notably Curme's *Syntax*. It does attempt to do just one thing—set up for the user a simple system by means of which he may intelligently interpret for himself what happens when words get together to form sentences. No *simple* system could possibly be devised that would cover every linguistic situation. What Mr. C. H. Ward has to say about definitions (see p. 3) might be paraphrased to read:

> Statements regarding constructions are provisional, are mere statements of what is typical and usual; they are not, cannot be, all-inclusive containers of the full truth about constructions. These statements are only a convenience; exceptions and anomalies will crop up later. No statement in this book is an eternal truth; it is a preliminary and partial explanation of what is characteristic.

This book inverts the usual order and places the section on constructions (that is, syntax) first, with the section on forms and usages following. It has been found through long experience that if a student once gains a mastery of the basic constructions of sentences, he is likely then to become much more interested in forms and usages and to be able to make a much more intelligent study of them than would be the case if the usual order were followed. Too often the student who is first put to work on forms is so bogged down in the welter of relatively uninteresting details that he has little enthusiasm left for that aspect of grammar which could be of assistance to him in building accurate and effective sentences.

Because this book is intended for him who has little or no previous experience with a study of formal grammar, it is very explicit and very detailed (and at times undoubtedly very dogmatic) in its explanations. It will be noted that examples are far more abundant and are much more fully explained than is usually the case in such a book. Examples of constructions have not merely been placed on the page and left there: they have been, in each instance, explained in detail. In fact, it is the wealth of examples, with their full explanations, that goes far in justifying this new treatment of a very old subject. For the book is first of all and above all directed to the learner.

The author believes that a simply constructed diagram is the most efficient method, many times, of making clear to oneself how a given expression works in a given sentence. A diagram is the same kind of means to an end as a map in a history book or a chart in a laboratory manual. For those who feel as the author does, there is a section in which the sentences used earlier as illustrative material have been diagrammed (see pp. 367 ff.). This section has been placed at the end of the book for those who wish it. Thus the diagram need not annoy anyone who may feel that it is too mechanical and arbitrary a device with which to represent as artistic and illusive a thing as the English sentence.

But one cannot come to a genuine mastery of English grammar by merely reading about grammar. He must go to work on the subject on his own to make it really his. Hence, there are exercises scattered through the book, so that he may see first-hand how words actually do work in sentences.

If, then, this book will introduce the student to a simple system by means of which he may come to some comprehension of how words work in an English sentence; if it will provide him with a body of fact on the basis of which he may make intelligent decisions regarding correct and effective discourse; if it will serve as a convenient reference book until with his advancing knowledge of the language he becomes his own reference book, it will have reached the goal its author originally set for it.

The author's indebtedness to many can be merely suggested here. There are those who have used parts of the book in mimeographed form in their classes; those who have sat in the author's courses in grammar in his own institution and in the State College of Washington, where he has been a member of the summer faculty on several occasions; the author's colleagues—especially Professors Virginia A. Harlow, Edna Taylor, and Jerome C. Hixson. His thanks go to them, and to many others, for valuable suggestions. But, as final decisions had to be his, his must be the responsibility for all shortcomings.

R. W. P.

Greencastle, Indiana

TABLE OF CONTENTS

PREFACE *to the Second Edition*   iii

PREFACE *to the First Edition*   iv

Part One   Syntax

1. Definitions   3
   A. *Grammar*   3
   B. *The Sentence*   3
   C. *Parts of Speech*   5
   D. *Shifts*   8
   E. *The Sentence Again*   8
   F. *Clause and Phrase*   12
   G. *Main and Subordinate Clauses*   13
   H. *Compound Expressions*   14
   I. *Grammatical Types of Sentences*   16
   J. *Rhetorical Types of Sentences*   19
   K. *Equivalent Names for Grammatical Terms*   20
   EXERCISES   22

2. Functions of the Parts of Speech in a Sentence   33
   A. *Nouns and Pronouns (Substantives)*   33
       EXERCISES   38
   B. *Verbs*   39
       EXERCISES   76
   C. *Adjectives*   87
       EXERCISES   96

D. *Adverbs*   98
   EXERCISES   109
E. *Prepositions*   111
   EXERCISES   122
F. *Conjunctions*   123
   EXERCISES   132

3. Shifts, Absolute Constructions, Expletives,
     Ellipsis, and Inverted Order   134
A. *Shifts*   134
   EXERCISES   137
B. *Absolute Constructions*   138
   EXERCISES   143
C. *Expletives*   144
   EXERCISES   150
D. *Ellipsis*   151
   EXERCISES   155
E. *Inverted Order*   156
   EXERCISES   158

4. The Grammar of Subordinate Clauses   160
A. *Noun (Substantive) Clauses*   161
   EXERCISES   168
B. *Adjectival Clauses*   169
   EXERCISES   177
C. *Adverbial Clauses*   179
   EXERCISES   190

Part Two   Form and Usages

5. Nouns   199
A. *Classes of Nouns*   199
B. *Properties of Nouns*   201

6. Pronouns   218
  A. *Classes of Pronouns*   218
  B. *Agreement*   234

7. Verbs   247
  A. *Definitions*   247
  B. *Properties of Verbs*   tense sequence   247
  C. *Auxiliaries*   275
  D. *Inflections*   284
  E. *Verbals*   303

8. Adjectives   322
  A. *Classes of Adjectives*   322
  B. *Expressions Used as Adjectives*   325
  C. *Comparison of Adjectives*   327
  D. *Usages in Adjectives*   330

9. Adverbs   337
  A. *Kinds of Adverbs*   337
  B. *Meanings of Adverbs*   337
  C. *Forms of Adverbs*   339
  D. *Comparison of Adverbs*   340
  E. *Usages in Adverbs*   342

10. Prepositions   344
  A. *Kinds of Prepositions*   344
  B. *Usages in Prepositions*   345

11. Conjunctions   354
  A. *Kinds*   354
  B. *Meanings of Conjunctions*   357
  C. *Usages in Conjunctions*   357

12. Interjections   365
  Usages in O and Oh   365

Appendix: Diagramming

The Diagram in Grammatical Analysis   369

1. *Simple Sentence*   370
2. *Compound Subjects, Verbs, and Modifiers*   371
3. *Complements of Transitive Verbs*   372
4. *Complements of Intransitive Verbs*   374
5. *Participle*   376
6. *Gerund*   377
7. *Infinitive*   379
8. *Connectives between Coordinate Elements of a Sentence*   389
9. *Connectives Introducing Subordinate Clauses*   391
10. *Noun Clauses*   397
11. *Adjective Clauses*   402
12. *Adverbial Clauses*   407
13. *Shifts*   411
14. *Absolute Constructions*   412
15. *Expletives*   415
16. *Ellipsis*   420
17. *Loose Modifiers*   424
18. *Inverted Order*   425
    INDEX   427

PART One

SYNTAX

CHAPTER I

Definitions[1]

A. *Grammar*

Grammar is the science of language that treats of the constructions, forms, and usages of words. That aspect of grammar which deals with constructions of words in sentences is called syntax. Grammar also concerns itself with the forms of words (sometimes called accidence) and usages. We shall first of all try to familiarize ourselves with matters of syntax; then we shall be able to approach the problems of forms and usages.

B. *The Sentence*

Inasmuch as syntax has to do with the *relationship of words in sentences*, initially we need to know, at least in a general way, what a sentence is. Further, we shall find that we cannot get very far in applying our knowledge to the problems of composition, written and spoken, unless we understand what a sentence is and how it works. For the sentence is the basic unit of discourse; hence, it is the basic unit for the study of syntax.

---

[1] "Definitions in grammar are provisional, are mere statements of what is typical and usual; they are not, they cannot be, all-inclusive containers of the full truth about the parts of speech. . . . A definition is only a convenience . . . exceptions and anomalies will crop out later. . . . A definition is not an eternal truth. It is a preliminary and partial statement of what is characteristic." —C. H. Ward, *Grammar in Composition* (Chicago: Scott, Foresman and Company, 1933), p. 145.

We may start by saying that a sentence is a group of words that makes a complete statement of some kind. Probably this will become clearer if we examine groups of words to see how some of them make statements, whereas others do not. "It is raining," "Jim became homesick," and "The sun is setting in the west" make statements; that is, each one is a grammatically complete sentence. But "to make a long story short," "when the postman arrives," "in fighting the high cost of living," and "because he couldn't see the road" leave us wondering in each case what the complete idea was that we were supposed to gather. That is, these groups do not make statements; hence, they are not sentences. No one of them satisfies the demand that a thought be complete. For our immediate purpose, then, we may define a sentence thus:

A sentence is a group of words that expresses a complete thought.

From the point of view of grammar, a group of words, if it is to express a complete thought, must contain a subject and a predicate—something talked about and some declaration made about that "something." (These two indispensable components of a grammatically complete sentence will be discussed shortly; see pp. 8 ff.)

The important thing here is that we develop a clear perception of the difference between groups of words that are grammatically complete sentences and those groups that are only fragments of sentences. For until we perceive this difference, it is futile to proceed to any other matter of grammar, inasmuch as that aspect of grammar we are now studying has to do with the relationship of words in *sentences*.[2]

[2] It is true that experienced writers frequently use fragments of sentences as the rhetorical equivalent of complete sentences and begin such fragments with capitals and end them with periods. But our immediate problem is to comprehend what is meant *grammatically* by the term "sentence." And such fragments are not, from a grammatical point of view, sentences. We may call them rhetorical sentences. That is, for the intended reader or listener, who readily fills in the ellipsis involved (see pp. 151 ff. for Ellipsis), these fragments of sentences become in meaning the equivalent of grammatically complete sentences.

The words that make up a sentence (and from now on when we use the term "sentence" we shall mean a group of words that is complete from a grammatical point of view) have various functions to perform; and on the basis of these functions words are classed as "parts of speech." Hence, it will be well for us at this point to have brief working definitions of these parts of speech, seven in number.[3] Do not be disturbed if these brief definitions fail to bring to you a full comprehension immediately. For we shall continue to add information about each one of these parts of speech as we go along until full comprehension shall have been attained.

From the brief definitions that follow we may see that the parts of speech fall into four groups:

1. Nouns and pronouns (conveniently called substantives), which name;
2. Adjectives and adverbs, which qualify;
3. Verbs, which assert;
4. Prepositions and conjunctions, which connect.[4]

c. *Parts of Speech*[5]

1. NOUN

A noun is the name of anything: *boy, Mary, loveliness, sun, alacrity.* (Inasmuch as a noun is the name of anything that may be the subject of discourse, by an extension of this definition phrases and clauses may function as nouns. See pp. 161 ff.)

---

[3] The interjection is frequently included as an eighth part of speech. (See p. 7.)

[4] Or, we might just as readily group them in this fashion:
I. Nouns and pronouns (substantives) and adjectives (qualifiers of substantives);
II. Verbs and adverbs (qualifiers of verbs);
III. Prepositions and conjunctions (connectives).

[5] Note that these definitions designate *functions* that words have in sentences. It is fair to say that words belong to no part of speech until they are used in sentences.

2. PRONOUN

A pronoun is a word that is used as a substitute for a noun: *he, she, it, which, that, these.*

John took out the coat and hat *that he* had so carefully put away in *his* closet the night before.

3. VERB

A verb is a word (or phrase) that expresses action (Birds *fly*), being (I *am*), or state of being or occurrence (I *become*; he *seems*; she *died*). (For various kinds of verbs see pp. 56 ff.)

4. ADJECTIVE

An adjective is a word that describes (that is, modifies) a noun: *pretty* girl; *dusty* road; *sunshiny* day; *great* excitement. The articles, *a, an,* and *the,* are regarded as adjectives.

I maintained *a steady* pace.
He is *a* child.
He is *an intelligent* child.

NOTE.   The term "modify" in grammar means "to qualify, limit, or restrict." That is, a modifier usually narrows the conception of the thing modified. *Blue sky* is a narrower conception than *sky; unruly children* is a narrower conception than *children; she danced gracefully* is a narrower conception than *she danced.* Anything, then, that limits, restricts, or qualifies—that is, narrows the conception of—an expression is grammatically a modifier.

5. ADVERB

An adverb is a word that describes or modifies a verb, an adjective, or another adverb: work *hard;* drive *carefully; too* ill; drive *very* carefully.

He will come *soon.* [An adverb modifying the verb *will come*]
He will come *very* soon. [An adverb modifying the adverb *soon* (which in turn modifies *will come*)]
She is *extremely* patient. [An adverb modifying the adjective *patient*]

6.   PREPOSITION

A preposition is a word used with a substantive (that is, a noun or a pronoun), called its object, to form a phrase, called a prepositional phrase: "*in* the dark," "*up* the stairs," "*across* the street," "*without* a doubt," "*toward* me." (The functions of prepositional phrases will be discussed later; see pp. 116 ff.)

7.   CONJUNCTION

A conjunction is a word that joins one element in a sentence to another. A conjunction may join words, phrases, clauses, or whole statements. A conjunction that joins elements that are grammatically equal is called a coordinating conjunction. A conjunction that joins an element of less grammatical importance (such as a subordinate clause) to an element of greater grammatical importance (such as a main clause) is called a subordinating conjunction.

Frank *and* Henry are brothers. [The coordinating conjunction *and* joins two nouns, *Frank* and *Henry*.]
Up hill *and* down dale they went. [The coordinating conjunction *and* joins two phrases, *up hill* and *down dale*.]
The wind blew *and* the rain fell. [The coordinating conjunction *and* joins two clauses, *The wind blew* and *the rain fell*.]
Jim may come *if* he secures his furlough. [The subordinating conjunction *if* joins the subordinate clause *he secures his furlough* to the main clause *Jim may come*.]

8.   INTERJECTION

An interjection is an exclamatory word that usually expresses strong emotion: *Ah! Alas! Oh!* An interjection has little or no grammatical function in a sentence; in fact, an interjection is often written as if it were a complete sentence.

Heavens! What a mess!

Expletives
p. 144

D.   *Shifts*

As will be seen later (pp. 134 ff.), words in English easily cross from one part of speech to another. In fact, this shift of a word from a customary part of speech to another part of speech has been one of the characteristic methods of growth in the English language. When the dictionary lists a word as a noun or a verb or an adjective, it is merely recording the *customary* function of the word in a sentence. For, actually, a given word does not belong to any part of speech until it is used in a sentence.

The ball went *over* the fence. [Preposition]
His joke did not go *over*. [Adverb]
The first term is nearly *over*. [Adjective]
He is sitting *in* the sun. [Preposition]
Walk *in*, please. [Adverb]
You work too *hard*. [Adverb]
You are a *hard* worker. [Adjective]
The raccoon ran up a *tree*. [Noun]
Please show me a *tree* toad. [Adjective]
My dog can *tree* a raccoon any night. [Verb]
That typewriter belongs to me. [Adjective]
That is my typewriter. [Pronoun]
I know *that* the typewriter is mine. [Conjunction]
I never saw the *like* of it before. [Noun]
Your raincoat does not look *like* mine. [Preposition]
Do you *like* to read stage plays? [Verb]

E.   *The Sentence Again*

1.   SUBJECT AND PREDICATE

We defined a sentence as a group of words expressing a complete thought (p. 4). If we examine groups of words that meet our test for a sentence, we shall find that in every case there are two characteristic parts: first, there is something talked about; second, there is some declaration made about this "something." The first is called the subject; the second is called the predicate. The subject is a substantive — a noun or anything (such as a pronoun, a phrase, or a clause) that functions like a noun. The main element (sometimes the only element) of a predicate is a verb. We cannot have a grammatically complete sentence, then, without having these two essential ingredients — a subject and a predicate. But this must not lead us to the erroneous conclusion that every group of words containing a subject and a predicate is by that fact a sentence. For if we will examine the groups listed above (p. 4) that we agreed were not sentences, we shall note that some of them contain subjects and predicates — "When the mailman arrives," "Because we couldn't see the road" — and yet do not meet our test for a sentence. These groups, which are called subordinate clauses, will be discussed later (see pp. 13 f.).

a. Subject. First, then, in a sentence there must be something talked about, which we call the subject. This subject is expressed by a word, or a group of words, that functions as a noun.

> The *sky* is blue. [Single word as subject]
> *To go now* is impossible. [Group of words functioning as a subject]
> *That we shall have some opposition* is to be expected. [Group of words functioning as a subject]

b. Predicate. The second requisite, if a group of words is to be a sentence, is some declaration about the subject. Such a declaration is called the predicate. Sometimes a single word, called a verb, can become a predicate ("Birds *fly*"). But more often than not this single word (or word group), called a verb, is not sufficient; something is required to complete the predication that it, the verb, has merely begun. Thus a predicate is often made up of a verb plus what is called a complement, something that completes the verb (hence the spelling *compl-e-ment*). (We shall discuss shortly the various kinds of complements that verbs may demand; see pp. 45 ff.) But

verb must be inflected, personal endings must be finite verb

whether or not the verb requires something to complete the predication that it has begun, the verb plus any such helpers becomes the predicate of the sentence.

The wind blew. [*Blew* a verb, is the predicate.]

They hoisted the Stars and Stripes. [*Hoisted*, a verb, with its complement, *Stars and Stripes*, is the predicate.]

We became greatly alarmed. [*Became*, a verb, and its complement, *alarmed*, with its modifier *greatly*, make up the predicate.]

After the dance we thanked our hostess and returned home. [The predicate in this sentence includes every word except the subject *we*. Notice that part of the predicate may precede the subject.]

A predicate is, then, the second requisite if a group of words is to become a sentence.

c. *Modifiers.* If we look back over some of the sentences that have been used as illustrative material, we shall find that while a subject and a predicate are indispensable to a sentence, more often than not a sentence contains something besides, something that upon examination proves to be an elaboration, a limitation, or a qualification of the subject or of the predicate. Anything that elaborates, limits, or qualifies another sentence unit, such as a subject or verb or complement, is called a "modifier."

We saw from our brief definitions above (p. 6) that anything that modifies a noun is an adjective in function and that anything that modifies a verb is an adverb in function. Hence, it should be clear that many of the words in a sentence are adjectival or adverbial modifiers. As we shall see later, these adjectival and adverbial modifiers may be single words, or they may be groups of words (phrases and clauses).

d. *Three major groups — subject, predicate, modifiers.* It is evident, then, that a sentence is composed of two absolutely indispensable parts — a subject and a predicate — and usually, but not necessarily, of a third — modifiers, which may belong to either the subject or the predicate. In fact, we may say that a subject, a predicate, and modifiers constitute nearly all of the grammar of any group of words making a sentence. (There are, to be sure, a few odds and ends — expletives, particles of various kinds — that we do not need to bother with at this point.)

A simple outline may help make evident the basic grammar of a sentence.

A SENTENCE

99·44% {
I. Subject (indispensable)
II. Predicate (indispensable)
   A. Verb (indispensable)
   B. Complement (often demanded but not always)
III. Modifiers of either subject or of predicate (not indispensable but usually present)

·56% { IV. Odds and ends (may be disregarded at this stage)

Or, we may regard a sentence from another point of view and see that it is divided into two great parts — the subject with such modifiers as may be attached to it, and the predicate with such modifiers as may be attached to it. The essential subject is the subject without any modifiers; the essential predicate is the verb plus any required complements without any modifiers of the verb or of the complements. The complete subject is the essential subject plus all the modifiers attached to it; the complete predicate is the essential predicate plus all the modifiers attached to the verb and to its complements.[6] Hence, everything that appears in a sentence is a part of a complete subject or of a complete predicate. Or, to restate the matter in another way, we may say that from the point of view of its grammatical structure a sentence falls into two distinct parts — a complete subject and a complete predicate.

Little birds that nest in the north in the summertime fly south when the cold winds begin to blow. [*Birds* is the essential subject; *fly* is the essential predicate. *Little birds that nest in the north in*

[6] Sometimes the term "simple predicate" is used to designate the verb of the predicate taken by itself. But the term seems to have little real value. Hence, this book has preferred to use the terms "essential subject" and "essential predicate" and define them as here.

the summertime is the complete subject; *fly south when the cold winds begin to blow* is the complete predicate.]

The office workers of the zinc mill gave their very efficient sales manager a handsome gold watch when he left them. [*Workers* is the essential subject; *gave manager watch* is the essential predicate. *The office workers of the zinc mill* is the complete subject; *gave their very efficient sales manager a handsome gold watch when he left them* is the complete predicate.]

The new Methodist church is remarkably beautiful in the simplicity of its architecture. [*Church* is the essential subject; *is beautiful* is the essential predicate. *The new Methodist church* is the complete subject; *is remarkably beautiful in the simplicity of its architecture* is the complete predicate.]

F.   Clause and Phrase

It will be of help if we have convenient terms with which to designate groups of related words that contain subjects and predicates and groups that do not contain subjects and predicates. To the first is applied the term "clause"; to the second the term "phrase." We may define the two thus:

A clause is a group of related words containing a subject and a predicate. (finite verb)

Note that what characterizes a clause is solely the presence of a subject and a predicate. (See pp. 13 f. for the difference between a clause that expresses a complete thought and a clause that does not express a complete thought.)

It is raining.
. . . when the clock strikes four . . .
Mac was surprised . . .
Since Alice left . . .

A phrase is a group of related words not containing a subject and a predicate.

The principal kinds of phrases are prepositional phrases (see pp. 111 ff.) and verbal phrases (participial, gerund, and infinitive phrases; see pp. 58 ff.). But any group of two or more related words constitutes a phrase. Hence, we have such phrases as verb phrases (a principal verb and its auxiliaries: He *has been promoted*), phrasal prepositions (*in accordance with*), and phrasal conjunctions (*in order that*), all of which will be discussed in due time.

> . . . in the morning . . .
> . . . at ten o'clock . . .
> Coming down the street . . .
> . . . to have seen such a sight . . .
> After mailing your complaint . . .
> It being a nice day . . .

Inasmuch as a phrase never contains a subject and a predicate, a phrase can never express a complete thought; hence, a phrase normally does not stand by itself with a capital at the beginning and a period at the end. Ability to distinguish between phrases and clauses is important. The principal thing to remember here is that a phrase never contains a subject and a predicate, that a clause always contains both; that some clauses express complete thoughts and can stand by themselves and other clauses do not express complete thoughts and so cannot stand by themselves.

G.   *Main and Subordinate Clauses*

Some groups of related words containing a subject and a predicate express complete thoughts and so can stand by themselves with capitals at the beginning and periods at the end. Such groups are called main (or independent or principal) clauses. Other groups of related words may contain subjects and predicates and yet not express complete thoughts. Such groups, which normally do not stand by themselves with capitals at the beginning and periods at the end, are called subordinate (or dependent) clauses. Hence, our definitions may be framed thus:

> *A main clause is any group of related words containing a subject and a predicate and expressing a complete thought — one that may stand as a complete sentence, with a capital at the beginning and a period at the end.*

Birds fly. It is raining. Ice is cold. Dogs bark.

The man holding up his hand is trying to quiet the people milling around at the entrance to the stadium.

> *A subordinate clause is any group of related words containing a subject and a predicate but not expressing a complete thought — one that cannot stand as a complete sentence with a capital at the beginning and a period at the end.*[7]

A subordinate clause will be introduced by some kind of expression, stated or implied, that makes clear its subordinate character (see also pp. 160 ff.).

when we were very young	*if* it doesn't rain
because my watch was slow	*who* wrote *Barchester Towers*
so that I had to walk fast	*that* James might have a chance

The ability to distinguish between (*a*) clauses that express complete thoughts and so are main clauses, and (*b*) clauses that do not express complete thoughts and so are subordinate clauses, is basic to any further consideration of grammar. It is likewise basic to any real understanding of the art of effective expression.

H.   Compound Expressions

Compounding (from the Latin *componere*, "to place together") is making a unit of two or more expressions that are alike in rank and function. The elements so joined are said to be coordinate. Usually they are joined by coordinating conjunctions (see pp. 123 f.). Almost any element of a sentence

---

[7] We shall see later (pp. 161 ff.) that every subordinate clause is a noun, an adjective, or an adverb in function.

may appear as a coordinate unit—subjects, verbs, modifiers, complements, phrases, and clauses.

For diagrams of compound units see pp. 389 ff.

1. SUBJECTS, VERBS, AND COMPLEMENTS COMPOUNDED

Mr. Adams and Mr. Jones own and operate a grocery store and a lumber mill. [*Mr. Adams* and *Mr. Jones* are compounded as the subject of the compounded verb *own* and *operate;* and *grocery store* and *lumber mill* are compounded as the object of *own* and *operate.*]

2. ADJECTIVES AND ADVERBS COMPOUNDED

The shy and timid animal approached the food hesitatingly and even fearfully. [The adjectives *shy* and *timid* are compounded as an adjectival modifier of *animal;* and *hesitatingly·*and *even fearfully* are compounded as an adverbial modifier of *approached.*]

3. PHRASES COMPOUNDED

Jane ran into the house and up the stairs. [The prepositional phrases *into the house* and *up the stairs* are compounded as an adverbial modifier of *ran.*]

He likes best to eat and to sleep. [The infinitive phrases *to eat* and *to sleep* are compounded as the direct object of *likes.*]

Eating your cake and having it too is not possible in this life. [The gerund phrases *Eating your cake* and *having it too* are compounded as the subject of *is.*]

The man standing on the corner and waving his arms is Mr. Simmons. [The participial phrases *standing on the corner* and *waving his arms* are compounded as an adjectival modifier of *man.*]

4. CLAUSES COMPOUNDED

If it doesn't rain and if it doesn't seem too cold we can have our picnic on the lawn. [*If it doesn't rain* and *if it doesn't seem too cold,* subordinate clauses, are compounded; the unit functions as an adverbial modifier of *can have.*]

Mary cleared away the dishes, I started to mow the lawn, and Mother went to do the marketing. [*Mary cleared away the dishes,*

I started to mow the lawn, and *Mother went to do the marketing,* main clauses, are compounded.]

I haven't a cent in cash; hence, I must get a check cashed. [*I haven't a cent in cash* and *I must get a check cashed,* main clauses, are compounded. (For the use of the transitional adverb *hence,* see pp. 105 f.)]

I.   *Grammatical Types of Sentences*

On the basis of the kind of main or subordinate clauses, or both, that enter into a sentence, sentences are classed as simple, compound, and complex.

1.   SIMPLE SENTENCE

Sometimes a single clause can express a complete thought (with. a capital at the beginning and a period at the end). A sentence made up of such a clause, no matter how long or short it may be, is called a simple sentence. Our definition may be framed thus:

> A *simple sentence is a sentence made up of a single clause that expresses a complete thought.*

Birds fly..

Tossing away his cigarette, he strode briskly through the open door into the office at the end of the hall.

2.   COMPOUND SENTENCE

Sometimes a sentence is composed of two or more clauses each of which is an independent statement. A sentence made up of two or more main clauses is called a compound sentence. Any one or all of the main clauses making up a compound sentence may be modified by subordinate clauses. But if the whole sentence has as a minimum at least two main clauses it is called a compound sentence. We may now frame our definition thus:

> A *compound sentence is any sentence that contains at least two main clauses.*

Birds fly, but fish swim. [*Birds fly* is one main clause; *fish swim* is another.]

A car that runs only when it feels like it is a nuisance; but a car that runs whether it rains or shines is a joy. [*A car . . . is a nuisance* is one main clause; *a car . . . is a joy* is another main clause; *when it feels like it* and *that runs* and *whether it rains or shines* are all subordinate clauses.]

The clauses of a compound sentence may (*a*) have no word connecting them; (*b*) have a coordinating conjunction; (*c*) have a transitional adverb (see pp. 105 f.). (For the punctuation between the clauses of a compound sentence, see p. 105, *Note*.)

You stay here; I'll go in search of him. [No connective]

You stay here, *and* I'll go in search of him. [Coordinating conjunction]

You stay here; *however*, I'll go in search of him. [Transitional adverb]

NOTE. It may be well to point out again that either of the indispensable elements of a sentence (the subject or the predicate) or both may be compounded (See also pp. 14 f.)

Whether a subject or a predicate is compounded has nothing to do with whether a sentence is simple, compound, or complex. In the simple sentence *Jack and Jill came up the hill* the subject, composed of *Jack* and *Jill*, is said to be compounded. In the simple sentence *Birds fly and sing* the predicate composed of *fly* and *sing* is said to be compounded. No matter whether a subject or a predicate (or both) is compounded, a sentence is not a compound sentence unless there are present in it at least two independent clauses, each with its own subject (which may be compounded) and with its own predicate (which may be compounded).

Jack and Jill came up the hill. [Simple sentence with a compound subject]

Jack came up the hill and went down again. [Simple sentence with a compound predicate]

Jack and Jill came up the hill and then went down again. [Simple sentence with a compound subject and a compound predicate]

Jack came up the hill, but Jill went down the hill. [Compound sentence]

Jack and Jill came up the hill, but they went down again. [Compound sentence, in the first clause of which the subject *Jack and Jill* is compounded]

3.   COMPLEX SENTENCE

Sometimes a sentence is composed of one main clause and one or more subordinate clauses. Such a sentence is called a complex sentence. A sentence to be a complex sentence may not have more than one main clause; otherwise it would become a compound sentence. But it must have as a minimum one subordinate clause. We may frame our definition thus:

> **A complex sentence is one that contains one and only one main clause and at least one subordinate clause.**

When winter comes, most birds fly south. [*Most birds fly south* is the main clause; *when winter comes* is a subordinate clause.]

A man who will not respond to his country's call when her safety is threatened is not worthy of citizenship. [*A man . . . is not worthy of citizenship* is the main clause; *who will not respond to his country's call* and *when her safety is threatened* are subordinate clauses.]

NOTE.   Some texts have used the term "complex-compound" in such a way as to give the impression that this is a fourth, parallel grammatical type of sentence. Of course, there are just the three named above: simple, compound, and complex. Every sentence is basically one of these. If the term "complex-compound" is to be used, it ought to be paralleled by a term "simple-compound." Then "simple-compound" would mean any compound sentence that did not contain any subordinate clauses; and "complex-compound" would mean any compound sentence that contained at least one subordinate clause. An outline will make the matter clear.

A. Simple sentence
   Birds fly.
B. Compound sentence
   1. Simple-compound
      Birds fly, but fish swim.
   2. Complex-compound
      Birds fly when the whim seizes them, but fish swim only when they are hungry.
C. Complex sentence
   Rains come when we seem to need them.
But, because of the confusion it causes, the term "complex-com-

pound" does more harm than good and had best be dispensed with
entirely.

J. Rhetorical Types of Sentences

On the basis of their meaning and purpose sentences
may be classified as declarative sentences and interrogative sentences.

1. DECLARATIVE SENTENCE

A declarative sentence is one that makes an assertion.
A declarative sentence is regularly followed by a period.

It is snowing. I became conscious of a dull thud. She seems to
be having a good time. Jackson has been selected as a delegate to
the convention. She asked me if I knew Mr. Hall.

NOTE. An imperative sentence is a declarative sentence that expresses
a command. *You*, the subject of an imperative sentence, is generally
understood. When *you* as the subject of a command is expressed it is
usually for emphasis. But some grammarians prefer to regard the imperative as a third rhetorical type of sentence. (See also under Mood,
pp. 256 f.)

Go. Shut the door. You do as I say.

2. INTERROGATIVE SENTENCE

An interrogative sentence is one that asks a question.
An interrogative sentence is followed by a question mark.

Didn't you hear the bell ring? What time is it? Have you a
match? Whom were you speaking of?

NOTE. An interrogative sentence will have the verb preceding the subject or will begin with an interrogative word (pronoun, adjective, or
adverb), which is a signal word preparing the reader or listener for a
question rather than a statement. As a result, the main sentence units of
many interrogative sentences do not follow the usual subject-verb-
complement pattern. Changing an interrogative sentence to the declarative form will show the grammatical relation of the parts. Thus *Didn't
you hear the bell ring?* becomes for analysis *You didn't hear the bell ring?*
What time is it? becomes *It is what time? Have you a match?* becomes

You have a match? Whom were you speaking of? becomes *You were speaking of whom?* But in *Who called me?* the grammatical subject comes first; hence, the parts of the sentence follow the normal order.

K.   Equivalent Names for Grammatical Terms

Something that has caused needless confusion for the beginning student of English grammar is the multiplicity of names for what turns out to be, in many cases, the same thing. Too frequently the student feels like giving up in despair when he discovers, for instance, often by pure accident, that "factitive complement," "factitive object," "objective attribute," and "objective predicate" are only different names for the construction that he may have come to recognize under the name of "objective complement."

The following list of common names for various constructions and grammatical functions may be of value. But it must be noted that the terms are not always perfect synonyms for one another. For instance, a weak verb is not the same thing as a regular verb; the genitive case is not identical with possessive case.

This book has attempted to employ throughout terms that are likely to be most familiar to the user; these terms have been printed below in boldface type.

Accusative, **direct object**
Accusative case, **objective case**
Additive clause, **nonrestrictive clause**
Adverbial accusative, adverbial noun, adverbial object, adverbial objective, **noun functioning as an adverb**
Adverbial conjunction, **transitional adverb**
Asserting verb, **link verb**
Assertive sentence, **declarative sentence**
Attribute adjective, attribute complement, attribute noun, attribute pronoun, **subjective complement**
Attributive adjective, attributive complement, attributive noun, attributive pronoun, **subjective complement**
Complementary object, **objective complement**

Conjunctive adverb, **transitional adverb**
Copula, copulative verb, **link verb**
Declarative sentence, assertive sentence
Direct address, nominative of address, vocative
Direct object, accusative, object accusative, object complement,
    objective accusative
Double object, secondary object
Essential clause, **restrictive clause**
Factitive complement, factitive object, **objective complement**
Full verb, **notional verb**
Genitive case, **possessive case**
Gerund, infinitive ending in -*ing*, participial infinitive, participial
    noun, verbal noun
Infinitive ending in -*ing*, **gerund**
Irregular verb, strong verb
Limiting clause, **restrictive clause**
Link verb, asserting verb, copula, copulative verb, linking verb
Linking verb, **link verb**
Nominative of address, **direct address**
Nonessential clause, **nonrestrictive clause**
Nonfinite verb, **verbal**
Nonlimiting clause, **nonrestrictive clause**
Nonrestrictive clause, additive clause, nonessential clause, non-
    limiting clause
Notional verb, full verb, principal verb
Noun clause and **substantive clause**
Noun functioning as an adverb, adverbial accusative, adverbial
    noun, adverbial object, adverbial objective
Noun phrase and **substantive phrase**
Object accusative, object complement, **direct object**
Objective accusative, **direct object**
Objective attribute, objective predicate, **objective complement**
Objective case, accusative case
Objective complement, complementary object, factitive comple-
    ment, factitive object, objective attribute, objective predicate,
    predicate objective
Participial adjective, **participle**
Participial infinitive, participial noun, **gerund**
Participle, participial adjective, verbal adjective

Possessive case, genitive case
Predicate adjective, predicate complement, predicate nominative, predicate noun, predicate pronoun, **subjective complement**
Predicate objective, **objective complement**
Principal verb, **notional verb**
Regular verb, weak verb
Restrictive clause, essential clause, limiting clause
Secondary object, **double object**
Strong verb, **irregular verb**
Subjective adjective, subjective noun, subjective pronoun, **subjective complement**
Subjective complement, attribute adjective, attribute complement, attribute noun, attribute pronoun, attributive adjective, attributive complement, attributive noun, attributive pronoun, predicate adjective, predicate complement, predicate nominative, predicate noun, predicate pronoun, subjective adjective, subjective noun, subjective pronoun
Substantive clause and **noun clause**
Substantive phrase and **noun phrase**
Transitional adverb, adverbial conjunction, conjunctive adverb
Verbal, nonfinite verb, verbid
Verbal adjective, **participle**
Verbal noun, **gerund**
Verbid, **verbal**
Vocative, **direct address**
Weak verb, **regular verb**

EXERCISES

Sentences and fragments of sentences

Indicate which you regard as grammatically complete sentences and which as fragments of sentences.

1. He carried his coat over his arm.
2. On a very cold night.
3. If we can only have turkey for Thanksgiving.
4. The clock that is striking three.

5. On the back of a horse that once was a racing horse.
6. Thinking of oneself only.
7. A better way to catch trout.
8. The amount of paper that goes into the printing of an edition of three thousand copies of a book of approximately four hundred pages.
9. In planning a garden for a family of four.
10. All parts have been securely welded.
11. Mr. Alcord plans building a new garage. A two-car garage, by the way.
12. When I was a child.
13. A beautiful green vine of some kind. Growing up the north side of the house it was.
14. Father sent me a check. To cover all my expenses for the first semester.
15. Her dining room was decorated in green and gold.
16. A sober-dressing man who exhibited his vanity only in the dull perfection of his clothes and the wearing always of a corded edge to his waistcoat.
17. In this book on the technique of the novel in which I have taken the clock apart in an effort to show the functions of the wheels, screws, and levers composing its mechanism.
18. There is something almost terrifying about the way spring comes to Thunder Cove, terrifying and demoralizing in the literal meaning of the word.
19. Jane arrived twenty minutes late. Having stopped at the barge to kiss her sister and peep at her birthday presents.
20. Across the table the two faced each other in silence, the gaunt man, with his tremendous loosely hung frame with the stoop that comes from bending down to converse with shorter people, and the slender, buoyantly lovely girl.
21. In quick succession he registered many emotions. And there is not the slightest doubt about the state of his mind.
22. The *Blackbird* was an old London River sailing barge. Though now it had neither mast nor rigging but lay, a sheer hulk, against Valentine Wharf, a little below the "Black Swan" inn.
23. The interior of Tantamount House is as nobly Roman as its façade. Round a central quadrangle running two tiers of open arcades with an attic, lit by small square windows, above.
24. Walt Whitman—a tall, heavy figure, like a heroic statue, well-shaped, full-chested, broad-shouldered, unafraid.

25. An old plantation with smooth-planted fields and rich woodlands and pastures where little shaded streams ran.
26. Finally the sun, creeping softly as if to effect some diurnal surprise, repetitious but always new. All of which was exciting to the eyes of a small boy who had risen early to go fishing.
27. Duncan saw through the deception. When she failed to recognize you and you failed to recognize her.
28. Once more she flashed her eyes in quick appraisal of the two men, then stepped forward until she was standing within two feet of Duncan, who kept his left hand on the knob of the partially opened door.
29. To think that he would do such a thing!
30. The crate suddenly fell apart. All the spikes having been removed.
31. Plans for the meeting today have been abandoned. A call for a new meeting some time next week to go out this coming Saturday.
32. She swept through the door. Duncan, still grinning, pulling it shut behind her.
33. He eventually shows up. Usually some time around the Fourth of July.
34. Behind the coal dock, protected by a tall fence from the eyes of impressionable passengers, waited the wrecker, that train which always stands ready on any railroad worthy of its freight to swing down the track and cope with the emergency.
35. It was the night that the Chicago Limited piled into an eastbound beef train just above Highboy Bridge, that Amos Shoaff first gave special heed to Michael Ahearn. They talk of that night still around the cannon stoves in snug cabooses. February fourteenth it was, in 1909.

Subject and predicate

Indicate in the following sentences what you regard as the essential subject and what the essential predicate; what the complete subject and what the complete predicate. Sometimes the subject follows rather than precedes the predicate.

1. Mr. Myers spoke for about fifteen minutes.
2. I wish to go to work at once.
3. He confessed that he was disappointed.
4. I just walked and walked all afternoon.
5. The history of deep-sea diving has always fascinated me.
6. Herbert became adept at horseshoe pitching.
7. Not a trace of a breeze could I detect.

8. For seven years Hamblen clerked in a small grocery store.
9. A royal road to a reputation for originality is to impugn the verdicts of the past.
10. The brilliant and fascinating studies of Mr. Strachey have been followed by all kinds of biographical efforts.
11. Never before in the history of this country has there been such enthusiasm for schooling.
12. High in the cab window a motionless figure peers ahead into the night.
13. New York is a great city, the only one in America with the possible exception of Chicago.
14. The car slid down into a broad, shallow valley where a broad, shallow stream ran beneath a stone bridge.
15. The stream was bordered by squat willows and big maples.
16. The face was warped and cracked with age but looked pleasant in the morning sun.
17. Looking down from the top of the pass we saw the barren land spread magnificently before us.
18. An enormous cloud, heavy and black underneath but billowy on top, pressed down over a small bit of the plain to the south.
19. Dairy farms and market gardens upon its slopes helped to feed the populace in the busy valley below.
20. She could drive an automobile; she danced well and cooked capably out of cans.
21. The question of selection from their joint wardrobes occupied the two ladies most of the day; and all afternoon he and Mr. Hedge drove apathetically through the city's parks and about the suburbs.
22. The beast came on with a new fire, closer and closer.
23. Most of the railroad men went to work at seven-thirty in the morning, quit at four-thirty, and dined immediately.
24. Nothing was seriously injured except my nerves.
25. Another month of hot weather gradually wore away.

Modifiers

Indicate what you consider to be modifiers of the subject and what modifiers of the predicate.

1. We shot down the incline at an alarming speed.
2. The little room with its single window seemed a veritable prison to him.
3. Such nice books deserve better treatment.
4. He hurriedly adjourned the meeting of the committee.

5. She stood absolutely still for a single moment.
6. Without another word the little girl tripped lightly down the dusty road.
7. A resonant voice will be a great help to you in radio work.
8. That's a very fine old institution.
9. The smoking chimney did not exactly commend the old house to our favor.
10. I am going to buy immediately a heavy woolen flannel shirt.
11. James was tall, lean, dark, clean-shaven.
12. He lived in Chestnut Hill in a large expressionless house surrounded by clipped lawns and flower beds.
13. In a moment of disgust Stephen had once described James as "an Episcopalian Republican from Pennsylvania."
14. A little water wheel turned slowly with the stream from the spring.
15. On starlit nights there were thousands of fireflies.
16. Grayson was a medium-sized, sharply featured, cigar-smoking, stay-up-late, human-loving fellow.
17. It was the first stone wall, festooned with wine-red woodbine, surrounding a scrubby clearing overgrown with yellow sweet fern and dotted with silver-gray rock.
18. The country was changing from New York to New England insensibly.
19. The very men and women, walking the village streets, were racially different from the flat-faced, stolid descendants of the Dutch farmers and patroons who had settled the Hudson Valley.
20. At last a leading university has had the courage to break with commercialized and overemphasized athletics.
21. Elmer Davis described in the *New Republic* the empty city above the twelfth floor in New York skyscrapers.
22. Another invention in the printing trade gives a fresh threat of technological unemployment.
23. The Indians are presumed to be incapable of managing their own affairs and are therefore made wards of the Federal Government.
24. In the sixteenth century Louise Labe got a bit bored with the routine life of a well-to-do merchant's daughter at Lyon.
25. Chaucer, with all his ability to photograph the life and characters of fourteenth-century England, used French models during the first part of his career and Italian during the second, and borrowed unblushingly from Dante and Boccaccio.

Clauses and phrases

Indicate what groups of words you regard as phrases and what as clauses.

1. At precisely eight o'clock every morning he enters his office.
2. To me it seems a labor of love.
3. If the bus does not leave until ten, we have plenty of time.
4. When the bell rings, make for the stairway.
5. I shall go where I wish to go.
6. Since he is only a child, we must overlook some of his peculiarities.
7. You can't make money by buying dear and selling cheap.
8. In this sort of project you must take into consideration the greatest good to the greatest number.
9. There is no good reason why you should take a position of opposition.
10. I am going to make the attempt because I think I owe something to those who have encouraged me thus far.
11. Ariosto tells a pretty story of a fairy, who, by some mysterious law of her nature, was condemned to appear at certain seasons in the form of a foul and poisonous snake.
12. At the end of the road the land rose sharply into a crescent-shaped hill, one horn of which dipped into the water.
13. A few bedraggled hemlocks and spruce marked what had once been a lawn, and a row of giant butterwoods faced the stream.
14. It was the useless hour of three o'clock, and the day was used up and full of old smells that drifted in through the dusty sunlight of the September afternoon.
15. Below Big Gully Hill a great wound lay alongside of the slope, dripping red clay like blood on the green scrub.
16. It is a land of high hopes and mystic allegiances, where one may stroll through forests of Arden and find heaths and habits like those of olden England.
17. Just as cynicism is essentially a masculine achievement, to which the female mind rarely even aspires, so selfishness is essentially a feminine virtue, whose supreme flights are far beyond the reach of the average healthy male.
18. In lecture courses I had my notebooks so arranged that one-half of the page could be devoted to drawings of five-pointed stars (exquisitely shaded), girls' heads, and ticktacktoe.
19. His candle is lit at both ends, and it burns with a clear blue flame.
20. Women consulted neither politicians nor psychologists; they had yet to see a time clock and call it economic independence.
21. But when women compete with men, the healthy male is gravely handicapped by his unfamiliarity with the primordial feminine virtue of selfishness.
22. I have already found engaging trifles for essays in a Monday's wash

as it swings on a neighbor's line, and a bit of fluttering lace has been a prologue to a paragraph on vanity.

23. I find that a leisured stride is the best rhythm to start an essay, for it is by an easy vibration and tuning of the legs that the message flashes with the least interference out of space.

24. Adversity is the most social force in the world; nothing brings people together like it.

25. The maid announced that dinner was served; and, while Mrs. Turner was giving her some last-minute instructions, our host came in, full of apologies, and hurriedly shook hands all around.

Compound expressions

Go through any of the previous or following exercises and point out expressions that have been compounded.

Main clauses and subordinate clauses

Indicate in the following what you regard as main clauses and what as subordinate clauses.

1. A joke that needs to be explained is not much of a joke.
2. The poem, which I thought was very good, the publisher returned.
3. In Chicago, where the convention was held, the temperature reached 101.
4. That Jim has the making of a baseball player is evident.
5. Since no one is willing to second my motion, I'll withdraw it.
6. Most of my friends are buying new cars this year, but I am convinced that my old station wagon will give me good service for several more years.
7. I always like to do what I am told to do.
8. Nobody cares to be told that he is unpopular.
9. Seeing that the storm was about over, we began to make preparations to leave.
10. I don't know how you feel about the election.
11. A man who is so blunt in his speech is likely to make many enemies.
12. This volume satisfies the mental appetite without sating it, and when you come to the end you lay it down with the resolve you'll read it again.
13. You can see what I mean when I say that it is much easier to write about a book than to write the book itself.
14. How long he stood there he could not afterward remember.
15. The three of them stood there as though they awaited a sign or a miracle.

16. A bell clanged; immediately the signal lights winked red.
17. Alan stood with clenched fist, fighting back the cry that rose to his lips.
18. For a little while the sound rose and fell and seemed to die away in unmeasured distances.
19. There were guttural ejaculations, the clank of metal; then scream on scream pierced the paralyzed listener through and through.
20. It seemed ages until the crowning terror came and wiped out sense of time from his stricken mind.
21. It is foolish to generalize, but I think a writer serves himself best by sticking to his own soil.
22. Every western town has a few representatives in New York who lie in wait for old friends from home on whom to effect a light and graceful touch.
23. Most of the inspirational literature with which we are deluged is dangerous stuff.
24. The wheezy old clock in the kitchen struck four with a rattle of chains and weights that could be heard all over the barnyard.
25. There below him stretched the valley and strung across it, like a chain hanging from the churchyard steps, the village street, which, but for one little compact offshoot of houses to the right, was the village.
26. If I don't find what I want in Indianapolis, it's only a step over to Crawfordsville, where I was born.
27. A short circuit in a power house at Fiftieth Street started a tiny fire but a smoky one. Almost instantly all power left the Grand Central Station. Throughout the night no train could move in or out.
28. The example I have given is rather long; so there isn't room left for a real discussion of the problem.
29. Through increasing knowledge of natural laws man has increased his control over his environment.
30. I have quarreled violently with a friend who worked in a big department store simply because I claimed to have bought an article cheaper elsewhere.
31. It is significant that foreign challenge to English industrial supremacy became effective at the moment when the alliance between the aristocracy and the middle class became an essential feature of English life.
32. I have just had the opportunity to read a letter from a distinguished judge of the State of New York to an acquaintance of his, a New Zealander, who had written to him from England, where he was paying a visit.

33. Whether there is any truth in what the judge says of America I don't know.
34. This insistence upon the security of his personal privacy is of a piece with the Englishman's insistence upon the security of his personal rights.
35. Americans are queer people: they can't rest.

Simple, compound, and complex sentences

Indicate which you regard as simple, compound, and complex sentences.

1. I can't see who it is, but I believe it must be my brother.
2. I must run when the clock strikes.
3. Having put the children to bed, she proceeded to write a letter to her husband narrating the happenings of the day.
4. Come when you are called; do what you are told to do; and keep in a cheerful mood when things don't go as you think they should.
5. You may call that having fun; but I call it downright rowdyism.
6. But before I signed the contract my wife suggested that it might be a good thing for her to go through it carefully to see what its provisions actually were.
7. In reaching such a conclusion I was largely guided by those intuitions commonly thought of as belonging only to women.
8. Although literature today is in the doldrums, there are two groups at least of writers who are reacting as best they can to the new conditions of corporate society.
9. Bernard Shaw is recorded as having said that when people ask him what has happened in his long lifetime he does not refer them to the newspaper files or to the authorities but to Upton Sinclair's novels.
10. Mr. Brown gives us a vivid picture of the behavior of a group of men set down in a strange country to carry out an isolated assignment which tends to seem unreal and irrelevant.
11. The American Society of Newspaper Editors adopted a handsome code of ethics; it has held annual meetings; and some of its members believe that it has made conspicuous progress.
12. Glen Hazard is not a specially likely place for a town; but when coal takes it in its head to run out to the top of the earth a town grows there.
13. Now the misted sunlight was made ugly by the shrieking of the great steam shovel that bit nearer to the old farm with every scoop of its hungry mouth.

14. The busy roadmen squirmed around and burrowed under a great boulder that lay next to the path and directly were wriggling up or down the mountainside out of harm's way; and the foreman lighted the fuse and went running down the gash as fast as his legs might take him.

15. She was a majestic woman; her eyes demanded your homage; her nose commanded it.

16. Once I did go away and try to adjust myself to a new environment; but the virulence of my nostalgia nearly killed me, and I only saved myself by putting in my leisure time writing a book about Indiana.

17. Now it would be idle to pretend that I have more than one white waistcoat; and even my stiff evening shirts are limited in number.

18. A young friend who is engaged in the manufacture of door and window screens has been feeling the decline in the market for such luxuries.

19. But he also makes a few washboards on the side, and all of a sudden a tremendous demand for these appliances has developed.

20. Why don't these people give you a chance to tell them who it is you know?

21. Your wife inquires why you bother to fill in all these details.

22. A banker who had lived in New York for forty years once asked me diffidently if I knew a certain Western senator who, he thought, could assist in advancing a piece of legislation in which he was interested.

23. The ideal place in which to live happily and comfortably in America is a town of not more than ten to twenty thousand people.

24. Industry is represented by a flour mill, a strawboard factory, a cannery, a creamery, and a flourishing brickyard, and there are sure to be a few restless young persons who yearn to make a bigger town of it; and, unless the horned money devils of Main Street succeed in their earnest efforts to discourage them, they are very likely to accomplish it.

25. All safety devices were working; but the switchman's normal reflexes were momentarily in abeyance.

26. Originally the appeal was directed at the farmers alone, but their political strength by itself may not have been considered sufficient.

27. So, with some modifications, the amendments came back and were ultimately approved in flood control and in rivers and harbors bills.

28. She was up the next morning at half past seven, up and nearly dressed, when a knock rattatted on the front door of the flat and a high voice called through the panel.

29. The telephone stood on the top of a medicine cabinet, which in

turn stood atop a buffet, and as you talked into it you leaned against an icebox and rested your foot on the rung of a baby's crib.

30. The United States of America somehow seems remote as I walk the streets of New York, and lately I experienced in Chicago the same feeling of being an alien.

31. Somebody had turned on the radio, and somewhere the Better Biscuit String Ensemble was playing a Brahms Hungarian dance.

32. It is in a way absurd to discuss any great social movement in logical terms.

33. There is a possibility that society gets what it wants; and, when large sections of society find that what they want is illegal, they simply devise their own ways of nullifying laws.

34. Since then he has sent me the new lock, and I should have already put it in the kitchen door except that something must be done about the door.

35. The new lock fits nicely into the cavity, but the keyholes do not coincide with those in the door.

CHAPTER 2

Functions of the Parts
of Speech in a Sentence

We are now ready to consider in some detail how the various parts of speech function in a sentence. With a mastery of these aspects of grammar we shall have taken care of roughly ninety per cent of the content of syntax.

A. *Nouns and Pronouns (Substantives)*[1]

A noun is the name of anything that may be the subject of discourse: *boy, gentleness, thought, air, typewriter, dexterity.*
A pronoun is an expression that may be used as a substitute for a noun: *he, they, anybody, one, whoever, that, what.* A noun designates a person, place, or thing by naming it; a pronoun designates a person, place, or thing without naming it.
"Substantive" is a convenient term used to designate anything that may function as a noun; hence, "substantive" includes both nouns and pronouns. Further, phrases and clauses used as nouns may be referred to as "substantive phrases" and "substantive clauses," although in this book the shorter names "noun phrase" and "noun clause" will ordinarily be used.
The noun to which a pronoun refers is called its antecedent.

---

[1] For forms and usages in nouns see pp. 199 ff.; for forms and usages in pronouns see pp. 218 ff.

John took his friend with him. [*John* is the antecedent of the pronouns *his* and *him*.]

In his ability to write deathless prose Lincoln is unexcelled. [*Lincoln* is the antecedent of the pronoun *his*.]

A noun or a pronoun (that is, a substantive) may be used in the following constructions.

1. **SUBJECT OF A FINITE VERB**

(Or of an infinitive; see pp. 70 ff.)

Dogs bark. [Noun]

Honesty is the best policy. [Noun]

The Board ordered *him* to speed up production. [Pronoun, the subject of the infinitive *to speed*]

2. **OBJECT OF A PREPOSITION**

Mr. Herrod has just arrived from *Alaska*. [Noun]

Did you receive a letter from *me?* [Pronoun]

It is an accomplishment of *which* I am proud. [Pronoun]

3. **APPOSITIVE**

(See p. 167.) *identity*

Harry, the *scamp*, laughed. [Noun]

I prefer that pen, the *one* with the short nib. [Pronoun]

4. **DIRECT ADDRESS**

Open the door, *Mary*. [Noun]

You, what seems to be the trouble? [Pronoun]

5. **NOMINATIVE ABSOLUTE**

(See pp. 61 f.)

The *day* being delightful, we went on a picnic. [Noun]

I being noncommittal, they turned to my brother. [Pronoun]

6. **POSSESSIVES AS ADJECTIVAL MODIFIERS**

I don't like *Steve's* companion. [Noun]

He is a man *whose* ideals I respect. [Pronoun]

7. POSSESSIVES AS SUBSTANTIVES

He is a companion of *Steve's*. [The possessive *Steve's* functions as the object of the preposition *of*. (See also pp. 113 f.)]

He is no friend of *mine*. [The possessive *mine* functions as the object of the preposition *of*. (See also p. 221.)]

I like *yours*, but I don't like *John's*. [The possessive *yours* functions as the object of the first *like*; the possessive *John's* functions as the object of the second *like*.]

8. COMPLEMENTS OF VERBS[2]

a. Direct object

I enjoyed my *vacation*. [Noun]
The President introduced *her* to the audience. [Pronoun]

b. Indirect object

Give *Helen* your scarf. [Noun]
Make *me* a bookmark like yours. [Pronoun]

c. Objective complement

We elected Jim *secretary*. [Noun]
I'd call that a mean *trick*. [Noun]
(A pronoun does not normally function as an objective complement.)

d. Cognate object

The boys ran a lively *race*. [Noun]
In that moment I died a thousand *deaths*. [Noun]
(A pronoun does not normally function as a cognate object.)

e. Double objects

The teacher asked the *boy* a *question*. [Nouns]
Father taught *me* Greek. [Pronoun and noun]

[2] Complements of verbs have been listed here in order that this list for ready reference may be complete. Complements of verbs will be discussed in detail after certain necessary information about verbs has been presented. Hence, if desired, the material on pp. 35 f. may be passed over for the time being.

(marginal handwritten note: always appears with passive voice)

    f. *Retained object or retained indirect object*

        I was given a *prize*. [Noun]
        A prize was given *me*. [Pronoun]

(marginal handwritten notes: occurs only with pronouns; action does not originate in the subject)

    g. *Subjective complement*

        My father has become *chairman* of the committee. [Noun]
        She is *someone* that I ought to know. [Pronoun]

9. NOUNS FUNCTIONING AS OTHER PARTS OF SPEECH

Words that normally function as nouns may function as other parts of speech — especially as adjectives (see p. 94 and pp. 134 ff.) and as adverbs (see pp. 106 f.).

    He is a Brooklyn ball-player. [*Brooklyn* functions as an adjectival modifier of *ball-player*.]
    One day we walked ten miles. [*Day* and *miles* function as adverbial modifiers of *walked*.]
    I thumbed my way to the city. [*Thumbed* functions here as a verb.]

10. OTHER PARTS OF SPEECH FUNCTIONING AS NOUNS

Any expression can, of course, function as a noun. But adjectives become nouns with especial ease (see pp. 135 f.). In colloquial language verbs and adverbs are commonly used as nouns. (See also pp. 135 ff.)

    There are too many *ands* and *buts* and *notwithstandings* in your manuscript; and I don't like *&'s* in a formal paper. [*Ands*, *buts*, *notwithstandings*, and *&'s* here function as nouns.]
    The living and the dead have paid and are paying the price of our stupidity. [The adjectives *living* (originally a participle) and *dead* here function as nouns, the subject of *have paid and are paying*.]
    We all have our ups and downs. [The adverbs *up* and *down*, here pluralized like regular nouns, function as nouns, the objects of *have*.]
    That house is a good buy at six thousand dollars. [The verb *buy* here functions as a noun, the subjective complement of *is*.]

11. NOUN PHRASE *noun with modifiers can be a phrase*

A phrase may function as a noun; such a phrase is known as a noun phrase or a substantive phrase. Common noun phrases are infinitive phrases (see p. 65), gerund phrases (see p. 63), and prepositional phrases (see p. 118).

Crossing the street against the red light is a violation of law. [The gerund phrase *crossing the street against the red light* functions as a noun phrase, the subject of the main verb *is*.]
I like to go on picnics. [The infinitive phrase *to go on picnics* functions as a noun phrase, the object of *like*.]
After lunch is the best time for a short snooze. [The prepositional phrase *after lunch* functions as a noun phrase, the subject of *is*.]
The men were told to wait at the station. [The infinitive phrase *to wait at the station* functions as a noun phrase, the retained object.]
His intention, to cause her embarrassment, backfired. [The infinitive phrase *to cause her embarrassment* functions as a noun phrase in apposition with *intention*.]
After painting half of the fence, I was ready to quit. [The gerund phrase *painting half of the fence* functions as a noun phrase, the object of the preposition *after*.]

12. NOUN CLAUSE

A clause may function as a noun; such a clause is known as a noun clause or a substantive clause. A noun clause (which, of course, is always a subordinate clause) is joined to the main clause by some kind of connective. (See also under Noun Clauses, pp. 161 ff.)

That we had to do something in a hurry became evident. [The subordinate clause *that we had to do something in a hurry* functions as a noun clause, the subject of the main verb *became*.]
I think that crossing the street against the red light is a violation of law. [The subordinate clause *that crossing the street against the red light is a violation of law* functions as a noun clause, the object of the main verb *think*.]

The fact that our agreement was verbal is important. [The subordinate clause *that our agreement was verbal* functions as a noun clause in apposition with *fact*.]

The girls were taught that anything worth doing is worth doing well. [The subordinate clause *that anything worth doing is worth doing well* functions as a noun clause, a retained object.]

EXERCISES

Nouns and pronouns

State the function of every substantive (noun and pronoun) in the following, pointing out all substantives used as subjects of verbs, as objects of prepositions, as appositives, possessives used as adjectival modifiers, possessives used as nouns, phrases and clauses used as nouns. (Complements will be taken up and exemplified later; see pp. 45 ff.)

1. Mary has Jack's hat on.
2. Mary, give the hat back to your brother.
3. On my table you will find an orange.
4. Sam Jenkins, the town marshal, reported the theft.
5. Here are two notebooks. One is John's and the other must be yours.
6. I like sleeping late in the wintertime.
7. I think that I must have lost my gloves. I thought I had left them on the table in your room.
8. The fact which we must always bear in mind is our relative unpreparedness to meet an emergency.
9. Little boy, is your father at home?
10. The best time to work in a garden is from five o'clock to six o'clock in the evening.
11. Adversity is a fine art.
12. Paying cash has no pleasurable social aspect.
13. I have been living in one town for fifteen years.
14. My idea about a good time is evidently not the same as yours.
15. Ohio, the Buckeye State, is a state of many industries.
16. My star has six points; yours has only five.
17. That we have progressed in a gratifying manner is very obvious.
18. He came to within a hairbreadth of success.

19. From Friday noon until Monday morning makes an ideal weekend.
20. Matt, bring me a wrench.
21. Europe's responsibility is extensive; ours is intensive.
22. Did you notice that new hat of Father's?
23. Whether we go or stay is the question before us.
24. Carrying the attack to the enemy produced results.
25. To have seen a sunrise in the Rockies is a thrilling experience.

B. Verbs[3]

The dynamic part of a sentence is usually a verb — a word that represents an action, a state of being, or an occurrence. Because a large portion of the grammar of a sentence is concerned with the verb, we must have a full understanding of everything about a verb in order to analyze a sentence intelligently. Therefore, we shall give much attention here to a study of the verb. And in the light of the new information we gather about the verb we shall review in detail some things that have been discussed only very briefly heretofore.

1. SIMPLE VERBS AND VERB PHRASES

Sometimes the verb is a single word ("The sun *shines*"). Often the verb is accompanied by other verb forms to indicate tense, mood, or voice ("The sun *has been shining* more than an hour"). All the words that go to make up a complete verb constitute a verb phrase.

2. NOTIONAL VERBS AND AUXILIARY VERBS

A notional (or principal or full) verb is one that has a full meaning of its own. In a verb phrase it will be the last word, the part of the phrase which expresses the main notion or idea as distinguished from those parts which are auxiliary or helping verbs.

He should have been invited. [*Should* and *have* and *been* are auxiliaries; they help the notional verb *invited*.]

---

[3] For forms and usages see pp. 247 ff.; for diagramming verb constructions, including complements, see pp. 370 ff.

I do insist that I am leaving this afternoon. [*Do* is an auxiliary helping to make the emphatic conjugation of *insist* (see p. 302); *am* is an auxiliary helping to form the progressive conjugation (see pp. 301 f.) of the verb *leave*. *Insist* and *leaving* are notional verbs.]

NOTE *Do, have,* and *be* have important auxiliary functions; they also can function as notional verbs and have full meanings of their own.

I did the work yesterday. [*Did* is a notional verb.]
Did you work today? [*Did* is an auxiliary; *work* is the notional verb.]
I have only a dime left. [*Have* is a notional verb.]
I have spent nearly all my money. [*Have* is an auxiliary; *spent* is the notional verb.]
To be or not to be, that is the question. [*To be* in both cases and *is* are notional verbs.]
There was some confusion later. [*Was* is a notional verb.]
I am merely making a suggestion. [*Am* is an auxiliary; *making* is the notional verb.]
The package was mailed yesterday. [*Was* is an auxiliary.]

3.   FINITE AND NONFINITE VERBS

On the basis of whether a verb is capable of making an assertion verbs are classed as finite and nonfinite. The more common name for a nonfinite verb is "verbal." A finite verb is one that makes an assertion. Such a verb undergoes change to show person and number; hence the term "finite" (from the Latin *finire,* "to limit").

He walks slowly. [*Walks* has been changed from *walk* to show third person singular number. Further, *walks* makes an assertion; hence it functions as a finite verb.]

A verbal (nonfinite verb) is one that is incapable of making an assertion. Such a verb undergoes no change to show number or person. The three nonfinite verbs are (*a*) participle, a verbal adjective (see pp. 59 ff.); (*b*) gerund, a verbal noun (see pp.

63 ff.); and (c) infinitive, usually preceded by *to*, called its sign (see pp. 65 ff.).

> *coming* to see you [Verbal; *coming* is incapable of making an assertion.]
>
> in *coming* to see you [Verbal; *coming* is incapable of making an assertion.]
>
> *to come to see* you [Verbals; *to come* and *to see* are incapable of making assertions.]

NOTE. Inasmuch as English, unlike Latin and Greek, is largely an uninflected language the learner cannot make much use of the statement that a finite verb is one that undergoes change to show person and number. Probably the simplest thing for the learner to do is to remember that there are just three nonfinite verbs — namely, the participle, the gerund, and the infinitive — and that, consequently, all other verbs are finite verbs.

Or, inasmuch as the subject of a finite verb is always in the nominative case, we may say that any verb that takes a subject in the nominative case is by that fact a finite verb.

> I came at ten o'clock. [The subject of *came* is *I*, which is in the nominative case; hence, *came* is a finite verb.]
>
> Mac ordered me to come at ten o'clock. [The subject of *to come* is *me*, which is in the objective case; hence, *to come* is a nonfinite verb (an infinitive).]

4. VERBS OF COMPLETE AND INCOMPLETE PREDICATION

As was pointed out earlier (p. 9), some verbs may make complete predications by themselves ("The wind *shrieked* and *howled*"; "The door *had been locked*"). But other verbs require help of some kind to make complete predications ("He *closed* the *door*"; "Betty *is* very *quiet* today"; "We *were given* a *permit*"). Verbs that require nothing to complete their predication are called verbs of complete predication; verbs that require something to complete their predication are called verbs of incomplete predication. Anything that completes the predication begun by a verb is termed a "complement."

Before we can discuss the various kinds of complements that verbs may require, we must understand certain functional differences in verbs, differences that determine whether a verb is transitive or intransitive, linking, or passive.

5. TRANSITIVE AND INTRANSITIVE VERBS

On the basis of whether or not they represent an action as "passing over" (*transitive*, from the Latin *transire*, "to pass over") to a grammatical object, verbs are classed as transitive and intransitive.

A transitive verb is one that represents an action as passing over to (that is, being performed on) a grammatical object. In other words, any verb that takes a direct object is a transitive verb; any verb that does not take a direct object is an intransitive verb. Of course, a verb may be transitive in one sense and intransitive in another. (For a transitive verb that becomes intransitive when used absolutely see pp. 56 f.)

> John *painted* the fence. [Transitive; the action of the verb *painted* passes over to — that is, is performed upon — *fence*, the direct object.]
>
> The fence *sparkles* in its new coat of paint. [Intransitive; the verb *sparkles* does not take a direct object.]
>
> The fence *was painted* white. [Intransitive; the verb *was painted* does not take a direct object. (*White* is a subjective complement.)]
>
> They *elected* John chairman. [Transitive; the action of the verb *elected* (with its objective complement *chairman*) passes over to *John*, the direct object.] .
>
> John *was elected* chairman. [Intransitive; the verb *was elected* does not take a direct object. (*Chairman* is a subjective complement.)]

6. ACTIVE AND PASSIVE VOICE

Voice is that property of a verb which makes clear whether the subject of the verb performs the action or receives the action described by the verb.

If the subject performs the action (or is in the state or condition) described by the verb, the verb is said to be in the active voice. If the subject receives the action, the verb is said to be in the passive voice. A transitive verb may be turned into the passive voice, in which case it becomes an intransitive verb (see p. 42). But an intransitive verb in the active voice is usually incapable of being turned into the passive voice.

The passive voice employs the auxiliary verb *be* combined, in any of its forms, with the past participle of the notional verb. (See also p. 248.)

> John *hit* James. [Active voice (transitive). The subject *John* performs the action of *hit*.]
> James *was hit* by John. [Passive voice (intransitive). The subject *James* receives the action of *hit*.]
> Professor Nicholson *has discovered* a new star. [Active voice (transitive)]
> A new star *has been discovered*. [Passive voice (intransitive)]
> Mother *appears* nervous. [Active voice (intransitive)]
> It *is raining* hard now. [Active voice (intransitive)]

NOTE. An apparent exception to the statement that an intransitive verb is incapable of being turned into the passive voice is seen in the case of a few verbs, normally intransitive, which may be followed by adverbs so closely welded to them that the following substantives are objects of the verb plus its adverb. The active construction "They laughed at me" can be turned into the passive voice ("I was laughed at") because in the active form *me* is the object of *laughed* plus *at*; it is not the object of a preposition. See p. 55.

7. LINK VERBS

Any verb which does not require a direct object is an intransitive verb. Some such verbs may be verbs of complete predication ("The sun *shines*"; "The leaves *were falling*"). Other intransitive verbs are verbs of incomplete predication and must be completed by a subjective complement (see pp. 51 ff.), a sentence unit which renames or describes the subject. The intransitive verb used in this kind of predication is called the link (or linking, or copulative) verb.

The most commonly used link verb is *be*. It must be remembered that *be* may also be used as a complete verb, in the sense of "exist." It is so used as a verb of complete predication with the expletive *there* especially.

At one time Tom *was* my closest friend. [Link verb, linking *friend* to *Tom*]

Lately he *has been* unfriendly. [Link verb, linking *unfriendly* to *he*]

There *are* two ways to silence a talkative roommate. [Verb of complete predication. That is, "Two ways to silence a talkative roommate are" (= "exist").]

Your guests *are* in the living room. [Verb of complete predication]

Whatever *is* is right. [The first *is* is a verb of complete predication; the second *is* is a link verb, joining *right* to the noun clause *whatever is*.]

The function of the two verbs *seem* and *become* is almost always a link function. Many other verbs, such as *appear, remain, prove, grow, come, turn, get;* certain verbs having to do with the senses or with health, such as *look, taste, smell, feel, sound;* and some verbs in the passive voice may have the linking function. Any verb that is completed by a subjective complement, a unit renaming or describing the subject, is a link verb.

Notice in the following examples that most of these verbs have non-linking uses also.

Lucy *seems* unhappy about something. [Link verb, linking *unhappy* to *Lucy*]

Remember, even you *might become* president. [Link verb; *president* is a subjective complement renaming *you*.]

Such petty arguing hardly *becomes* you. [Transitive verb; *you* is the direct object.]

Mrs. Allen *appeared* in the doorway. [Intransitive verb of complete predication]

She *appeared* somewhat distraught. [Link verb, linking *distraught* to *she*]

He *remained* my partner for twenty years. [Link verb; *partner* renames *he*.]

At times I *grow* despondent. [Link verb; *despondent* describes *I*.]

Your son *is growing* rapidly. [Intransitive verb of complete predication]

Larkin *grows* prize-winning dahlias. [Transitive verb; *dahlias* is the direct object.]

Pearson's prophecy *came* true. [Link verb; *true* is the subjective complement.]

Peace finally *came* to our troubled land. [Intransitive verb of complete predication]

The days *are getting* colder. [Link verb; *colder* is the subjective complement.]

Martha *tasted* the soup critically. [Transitive verb; *soup* is the direct object.]

"This soup *tastes* insipid," she remarked. [Link verb; *insipid* describes the subject, *soup.*]

Your plan *sounds* workable. [Link verb; *workable* is a subjective complement.]

Feel this sample of cloth. [Transitive verb]

The child's hand *felt* soft. [Link verb; *soft* describes *hand.*]

I *feel* bad; in fact, I *feel* downright ill. [Link verbs, linking *bad* to *I* and *ill* to *I*]

Joe *is considered* trustworthy. [Passive verb linking *trustworthy* to *Joe*]

Herb *was chosen* leader. [Passive verb; *leader* is a subjective complement.]

The barn *has been painted.* [Passive verb of complete predication]

The barn *has been painted* red. [Passive verb used also as a link verb]

8.   COMPLEMENTS OF TRANSITIVE VERBS[4]

A verb to be a transitive verb must take a direct object (see p. 42). But a transitive verb may have other complements in addition to a direct object.

For diagrams of complements of transitive verbs see pp. 372 ff.

a. Direct object.   A direct object is a word or group of words

---

[4] It is strongly urged that at this point the student familiarize himself with a simple method of diagramming a sentence, so that he may see at a glance its complete syntactical make-up. See pp. 369 ff.

upon which the action described by the verb is performed. That is, the action of the verb is said to "pass over" to the direct object. This direct object will be a noun or a noun equivalent (that is, a substantive).

NOTE. A direct object never names the same thing as the subject except in the case of a reflexive — *I hurt myself*. Therefore, a direct object need never be confused with a subjective complement (see p. 51), which always renames or describes the subject.

A single word, a phrase, or a clause may function as a direct object.

1. Single word

Bill hit the *ball* squarely.
He owns several racing *cars*.
What do you think of the news from Washington?

2. Phrase

My brother likes *to drive fast*.
Colby enjoys *walking in the rain*.

3. Clause

I can't believe *that our time has been wasted*.
I cannot understand *why he refused my offer*.

NOTE. When a direct object renames an idea inherent in the verb, such an object is sometimes termed a "cognate" object. That is, the meaning of the direct object is "cognate" with the verb. But it is usually sufficient simply to call all such objects direct objects. In fact, the only odd thing about the construction is that the verb without such an object normally functions as an intransitive verb. (See also p. 57.)

Phrases and clauses normally do not function as cognate objects.

Will you sing a song for us? [*Song* is a direct object (a cognate object) of *sing*, which here functions as a transitive verb.]
She sings beautifully. [*Sing* here is an intransitive verb.]
Live the good life. [*Life* is a direct object (cognate object) of *live*, which here functions as a transitive verb.]
He lives from one day to the next. [*Lives* is here an intransitive verb.]

b. Indirect object. An indirect object names, without an expressed preposition, the person or thing to whom or for whom the action described by the verb is performed. An indirect object in a main clause usually precedes a direct object.

There is no preposition with a true indirect object.[5] In fact, the indirect object existed before prepositions had come into common use. If a preposition is expressed, then the construction becomes a prepositional phrase (see p. 111) functioning as an adverbial modifier of the verb. The alteration in word order has no real effect upon the meaning of the sentence; the form used may be determined by the stylistic or emphatic effect desired by the writer or speaker.

He gave the book to me. [*To me* is a prepositional phrase functioning as an adverbial modifier of *gave*.]

He gave me the book. [*Me* is a true indirect object of *gave*.]

She made a lovely scarf for my mother. [*For my mother* is a prepositional phrase functioning as an adverbial modifier of *made*.]

She made my mother a lovely scarf. [*Mother* is a true indirect object of *made*.]

An indirect object is usually a single word, rarely a phrase or clause.

1. Single word

James gave me a book. [*Me* is an indirect object of *gave*.]

My mother made my sister a lovely sweater. [*Sister* is an indirect object of *made*.]

2. Phrase

He brought Stratford on Avon lasting fame. [*Stratford on Avon* is an indirect object of *brought*.]

---

[5] Some grammarians prefer to disregard the indirect object as a form of complement and explain the construction in either of two ways. Some supply a preposition to govern the substantive and explain the prepositional phrase resulting as an adverbial modifier of the main verb. Others explain *me* in "He gave me a book" as an adverbial modifier of *gave* rather than as a complement of *gave*, an excellent explanation which shows how close complements and adverbial modifiers really are.

3. Clause

My father always gave whoever came a warm welcome. [The clause *whoever came* is an indirect object of *gave*.]

Occasionally an indirect object is used without any direct object appearing in the statement.

I'll write him as soon as I have paid the workmen. [*Him* and *workmen* are indirect objects. The intended meaning is clear without expressed direct objects.]

c. Double objects. A few verbs seem to take two direct objects. This comes from the fact that the verb is being used in two slightly different senses at the same time, in one sense taking one substantive as its direct object and in another sense taking the other substantive as its direct object. The two commonly used verbs that may thus take two direct objects are *ask* and *teach*.

Double objects may be single words, phrases, or clauses.

1. Single word

He asked me a puzzling question. [In one sense of *ask*, *question* is the direct object; in another sense of *ask*, *me* is the direct object.]

Mr. Brammar taught my brother penmanship. [In one sense of *taught*, *brother* is a direct object; in another sense of *taught*, *penmanship* is a direct object.]

2. Phrase

Alice taught her sister how to dance. [In one sense of *taught*, *sister* is a direct object; in another sense of *taught*, the infinitive phrase *how to dance* is a direct object.]

Ask the manager where to file your application. [In one sense of *ask*, *manager* is a direct object; in another sense of *ask*, the infinitive phrase *where to file your application* is a direct object.]

3. Clause

Don't ask me what I am doing. [In one sense of *ask*, *me* is a direct object; in another sense of *ask* the subordinate clause *what I am doing* is a direct object.]

Teach whoever applies what you know about welding. [In one sense of *teach* the subordinate clause *whoever applies* is a direct object; in another sense of *teach* the subordinate clause *what you know about welding* is a direct object.]

NOTE. The pattern of the sentences using the verbs *ask* and *teach* is essentially that of the sentence with an indirect object followed by a direct object; the distinction between the two patterns is of minor interest to anyone except the language specialist. There are, similarly, some other transitive verbs which take two objects which have a slightly different relation to the verb from that in the verbs exemplified in *b* above. The difference comes from the fact that of the two objects following the verb the first one does not lend itself satisfactorily to the convenient "to whom?" or "for whom?" test which helps us recognize most indirect objects. In each of the following sentences, for example, the italicized object, although it is in the normal position of the indirect object, would not allow an idiomatically acceptable *to* or *for* prepositional phrase as an alternate pattern:

Many people envy *him* his prospects.
Forgive *us* our debts.
I struck *him* a resounding blow.
We must deny *him* his simple request.
She led *Luther* a merry chase.
I must remind *you* that I am the chairman.

All of these sentences are alike in the arrangement of the main units: the transitive verb is followed by two substantives, each of which receives, or is in some way affected by, the action named in the verb. For purposes of functional sentence analysis, it is usually sufficient to consider the first of the substantives following the verb in this pattern the indirect object and the second the direct object.

d. Objective complement. Some transitive verbs require in addition to a direct object a substantive or an adjective to complete the predication begun by the verb.[6] Such a substantive or adjective is termed an "objective complement." If the objective complement is a substantive, it will rename the direct object (or act as the equivalent of it); if it is an adjective, it will qualify (that is, modify) the direct object. Although an objective complement usually follows the direct object, it may actually at times precede the direct object.

[6] Verbs — such as *make, call, name, choose* — that take an objective complement in addition to a direct object are sometimes called factitive verbs.

NOTE. It may be noted that an objective complement often designates a result produced by the verb acting on the direct object; that is, what the direct object has been made into by the action of the verb. In other words, the direct object receives the action of the verb plus the objective complement rather than the action of the verb alone.

> He washed the window clean. [That is, "He washed the window so that it is now clean." *Window* is the object of *washed + clean* rather than of *washed* alone.]
>
> They elected Hendricks mayor. [That is, "They elected Hendricks so that he is now mayor." *Hendricks* is the object of *elected + mayor* rather than of *elected* alone.]

An objective complement may be a single word, a phrase, or a clause. An objective complement may be introduced by the expletive *as* and, in a few set expressions, by the expletive *for*.

(1.) Single word

The court rendered the law null and void. [The adjectives *null* and *void* are objective complements. They qualify the direct object *law*; and they complete the predication begun by the verb *rendered*.]

We elected Kenneth secretary-treasurer. [The noun *secretary-treasurer* is an objective complement. It renames the direct object *Kenneth*; and it completes the predication begun by the verb *elected*.]

(2.) Phrase

We found him strumming a guitar. [The participial phrase *strumming a guitar* is an objective complement. It qualifies the direct object *him*; and it completes the predication begun by the verb *found*.]

His action renders our protest of no avail. [The prepositional phrase *of no avail* is an objective complement. It qualifies the direct object *protest*; and it completes the predication begun by the verb *renders*.]

(3.) Clause

His wife made him what he is. [The noun (substantive) clause *what he is* is an objective complement. It renames the direct object *him*; and it completes the predication begun by the verb *made.*]

4. Objective complement preceding a direct object

We have found effective in such cases a mild salt solution. [*Effective* is an objective complement. It qualifies the direct object *solution*; and it completes the predication begun by the verb *have found.*]

5. Objective complement introduced by expletives *as* and *for*. (See also p. 149.)

We choose Bill as our spokesman. [Compare "We choose Bill to be our spokesman." *Spokesman,* an objective complement, is introduced by the expletive *as.*]

He apparently took me for my younger brother. [Compare "He apparently took me to be my younger brother." *Brother,* an objective complement, is introduced by the expletive *for.*]

9. **COMPLEMENTS OF INTRANSITIVE VERBS**

As we saw above (p. 41), there are many verbs that are capable of making complete predications without any complements ("Birds *fly*"; "John *hesitated*"; "Frank *departed*"). But there are also many intransitive verbs that require something to complete the predication that the verb itself has merely begun.

For diagrams of complements of intransitive verbs see pp. 374 ff.

a. Subjective complement.[7] Some intransitive verbs require a noun or an adjective to complete the predication begun by the verb. Such a complement is called a subjective complement — that is, something that refers to the subject and at the same

[7] "Subjective complement" is a convenient term to designate anything — noun, adjective, phrase, clause — that completes the predication begun by an intransitive verb; and usually it is sufficient. But some grammarians use the term "predicate noun" to designate a noun functioning as a subjective complement and "predicate adjective" to designate an adjective functioning as a subjective complement. The term "predicate nominative," sometimes used, is unfortunate, for a "predicate nominative" is not always in the nominative case. After an infinitive in an infinitive clause (see pp. 240 f.) the subjective complement *me* is actually in the objective case —"They believed him to be me." Hence, the term "predicate nominative" is not used in this book.

time completes the predication. If the subjective complement is a substantive, it renames (or is the equivalent of) the subject; if it is an adjective, it qualifies (that is, modifies) the subject.

A verb that is used with a subjective complement is called a link (or linking) verb (see also pp. 43 ff.).

A subjective complement may be a single word, a phrase, or a clause.

1. Single word

Mother is gentle and kind. [The adjectives *gentle* and *kind* are subjective complements; they both qualify *Mother*, the subject, and complete the predication begun by the verb *is*.]

Tennis is my choice. [The noun *choice* functions as a subjective complement; it both renames the subject *tennis* and completes the predication begun by the verb *is*.]

The only guests I had met before were you and she. [The pronouns *you* and *she* function as subjective complements; they rename the subject *guests* and complete the predication begun by the verb *were*.]

2. Phrase

Your question seems to be irrelevant. [The infinitive phrase *to be irrelevant* functions as a subjective complement; it both qualifies the subject *question* and completes the predication begun by the verb *seems*.]

Her gown is of expensive silk. [The prepositional phrase *of expensive silk* functions as a subjective complement; it both qualifies the subject *gown* and completes the predication begun by the verb *is*.]

3. Clause

His answer is not what one might have expected. [The subordinate clause *what one might have expected* functions as a subjective complement; it both renames (or qualifies) the subject *answer* and completes the predication begun by the verb *is*.]

b. Subjective complement after a passive verb.   When a sentence containing a direct object and an objective complement is turned into the passive voice, the direct object becomes the subject of the passive verb and the objective complement becomes a subjective complement.[8] The passive verb has a link function and joins a subjective complement to a subject.

A subjective complement following a passive verb may be a single word, a phrase, or a clause.

1. Single word

Mr. Smith was appointed manager. [*Manager,* a subjective complement after the passive verb *was appointed,* was an objective complement in the active construction — "They appointed Mr. Smith manager."]

The slate was wiped clean. [The adjective *clean,* a subjective complement after the passive verb *was wiped,* was an objective complement in the active construction —"He wiped the slate clean."]

2. Phrase

Grandfather was found in excellent health. [The prepositional phrase *in excellent health,* a subjective complement after the passive verb *was found,* was an objective complement in the active construction —"We found Grandfather in excellent health."]

3. Clause

He was made what he is today by circumstances beyond his control. [The subordinate clause *what he is today,* a subjective complement after the passive verb *was made,* was an objective complement in the active construction —"Circumstances beyond his control made him what he is today."]

c. Retained object.   When a verb with an indirect object and a direct object is turned into the passive voice, one of the objects becomes the subject of the passive verb and the other object remains; and this object that remains is known as a retained object. If it is an indirect object that is retained, this

---

[8] A subjective complement after a passive verb might be regarded as a "retained objective complement" by analogy with the "retained object" discussed in section *c* — that is, as an objective complement "retained" from the active construction.

may be called a retained indirect object. (The retained object also appears when an infinitive clause construction is turned into the passive voice; see p. 73.)

A retained object may be a single word, a phrase, or a clause.

1. Single word

He was given a reward. [The indirect object of the active construction ("They gave him a reward") has become the subject of the passive verb, and the direct object *reward* has been retained.]

A reward was given him. [The direct object of the active construction ("They gave him a reward") has become the subject of the passive verb, and the indirect object *him* has been retained.]

2. Phrase

I was ordered to report for duty. [*Me*, the subject of the infinitive clause in the active construction ("They ordered me to report for duty") has become the subject of the passive verb *was ordered* and the infinitive phrase *to report for duty* has been retained. (See also p. 73.)]

He was given until Saturday night. [*Him*, the indirect object of the active construction ("They gave him until Saturday night") has become the subject of the passive verb *was given* and the prepositional phrase *until Saturday night* (the direct object in the active construction) has been retained.]

3. Clause

I was taught that I should respect my elders. [*Me*, one of the double objects in the active construction ("Mother taught me that I should respect my elders") has become the subject of the passive verb *was taught* and the other object, the subordinate clause *that I should respect my elders*, has been retained.]

NOTE. There is a persistent feeling on the part of some who are uncertain about English usage that retained constructions are grammatical errors of some kind, whereas the fact is that they are well-established locutions. Of course, the construction can be abused by one who is overinclined to use the passive voice; for the passive voice is by its very nature a weaker form of expression than the active voice.

10. VERB + ADVERB COMBINATIONS

Shakey construc.

Sometimes such an adverb as *up, down, in, out,* is so closely welded to a preceding verb that a following substantive is really the object of the verb plus the adverb rather than of the verb alone. (Such an adverb must not be mistaken for a preposition governing the following substantive.) This explains why such constructions can readily be turned into the passive voice. (See pp. 352 f. for adverbs — and prepositions — at ends of statements.) These verb + adverb combinations are especially common in colloquial discourse.[9]

cf. reached for

He put down the rebellion in short order. [*Down* is an adverb attached to *put,* not a preposition governing *rebellion,* so that *rebellion* is really the direct object of *put+down.* Note that the position of *down* may be shifted —"He put the rebellion down. . . ." Note also the possible passive voice —"The rebellion was put down."]

I have closed out my business. [*Out* is an adverb attached to *have closed,* not a preposition governing *business,* so that *business* is really the direct object of *closed+out.* Note that the position of *out* may be shifted —"I have closed my business out." Note also the possible passive voice —"My business has been closed out."]

They have put off the play. [*Off* is an adverb attached to *put,* not a preposition governing *play,* so that *play* is really the direct object of *put+off.* Compare "They postponed the play." Note the possible passive voice — "The play has been put off."]

11. VERB + PREPOSITION COMBINATIONS

cf. reached for

Sometimes a preposition-like word is so closely welded to a preceding verb that a following substantive is really the object of the verb plus the preposition rather than the object of the preposition alone. That is, the preposition is almost a

[9] It may be noted that an adverb so used has much the effect of an objective complement. Note that *out* in "They put the fire out" completes the predication begun by the verb *put* much in the way in which a regular objective complement completes the predication begun by the verb —"They scrubbed the floor clean." Such an adverb as *out* might very well be construed in the sentence given as an adverb functioning as an objective complement. Once again we see how close adverbial modifiers and complements really are.

suffix of the verb. This explains why some intransitive verbs become transitive when such a preposition is closely welded to them and why such verbs may readily be turned into the passive voice with the preposition "retained" after the passive verb (see p. 121). (See pp. 352 f. for prepositions at ends of statements.)

They laughed at me. [*At* is a preposition attached to *laughed*, so that *me* is really the object of *laughed+at* rather than of *at* alone. Compare "They ridiculed me." Note the possible passive voice — "I was laughed at" — with the preposition *at* "retained."[10]]

I cannot put up with your conduct any longer. [*Up* is an adverb and *with* a preposition, attached to *put*, so that *conduct* is virtually the direct object of *put+up+with* rather than the object of the preposition *with* alone. Compare "I cannot tolerate your conduct." Note also the possible passive construction —"Your conduct cannot be put up with"— in which *with* becomes a retained preposition.]

NOTE. Transitive verbs likewise may thus combine with prepositions.
We should not make fun of him. [*Him* is virtually the object of *make+fun+of*. Compare "We should not ridicule him." Note also the possible passive construction "He should not be made fun of."]
You should make much use of the dictionary. [*Dictionary* is virtually the object of *make+use+of*. Compare "You should consult the dictionary." Note also the possible passive construction "The dictionary should be made much use of."]
We will take good care of you. [*You* is virtually the object of *take+care+of*. Compare "We will safeguard you." Note also the possible passive construction "You will be taken good care of."]

12.   VARIOUS KINDS OF VERBS

Verbs may be classed according to their basic ideas, their relationship to other verb forms, and their relationship to their complements.

a. Absolute verb. Some grammarians use the term "absolute" to designate a verb, normally transitive, that becomes

---

[10] Some grammarians prefer to say that this preposition-like word becomes an adverb in the passive construction rather than to call it a retained preposition as we have called it in this book.

intransitive when used without an object to describe a customary or habitual action. But it is simpler to regard all such
verbs — any verb that does not take a direct object — as intransitive verbs.

Does he *smoke?* [Intransitive]
That dog certainly likes *to eat.* [Intransitive]
A stop should be put to illegal *drinking.* [Intransitive]

b. Cognate verb. A cognate verb is one, normally intransitive, that becomes transitive when it takes an object that is
akin to it in meaning (that is, is cognate in meaning). (See
also p. 46.)

Fight the good fight. [*Fight,* here a transitive verb, takes the
noun *fight* as its direct object.]
He slept the sleep of the just. [*Slept,* here a transitive verb,
takes *sleep* as its direct object.]

Similar constructions are *die a death, live a life, pray a prayer,
run a race, sing a song.* The distinction is not an important one;
for, as far as grammar is concerned, the verbs, taking direct
objects, function in such situations like any other transitive
verbs; hence, the substantive may be regarded as merely a direct
object.

c. Causative verb. A verb normally intransitive may become
transitive when it is used in a causative sense.

He ran his car into the garage. [That is, "He caused his car to
run into the garage."]
She watered the flowers. [That is, "She caused the water to
flow on the flowers."]
I grow dahlias for a hobby. [That is, "I cause dahlias to grow."]

NOTE. The verb *to fell* is sometimes said to be the causative of *to fall* —
"He felled the tree"; that is, "He caused the tree to fall."
To set is a causative of *to sit*—that is, "to set the vase on the table" is
"to cause the vase to sit on the table." "To lay the book on the table" is
"to cause the book to lie on the table."
Verbs in *-en* — *blacken, whiten, brighten, shorten* — are sometimes
called causative verbs.

d. Impersonal verb. An impersonal verb is one that has an indefinite *it* (see p. 219) as its subject. Such verbs frequently help to make statements about the weather or about time. (For other uses of *it* see also pp. 219 f.)

> It is raining. [*Is raining* is an impersonal verb.]
> It is nearly midnight. [*Is* is an impersonal verb.]
> It looks like a storm. [*Looks* is an impersonal verb.]
> I am always happy when it snows. [*Snows* is an impersonal verb.]
> It feels as if we might have some hot weather. [*Feels* is an impersonal verb.]
> It seems as if it were later than ten o'clock. [*Seems* is an impersonal verb.]

e. Defective verb. A defective verb is one that does not have the necessary forms to make up a complete conjugation, that is, a systematic arrangement of all possible forms of a verb. The verb *be* and the auxiliaries, with the exception of *do* and *have,* are defective verbs.

The verb *be* has no passive voice. The auxiliaries *may, might, can, could,* have only the active voice. They have the present and past but no future and no perfect tenses; they lack infinitive and participle forms. The auxiliary *must* has only this one form. The auxiliary *ought* has only this one form.

f. Redundant verb. A redundant verb is one that has more than the necessary forms for a complete conjugation. It may have two forms for the past tense or two or more forms for the past participle or both. Thus we have both *awaked* and *awoke* for the past tense and past participle of *awake; burnt* or *burned* for the past tense and past participle of *burn; dreamed* or *dreamt* for the past tense and past participle of *dream.* (See the list on pp. 287 ff. for other instances.)

13. VERBALS (NONFINITE VERBS)

There are three nonfinite verb forms in English, called verbals — namely, the participle, the gerund, and the infinitive. They are like finite verbs in that they may be transitive or intransitive, complete or link, may exist in the active and passive voices, and may take complements and adverbial modifiers. But they are unlike finite verbs in that they cannot by themselves make assertions. Because they are not limited in form as to person and number and do not represent time in the same way in which a finite verb does, they are called infinite or nonfinite verbs.[11]

Although they cannot make assertions by themselves, verbals, constituting as they do one of the most valuable linguistic resources we have in English, are very important. Hence, a mastery of them is highly important for anyone who wishes to write with precision and effectiveness.

a. Participle.[12]   A participle is a verb form that may be used as a modifier of a substantive — that is, may be used as an adjective. Most participles thus used have an *-ing* ending either in the notional verb (*seeing*; see pp. 267 f.) or in an auxiliary expressed or easily supplied (*having seen*; *having been seen*; see pp. 267 f.). A verbal, then, in *-ing* that functions as an adjective is a participle and is to be distinguished from a gerund (see p. 63), also ending in *-ing* but functioning as a noun.

The participle, like the other verbals, is a hybrid; for it takes on the characteristics of two different parts of speech at the same time. Derived from a verb as it is, a participle has the sense of a verb and may take any kind of complements and any kind of adverbial modifiers that a finite verb may take. A participle with any complements and any adverbial modifiers it may take constitutes a participial phrase.

But in addition to this sense of a verb a participle has the function of an adjective and attaches itself to — that is, modifies — a substantive in the statement in which it appears.

For diagrams of participial constructions see pp. 376 f.

1. Dual nature.   The dual nature of the participle can be seen in some of the examples given below.

a) As a verb.   In its sense as a verb, a participle may take

---

[11] See pp. 269 ff. for the relative time expressed by a verbal.
[12] For forms and usages see pp. 267 ff. and pp. 303 ff.

any kind of complement and any kind of adverbial modifier that the corresponding finite verb might take.

Having had no sleep for the last twenty-four hours, Bill is now in no mood for frivolity. [The participle *having had*, in its verb capacity, takes *sleep* as its direct object and *for the last twenty-four hours* as an adverbial modifier; in its adjectival capacity it attaches itself to (that is, modifies) the substantive *Bill*, subject of the main verb.]

Becoming serious for a moment, Father added a final word of advice. [The participle *becoming*, in its verb capacity, takes *serious* as a subjective complement and *for a moment* as an adverbial modifier; in its adjectival capacity it attaches itself to (that is, modifies) *Father*, subject of the main verb.]

b) As an adjective. In its capacity as an adjective a participle may function as either an attribute or an appositive modifier (see pp. 89 f.); or it may function as a subjective complement or an objective complement. Or it may be used to modify a noun that is used absolutely (see below).

(1) As an attribute modifier

Barking dogs don't bite. [*Barking* is an attribute modifier of *dogs*.]

The man wearing a topcoat is Mr. Seaman. [*Wearing* functions as an attribute modifier of *man*.]

It was like a burning fire in his bones. [*Burning* is an attribute modifier of *fire*.]

It was like a fire burning in his bones. [*Burning* is an attribute modifier of *fire*.

(2) As an appositive modifier[13]

Our team, outweighed and outplayed, lost by a big score. [*Outweighed* and *outplayed* are appositive modifiers of *team*.]

Harassed and terrified, he knew not which way to turn. [*Harassed* and *terrified* are appositive modifiers of *he*.]

Putting on his cap, Jim started down the steps. [*Putting on his cap* is an appositive modifier of *Jim*.]

[13] Note commas to set off an appositive modifier. See Note, p. 91.

(3) As a subjective complement

The situation was encouraging. [*Encouraging* is a subjective complement after *was*.]

The refugees looked starved. [*Starved* is a subjective complement after *looked*.]

The children came running into the house. [*Running* is a subjective complement after *came* (which here functions as a link verb.)][14]

(4) As an objective complement

Dad found his car gone. [*Gone* looks back to and modifies *car* and at the same time completes the predication begun by the verb *found*.]

He declared the meeting adjourned. [*Adjourned* looks back to and modifies *meeting* and at the same time completes the predication begun by the verb *declared*.]

NOTE. The participles used in (1), (2), (3), and (4) above are unmistakably adjectival in function. But other participial constructions, especially the introductory participial phrase, show a somewhat more complex modifying function, a relationship which makes the participial phrase a very versatile linguistic tool. In such a sentence as "Having paid my fees, I considered my registration finished," the introductory participial phrase does, of course, tell something about *I*; the adjectival relationship is demonstrated by the fact that a reordering of parts — e.g., "Having paid my fees, my registration was finished" — results in a dangling modifier. (See p. 306.) But the phrase tells more: it suggests the *time* of the considering and the *reason* for the considering, modifying functions normally associated with adverbial modifiers.

2. The nominative absolute construction. A participle may modify a substantive that has no grammatical function of its own in the statement in which it appears; that is, the substantive

[14] Originally *running* was a gerund in this construction. Compare "came a-running" and "went a-fishing," the gerunds originally fuctioning as objects of a preposition *a* (= "on"), and the prepositional phrases functioning as adverbial modifiers of the verbs. But today the *-ing* word is usually regarded as a participle functioning as a subjective complement after a verb like *came* or *went* (functioning as a link verb). Or, the *-ing* word may be regarded as a gerund functioning as an adverb and modifying *came* (see p. 106). Again we see that often there is more than one good explanation for a construction in English grammar.

is said to be used absolutely (see pp. 138 ff.). Inasmuch as a substantive used absolutely is always in the nominative case, the construction is known as the nominative absolute.

Today being the Fourth of July, the banks are closed. [The noun *today* is modified by the participle *being; Fourth of July* is a subjective complement with *being.* The whole phrase *today being the Fourth of July* is a nominative absolute, for it has no grammatical function in the statement *the banks are closed.*]

The bank having closed, we can't get our checks cashed. [The noun *bank* is modified by the participle *having closed.* The whole phrase *the bank having closed* is a nominative absolute, for it has no grammatical function in the statement *we can't get our checks cashed.*]

She not being a member, we must be guarded in our remarks. [*She,* a pronoun in the nominative case, is modified by the participle *being; member* is a subjective complement with *being.* The whole phrase *she not being a member* is a nominative absolute, for it has no grammatical function in the statement *we must be guarded in our remarks.*]

The truck raced down the hill, the helpless driver frantically trying to bring it under control. [*The helpless driver frantically trying to bring it under control* is a nominative absolute. The construction commonly occurs after, or sometimes in the interior of, the main predication.]

The bereaved woman waited quietly, her eyes still red from weeping. [*Her eyes still red from weeping* is a nominative absolute. The participle (usually *being*) in such a phrase is sometimes not expressed, so that the substantive in the phrase may be followed by some other grammatical unit such as an adjective, an adverb, or a prepositional phrase.]

NOTE. The nominative absolute is a perfectly proper construction as far as grammar is concerned. In the hands of skilled writers it is an effective device for the unobtrusive insertion of descriptive and narrative details. However, it can easily call attention to itself and thus become ungraceful in the hands of an inexpert writer. Although a nominative absolute has no *grammatical* function in the statement in which it appears, it should have a logical function. It usually expresses an idea that might have been expressed by a subordinate clause modifying the main verb. That is, it usually expresses a notion of time, condition, cause, or concession.

> It being a nice day, let's have a picnic. [That is, "Since it is a nice day, let's have a picnic."]
> Weather permitting, we will have the picnic. [That is, "If the weather permits, we will have the picnic."]

Failure to express clearly some notion of time, condition, or concession of a nominative absolute may result in confused writing.

> Although the door was unlocked, he chose to crawl through a window. [*Not:* "The door being unlocked, he chose to crawl through a window." For it is not clear here whether the notion of the nominative absolute is one of time, reason, or concession.]

3. <u>Dangling participle</u>. For the dangling participle, sometimes confused with the nominative absolute, see pp. 306 f.

<u>b. Gerund.</u>[15] A gerund is a verb form that is used as a noun. A gerund has an *-ing* ending either in the notional (principal) verb (*seeing*) or in one of its auxiliaries, expressed or easily supplied (*being seen, having been seen*). A gerund is identical in form with the participle but differs from the participle in that, whereas the participle functions as an adjective and modifies a noun (see p. 60), a gerund functions as a noun.

The gerund, like the participle and the infinitive, is a hybrid, for it takes on the characteristics of two different parts of speech at the same time. Derived from a verb as it is, it has the sense of a verb and may take any kind of complement and any kind of adverbial modifier that a finite verb may take. A gerund with any complements and any adverbial modifiers it may take constitutes a gerund phrase.

But in addition to this sense of a verb, a gerund has the function of a noun in the statement in which it appears.

For diagrams of gerund constructions see pp. 377 f.

1. Dual nature. The dual nature of a gerund may be seen in some of the examples given below.

> Examining specimens critically requires a strong magnifying glass. [The gerund *examining* takes *specimens* as a direct object

[15] For forms and usages see pp. 268 and 309 ff.

and *critically* as an adverbial modifier and at the same time functions as a noun, the subject of the main verb *requires*.]

I like teaching grammar to beginners. [The gerund *teaching* takes *grammar* as a direct object and the prepositional phrase *to beginners* as an adverbial modifier; the gerund at the same time functions as a noun, the direct object of the verb *like*.]

Such becomes merely carrying coals to Newcastle. [The gerund *carrying* takes *coals* as a direct object and *to Newcastle* as an adverbial modifier; the gerund at the same time functions as a noun, the subjective complement of *becomes*.]

They talked about playing the game at night. [The gerund *playing* takes *game* as a direct object and *at night* as an adverbial modifier; the gerund at the same time functions as a noun, the object of the preposition *about*.]

In guessing accurately a person's weight you must take into account his age. [The gerund *guessing* takes *weight* as a direct object and *accurately* as an adverbial modifier; the gerund at the same time functions as a noun, the object of the preposition *in*. (The prepositional phrase *in guessing accurately a person's weight* functions as an adverbial modifier of the main verb *must take*.)]

I'll overlook your first deception, selling Bob your worthless old car. [The gerund *selling* takes *Bob* as an indirect object and *car* as a direct object; the gerund at the same time functions as a noun, in apposition with *deception*.]

2. Gerund used absolutely. A gerund used absolutely is really a nominative absolute (see pp. 61 f.). The gerund functions as the substantive in the construction and is modified by the participle. Like any other nominative absolute, the whole phrase is used absolutely. Because the gerund absolute, although possible grammatically, may not be a particularly graceful expression, it is rarely encountered.

[handwritten margin note: usually near the subj.]

Dissuading him from his intent proving impossible, we must resort to something else. [The gerund *dissuading* (with its object *him* and its adverbial modifier *from his intent*) is modified by the participle *proving* (with *impossible* as its subjective complement). The whole phrase *dissuading him from his intent proving impossible* has no grammatical function in the statement *we must resort to something else.* Actually, then, the phrase becomes a nominative absolute construction.]

3. Dangling gerund. For the "dangling gerund" see p. 310.

c. Infinitive.[16] The third verbal (or nonfinite verb form) is the infinitive—usually accompanied by *to*, called its sign. (For the omission of *to* see p. 72).

The infinitive, like the participle and the gerund, is a hybrid, for it takes on the characteristics of two parts of speech at the same time. Derived from a verb as it is, the infinitive has the sense of a verb and may take any kind of complement and any kind of adverbial modifier that a finite verb may take. An infinitive with any complements and any adverbial modifiers it may take constitutes an infinitive phrase.

In addition to this verb function, an infinitive may have the function of a noun, of an adjective, of an adverb; and in a construction known as the infinitive clause it may have the function of a verb and take a grammatical subject of its own.

For diagrams of infinitive constructions see pp. 379 ff.

1. Dual nature.   The dual nature of the infinitive may be seen in the examples given below.

a) Noun use

(1) As a subject

To make a mistake unwittingly is pardonable. [The infinitive *to make* takes *mistake* as its direct object and *unwittingly* as an adverbial modifier and at the same time functions as a noun, the subject of the main verb *is*.]

(2) As an appositive

His plan, to appoint a new supervisor, ran into much opposition. [The infinitive *to appoint* takes *supervisor* as its direct object and at the same time functions as a noun, in apposition with *plan*.]

(3) As a subjective complement

[16] For forms and usages see pp. 268 ff. and pp. 317 ff.

Our plan is to wait until next Sunday. [The infinitive *to wait* takes *until next Sunday* as an adverbial modifier and at the same time functions as a noun, the subjective complement of the main verb *is*.]

(4) As a direct object

It began to rain just as I was starting for home. [The infinitive *to rain* takes the subordinate clause *just as I was starting for home* as an adverbial modifier and at the same time functions as a noun, the direct object of the main verb *began*.]

(5) As a retained object   *passive*

The young lady was asked to start the song. [The infinitive *to start* takes *song* as its direct object and at the same time functions as a noun, the retained object after the passive verb *was asked*.]

(6) As the object of a preposition

I have done everything except use force. [The infinitive (*to*) *use*, with its object *force*, functions as the object of the preposition *except*. (For the omission of *to* see pp. 72 f.)]

(7) Introduced by adverb, adjective, or pronoun. Infinitive phrases may be introduced by such adverbs, adjectives, and pronouns as *where, when, how, which, what, whom.*

The problem is where to find such leaders. [The infinitive *to find*, introduced by and modified by the adverb *where*, takes *leaders* as a direct object and at the same time functions as a noun, as a subjective complement of the main verb *is*.]

We must think about when to start the campaign. [The infinitive *to start*, introduced by and modified by the adverb *when*, takes *campaign* as its object and at the same time functions as a noun, the object of the preposition *about*.]

How to raise that much money is the question. [The infinitive *to raise*, introduced by and modified by the adverb *how*, takes *money* as a direct object and at the same time functions as a noun, the subject of the main verb *is*.]

One problem — which hat to wear to church — worried Lucy for hours. [The infinitive *to wear* is introduced by the adjective *which,* which modifies *hat,* the direct object of the infinitive. The infinitive phrase is used as a noun, in apposition with *problem.*]

I do not know what to do next. [The infinitive *to do,* introduced by its direct object, the pronoun *what,* functions as a noun, the direct object of the main verb *do know.*]

The girls argued about whom to invite. [The infinitive *to invite* is introduced by the pronoun *whom,* which is used as the direct object of the infinitive. The infinitive phrase is used as a noun, the object of the preposition *about.*]

NOTE. Very probably the infinitive in such sentences represents an ellipsis and a substitution. The infinitive has been substituted for the finite verb of a subordinate clause and the subject of this finite verb has been dropped. *He does not know which course to choose* probably developed from "He does not know which course he should choose." Again we see in an infinitive construction the natural tendency of language toward shortened forms of expression. (For ellipsis see pp. 151 ff.)

(8) Infinitive phrase introduced by the expletive *it.* The expletive *it* (see pp. 145 f.) may introduce a sentence in which the infinitive functions as a noun, the true subject of the main verb.

It is necessary to count the books accurately. [The infinitive *to count,* with *books* as its direct object and *accurately* as an adverbial modifier, functions as the true subject of the main verb *is.* *It* is an expletive. The sentence for analysis reads "To count the books accurately is necessary."]

Another sentence pattern makes use of the expletive *it* followed by an objective complement plus an infinitive, in which case the infinitive is the true direct object of the verb.

I find it impossible to like him. [The infinitive *to like,* with *him* as its direct object, functions as the true direct object of *find.* *It* is an expletive and *impossible* is an objective complement. The sentence for analysis reads "I find to like him impossible."]

b) Adjective use. An infinitive may modify a noun.

You have a task to perform. [The infinitive *to perform* functions as an adjectival modifier of *task.*]

A program to meet this emergency must be formulated at once. [The infinitive *to meet*, with its direct object *emergency*, functions as an adjectival modifier of *program*.]

The accused had nothing to say. [The infinitive *to say* functions as an adjectival modifier of *nothing*.]´

c) Adverb use. An infinitive may modify a verb, an adjective, or an adverb. An infinitive modifying a verb and expressing purpose is often introduced by *in order* or, expressing result, by the conjunction *so as*.

Purpose We went to have a good time. [The infinitive *to have*, with its object *time*, functions as an adverbial modifier of the main verb *went*. (The infinitive expresses purpose.)]

In order to draw well one must have a natural aptitude. [The infinitive *to draw*, with its adverbial modifier *well*, introduced by the preposition *in order*, functions as an adverbial modifier of the main verb *must have*.]

He acted so as to make himself obnoxious. [The infinitive *to make*, with its object *himself* and its objective complement *obnoxious*, introduced by the conjunction *so as*, functions as an adverbial modifier of the main verb *acted*.]

A good tire is hard to find nowadays. [The infinitive *to find*, with its adverbial modifier *nowadays*, functions as an adverbial modifier of the adjective *hard* (which in turn is a subjective complement of *is*.)]

You are certain to be well received. [The infinitive *to be received*, with its adverbial modifier *well*, functions as an adverbial modifier of the adjective *certain* (which in turn is a subjective complement of *are*.)]

The dean is ready to see you. [The infinitive *to see*, with its object *you*, functions as an adverbial modifier of the adjective *ready* (which in turn is a subjective complement of *is*.)]

I was not close enough to identify him. [The infinitive *to identify*, with its object *him*, functions as an adverbial modifier of the adverb *enough* (which in turn is a modifier of the adjective *close*, a subjective complement of *was*.)]

Father is too tired to go to the movies tonight. [The infinitive *to go*, with its adverbial modifiers *to the movies* and *tonight*, functions as an adverbial modifier of the adverb *too* (which in turn modifies the adjective *tired*.)]

I did not stay long enough to see the last act. [The infinitive *to see*, with its object *act*, functions as an adverbial modifier of *enough* (which in turn is an adverbial modifier of *long*, *long* being an adverbial modifier of the verb *did stay*.)]

He left too quickly to obtain a clear view of the situation. [The infinitive *to obtain*, with its object *view*, functions as an adverbial modifier of *too* (which in turn is an adverbial modifier of *quickly*, *quickly* being an adverbial modifier of the verb *left*.)]

2. Complementary infinitive. An infinitive often forms with a finite verb such a close connection that the primary purpose of the infinitive seems to be to complete the predication begun by the verb. When the infinitive is combined with *use*, *have*, *go*, *is*, *happen*, *about*, *ought*, in such expressions as "used to go," "have to go," "going to go," "is to go," "happen to go," "about to go," "ought to go," etc., the infinitive becomes part of the verb phrase. In these uses the infinitive is called a "complementary infinitive."

For diagrams of complementary infinitives see p. 384.

I used to read Latin at sight. [The infinitive *to read*, with its object *Latin* and its adverbial modifier *at sight*, may be regarded as a complementary infinitive, the main function of which is to complete the predication begun by the finite verb *used*.]

It is going to rain. [The infinitive *to rain* may be regarded as a complementary infinitive, completing the predication begun by the finite verb *is going*.]

You are to leave in an hour. [The infinitive *to leave*, with its adverbial modifier *in an hour*, may be regarded as a complementary infinitive completing the predication begun by the finite verb *are*.]

I have to make a speech. [The infinitive *to make*, with its direct object *speech*, may be regarded as a complementary infinitive completing the predication begun by *have*.]

You ought not miss the celebration. [The infinitive *miss* (without its sign *to*), with its direct object *celebration*, may be regarded

as a complementary infinitive completing the predication begun
by *ought*.]

We are about to have a storm. [The infinitive *to have*, with its
direct object *storm*, introduced by its adverbial modifier *about*,
may be regarded as a complementary infinitive completing the
predication begun by *are*.]

3. Infinitive clause.   An infinitive may function in a kind of
semi-clause with a grammatical subject of its own. But it differs
from a finite verb in this very important respect: the subject
of an infinitive (when the infinitive takes a grammatical subject) is always in the objective case. This grammatical subject
of an infinitive indicates the agency of the infinitive.[17]

For diagrams of infinitive clause constructions see pp. 385 ff.

a) Similar to a shortened clause.   An infinite clause is
roughly equivalent to a regular subordinate clause. Sometimes
to (the sign of the infinitive) is omitted, especially after verbs
such as *see, hear, make*. (See also pp. 72 and 315.)

We thought him to be the best player. [The infinitive clause
him to be the best player is roughly equivalent to the subordinate
clause "that he was the best player."]

The dean requested me to report at once. [The infinitive clause
me to report at once, in which *me* is the grammatical subject
of *to report*, functions as the direct object of the main verb *requested*.]

The major ordered the bridge to be taken at any cost. [The
infinitive clause *the bridge to be taken at any cost*, in which *bridge*
is the grammatical subject of *to be taken*, functions as the direct
object of the main verb *ordered*.]

I believe her preference to be to play one more game. [*Preference* is the subject of the infinitive *to be*; *to play one more
game* is an infinitive phrase functioning as a subjective complement of *to be*; the infinitive clause *her preference to be to play
one more game* functions as the direct object of the finite verb
believe.]

---

[17] That is, the doer of the action (He told *us* to leave), the thing being re-
named or described (He wanted his *son* to be president some day), or the re-
ceiver of the action of a passive form (I expect *him* to be promoted soon).

He left too quickly for me to get a good look at him. [The infinitive clause *me to get a good look at him*, in which *me* is the grammatical subject of *to get*, functions as the object of the preposition *for* (the whole prepositional phrase *for me to get a good look at him* functioning as an adverbial modifier of the adverb *too*, or *too quickly*.)]

NOTE. Of course, no one explanation will fit exactly every case. After such verbs as *believe, know, think, order*, and the like, the infinitive construction is clearly a kind of semi-clause, with the noun that indicates the agency of the infinitive functioning as the grammatical subject of the infinitive—*They believed me to have lost the key.*

Inasmuch as the two special verbs *ask* and *teach* are capable of taking two direct objects (see p. 48), the substantive may be regarded as one of the double objects and the infinitive as the other.

He asked me to go. [*Me* and *to go* may be regarded as double objects after the verb *asked*. Or, in view of the fact that the sentence means roughly "He asked that I go," *me to go* may be regarded as an infinitive clause functioning as the direct object of the main verb *asked* (*me*, with this interpretation, being the subject of the infinitive *to go*).]

She taught me to dance. [*Me* and *to dance* may be regarded as double objects after the verb *taught*. Or, *me to dance* may be regarded as an infinitive clause functioning as the direct object of the main verb *taught* (*me*, with this interpretation, being the subject of the infinitive *to dance*).]

After such verbs as *make, hear, see*, the infinitive (usually appearing without its sign *to*) closely resembles an objective complement construction.

He made me go. [*Me* may be regarded as the object of *made* and *go* (without its sign *to*) as a kind of objective complement. Or, *me (to) go* may be regarded as an infinitive clause functioning as the direct object of the main verb *made* (*me*, with this interpretation, being the subject of the infinitive *(to) go*).]

Although there are these other thoroughly acceptable explanations, in the interests of simplicity it will serve all ordinary purposes to regard as an infinitive clause any construction in which a substantive preceding an infinitive indicates the agency of the infinitive, the substantive then to be interpreted as the grammatical subject of the infinitive. However, we must bear in mind that not all substantives preceding infinitives indicate the agency of the infinitive. Such substantives, of course, cannot function as grammatical subjects of infinitives.

We promised her to come. [*Her* is the indirect object after *promised*, not the grammatical subject of *to come*, which is the direct object of *promised*.]

My father has a house to rent. [*House* is the direct object of *has*, not the grammatical subject of *to rent*. *To rent* is an adjectival modifier of *house*.]

Congress needs another argument to be convinced. [*Argument* is the direct object of *needs*, not the grammatical subject of *to be convinced*. *To be convinced* functions as an adverbial modifier of *needs*.]

b) *To* sign omitted.   The infinitive without *to* (called the "simple" infinitive) is often used in infinitive clauses following certain verbs, such as *let, help, make, see, hear*, etc. (See pp. 315 ff. for other uses of the simple infinitive.)

Let him come back tomorrow. [*Him* is the subject of (*to*) *come*; the infinitive clause *him* (*to*) *come back tomorrow* functions as the direct object of the main verb *let*.]

I might be able to help you convince her. [*You* is the subject of (*to*) *convince*; the infinitive clause *you* (*to*) *convince her* functions as the direct object of the infinitive *to help*.]

That curbing made me stumble. [*Me* is the subject of (*to*) *stumble*; the infinitive clause *me* (*to*) *stumble* is the direct object of the main verb *made*.]

Seeing Bob act in such a childish manner shocked all of us. [*Bob* is the subject of (·*to*) *act*; the infinitive clause *Bob* (*to*) *act in such a childish manner* functions as the direct object of the gerund *seeing*.]

I never heard her make an unkind remark about anybody. [*Her* is the subject of (*to*) *make*; the infinitive clause *her* (*to*) *make an unkind remark about anybody* functions as the direct object of the main verb *heard*.]

c) Introduced by the expletive *for*.   Sometimes an infinitive clause is introduced by the expletive *for* (see also pp. 148 f.).

For me to go now is impossible. [The infinitive clause *me to go now*, functioning as the subject of the main verb *is*, is introduced by the expletive *for*.]

It is difficult for us to trust his word. [The infinitive clause *us to trust his word,* functioning as the true subject of *is,* is introduced by the expletive *for;* and the whole statement is introduced by another expletive, the expletive *it* (see also pp. 145 f.).]

His plan is for us to go first. [The infinitive clause *us to go first,* functioning as a subjective complement of *is,* is introduced by the expletive *for.*]

I know no way except for us to voice our objections in person. [The infinitive clause *us to voice our objections in person,* functioning as the object of the preposition *except,* is introduced by the expletive *for.*]

The time for us to assert ourselves has come. [Here the infinitive clause *us to assert ourselves* is the object of the preposition *for;* and the prepositional phrase *for us to assert ourselves* functions as an adjectival modifier of *time.*]

NOTE. Some grammarians prefer to regard *for* introducing an infinitive clause as a preposition, with the infinitive clause functioning as its object, under all circumstances. But there is a real difference in meaning between *for* functioning as an expletive and *for* functioning as a preposition, a difference worth maintaining.

It is difficult for me to judge. [The sentence for analysis reads "For me to judge is difficult." Here *for* functions as an expletive introducing the infinitive clause *me to judge.*]

I waited for him to speak. [Here *for* clearly functions as a true preposition, taking the infinitive clause as its object, the whole prepositional phrase *for him to speak* functioning as an adverbial modifier of the main verb *waited.*]

d) Construction with the passive voice. When a construction containing an infinitive clause is turned into the passive voice, the grammatical subject of the infinitive becomes the grammatical subject of the passive verb and the infinitive remains; that is, the infinitive may be said to become a retained object (see also p. 54).

I was ordered to report for duty. [The infinitive *to report* (with its adverbial modifier *for duty*) functions as a retained object after the passive verb *was ordered.* (The active construction reads "They ordered me to report for duty.")]

He was thought to be the right man. [The infinitive *to be* (with its subjective complement *man*) functions as a retained object after the passive verb *was thought.* (The active construction reads "They thought him to be the right man.")]

I was taught to make my own bed. [The infinitive *to make* (with its direct object *bed*) functions as a retained object after the passive verb *was taught.* (The active construction reads "My mother taught me to make my own bed.")]

4. Infinitive phrase or clause used absolutely. Infinitive phrases and infinitive clauses are sometimes used absolutely (see pp. 139 f.) — that is, without any grammatical function in the statements in which they appear. (For diagrams of infinitive phrases and clauses used absolutely see pp. 412 f.)

To make a long story short, I do not know any such person. [The infinitive phrase *to make a long story short* is used absolutely; it has no grammatical function in the statement *I do not know any such person.*]

To think that she would believe such a report! [The infinitive phrase *to think that she would believe such a report* is used absolutely; it is used here as an exclamation.]

Our house, to be sure, is a bit old-fashioned. [The infinitive phrase *to be sure* is used absolutely; it is used here parenthetically.]

The judges have already departed, their decision to be announced tomorrow. [The infinitive clause *their decision to be announced tomorrow* is used absolutely; it has no grammatical function in the statement *the judges have already departed.*]

5. Miscellaneous constructions. The infinitive in English lends itself readily to the tendency of language toward shortened locutions. As a result many infinitive constructions must be regarded as idioms, for in such cases we can only guess at the original form from which the idiom came. That is, many constructions that we must now regard as idioms probably involved originally some kind of ellipsis (see pp. 151 ff.).

a) Infinitive with *than*

I should rather save my money than spend it. [The infinitive phrase (*to*) *spend it* may be regarded as an adverbial modifier of the adverb *rather,* joined to it by the conjunction *than.*]

She prefers to drop out rather than to face defeat. [The infinitive phrase *to face defeat* may be regarded as an adverbial modifier of the adverb *rather*, joined to it by the conjunction *than*.]

There can be no greater thrill than to discover that you were right all the time. [Probably the full sentence was "There can be no greater thrill than to discover that you were right all the time would be a thrill." But in the interest of simplicity the infinitive phrase may be regarded as an adverbial modifier of the adjective *greater*, joined to it by the conjunction *than*.]

b) Infinitive after *as* to complete a comparison begun by *so* or *such*

His explanation was such as to amaze the most skeptical. [Probably the infinitive *to amaze* originally was the subject of an understood finite verb — "His explanation was such as to amaze the most skeptical would be." But in the interest of simplicity the infinitive phrase may be regarded as an adverbial modifier of the adjective *such*, joined to it by the conjunction *as*.]

He surely will not be so foolish as to run away. [Probably the infinitive *to run away* was originally the subject of an understood finite verb — "He surely would not be so foolish as to run away would be foolish." But in the interest of simplicity the infinitive phrase may be regarded as an adverbial modifier of the adverb *so*.]

c) Infinitive after *as if*

He made a motion as if to throw the ball. [Probably there is an ellipsis here for something like "He made a motion as he would make if he were going to throw the ball." But in the interest of simplicity the infinitive phrase may be regarded as an adjectival modifier of *motion* (for the infinitive phrase describes the kind of motion), joined to it by the conjunction *as if*.]

6. Dangling infinitive. For the "dangling infinitive" see pp. 318 f.

EXERCISES

Verbs

I. In the sentences printed below point out what you regard as simple finite verbs and what as finite verb phrases.

1. I take a walk every morning.
2. Getting up at five o'clock on a cold morning is not what I call fun.
3. Around seven o'clock the Piticcos, looking out their windows, saw that their neighbors had also been preparing to leave.
4. The other day we were in a taxicab that just missed a collision with a cab that cut in ahead of it.
5. After standing empty for a matter of eleven years, the old Army and Navy Club building has been fixed up and reopened as the United States Maritime Service Center.
6. There was one small dog which was not only willing to sit down but insisted on holding its front paws up at the same time.
7. The new station can sleep two hundred and forty men.
8. Sometimes the men don't stay overnight but are shipped out after a couple of hours.
9. Mr. Staunton has just been appointed revenue collector for Ohio.
10. Weismuller was making his debut on the vaudeville stage at the Capitol Theater in New York.
11. It was not known what talk the two men may have had together.
12. Ben Lander, who stood the night trick himself, waddled around the end of the bar, tossed his apron back over his shoulder in a social mood, and accepted a drink from Michael.
13. I am aware of the fact that my remarks could have been misinterpreted.
14. Could anyone really believe that I was running away?
15. I have been told that I have unusually expressive eyes.

II. Examine each verb in the following sentences. Determine which are transitive verbs, which are link verbs, and which are passive verbs. Remember that some passive verbs may also be link verbs.

1. He must have burned his papers; we could find only a few charred remains.
2. He looked fine when I saw him last.

3. We decided that the delicate machinery had been tampered with.
4. The report was received with little enthusiasm; to some of us it seemed quite incomplete.
5. If you make your fence ten feet high, I am afraid that you might be considered antisocial by your neighbors.
6. I have only one request to make: that my personal papers be left unpublished for one hundred years.
7. The clerk apparently felt that a sale was imminent. "Just feel the texture of this material," he said. It felt quite ordinary to me.
8. I felt uncomfortable when I gave him the news that his plan had been declared unworkable.
9. Now that the leaves are turning green, my daily routine seems almost unbearably tedious.
10. We had been told that the property would require practically no improvements.
11. I cannot accept the doctrine that "whatever is is right."
12. The sorrel horse, number 3, was finally adjudged the winner.
13. I have been given a new fountain pen; now I have three good ones.
14. You should have been more careful; you could have been arrested for reckless driving.
15. Our accommodations proved disappointing, but later we located another resort that friends had told us about.
16. I now own ten shares of common stock; I have become a capitalist.
17. Undoubtedly someone will be appointed temporary chairman at our next meeting.
18. I am afraid that my remarks may have sounded almost heartless to the unfortunate survivors.
19. The soft, warm winds of the Piedmont Plain proved most welcome after the Alpine blasts which had been chilling us.
20. This is, I believe, the first time that I have ever been called a diplomat.

III. Identify all of the complements in the following sentences.[18]

1. He is the new senator from Oregon.
2. The ground feels dry.
3. Jim was elected president on the third ballot.
4. They call their son Jasper.
5. She seems to be mistress of the situation.
6. Give me the ball; you take the bat.

[18] For this exercise, and for the remaining exercises in the book, diagram forms could be used as an effective and time-saving means of showing the construction of sentences. See pp. 370 ff. for examples of diagram forms.

7. He is not the man we are looking for.
8. Live the good life.
9. I was promised a promotion.
10. I was taught Latin by a master hand.
11. I wish to ask you three questions.
12. This apple tastes sweet.
13. She smiled a happy smile.
14. We were told that we could not enter.
15. You certainly ran a good race.
16. My dog is named Shep.
17. The lilacs smell strong.
18. Your plan sounds good.
19. I chose Professor Mills as my adviser.
20. Please wipe the dishes dry.
21. They were informed that their plan was unconstitutional.
22. This pen point has become bent.
23. She grew worse each hour.
24. This box must be packed full.
25. Don't throw everything to the four winds.
26. The man was voted guilty.
27. I am called Tack by my friends.
28. None of us likes to be considered eccentric.
29. My mother taught me that I must respect my elders.
30. I consider the man a genius.
31. We found our car unharmed in any way.
32. I feel fine; but you look bad. Are you ill? You look ill.
33. Mr. Hobbs was elected county treasurer.
34. Consider him what you will, he is at least a scholar.
35. Tie the rope tight.
36. We found the house in poor repair.
37. She considered him the best man in the world.
38. Such inventions have made food plentiful and cheap.
39. Don't call me a fool.
40. He felt himself unequal to the task.
41. The truth shall make you free.
42. He calls himself a liberal.
43. Such taxes make capital secretive.
44. I pronounce you husband and wife.
45. The ring was found to be of brass.
46. Having been given a salary increase, he looked about for ways to spend the increase.
47. To be given such a tongue-lashing in public was most embarrassing.

48. The agent told us that we would have to wait for the second section of the limited.
49. My experience taught me that I should be careful about talking with strangers.
50. De Lawd in *The Green Pastures* said "Bein' God ain't no bed of roses."
51. We were informed that there were no more prewar bicycles available.
52. Did you ask him when we might be able to buy some bananas?
53. To be given an honorary degree by such a distinguished college is something to be very proud of.
54. Being deprived of his privileges made him very angry.
55. I tried to discover when the name was first used.
56. He blurts out whatever seems to come into his mind.
57. We found that the left rear tire had gone flat during the night.
58. I can show you how to make yourself popular with your classmates.
59. Edward has become one of our most energetic workers.
60. She made him a good wife, because she made him a good husband.
61. Brenda will not remain inconspicuous long; she has tinted her hair a startling shade of orange.
62. Tell me how you intend to raise sufficient funds.
63. When I made my announcement, Mr. Conway looked startled and uncomfortable.
64. You will have plenty of time to make out a detailed itinerary.
65. It seems hardly fair that I should be assigned the worst room in the dormitory.

IV. Explain all verb + preposition and verb + adverb combinations you find in the following sentences.

1. We can't put off our departure any longer.
2. The play took in four hundred dollars last night.
3. Have you disposed of your bicycle yet?
4. The factory has shut down for a week.
5. I'll close out the rest of the stock at fifty cents on the dollar.
6. You can't laugh at such a man.
7. You seem to have great luck in standing off your creditors.
8. If you will close the windows you will shut out the heat.
9. The race will be run off at ten o'clock.
10. We were laughed at for our pains.
11. My business with you can be disposed of in five minutes.
12. The Giants were shut out for the third successive day.
13. I don't propose to be taken in by any such excuse.

14. You may leave out the last two questions of the examination.
15. Such conduct can't be put up with any longer.
16. Dr. Thompson has taken over Dr. Harlow's practice for the month of June.
17. Such criticism can't be laughed off.
18. You surely won't sneeze at such a chance, will you?
19. If you will put up the money, we can start work at once.
20. But until the money is actually put up, we can't begin.
21. The sheriff deputized some citizens to help him put down the riot.
22. I shall look over the applications before the end of the week.
23. Several of my good neighbors helped out at harvest time.
24. Before long Grandfather will surely turn over the business to me.
25. I promised him that I would look into the matter of the oil leases for him.

V. Explain fully all the participial constructions in the following sentences, explaining the function of the participle itself and indicating any modifiers and any complements the participle may take.

1. Borrowing a few dollars here and a few dollars there, he finally had enough to make the down payment.
2. Wrapped in a great coat of fur, he looked like a huge bear.
3. Having been scooped on that assignment, Ben did not propose to be caught napping a second time.
4. Acquitted on one charge, he has to stand trial on another.
5. On the third floor are two large rooms connected by a narrow hall.
6. It being the first of the month, I'll have some money to spend.
7. He finally reached the goal he had set for himself, never turning aside for a single moment.
8. The bank having closed, we shall have to wait until tomorrow to cash our checks.
9. Sensing the peril, he leaped quickly to one side.
10. Harried by first one inquisitor and then another, he maintained his claim of innocence.
11. Being of a genial nature, he took no offense at the remark.
12. I mean the bank fronting on Main Street.
13. He told a story reminding me of one that Grandfather once told me.
14. All rubbish having been cleared away, we started to lay the foundation for our cabin.
15. Bananas kept in a paper sack will ripen nicely.
16. Catching hold of the bar, he pulled himself to the top.
17. The little girl went down the walk singing at the top of her voice.
18. I kept fingering the cloth and wondering at the price.

19. I felt myself struggling against an unseen force.
20. We saw him laughing and gesticulating at the top of the hill.
21. There being no objection, we will stand adjourned until next Monday.
22. My tie has come untied.
23. The man wearing a Panama is my uncle.
24. A mass tangled up like that is beyond me.
25. As they stepped to the dock, Hester grimly refusing assistance, they started at the appearance of what at first glance seemed to be a ghost.

VI. Explain fully all the gerund constructions in the following sentences, explaining the function of the gerund itself and indicating any modifiers and any complements that the gerund may take.

1. My mother used to talk about carrying coals to Newcastle.
2. After mailing your complaint wait a full week before taking further steps.
3. By economizing carefully I can make my money last for a year.
4. His usual activity was whittling an old stick.
5. I call that being downright mean.
6. Your proposition is worth considering carefully.
7. Be sure to have the water boiling hot.
8. Hank was fighting mad.
9. I have been worried about his coughing so much.
10. You must use great care in paddling a canoe if you don't want a ducking.
11. In making fudge don't forget the essential pinch of salt.
12. By taking a little exercise every day the average person can keep himself in fit condition.
13. We can save as much as five minutes by taking the short cut through the woods.
14. His one obsession, grabbing every dollar he sees, is getting the best of him.
15. Shelling peas for a large family is my idea of doing stupid work.
16. By taking a stitch in time you are supposed to save nine.
17. The high gods have been capricious in handing down their favors.
18. The boy was confronted with the problem of finding a job at once.
19. He eyed the boy craftily with an eye to trying him out.
20. Motoring across Minnesota has its compensations.
21. I like living in a state where the political pot is always at the boiling point.
22. It won't be necessary at his passing for the mortician's assistants to do the pallbearing.

23. The very word "Christmas" was inseparable from her memory of the elder Ottendorfs' great golden-oak dining room on Christmas Eve.
24. Hoarding money can be as destructive as squandering it.
25. Citizens shifted in and out and fell to quarreling over nothing.

VII. Explain fully all the infinitive constructions in the following sentences, explaining the construction of the infinitive itself and indicating any modifiers and any complements that the infinitive may take.

1. Nobody seemed to want to make the first move.
2. It is hard to decide what measures to take in such a situation.
3. To be ready to answer all questions promptly you must have made adequate preparation.
4. I went to the doctor to get him to give me something to make me sleep.
5. It will be foolish to attempt to persuade him to join us.
6. How we are going to make both ends meet is beyond me.
7. Let my mother decide where to hold the picnic.
8. He seems to prefer very much to have a dog for a pet.
9. We waited to see them to determine what to do with the remainder.
10. They were permitted to have flower gardens.
11. Brother taught me to skate in three lessons.
12. Do you know where to find his raincoat?
13. I was taught how to hold the club correctly.
14. I'd hate to think that I would do anything just to get money.
15. It was a relief to discover that nothing was missing.
16. Maxine was asked to become the new secretary.
17. She seems to have nothing to do except read and sleep.
18. He soon began to realize his predicament.
19. The company now occupying the building was asked to vacate.
20. I believe that it will be difficult to convince him of his error.
21. I see no good reason to grant your request.
22. The rain came too swiftly for us to get all the hay in.
23. His plan, to block the President's scheme, was thwarted just in time.
24. The commanding officer ordered the bridge to be blown up.
25. Did you ever hear her sing?
26. It is impossible for all of us to go in one car.
27. We have three courses before us — to go forward, to turn back, or to stand still.
28. It is easy to make a checkerboard.
29. A checkerboard is easy to make.

30. It is useless for you even to plan to attempt to refuse to learn to swim.
31. She waited for me to make the telephone call.
32. I have my work to do.
33. Such a course is to be warmly commended.
34. The prisoners were thought to be the bank robbers.
35. To put the matter bluntly, why delay longer?
36. I should like to have attended your birthday party.
37. She should be allowed to pursue her own way.
38. It is a situation to be avoided at any cost.
39. To tell the truth, I need the money.
40. They were too strong for any of us to wish to start a fight.
41. To make a long story short, I was asked not to play my trombone after nine o'clock.
42. Our plan was for them to take the initiative.
43. I do not like to seem to be ungracious.
44. The contract has been let, the work to be completed by May first.
45. Let's decide now where to meet.
46. That makes me laugh.
47. There is nothing to do here but fish and swim.
48. There is nothing for us to do but keep our mouths closed.
49. The heat caused the pavement to explode.
50. He is entirely too young to drive a car.
51. We got there early enough to see the last act.
52. We were just about to give you a ring.
53. Political parties ought to live up to their platforms.
54. I am going to make a motion that we lay the matter on the table.
55. We are going to have a pep session Friday evening.
56. I have to file a report this afternoon.
57. He came to see my sister.
58. I did my best to convince him of his mistake.
59. He did not hesitate to ask the men to be quiet.
60. She is to become the new dean of women.
61. He is sure to cross our path some day.
62. You know my orders, one man to stand guard at each door and two men to enter the building itself.
63. I believe it to be evident that he made a motion as if to draw a deadly weapon.
64. He did no more than to outline the scheme to us.
65. We dare not hesitate now.

VIII. Explain fully all the verbal constructions in the following sentences, explaining the function of the verbal itself and then indicating any modifiers and any complements that the verbal may take.

1. I can see the limited coming several miles away, its powerful headlight fingering rails and telegraph wires with a shimmer of light.
2. And then, looming black against the night sky, it smashed past, and in the swing of drivers and connecting rods I think of a greyhound, or race horse, thundering down the final stretch.
3. I recall participating in a spelling bee.
4. He continued on his way like a big-breasted galleon, Stephen following like a captured corsair.
5. She could hear the cuckoo clock striking six in the hall and feel the boys tugging at her hands and see the sliding dining-room doors rolling back to reveal the tall tinsel-hung Christmas tree, twinkling with wax candles, rising from piles of white-papered, red-ribboned Christmas gifts.
6. There were the bewildering smells of sap, crushed leaves, and decaying wood; acrid, sweet, spicy, and suffocating, some like musty books, others recalling the paint on the Noah's Ark of one's nursery.
7. He never at any time lost entirely that disheveled appearance of being undusted, a little tumble-down, unbrushed, and uncombed.
8. There's always plenty of work to be done in any small town.
9. Having discussed the story, we can now turn to a more interesting topic, the actors.
10. The job is for those strong enough to bend the bow to drive the unerring arrow to the center of the target.
11. My main design in writing this article is to address a word of exhortation to our feminists.
12. Modern feminism has contented itself with asserting the thesis of women's ability and right to do everything that men can do.
13. At any period in history one may find women living their own lives.
14. His greatest ambition is to follow in his father's footsteps.
15. It is difficult to be as frank in talking with women as with men, because women tend more than men to hold a preconceived idea of one's character and tastes; and it is difficult to talk simply and naturally to anyone who has formed a mental picture of one, especially if one is aware that it is not correct.
16. But men are slower to form impressions; moreover, in talking with men one encounters more opposition.
17. You are tempted to emphasize good and bad qualities beyond the truth simply to impress the reader and make a telling picture.
18. Everybody appreciates how prone to yield to it Macaulay was.
19. It is so easy to use a strong adjective unqualified, so easy to make a white virtue out of a casual complacency, or to turn a regretted and forgotten error into blasting sin.

20. The plodding storekeeper, ambitious for his son, hoped to make a doctor or lawyer of him.
21. In the orange light I can see the fireman swing back and forth as he feeds his fire.
22. Through swirls of dust I watch the two red lights sink down the track.
23. We must not shrink from exploring even the retreats of misery.
24. It would be possible to present a long list of officeholders who have had their sons educated free at West Point and Annapolis.
25. Writing in the plainest manner, he manages to do what more artful authors merely try to do — he gives his world that simple, solid reality and permanence which it would seem we cannot give a thing when we are aware of wanting to do so.
26. Sunk between Cragg Hill and Red Hill, Glen Hazard had the look of being dropped in the hollow and mixed by the four winds.
27. She shut the door softly and sat herself down upon the edge of the porch, her mind quivering with the uneasiness of sleep that had run away too soon.
28. He'd brought Dell all the honey he was going to bring. He wasn't going out honey-gathering every morning any longer.
29. We have much to learn from one another.
30. Feminism has been content with demanding the right to vote, to practice politics and hold public office, to enter commerce, finance, and the learned professions, and the trades, on equal terms with men, and to share men's social privileges and immunities on equal terms.
31. The thing now is to measure the strength of this new factor.
32. Woman's economic status has a great deal to do with defining and establishing her social status.
33. Having found my first snowdrop of the year, I did what I always do with that flower of promise: I held it above my head to look within its green lines and again to marvel at the beauty of it.
34. Making allowances for the conscious exaggeration of a delightful writer, there is a great deal of truth in this paradox.
35. They even take the liberty of inventing conversations between well-known men and of putting in their mouths sentences they never pronounced.
36. He seemed to spend all his waking hours in practicing scales on the piano.
37. The farmhouse stood off among tall trees, two red chimneys budding out of the roof.
38. She heard something crying far off, undetermined crying, sharp and

full of pain, but too far away to touch pity, the mere outline of a cry duplicated without feeling on the hot air.

39. Bisecting the hill like a precise center parting was the main turnpike road between Fleece and Bathwater Spa.

40. To call it a garden city suburb would be an anachronism.

41. With the coming of the terraces Button Hill was no longer the name, primarily, of a hill.

42. Henry used the trolley cars to go to the factory and return, leaving the sedan for Aurelia to use.

43. In the store she might spend an hour pricing things and perhaps matching a shred of silk, buying a pair of stockings or a small vial of perfume.

44. Then she would hurry to keep an engagement to lunch indigestibly with Stella Greeley at the confectioner's.

45. It didn't happen to be one of the days for hairdressing, manicuring, and facial beautifying.

46. Vicky saw that her own stock had risen with her secretary because of being lunched with by a young male member of the staff.

47. The question of their not being here on time never entered my mind.

48. The question of there not being enough food for all never entered my mind.

49. The time came for her to sing.

50. The time for her to sing came at last.

51. It became my unpleasant task to tell him that he would soon have to start supporting himself.

52. My work out of the way, I am now ready to have some fun.

53. What have you to say about my brother and me joining your club?

54. I never heard of it being done before.

55. I never heard of its being done before.

56. I think I heard Robert's hound baying.

57. They discussed briefly both plans, the question of which being the more prudent not having yet arisen.

58. I knew the groceries were closed; but I never thought of the bank being closed.

59. You should have thought of the bank's being closed on the Fourth of July.

60. His embarrassment in having been duped was very great.

61. Getting up early in the morning and taking a brisk walk requires a compelling kind of determination.

62. We must go ahead without having obtained permission first.

63. His habit of smacking his lips while eating a meal annoyed me.

64. His money all spent, he smiled a curious smile.

65. I saw her standing in the door leading to the library.
66. It took great patience to cope with such a man.
67. He knew where the earliest violets were to be found.
68. The desire to achieve ought to be found in every one of us.
69. We had to spend little time in locating his hiding place.
70. I am unable to make out what you are talking about, to speak frankly.
71. He was unusual in his ability to ward off criticism.
72. Abandoned by his friends and laughed at by his enemies, he tried to find solace in reading the great classics of literature.
73. Be sure to think carefully before making up your mind.
74. Speaking of jokes, have you seen Murphy recently?
75. His only interest in life seems to be making money and still more money.

c.   Adjectives[19]

As we saw earlier from our brief definition (p. 6), anything that qualifies (that is, modifies) a substantive (noun or pronoun) is adjectival in function and may be called an adjectival modifier. (For classes of adjectives see pp. 322 ff.)

1.   WORD, PHRASE, CLAUSE

A single word, a phrase (such as a prepositional phrase, a participial phrase, an infinitive phrase), or a clause may function as an adjectival modifier.[20] (For adjectival clauses see pp. 169 ff.)

a. Single words as modifiers

The tall and stately pine impressed everyone with its beauty. [*Tall* and *stately* are adjectival modifiers of *pine*.]
The lecture, dull and lengthy, wore people out. [*Dull* and *lengthy* function as adjectival modifiers of *lecture*.]
The lecture was dull and lengthy. [*Dull* and *lengthy*, subjective

[19] For forms and usages see pp. 322 ff.
[20] A single word functioning as an adjective usually precedes the noun it modifies; but a phrase or clause functioning as an adjective usually follows the noun it modifies.

complements (see pp. 51 f.), function as adjectival modifiers of *lecture*.[21]]

b. Phrases as modifiers

1. Prepositional (see also pp. 116 f.)

An officer from Annapolis is expected soon. [The prepositional phrase *from · Annapolis* functions as an adjectival modifier of *officer*.]

2. Participial (see also pp. 59 ff.)

The man wearing a straw hat is Mr. Hanna. [The participial phrase *wearing a straw hat* functions as an adjectival modifier of *man*.]

Rejected by the Marine Corps, Jim enlisted in the army. [The participial phrase *rejected by the Marine Corps* functions as an adjectival modifier of *Jim*.]

3. Infinitive (see also pp. 65 ff.)

I have an appointment to meet this afternoon and a train to catch in the morning. [The infinitive phrase *to meet this afternoon* functions as an adjectival modifier of *appointment*; and *to catch in the morning* functions as an adjectival modifier of *train*.]

c. Clauses as modifiers (see also pp. 160 ff.) When a clause functions as a modifier of a substantive, this clause is known as an adjectival clause or an adjective clause. An adjectival clause (which, of course, is always a subordinate clause) is joined to the element that it modifies by some kind of connective. (See also under Adjectival Clauses, pp. 169 ff.)

A man who will not take a risk will never get ahead. [The subordinate clause *who will not take a risk* functions as an adjectival modifier of *man*.]

Walla Walla, which is located in the southeastern part of Washington, is one of the oldest cities in the Pacific Northwest. [The subordinate clause *which is located in the southeastern part*

---

[21] Adjectives functioning as subjective complements are sometimes called predicate adjectives.

of Washington functions as an adjectival modifier of *Walla Walla*.]

2.   RELATIONSHIP TO SUBSTANTIVE

An adjective may bear several possible relationships to the substantive that it qualifies.

a. Attribute, appositive, predicate

1. Attribute.   An adjective may represent an attribute of the substantive, something that qualifies or limits or narrows the meaning of the substantive modified. It is then said to bear an attribute relationship to the substantive. A single-word attribute (*large* dog; *blue* sky; *stern* expression) usually precedes the substantive modified. But an attribute adjective that is modified by a phrase ("a man anxious about his children") usually has to be placed after its substantive. A prepositional or verbal phrase functioning as an attribute modifier ("the girl in the blue dress"; "the man wearing a red carnation"; "a house to rent") and any subordinate clause functioning as an attribute modifier ("the girl that is wearing a blue dress") must of necessity follow the substantive modified (see also pp. 175 f.).

The noisy and boisterous children rushed into the house. [*Noisy* and *boisterous* function as attribute modifiers of *children*.]

A courageous man would know how to meet such a situation. [*Courageous* functions as an attribute modifier of *man*.]

A man eager to meet such a situation would know what to do. [*Eager*, modified by the infinitive phrase *to meet such a situation*, functions as an attribute modifier of *man*.]

A man that had the necessary courage to meet the situation would know what to do. [The subordinate clause *that had the necessary courage to meet the situation* functions as an attribute modifier of *man*.]

That is the girl whose brother is my roommate. [The subordinate clause *whose brother is my roommate* functions as an attribute modifier of *girl* (the relative adjective *whose* modifying *brother* and looking back to *girl* as its antecedent.)]

I wish to visit the farm where I was born. [The subordinate clause *where I was born* functions as an attribute modifier of *farm* (the relative adverb *where* modifying *was born* and looking back to *farm* as its antecedent).]

There comes a time when a man must make a decision. [The subordinate clause *when a man must make a decision* functions as an attribute modifier of *time* (the relative adverb *when* modifying *must make* and looking back to *time* as its antecedent).]

2. Appositive. An adjective may represent an appositive idea; that is, it may bear an appositive relationship to the substantive modified, being in the nature of an afterthought, of something added, in which case it is called an appositive adjective. An appositive adjective whether a single word, a phrase, or a clause usually follows the substantive modified, although an appositive modifier may at times precede the substantive.

The children, noisy and boisterous, rushed into the house. [*Noisy* and *boisterous* function as appositive adjectival modifiers of *children*.]

Noisy and boisterous, the children rushed into the house. [*Noisy* and *boisterous* function as appositive adjectival modifiers of *children*.]

Stern but kindly, shy but gracious, Hamilton fascinated people. [*Stern, kindly, shy,* and *gracious* function as appositive modifiers of *Hamilton*.]

Mr. Hardy, courageous and even a bit daring, did not hesitate for a moment. [*Courageous* and *daring* function as appositive modifiers of *Mr. Hardy*.]

Mr. Baxter, of the State Department, is my authority for the statement. [The prepositional phrase *of the State Department* functions as an appositive modifier of *Mr. Baxter*.]

I shall see my boss, with whom I have an agreement about overtime work, to arrange the details. [The subordinate clause *with whom I have an agreement about overtime work* functions as an appositive modifier of *boss* (the relative pronoun *whom*, object of the preposition *with*, looking back to *boss* as its antecedent).]

He has gone to Seattle, where he will live in the future, and has opened a law office. [The subordinate clause *where he will live in the future* functions as an appositive modifier of *Seattle* (the relative adverb *where* modifying *will live* and looking back to *Seattle* as its antecendent).]

NOTE. The distinction between the attribute modifier and the appositive modifier is important in punctuation. An adjective unit functioning as an attribute modifier (also called a restrictive modifier) is never set off with commas. But an adjective unit functioning as an appositive modifier (also called a nonrestrictive or additive modifier) is always set off with commas or something stronger. A predicate adjective, naturally, is never set off.

The phrase or clause used as an attribute modifier is added to the substantive it modifies because further *identification* of the substantive is needed. The attribute modifier distinguishes the modified substantive from all other members of its class.

People sitting near the window saw the accident. [The participial phrase *sitting near the window* is vital for the identification of the noun *people*. It is an attribute (restrictive) modifier and is therefore not set off with commas.]

I envy anyone who can type and take shorthand. [The adjective clause *who can type and take shorthand* is vital for the identification of the pronoun *anyone*. It is therefore an attribute (restrictive) modifier and is not set off with commas.]

The appositive (nonrestrictive) modifier is added to a substantive to give additional descriptive information, but it differs from the restrictive modifier in that it is not necessary for the *identification* of the substantive.

My boss, sitting near the window, saw the accident. [The participial phrase *sitting near the window* is not necessary for the identification of the noun *boss* (which is already identified by the modifier *my*). It is therefore a nonrestrictive modifier and is set off with commas.]

I envy Linda Cooper, who can type and take shorthand. [The adjective clause *who can type and take shorthand* is not needed for the identification of the noun *Linda Cooper* (which, being a proper noun, is already identified). It is therefore a nonrestrictive modifier and is set off with commas.]

An adjective phrase or clause modifying a proper noun will normally be a nonrestrictive modifier, since a proper noun identifies a member of a class. But a proper noun can be followed by a restrictive modifier if further identification is needed:

The Joe Brown who was arrested last night for vagrancy is not the Joe Brown who works in our office.

3. Predicate. An adjective may serve to qualify a subject (or an object) and to complete the predication begun by the verb. Such an adjective is called a predicate adjective. If it qualifies the subject, it functions as a subjective complement; if it qualifies a direct object, it functions as an objective complement. An adjective may function as a predicate adjective after a verb in the active voice ("This apple tastes sweet") or after a verb in the passive voice ("He was found unconscious").

A single word or a phrase may function as a predicate adjective.

The children were noisy and boisterous. [*Noisy* and *boisterous* function as predicate adjectives; they both qualify *children* and complete the predication begun by the verb *were*.]

Mr. Hardy was courageous and even a bit daring. [*Courageous* and *daring* function as predicate adjectives; they both qualify *Mr. Hardy* and complete the predication begun by the verb *was*.]

This ring is of solid gold. [The prepositional phrase *of solid gold* functions as a predicate adjective; it both qualifies *ring* and completes the predication begun by the verb *is*.]

Your suspicion seems to be unfounded. [The infinitive phrase *to be unfounded* functions as a predicate adjective; it both qualifies *suspicion* and completes the predication begun by the verb *seems*.]

His equipment was found intact. [*Intact* functions as a predicate adjective; it both qualifies *equipment* and completes the predication begun by the passive verb *was found*.]

The rod was heated red-hot. [*Red-hot* functions as a predicate adjective; it both qualifies *rod* and completes the predication begun by the passive verb *was heated*.]

The situation made Mr. Hardy courageous and even a bit daring. [*Courageous* and *daring* function as predicate adjectives; they both qualify *Mr. Hardy* and complete the predication begun by the verb *made*. They are objective complements.)]

He tied the rope tight. [*Tight* functions as a predicate adjective;

it both qualifies *rope* and completes the predication begun by the verb *tied*. (*Tight* is an objective complement.)]

The jury found him guilty. [*Guilty* is a predicate adjective; it both qualifies *him* and completes the predication begun by the verb *found*. (*Guilty* is an objective complement.)]

We found Mr. Lander in excellent spirits. [The prepositional phrase *in excellent spirits* functions as a predicate adjective; it both qualifies *Mr. Lander* and completes the predication begun by the verb *found*. (The phrase is an objective complement.)]

NOTE. A subordinate clause used as a subjective complement or as an objective complement has a renaming relationship with the substantive rather than a modifying relationship. Clauses used in these positions will therefore be noun clauses, not adjective clauses.

My hope is that I shall receive a passing grade. [The clause *that I shall receive a passing grade* is a noun clause, since it renames the subject *hope*.]

These experiences made him what he is today. [The clause *what he is today* is a noun clause, since it renames the direct object *him*.]

b. Coordinate and cumulative. Adjectives may attach themselves to substantives in two different manners, either as coordinate or as cumulative modifiers. The distinction is particularly important to correct punctuation. Adjectives that are coordinate in function are separated with commas, like any other series of items; but adjectives functioning as cumulative modifiers are not so separated. When adjectives are coordinate in function each adjective modifies the substantive in exactly the same manner as the other. A simple test for adjectives functioning as coordinate and cumulative modifiers is whether *and* can be placed between them. If *and* can be placed between them, the adjectives are coordinate and should have commas between them. If *and* cannot be placed between them, the adjectives are cumulative in effect and no comma should appear between them.

He was entranced with the little old lady. [*Little* and *old* are cumulative in effect. That is, *old* modifies *lady*, and *little* modifies *old lady*.]

He is an honest, law-abiding, conscientious, and cooperative citizen. [*Honest, law-abiding, conscientious,* and *cooperative* are coordinate adjectives. Apply the *and* test and the sentence may read "He is an honest and law-abiding and conscientious and cooperative citizen."]

He wore a splendid new blue-striped shirt. [*Splendid, new,* and *blue-striped* are cumulative modifiers of *shirt.*]

She wore her brother's old overcoat. [*Brother's* and *old* are cumulative modifiers of *overcoat; her* modifies *brother's.*]

The boy presented a ragged, unkempt, somewhat disreputable appearance. [*Ragged, unkempt,* and *disreputable* are coordinate modifiers of *appearance;* hence, the commas between them.]

He was a pompous, belligerent, impetuous little old man. [*Pompous, belligerent,* and *impetuous* function as coordinate modifiers of *man;* hence, the commas between them. The first three adjectives and *little* and *old* function as cumulative modifiers of *man;* hence, no commas between them.]

3.   OTHER PARTS OF SPEECH FUNCTIONING AS ADJECTIVES

Because of the ease with which a word in English may change its customary part of speech, other parts of speech may readily function as adjectives. This is especially true of nouns. (See also pp. 36 and 134 ff.)

a. Nouns *(including gerunds;* see also p. 315.)

a *morning* meal   the *Fourth of July* celebration   the *United States* flag   a *railroad* station   a *high-school* course   the *college-entrance* requirements   a *dining* car

I prefer a Saturday holiday to one on Monday. [*Saturday,* a noun, here functions as an adjectival modifier of *holiday.*]

I favor the Senate bill, but I am opposed to the House bill. [*Senate* and *House,* nouns, here function as adjectival modifiers of *bill.*]

My friend always carries a walking stick. [*Walking,* a gerund, here functions as an adjectival modifier of *stick.*]

NOTE.   Some newspapers have carried this possibility of using a noun as an adjectival modifier to such extremes that a headline sometimes has to be read more than once before the reader is sure of its meaning – "The United States Senate Patent Committee Chairman Makes Report."

b. Adverbs (see also p. 109).

I prefer to wait for the through train. [The adverb *through* functions as an adjectival modifier of *train*.]

We have to be careful about the up and down drafts. [*Up* and *down*, adverbs, function as adjectival modifiers of *drafts*.][22]

c. Verbs

The would-be hero failed dismally in trying to be heroic. [The verb form *would-be* functions as an adjectival modifier of *hero*.]

For adjectival uses of participles and infinitives, see p. 59 and p. 67.

4. **ADJECTIVES AS OTHER PARTS OF SPEECH**

Adjectives may function as nouns especially (see pp. 36 and 134 ff.).

a. With "the" to form an abstract noun. An abstract adjective like *good, beautiful, right,* may be used with the article *the* and become the equivalent of an abstract noun.

The right eventually prevails.
The good that men do is oft interred with their bones.
We admire the good, the true, the beautiful.
The best is none too good for her.

b. With "the" to form a plural noun. The article *the* is frequently used with an adjective, or participle, to form a plural noun.

The poor have their problems; the rich have theirs. [*The poor* and *the rich* function as plural nouns.]

The wounded were removed to the hospital. [*Wounded*, originally a participle, with *the* functions as a plural noun.]

The uprooted, the downtrodden, the poverty-stricken are entitled to our sympathy. [The adjectives *uprooted, downtrodden,* and *poverty-stricken*, originally derived from participles (see p. 305), with *the* function as plural nouns.]

[22] Many such adverbs are attached to the noun, sometimes with a hyphen: *offshoot, show-off, outgrowth, overhead.*

c. *With "s" attached to form nouns.*   Some adjectives by the addition of s function as plural nouns: *eatables, particulars, valuables.*

The particulars are not yet available.
I keep my valuables at the bank.
Our kindergarten classes are held in portables.

EXERCISES

Adjectives

I. Indicate which expressions you regard as adjectival in function and state whether the expression is a single word, a phrase, or a clause. Make clear what the adjectival expression modifies. If the adjectival expression is a phrase, state whether it is a prepositional, participial, or infinitive phrase in form. (Adjectival clauses will be exemplified later; see pp. 169 ff.)

1. I mention these melancholy details not only for their own sake but also to emphasize the point that when I speak of students' dormitories and the larger life they offer, I speak of what I know.
2. The shops faced the oldest house on the estate, which stood back from the main road, sharing a strip of lawn and the communal crescent-shaped drive with carriage gates.
3. He had a hundred schemes in his head and a thousand impulses in his heart.
4. She knew an instant's pang of tenderness, poignant, exquisite.
5. Walking along slowly, very close together, oblivious and sunlit and young, they talked things over.
6. My analysis can be extended to encompass the economic relationships which play an important role in other fields of culture as well as in the motion-picture industry.
7. The rise of `Hollywood to the realm of culture is a phenomenon analogous to that of the triumph of machine production during the industrial revolution.
8. The second group of scientific philosophers brings us back to social criticism.
9. The man took off his old battered felt hat.

10. It was romantic hair – it was the kind of hair that made you feel it must have turned white in a single night.
11. Lank and lean, gaunt and a little grim, with the wistful shadow of unfulfillment on their shrewd faces, they were strangely evocative of their Puritan forebears.
12. It was the first stone wall, festooned with wine-red woodbine, surrounding a scrubby clearing overgrown with yellow sweet fern and dotted with silver-gray rock.
13. The most tantalizing odors were the wonderfully delicate and penetrating ones from some great burst of blossoms, odors heavy with sweetness, which seeped down from vine or tree high overhead, wholly invisible from below even in broad daylight.
14. His scanty hair, which fell away from a great dome of a forehead, was an indeterminate sandy-gray.
15. Along the moonlit trail there came wavering whiffs of orchids, ranging from attar of roses and carnations to the pungence of carrion, the latter doubtless distilled from as delicate and as beautiful blossoms as the former.
16. Any man's memory of his boyhood is the memory of a world which time refused to touch.
17. By noon the garden was hot and pungent and immensely sweet.
18. Very early over the dark and chestnut-covered hills in the distance and over the Lombardy poplars which marked the end of the garden, holding up close perpendicular branches like foliated silver cups to catch some cool light wine, the sun fell slantingly upon the white summerhouse with its pentagonal tin roof of red, upon damp paths of tan bark, and upon borders of flox, where silver dew and silver spider webs frosted the implacable green.
19. Back of the house was a barn, newly painted white, and the neatness of a freshly planted vegetable garden.
20. He was facetious and philosophical, allusive and alliterative, pointed and parenthetical, flowery and brief.
21. A dark green wrapper was pulled close around her slight-made body, and her uncombed hair flared above her puzzled eyes.
22. On the far edges the circling woods about the farmstead were slate-colored, for the heavy-footed time of year was come, and a spicy smell of late fall was crushed from the fields and forest trees around Glen Hazard.
23. There sat the old log house, the same that she had been born in.
24. New York had all the American faults and all the American virtues. It was brilliant, gallant, insouciant, cool, tolerant; it was generous, witty, sensitive, eager, and vivacious; it was unmellow, selfish, un-

humorous despite its wit, fierce, cruel, and contemptuous, not of habits, morals, or ideas, but of lack of intelligence and failure.

25. Having no mountains of its own, it had built mountains; but they were harsh mountains without any streams in them, or green open spaces, or hidden shadows.

26. It is almost impossible to distinguish between the prophet of bad news and the causer of bad events.

27. He beat his forehead with his hairy, prehensile hands; for the birth of something absolutely new in his mind was making his head ache.

28. And there have been countless minor incidents which have led other Congressmen to similar conclusions.

29. Valuable hand-carved furniture is made for the use of people of means.

30. The Missouri is the frontier's river, and it is still regarded with the passionate possessiveness the frontier felt for its few immediately available natural resources.

II. Go back over some of the previous sentences and point out which adjectives bear an attribute and which an appositive and which predicate relationships to the substantives that they qualify.

III. Go back over some of the previous sentences and point out which adjectives are coordinate in effect and which cumulative in effect.

D.   Adverbs[23]

As we saw earlier from our brief definition (p. 6), anything that qualifies (that is, modifies) a verb, an adjective, or another adverb is adverbial in function. (For classes of adverbs see p. 337.)

1.   SINGLE WORD, PHRASE, CLAUSE

A single word, a phrase, or a clause may function as an adverb.

a. Single words as modifiers

Jim folded his paper carefully. [*Carefully* functions as an adverbial modifier of the verb *folded*.]

[23] For forms and usages see pp. 337 ff.

One must be extremely careful. [*Extremely* functions as an adverbial modifier of *careful* (which is a subjective complement of *must be*).]

Jim folded his paper very carefully. [*Very* functions as an adverbial modifier of *carefully* (which in turn is an adverbial modifier of *folded*).]

b. Phrases as modifiers
1. Prepositional   *most commonly*

Harriet walked to the window. [The prepositional phrase *to the window* functions as an adverbial modifier of the verb *walked*.]

In helping others we help ourselves. [The prepositional phrase *in helping others* functions as an adverbial modifier of the main verb *help*.]

2. Infinitive

not as flexible

I am eager to know the result. [The infinitive phrase *to know the result* functions as an adverbial modifier of the adjective *eager* (which is a subjective complement of *am*).]

You came too late to see the parade. [The infinitive phrase *to see the parade* functions as an adverbial modifier of the adverb *too*, which in turn modifies the adverb *late* (an adverbial modifier of the verb *came*).]

c. Clauses as modifiers.
A clause that functions as a modifier of a verb, of an adjective, or of an adverb is known as an adverbial clause or an adverb clause. An adverbial clause (which, of course, is always a subordinate clause) is joined to the element that it modifies by some kind of connective. (See also under Adverbial Clauses, pp. 179 ff.)

When I arrived I found nothing but confusion. [The subordinate clause *when I arrived* functions as an adverbial modifier of *found*, the verb in the main clause.]

I am sure that Mason has forgotten our appointment. [The subordinate clause *that Mason has forgotten our appointment* functions as an adverbial modifier of the adjective *sure*.]

The weather was so cold that our water pipes froze. [The subordinate clause *that our water pipes froze* functions as an adverbial modifier of *so*, which in turn is an adverbial modifier of the adjective *cold* (the subjective complement of *was*).]

He is as honest as the day is long. [The subordinate clause *as the day is long* functions as an adverbial modifier of the adverb *as*, which in turn is a modifier of the adjective *honest* (the subjective complement of *is*).]

NOTE.   Adverbs have a wide range of functions. An adverb can be used independently or absolutely – that is, with little or no grammatical function in the statement in which it appears (see pp. 141 f.). Further, adverbs can modify single words, phrases, or even whole clauses. (One authority has said that he would not venture the statement that there is anything that an adverb may not at one time or another be found to modify.) The chances are, then, that any element that is not readily classed otherwise is adverbial in function.

A simple working principle may be of help in many cases. A prepositional or an infinitive phrase coming at the beginning of a statement, or a subordinate clause coming first in a sentence, which is not obviously a subject of the main verb, will very likely function as an adverbial modifier – usually of the main verb. Or, of equal value may be the fact that any phrase or any subordinate clause found in the body of a sentence (not obviously a noun clause) that can be placed first without changing the sense of the statement is proved by that fact to be adverbial in function.

In Janesville thousands of fountain pens are made daily. [The prepositional phrase *in Janesville* functions as an adverbial modifier of *are made*, the main verb.]

Men and women of Janesville make thousands of fountain pens daily. [The prepositional phrase *of Janesville* functions as an adjectival modifier of *men and women*. Note that the prepositional phrase cannot be placed first without changing the sense of the sentence.]

In Meharry Hall a bell will be rung at six. (The prepositional phrase *in Meharry Hall* functions as an adverbial modifier of *will be rung*, the main verb.]

The bell in Meharry Hall will be rung at six. [The prepositional phrase *in Meharry Hall* functions as an adjectival modifier of *bell*. Note that the prepositional phrase cannot be placed first without changing the sense of the sentence.]

To operate a car legally one must have a license. [The infinitive phrase *to operate a car legally* functions as an adverbial modifier of *must have*, the main verb.]

In opening a checking account you must deposit a minimum of one hundred dollars. [The prepositional phrase *in opening a checking account* (with the gerund *opening* functioning as the object of the preposition *in*) functions as an adverbial modifier of *must deposit,* the main verb.]

If the gong sounds, come in a hurry. [The subordinate clause *if the gong sounds* functions as an adverbial modifier of *come,* the main verb.]

Since there is to be no holiday, we must work as usual. [The subordinate clause *since there is to be no holiday* functions as an adverbial modifier of *must work,* the main verb.]

I know a store where we can buy a San Francisco paper. [The subordinate clause *where we can buy a San Francisco paper* functions as an adjectival modifier of *store.* Note that this subordinate clause cannot be placed first.]

2.   MODIFIER OF A PHRASE OR CLAUSE

An adverb may be used to modify a phrase or a clause.

The ball went just over the fence. [*Just* functions as an adverbial modifier of the prepositional phrase *over the fence.*]

He came only to ask you a question. [*Only* functions as an adverbial modifier of the infinitive phrase *to ask you a question.*]

Precisely what he had in mind I do not know. [*Precisely* functions as an adverbial modifier of the noun clause *what he had in mind* (which is the object of *do know*).]

Surely we ought to make an effort. [*Surely* functions as an adverbial modifier of the sentence *we ought to make an effort.*]

He jarred my arm just when I was making a shot. [*Just* functions as an adverbial modifier of the adverbial clause *when I was making a shot* (which modifies *jarred*).]

3.   SPECIAL KINDS OF ADVERBS

a. Interrogative. An interrogative adverb — such as *when, where, why, how* — may introduce a direct question and modify a verb, an adjective, or an adverb. An interrogative adverb may also introduce a phrase or a noun clause asking or implying an indirect question. (See also under Noun Clauses, pp. 165 f.)

When did you leave? [*When,* introducing the direct question, functions as an adverbial modifier of *did leave.* (The sentence for analysis reads "You did leave when.")]

How tall are you? [*How,* introducing the direct question, is an adverbial modifier of the adjective *tall*. (The sentence for analysis reads "You are how tall.")]

How fast was he driving? [*How*, introducing the direct question, functions as an adverbial modifier of the adverb *fast*. (The sentence for analysis reads "He was driving how fast.")]

I do not know how to tie a bow tie. [*How*, introducing the infinitive *to tie*, functions as an adverbial modifier of *to tie*.]

I wonder why he left early. [*Why*, introducing the noun clause, functions as an adverbial modifier of the verb *left*.]

b. Relative.   A relative adverb — such as *when, where, why* — may function as a modifier in a subordinate clause and join this clause to some element in the main clause. That is, a relative adverb serves as both an adverb and as a connective at the same time. If the adverb has an antecedent expressed in its sentence, it is called a relative adverb (or definite relative adverb); if it does not have an antecedent expressed in its sentence, it is called an indefinite relative adverb.

This is a time when we cannot dodge the issue. [*When* modifies *can dodge* in the subordinate clause and joins this clause to *time*, which the subordinate clause modifies. As *when* has an antecedent — *time* — expressed in its sentence, *when* is called a relative adverb (or definite relative adverb).]

I shall go when I am summoned. [*When* modifies *am summoned* in the subordinate clause and joins this clause to *shall go*, which the subordinate clause modifies. As *when* has no antecedent expressed in its sentence, *when* is called an indefinite relative adverb.]

I marvel at how patient he is. [*How* modifies the adjective subjective complement *patient* in the noun clause. Since *how* has no antecedent in the sentence, it is an indefinite relative adverb.]

c. Correlatives.   A pair of related adverbs — such as *as . . . as, not so . . . as, the . . . the, when . . . then, where . . . there* — are called correlative adverbs. The one that appears in the main clause and contains the antecedent idea functions as a simple adverb; the one that appears in the subordinate clause and contains the relative idea functions as a relative adverb. (See also pp. 185 f. For diagrams of correlative adverbs see pp. 395 f. and 410.)

He is as old as I am. [That is, "He is as old as I am old." The second *as* functions as a relative adverb, modifying *am* (*old*) and joining the subordinate clause to the main clause as an adverbial modifier of *as*. (The sentence might be expanded to read "He is old to that degree to which degree I am old.")]

I am not so sure as I was yesterday. [That is, "I am not so sure as I was sure yesterday." *As* functions as a relative adverb, modifying *was* (*sure*) and joining the subordinate clause to the main clause as a modifier of *so*, which in turn is an adverbial modifier of the adjective *sure*, the subjective complement of the verb *am*. (The sentence might be expanded to read "I am not sure to the degree to which degree I was sure yesterday.")]

When you signal, then I shall enter. [*When* functions as a relative adverb, modifying *signal* and joining its clause to the main clause *then I shall enter* (in which *then* functions as a simple adverbial modifier of *shall enter*) as an adverbial modifier of *shall enter*. (The sentence might be expanded to read "I shall enter at the moment at which moment you signal.")]

The correlative adverbs *the . . . the* (often mistaken for the article *the*) function frequently in such constructions as "the more the merrier," which involve an ellipsis (see pp. 151 ff.). This *the* is an old English adverb used correlatively to mean "in which degree," "in that degree." (See also pp. 126 f. and 181 f.)

The faster we walk the sooner we shall arrive. [The meaning is this: "In which degree we walk faster in that degree we shall arrive sooner." The first *the* functions as a relative adverb modifying *faster* and joins its clause to the main clause *the sooner we shall arrive*, in which the second *the* functions as a simple adverbial modifier of the adverb *sooner*.]

The more the merrier. [The sentence for analysis reads "The more people there are the merrier it will be." The meaning is this: "In which degree there are more people in that degree it will be merrier." The first *the* is a relative adverb modifying the adjective *more*. The second *the* is a simple adverbial modifier of the adjective *merrier*.]

The sooner he comes the better. [The sentence for analysis reads "The sooner he comes the better it will be." The meaning is this: "In which degree he comes sooner in that degree it will be better." The first *the* is a relative adverb modifying the adverb *sooner*. The second *the* is a simple adverbial modifier of the adjective *better*, which is a subjective complement of the understood verb *will be*.]

d. Independent.   Adverbs (words, phrases, or clauses) may be used independently or absolutely (see also pp. 138 ff.); that is, they may be used without any grammatical function in the statements in which they appear.

sentence modifier

There are three ways to make an outline. [*There* is an adverb that here functions as an expletive (see pp. 145 f.); that is, it has no grammatical function in the sentence "Three ways to make an outline are" (in which *are* = "exist"; see pp. 43 f.). Compare, however, "You will find your friend in there," in which *there* is an adverb functioning as a noun, the object of the preposition *in*. (See also p. 108.)]

In short, we have come to the end of our rope. [The prepositional phrase *in short* may be regarded as an adverbial phrase used in an absolute sense; that is, it has no grammatical function in the statement *we have come to the end of our rope*.]

He doesn't know what he is talking about, if I may speak my mind. [The subordinate clause *if I may speak my mind* is an adverbial clause used absolutely; that is, it has no grammatical function in the statement *he doesn't know what he is talking about*.]

Such expressions as *now, well, why,* and the affirmative *yes* and the negative *no* are to be regarded as adverbs used absolutely or independently.

Well, you may be right. [*Well* may be regarded as an adverb used absolutely; that is, it has no grammatical function in the sentence *you may be right*.]

No, I don't know him. [The negative *no* may be regarded as an adverb used absolutely or independently.]

Why, I didn't know you at first. [*Why* may be regarded as an adverb used absolutely or independently.]

e. Transitional.   Certain words like *therefore, however, more-over, nevertheless, consequently, hence,* are used to effect a logical transition between independent clauses, between whole sentences, or between paragraphs or sections of a discourse. Effecting as they do a rhetorical transition, they may be called transitional adverbs[24] and so be regarded as adverbs used absolutely or independently. (See also pp. 141 f.)

I don't believe it will work. Nevertheless, I am willing to give it a trial. [*Nevertheless* functions as a transitional adverb, an adverb used absolutely or independently to effect a rhetorical transition between the two sentences.]

She controls the money; therefore, he is powerless to resist. [*Therefore* functions as a transitional adverb, an adverb used independently or absolutely to effect a logical relationship between the two independent clauses.]

NOTE 1.   The distinction between transitional adverbs and coordinating and subordinating adverbs is important in the matter of punctuation. Whereas a comma is the usual mark between statements joined by coordinating or subordinating connectives, a semicolon is customarily used before a transitional adverb standing between independent clauses. In other words, the presence of a transitional adverb between two statements does not affect the punctuation demanded; the punctuation is precisely the same as it would be were no transitional adverb present. Further, transitional adverbs, being absolute elements, are often set off with commas.

You have had lots of experience; therefore, you act as our scorekeeper. [*Therefore* is a transitional adverb, not a coordinating conjunction; hence, nothing less than a semicolon will suffice.]

It is raining, but we will go anyway. [*But* is a coordinating conjunction; hence, a comma is correct.]

NOTE 2.   Inasmuch as a sentence is a complete grammatical entity, it cannot be thought of as being joined *grammatically* to another sentence, although, of course, it may be joined to another sentence rhetorically.

[24] The term "conjunctive adverb" has been discarded in this book because of its ambiguity. Some grammarians have used the term "conjunctive adverb" to designate what we have just termed "transitional adverb." But other grammarians have used the same term to designate a relative adverb like *where* or *when* that functions as an adverb in a subordinate clause and joins its clause to a main clause (see pp. 131 f.). Hence, it seems best not to use the term "conjunctive adverb" at all.

Hence, *and, but, for, or, nor,* at the beginning of a sentence may rightly be regarded as transitional adverbs rather than as conjunctions.[25] For they effect a rhetorical rather than a grammatical connection.

> It is raining. But we will go anyway. [*But* may be regarded as a transitional adverb, effecting a rhetorical transition between the two independent sentences.]
> Tim is a good gardener. And that's not all. [*And* may be regarded as a transitional adverb, effecting a rhetorical transition between the two independent sentences.]

4.   OTHER PARTS OF SPEECH AND ADVERBS

Various relationships may exist among adverbs and other parts of speech.

a. Noun.   A noun (often roughly equivalent to a prepositional phrase) may function as an adverb and modify a verb, an adjective, or an adverb.[26]

> I am going home. [*Home,* a noun, here functions as an adverbial modifier of *am going.* The meaning = "I am going to home."]
> He is six feet tall. [*Feet,* a noun, here functions as an adverbial modifier of the adjective *tall* (a subjective complement after *is*). The meaning = "He is tall to the extent of six feet."]
> My sister will arrive Saturday. [*Saturday,* a noun, here functions as an adverbial modifier of *will arrive.* The meaning = "My sister will arrive on Saturday."]
> I am going hunting. [*Hunting* may be regarded as a gerund functioning as an adverbial modifier of *am going.* The meaning = "I am going on hunting." (See also p. 61, footnote 14.)]
> The water is boiling hot. [*Boiling,* a gerund, here functions as an adverbial modifier of *hot* (a subjective complement after *is*). (See also p. 314.)]
> The package arrived the day before yesterday. [*Day,* a noun,

[25] Of the many myths concerning "correct" English, one of the most persistent is the belief that it is somehow improper to begin a sentence with one of these words. The construction is, of course, widely used today and has been widely used for generations, for the very good reason that it is an effective means of achieving coherence between sentences and between larger units of discourse, such as paragraphs.

[26] Such a noun is sometimes called an "adverbial objective." In this book it has been called a "noun functioning as an adverb."

modified by the prepositional phrase *before yesterday*, functions as an adverbial modifier of *arrived*. The meaning = "The package arrived on the day before yesterday."]

He arrived a month before Easter. [*Month*, a noun, here functions as an adverbial modifier of the prepositional phrase *before Easter*. The meaning = "He arrived before Easter by a month."]

We struggled all day long. [*Day*, a noun, modified by the adjective *all*, here functions as an adverbial modifier of *long* (which in turn is an adverb modifying *struggled*). The meaning = "We struggled long to the extent of a day."]

He ordered a steak an inch thick. [*Inch*, a noun, here functions as an adverbial modifier of the adjective *thick* (which in turn is an adjectival modifier of the noun *steak*). The meaning = "He ordered a steak thick to the extent of an inch."]

She is six years older. [*Years*, a noun, here functions as an adverbial modifier of the adjective *older* (which is a subjective complement after *is*). The meaning = "She is older to the extent of six years."]

Admission costs fifty cents. [*Cents*, a noun, here functions as an adverbial modifier of the verb *costs*. The meaning = "Admission costs to the extent of fifty cents."]

Your bicycle is not worth ten dollars. [*Dollars*, a noun, here functions as an adverbial modifier of the adjective *worth* (which is a subjective complement after *is*). The meaning = "Your bicycle is not worth to the extent of ten dollars."]

Sugar now costs six cents a pound. [*Cents*, a noun, here functions as an adverb modifying *costs*. *Pound*, a noun, also functions as an adverbial modifier of *costs*. The meaning = "Sugar now costs to the extent of six cents for a pound."]

The average person can read fifty pages an hour. [*Hour*, a noun, here functions as an adverbial modifier of *can read*. The meaning = "The average person can ready fifty pages to the hour."]

We should have arrived an hour sooner. [*Hour*, a noun, here functions as an adverbial modifier of *sooner* (which is an adverb modifying *should have arrived*). The meaning = "We should have arrived sooner by an hour."]

NOTE. Nouns in the plural may function as adverbs.
Father works *nights*. *Sundays* he goes to church.

b. "The . . . the."   For the correlative adverbs *the . . . the* sometimes mistaken for the article *the*, see p. 103.

c. Prepositions and adverbs.   Prepositions and adverbs are very closely related. In fact, many words may be used as adverbs in one sense and as prepositions in another. The basic difference between them is the fact that the preposition will have an expressed (or easily supplied) object, whereas the adverb will not. (See also pp. 118 f.)

Adverb	*Preposition*
Come *in*.	Come *in* the morning.
Tear *down* the fence.	Let's walk *down* the street.
I'll look *up* the word.	She ran *up* the steps.

NOTE.   That *down* is an adverb and not a preposition governing *fence* in "He tore down the fence" is seen in the fact that the position of the adverb *down* can be changed — "He tore the fence down," — a thing which would not be true where *down* is a preposition — "He poured the liquid down the drain."

NOTE 2.   In such constructions as "He has nothing to hope for," "I have much to be thankful for," "That is nothing to be proud of," *for* and *of* may most simply be treated as adverbs modifying the infinitives. Or they may be regarded as prepositions governing an understood pronoun *which* — "He has nothing for which to hope," "I have much for which to be thankful," "That is nothing of which to be proud."

d. Adverb as a noun.   Adverbs may function as nouns, especially as objects of prepositions. (See also p. 114.)

The man in there is my uncle. [*There*, an adverb, functions as a noun, the object of the preposition *in*.]

I shall do it at once. [*Once*, an adverb, functions as a noun, the object of the preposition *at*.]

I think we shall find it in here. [*Here*, an adverb, functions as a noun, the object of the preposition *in*.]

He has had many ups and downs. [The adverbs *up* and *down*, pluralized, function as nouns, direct objects of the verb *has had*.]

I do not know the how or the why of his departure. [The adverbs *how* and *why* function as the direct object of *do know*.]

e. Adverb as an adjective. An adverb may function as an adjective. (See also p. 95.)

These pictures illustrate the before and after appearances. [The adverbs *before* and *after* function here as adjectival modifiers of *appearances*.]

My stay there was unpleasant. [The adverb *there* here functions as an adjectival modifier of *stay*.]

5.   ADVERB + VERB COMBINATIONS
See pp. 55 f.

EXERCISES
Adverbs

I. Indicate what expressions you regard as adverbial in function and state whether the expression is a single word, a phrase, or a clause. Make clear what the adverbial expression modifies. If the adverbial expression is a phrase indicate whether it is a prepositional or infinitive phrase. (Adverbial clauses will be exemplified in detail later; see pp. 179 ff.)

1. The game fishermen in certain localities began to complain bitterly to their congressmen about the expanding distance between bites.
2. By selecting a site of high altitude, above the denser and more disturbed portion of the atmosphere, in a region but little affected by clouds and storms, we may greatly reduce these difficulties.
3. When Lord Rosse built his six-foot reflector in the forties of the last century he was compelled to work on his country estate without the aid of skilled opticians and machinists, or the methods and machine tools of modern engineering.
4. He advanced menacingly toward the smaller man.
5. Fields lush with cotton are enlivened by bright-turbaned black women.
6. One straggling rain-rutted fork runs along the edge of a field to a cluster of low, weather-beaten houses grouped under giant red-oak trees.

7. Its branches reached up to the sky.
8. The roots seem to grope deep down into the earth.
9. Illidge was painfully conscious of his appearance.
10. The music came to an end in an orgy of mathematical merrymaking.
11. On the table were to be seen a plate, a teapot, and a loaf of bread.
12. To swing the deal we need your help very much.
13. After fixing the print wash it in running water for an hour.
14. The floor was of bare boards, which Jane swept twice a day, and down the center ran the great square beam that was the keelson and foundation of the barge.
15. The second blast roared off, and the boulder was a scattering of rocks spurted into the air. Gravel came flying up as far as where Waits and Fayre were standing.
16. What the English academic discipline lacks in extent is made up in thoroughness.
17. An art school run like a factory is scarcely more ridiculous than a factory run like an art school.
18. One might go on at length with this romantic type of stream piracy.
19. On the other hand, he contained within him a reservoir of learning of such depth as to be practically bottomless.
20. It is the business of every American professor to chase his students along over a prescribed course at a prescribed pace like a flock of sheep.
21. Long after Burke lamented the passing of the age of chivalry in Europe, the South maintained the outward form and inward spirit of chivalry in the whole structure of ante-bellum social life; and when that was shattered, the chivalric attitude toward the gentler sex was maintained as a precious survival.
22. Today processes the refractory material of yesterday's heresy into the standard tissue of orthodoxy; and tomorrow reprocesses its remnants into the shoddy of the commonplace.
23. In citing the American man's traditional easiness with women European opinion may have had everything on its side in the days of Daisy Miller and may still have something on its side.
24. Everybody speaks quite freely of the relation between ownership and rulership.
25. Women are able to do as well with all these activities as men can do.

II. Classify any adverbs you find in the following sentences as interrogative, relative, correlative, independent, or transitional.

1. Where are you going?
2. At any rate, he is harmless.
3. I have so little time; hence, I must make the most of what I have.

4. I think the time has come when we must take stock of things. *relative*
5. She said that the more she saw of men the better she liked dogs.
6. There is always one right answer to a question.
7. In brief, I refuse to be a martyr.
8. He is so old that he does not remember when he was ever young.
9. I do not know how he came by such a nickname.
10. Confidentially, he hasn't a leg to stand on.
11. I wish I could find the place where Shakespeare says something about a candle throwing a light.
12. Where he takes his stand there I take mine.
13. I downed the liquid quickly; nevertheless, I know I made a wry face.
14. Please ask where we can find a garage. *expletive*
15. That, in a nut-shell, is the explanation that he gave me.
16. The deeper I go into the matter, the greater is my bewilderment at his sheer stupidity.
17. That was a time when even Lincoln was discouraged.
18. America was not so dependent on England's navy as she had been prior to 1940.
19. Why did this have to happen to me?
20. Where can we buy stationery like yours?
21. In a word, we need your help.
22. I think you are a simpleton, if I may speak my mind boldly.
23. You are older than I am; hence, you better do the talking when we get there.
24. There is one novel of Jane Austen's that I reread whenever I am low in spirit.
25. But all of us must remember that haste now might mean dollars saved later on.
26. I must ask you how I am to make such a boat for twenty-five dollars.
27. We wondered when you would arrive.
28. We will start the game as soon as our pitcher arrives.
29. I am not so sure as you seem to be that everything will be all right.
30. With the people of the United States, therefore, rest the decisions on what shall be done about the Missouri basin.

E. *Prespositions*[27]

1. **A PREPOSITION AND A PREPOSITIONAL PHRASE**

A preposition is an expression governing a substantive in the objective case and joining this substantive to some other element in the sentence. *Sign of what follows.*

[27] For forms and usages see pp. 334 ff.

The substantive governed by the preposition is said to be the object of the preposition. This substantive is usually in the objective case — occasionally in the possessive case. (See Object of a Preposition, p. 113.) If the object of the preposition is compounded, each element of the compound is in the objective case.

The preposition and the substantive that it governs and all the modifiers of either the preposition or the substantive (or of the whole prepositional phrase) constitute a prepositional phrase.

The idea came to me suddenly. [The preposition *to* governs *me*, a substantive in the objective case; the prepositional phrase *to me* functions as an adverbial modifier of *came*.]

It is a secret between my sister and me. [*Not:* It is a secret between my sister and I. For the preposition *between* governs both *sister* and *me*, and both must be in the objective case. The prepositional phrase *between my sister and me* functions as an adjectival modifier of *secret*.]

He registered just at the time when the call went out for men who would volunteer for service. [*Just at the time when the call went out for men who would volunteer for service* constitutes a prepositional phrase; *time*, the object of *at*, is modified by the adjectival clause *when the call went out for men*; and *men* is modified by the adjectival clause *who would volunteer for service*. (*Just* is an adverb modifying the whole prepositional phrase; see p. 101.)]

2.   PHRASAL PREPOSITION

A preposition may be composed of two or more words — *in accordance with, on account of, because of, as to, in regard to.* Such prepositions are called phrasal prepositions. (See pp. 344 f. for a list.)

He paid ten dollars in accordance with our understanding. [*In accordance with* is a phrasal preposition governing the substantive *understanding*, the whole prepositional phrase *in accordance with our understanding* functioning as an adverbial modifier of *paid*.]

The shed was made out of old packing cases and beaverboard. [*Out of* is a phrasal preposition governing the substantives *cases* and *beaverboard*, the whole prepositional phrase *out of old packing cases and beaverboard* functioning as an adverbial modifier of *was made*.]

3. OBJECT OF A PREPOSITION

Any part of speech or any phrase or clause which can function as a substantive may be used as the object of a preposition.

a. Noun or pronoun. A noun or pronoun may function as the object of a preposition.

He drove from Cincinnati to Denver in two days. [The nouns *Cincinnati*, *Denver*, and *days* are the objects, respectively, of the prepositions *from*, *to*, and *in*.]

This is a present from her and me. [The pronouns *her* and *me* are objects of the preposition *from*.]

b. Noun or pronoun in the possessive case. A noun or pronoun in the possessive case may function as the object of a preposition. (Usually analysis will show that the substantive which the possessive really modifies has been omitted by ellipsis.) (See pp. 151 ff.)

You will find it at Marshall Field's. [That is, "You will find it at Marshall Field's store."]

I am going to my sister's for Christmas. [That is, "I am going to my sister's home for Christmas."]

My car is being repaired; we'll go in yours. [The possessive pronoun *yours* is the object of the preposition *in*.]

NOTE. In the case of the so-called "double genitive" (see pp. 345 f.) in which possession is shown by means of an *of*-phrase and a possessive at the same time, the possessive is to be regarded as a substantive functioning as the object of the preposition rather than as a modifier of some understood substantive.

Meton is a friend of mine. [*Mine*, a possessive pronoun, functions as the object of the preposition *of*.]

She is an acquaintance of my mother's. [*Mother's*, a possessive noun, functions as the object of the preposition *of*. (Note the slight difference in meaning of "She is an acquaintance of my mother.")]

c. Other units as objects of prepositions.   Inasmuch as adjectives, adverbs, gerund phrases, infinitive phrases, prepositional phrases, and subordinate clauses may be used as substantives, these units may function as objects of prepositions.

She is a friend of the sick, the needy, and the blind. [The adjectives *sick, needy,* and *blind* function as nouns, objects of the preposition *of*. (Or they may be regarded as modifiers of some understood substantive like "persons.")]

My luck is going from bad to worse. [The adjectives *bad* and *worse* may be regarded as functioning as nouns, objects of the prepositions *from* and *to*.]

It measures exactly six feet from here to there. [The adverbs *here* and *there* function as substantives, objects of the prepositions *from* and *to* respectively.]

He used an indelible pencil in signing the check. [The gerund *signing* (with its object *check*) functions as the object of the preposition *in*.]

We can do nothing but wait. [That is, "We can do nothing but to wait." The infinitive *(to) wait* functions as the object of the preposition *but*.]

Let's talk about how to spend our vacation. [The infinitive phrase *how to spend our vacation* functions as the object of the preposition *about*.]

He moved to within a few feet of me. [The prepositional phrase *within a few feet of me* functions as the object of the preposition *to*.]

The dog came out from under the shed. [The prepositional phrase *under the shed* functions as the object of the preposition *from*. (*Out* is an adverb modifying *came*.)]

I am satisfied with whatever you are. [The subordinate clause *whatever you are* functions as the object of the preposition *with*.]

Give it to whoever is willing to take it. [The subordinate clause *whoever is willing to take it* functions as the object of the preposition *to*.]

d. Position of object.   The object of a preposition usually immediately follows the preposition. But when a relative pronoun or an interrogative pronoun is the object, the relative or interrogative pronoun may come first and the preposition be left to the end of the statement. (For the problem of case involved see pp. 239 ff.) Note the examples in section *e*. (For a discussion of prepositions coming at the end of statements see pp. 352 f.)

I am not impressed with the man whom she is engaged to. [The relative pronoun *whom*, introducing the subordinate adjectival clause *whom she is engaged to*, is the object of the preposition *to*.]

The new mechanic does not seem to know what that tool is for. [The interrogative pronoun *what*, introducing the noun clause *what that tool is for* (the object of the infinitive *to know*), is the object of the preposition *for*.]

e. Object understood.   The object of a preposition, clearly understood, is often omitted by ellipsis (see pp. 151 ff.). An object frequently precedes the preposition that governs it — especially when the object is understood.

He is not a man I am acquainted with. [That is, "He is not a man whom I am acquainted with."]

This is the house I delivered the package to. [That is, "This is the house which I delivered the package to."]

4.   **PREPOSITIONAL PHRASE MODIFIED BY AN ADVERB**

A prepositional phrase may be modified by an adverb.[28]

He worked far into the night. [The adverb *far* modifies the prepositional phrase *into the night*, the whole prepositional phrase *far into the night* functioning as an adverbial modifier of *worked*.]

The door just to the right leads to my office. [The adverb *just* modifies the prepositional phrase *to the right*, the whole prepositional phrase *just to the right* functioning as an adjectival modifier of *door*.]

Crane's Bond is made wholly from new white rags. [The adverb *wholly* modifies the prepositional phrase *from new white rags*, the whole prepositional phrase *wholly from new white rags* functioning as an adverbial modifier of *is made*.]

[28] Or such an adverb may be construed as a modifier of the preposition alone rather than of the whole prepositional phrase.

5. FUNCTIONS OF PREPOSITIONAL PHRASES

A prepositional phrase may function as an adjective, as an adverb, and occasionally as a substantive. A prepositional phrase may also be used as an independent or absolute element (see pp. 138 ff.).

a. Adjectival modifier.

1. Simple modifier.   As a simple adjectival modifier of a substantive a prepositional phrase will usually follow the substantive modified.

> The girl in the green dress is our cheerleader. [The prepositional phrase *in the green dress* functions as an adjectival modifier of *girl.*]
> I like a man with a grin from ear to ear. [The prepositional phrase *with a grin from ear to ear* functions as an adjectival modifier of *man* (the prepositional phrase *from ear to ear* functioning as an adjectival modifier of *grin*).]

2. Subjective or objective complement.   A prepositional phrase may function as a subjective complement or an objective complement, although it is not always easy to declare that such a complement is primarily adjectival rather than substantive in function. (See also pp. 92 f.)

> My watch is of solid gold. [The prepositional phrase *of solid gold* functions as a subjective complement of *is.*]
> He is completely without friends. [The prepositional phrase *without friends* functions as a subjective complement of *is.*]
> I consider his testimony of no consequence. [The prepositional phrase *of no consequence* functions as an objective complement referring to *testimony* and completing the predication begun by the verb *consider.*]
> He thinks this book to be of great value. [The prepositional phrase *of great value* functions as a subjective complement of the infinitive *to be.*]

Note the difference in grammar and in meaning between the following:

The explanation was over my head. [*Over my head* is a prepositional phrase functioning as a subjective complement.]
The mistletoe was over my head. [*Over my head* is a prepositional phrase modifying *was*.]

b. Adverbial modifier.   A prepositional phrase may function as an adverbial modifier of a verb or of an adjective, or rarely of an adverb.

1. Modifying a verb.   A prepositional phrase functioning as an adverbial modifier of a verb may occur at the beginning of a statement or it may follow the verb. (See also p. 100, Note.)

In the morning I take only a cup of coffee and two slices of toast. [*Or*] I take in the morning only a cup of coffee and two slices of toast. [*Or*] I take only a cup of coffee and two slices of toast in the morning. [The prepositional phrase *in the morning* in each case functions as an adverbial modifier of *take*.]
In choosing a golf partner you need to consider several matters. [*Or*] You need to consider, in choosing a golf partner, several matters. [*Or*] You need to consider several matters in choosing a golf partner. [The prepositional phrase *in choosing a golf partner* in each case functions as an adverbial modifier of *to consider*.]

2. Modifying an adjective.   A prepositional phrase functioning as a modifier of an adjective will normally follow the adjective modified.

He seems sure of himself. [The prepositional phrase *of himself* functions as an adverbial modifier of the adjective *sure*.]
He is not tactful in handling subordinates. [The prepositional phrase *in handling subordinates* functions as an adverbial modifier of the adjective *tactful*.]

3. Modifying an adverb.   A prepositional phrase may occasionally function as a modifier of an adverb.

He swung the boat as far to the right as he could. [The prepositional phrase *to the right* functions as an adverbial modifier of the adverb *far*, which in turn modifies *swung*. Or, *far* may be interpreted as an adverb modifying the prepositional phrase *to the right*. (See p. 101.)]

You catch on quickly for a beginner. [The prepositional phrase *for a beginner* functions as an adverbial modifier of the adverb *quickly*.]

c. Substantive. Occasionally a prepositional phrase may function as a substantive. It may function as the object of a preposition (see p. 114). It may function as the subject or the complement of a verb.

The man stepped from behind a tree. [The prepositional phrase *behind a tree* functions as the object of the preposition *from*.]

From Monday to Saturday is a long stretch. [The prepositional phrases *from Monday* and *to Saturday* function as the subject of *is*.]

I consider right at noon very inconvenient. [The prepositional phrase *at noon* (modified by the adverb *right*) functions as the direct object of *consider* (*inconvenient* being an objective complement).]

The best time is just before breakfast. [The prepositional phrase *before breakfast* (modified by the adverb *just*) functions as a subjective complement of *is*.]

d. Absolute constructions. A prepositional phrase may be used as an absolute or independent element (see p. 138) — that is, without any grammatical function in the statement in which it appears.

By all means, let's have all the facts. [The prepositional phrase *by all means* is used absolutely; that is, it has no grammatical function in the statement *let's have all the facts*.]

At any rate, I have my health. [The prepositional phrase *at any rate* is used absolutely.]

We have, on the whole, little to complain about. [The prepositional phrase *on the whole* is used absolutely.]

6. PREPOSITIONS AND OTHER PARTS OF SPEECH

Prepositions may serve as other parts of speech, especially as adverbs.

a. Adverb or preposition. Often the same word may serve as a preposition in one situation and as an adverb in another (see p. 108). The basic distinction is the fact that the preposition takes an object, expressed or clearly understood (see p. 113), whereas an adverb does not.

Preposition	Adverb
My dog walked *behind* me.	I left my dog *behind*.
We walked *up* the drive.	Hold your head *up*.

b. Adverb rather than preposition.   At times the preposition-like word, with a noun following it, is actually an adverb, the noun being the object of the preceding verb and not of the preposition-like word.

I'll look up the word. [*Up* is an adverb, not a preposition governing *word*; *word* is the direct object of *look* (or of *look + up*; see verb + adverb combinations, p. 55). Note that the position of *up* may be shifted — "I'll look the word up."]

They tore down the old bridge. [*Down* is an adverb, not a preposition governing *bridge*; *bridge* is the direct object of *tore* (or of *tore + down*; see verb + adverb combinations, p. 55). Note that the position of *down* may be shifted — "They tore the old bridge down."]

c. "Like," "unlike," "near."   Like, unlike, and near may, for convenience, be regarded as prepositions governing the substantives that follow them. Actually, these words are adjectives or adverbs, and the substantives that follow them are objects of "to" or "unto," a construction no longer idiomatic with *like* or *unlike* but still possible with *near*.

He is unlike his brother in every respect. [*Unlike* may be regarded as a preposition governing *brother*. (Actually *unlike* is an adjective functioning as a subjective complement after *is*; and *brother* is the object of an understood preposition such as "to." That is, the sentence for analysis might read, "He is unlike to his brother in every respect."]

He acted like a demented man. [*Like* may be regarded as a preposition governing *man*. (Actually *like* is an adverb modifying the verb *acted*; and *man* is the object of an understood preposition such as "unto." That is, the sentence for analysis might read, "He acted like unto a demented man.")]

The children played near the porch. [*Near* may be regarded as a preposition governing *porch*. (Actually *near* is an adverb modifying *played*, and *porch* is the object of some understood preposition like "to." That is, the sentence for analysis might read, "The children played near to the porch.")]

The original use of these words as modifiers is shown by the fact that they have comparative and superlative degrees, and prepositions, of course, do not have the property of degree.

He looks more like a football player than a teacher. [*Like* is here an adjective (the *more* puts it in the comparative degree) used as a subjective complement. *Player* is the object of the omitted preposition *to* or *unto*.]

Your last guess came nearest the truth. [*Nearest* is here an adverb in the superlative degree. *Truth* is the object of the omitted preposition *to*.]

NOTE. Some grammarians now treat *worth* in such a sentence as "His hat is worth ten dollars" as a preposition governing the substantive *dollars*. The usual explanation is that *worth* is an adjective functioning as a subjective complement and that *dollars* (with its modifier *ten*) is a noun functioning as an adverbial modifier of *worth*. (See also pp. 106 f.)

d. Preposition as an adjective.   A preposition may at times function as an adjectival modifier of a substantive as the result of an ellipsis (see pp. 151 ff.).

The basement below is used as a playroom. [*Below* may be regarded as a preposition functioning as an adjectival modifier of *basement*. (Actually *below* governs an understood substantive — "The basement below this floor is used as a playroom" — and it is the whole prepositional phrase "below this floor" that modifies *basement*.)]

e. "For."   *For* often functions as an expletive introducing an infinitive clause. (See also pp. 148 f.)   pg. 73

The plan is (for) me to attract his attention. [*For* functions here as an expletive (rather than as a preposition) introducing the infinitive clause *me to attract his attention.*]

f. Participle as a preposition. Certain forms, originally participles, are now used with the force of prepositions — such forms as *concerning, excepting, regarding, during.* (See also p. 306.)

I shall say just one thing concerning your proposal. [*Concerning* may be regarded as a preposition governing *proposal* (*concerning* = "about").]
I saw everybody excepting the executive secretary. [*Excepting* may be regarded as a preposition governing *secretary* (*excepting* = "except" or "but").]

7. RETAINED PREPOSITION

When a statement containing a preposition that is closely welded to a verb (see Verb + Preposition Combinations, p. 55) is turned into the passive voice, the object of the preposition becomes the subject of the passive verb and the preposition is "retained."[29]

His offer ought not be sneezed at. [*Offer*, the object of the preposition *at* in the active construction — "We ought not sneeze at his offer" — has become the subject of the passive verb and the preposition *at* has been retained.]
She is being made fun of. [*She*, the object of the preposition *of* in the active construction — "They are making fun of her" — has become the subject of the passive verb and the preposition *of* has been retained.]

8. PREPOSITION + VERB COMBINATIONS

See p. 55.

9. PREPOSITION AT THE END OF A STATEMENT

See pp. 352 f.

---

[29] Some grammarians prefer to call this "retained" preposition an adverb in the passive construction. Again we see how close adverbs and prepositions really are.

EXERCISES

Prepositions

In the following sentences point out all the prepositional phrases. Make clear the nature of the object of the preposition. Supply the object when the object has been omitted by ellipsis. Make clear the construction of the prepositional phrase itself; that is, state whether the prepositional phrase is adjectival, adverbial, or substantive in function.

1. I looked at him and thought I discovered a certain evasiveness in his inability to look me in the eye.
2. A friend of mine is not necessarily a friend of yours.
3. The rain falls on the rich and poor alike.
4. After scrubbing the floor with gasoline put on it a good coat of wax and polish with a weighted brush.
5. George does nothing but work from morning to night.
6. He is a man I have formed a partnership with.
7. You are the one I am depending on.
8. I don't like to be trifled with.
9. A former law partner of Father's wanted to see me early in the morning.
10. From here to there is a matter of ten or eleven inches.
11. We waited to within five minutes of train time.
12. Up to within a year of his graduation he had made no particular impression on anybody.
13. We went to talk about what we should do with those who had paid no attention to our letters.
14. We have done everything except notify the police.
15. He is very shy in manner but resolute in conduct.
16. That is the man whom I talked to last night.
17. In deciding the matter we had to take into account his wide range of experience.
18. He offered a reward for the return of his favorite pen.
19. At all events, we have cleared out one nest of spies.
20. Come out from behind that door.
21. The curtain went up at precisely eight-fifteen.
22. People around New York frequently have jobs in New York.
23. About the middle of May is the best time to plant sweet corn.

24. I have a house for sale, but I must sell it for cash.
25. He proved himself a man of unflinching courage.
26. Although he is quick in thought, he is slow in action.
27. Her lovely bracelet of silver coins neatly linked together attracted the attention of a man who buys for Marshall Field's.
28. I have not been in Boston since before Christmas.
29. He enjoys everything about college except studying.
30. Because of bad roads it took us six hours to make the trip.
31. It came to just under ten dollars.
32. I spent a trifle over six days in the hospital.

F.   Conjunctions[30]

A conjunction is a word (or word-group) used to connect words, phrases, or clauses. Unlike a preposition, a conjunction does not govern a substantive (see p. 111). In "She and I walked; but Ned ran" *and* functions as a conjunction joining the pronouns *she* and *I*; *but* functions as a conjunction joining the two main clauses *she and I walked* and *Ned ran*. But in "All walked except him" *except* functions as a preposition governing the substantive *him* in the objective case.

For diagrams of connectives see pp. 389 ff.

1.   KINDS

There are two principal classes of conjunctions, called coordinating conjunctions and subordinating conjunctions. Both coordinating conjunctions and subordinating conjunctions may be used in pairs, in which case they are called correlative conjunctions.

a. Coordinating. A coordinating conjunction connects words, phrases, or clauses of the same rank and usually of the same kind — that is, noun and noun, adjective and adjective, phrase and phrase, clause and clause.

The common coordinating conjunctions are *and, but, or, nor, and for.*[31]

---

[30] For forms and usages see pp. 354 ff.
[31] Some grammarians insist that *for* is a subordinating conjunction, their argument being that *for* never joins anything but clauses. It is true that the use of *for*, as an equivalent of *because* or *as*, to introduce a causal clause is quite common: "I left early, for I had a long drive before me." In this use the clause

You and I seem to have the same ideas. [*And* is a coordinating conjunction connecting the pronouns *you* and *I*.]

It works equally well on alternating current or on direct current. [*Or* is a coordinating conjunction connecting the two prepositional phrases *on alternating current* and *on direct current*.]

Man proposes, but God disposes. [*But* connects the two main clauses *man proposes* and *God disposes*.]

It makes no difference whether you pay cash or give me your note. [*Or* connects the parallel parts of the predicate *pay cash* and *give me your note*, of the subordinate clause. *Whether* is a subordinating conjunction joining the subordinate clause to the main clause.]

We have been most generous in our offer, for generosity is our middle name. [*For* is a coordinating conjunction connecting the two independent clauses of a compound sentence.]

NOTE. A coordinating conjunction at the beginning of a sentence, expressing as it does a logical rather than a grammatical connection with a previous sentence, may be regarded as a transitional adverb (see p. 141), although some grammarians prefer to call it a detached or transitional conjunction.

He is not here. Nor do I know where you can find him. [*Nor* may be regarded as a transitional adverb; or it may be called a detached or transitional conjunction.]

That's that. And so we come to the end of our story. [*And* may be regarded as a transitional adverb; or it may be called a detached or transitional conjunction.]

b. Subordinating.   A subordinating conjunction connects a subordinate clause to another clause on which it depends; that is, a subordinating conjunction connects clauses of unequal grammatical rank. A simple subordinating conjunction has as its sole function the joining of a subordinate clause to the element on which it depends. A functional connective (see below) is

---

introduced by *for* is a subordinate clause. In a somewhat different use a *for* clause gives evidence for the truth of a preceding statement: "Someone must have entered the house during our absence, for the lock on the front door has been broken." Because in this use *for* can stand at the beginning of an independent statement or even of a paragraph, it can be classed as a coordinating conjunction. *Yet* and *so* are now generally regarded as coordinating conjunctions — at least as far as punctuation is concerned.

[handwritten margin notes: "words and phrases as well as sentences"; "rhetorical connection"]

one that not only joins a subordinate clause to the element on which it depends but at the same time functions grammatically in its own clause as a substantive, an adjective, or an adverb.[32] *clause to clause basis*

I will donate five dollars if you will. [*If* is a simple subordinating conjunction introducing the subordinate clause *you will (donate)* and joining it to *will donate* in the main clause, which it modifies.]

I will donate five dollars when you do. [*When* is a functional subordinating connective. It joins the subordinate clause *you do (donate)* to the main clause and at the same time functions as an adverbial modifier of *do (donate)* in its own clause. (See p. 131.)]

NOTE.   Such words as *whereas* and *notwithstanding* function sometimes as subordinating conjunctions, sometimes as transitional adverbs. Only the sense and correct punctuation will make clear their meaning in given sentences. As a subordinating conjunction *whereas* has something of the meaning of "although"; as a transitional adverb it has something of the meaning of "on the other hand." As a subordinating conjunction *notwithstanding* has something of the meaning of "even though"; as a transitional adverb it has something of the meaning of "yet."

He long opposed women in the business office, whereas today he seems to tolerate them. [*Whereas* here functions as a subordinating conjunction, used in the sense of "although." Note the use of the comma which, with the end period, sets off the subordinate clause as an additive clause.]

The National League leads in batting; whereas the American League leads in fielding. [*Whereas* here functions as a transitional adverb, used in the sense of "on the other hand." Note the use of the semicolon to separate the independent clauses of a compound sentence.]

He insisted on enlisting, notwithstanding he had good reason for exemption. [*Notwithstanding* here functions as a subordinating conjunction, used in the sense of "even though."]

He made every effort to enlist; notwithstanding, he was rejected for physical disability. [*Notwithstanding* here functions as a transitional adverb, used in the sense of "yet."]

[32] See pp. 355 f. for lists of simple and functional subordinating connectives. Anything, including relative and interrogative pronouns, adjectives, and adverbs, that connects grammatically one clause to another is to that extent a conjunction. But to avoid any confusion the name "functional connective" has been given to these expressions that not only join but function grammatically in their own clauses. For discarding of the ambiguous term "conjunctive adverb" see footnote, p. 105.

c. *Correlatives.*   Correlative conjunctions are conjunctions used in pairs. They may be used as coordinating conjunctions; that is, they may be used to coordinate items that are grammatically parallel. They may also be used with items when one item is grammatically subordinate to the other, in which case one introduces the main clause and the other introduces the subordinate clause. (For correlative adverbs see pp. 102 f.)

two types

The principal coordinating correlatives are *not only . . . but also, either . . . or, neither . . . nor, both . . . and.*

The principal correlatives used in connection with subordinate clauses are *although . . . yet (still), though . . . still (yet), if . . . then, since . . . therefore.* The first of the pair is used to introduce the subordinate clause; the second is used in the main clause principally for emphasis.

> Either we hang together or we hang separately. [The correlatives *either* and *or* join the two main clauses *we hang together* and *we hang separately.*]
> Both New York and San Francisco have excellent harbors. [The correlatives *both* and *and* join the substantives *New York* and *San Francisco.*]
> Although there is much in his favor, yet I do not feel certain about him. [*Although,* the first of the correlatives, introduces the subordinate clause *there is much in his favor; yet,* the second of the pair of correlatives, is used in the main clause principally for emphasis.]
> If you are right, then I am wrong. [*If,* the first of the correlatives, introduces the subordinate clause *you are right; then,* the second of the pair of correlatives, is used in the main clause principally for emphasis.]

When correlative adverbs such as *as . . . as, not so . . . as, the . . . the, when . . . then, where . . . there* (see pp. 102 f.) are used with main and subordinate clauses, one functions as a simple adverb in the main clause and the other functions as an indefinite relative adverb in the subordinate clause and so to this extent is a functioning connective. (See also pp. 181 f.)

She is as witty as she is pretty. [That is, "She is witty to that degree to which degree she is pretty." The first *as* functions as a simple adverbial modifier of *witty* in the main clause; the second *as* functions as an indefinite relative adverb, modifying *pretty* in the subordinate clause and referring to the first *as* in the main clause and so joining its own, the subordinate, clause to the main clause as an adverbial modifier of the first *as*. Hence, the second *as* is an indefinite relative adverb — that is, a relating adverb.]

2.   FUNCTIONS OF CONNECTIVES IN CLAUSES

In order to understand the grammar of subordinate clauses (see pp. 160 ff.) it is necessary to understand how subordinate clauses are attached to the rest of the sentence. For a subordinate clause must be attached to another clause in such a way as to make obvious the dependent character of the clause being attached and at the same time to make evident how the connection is made.

Of course, anything that attaches a subordinate clause to another clause is to that extent a conjunction or a connective. But a connective may have its own function to perform in the subordinate clause.

We may list here, for convenience, the various kinds of subordinating connectives, showing at the same time the various ways in which subordinate clauses are attached to other clauses.

a. Simple subordinating conjunctions.   The sole function of some expressions is to establish a connection between a subordinate clause and another clause. Such words as *if, unless, because, as if, since, though, although, so that, in order that,* are simple conjunctions. Their only function is to connect the subordinate clause that they introduce to another clause; they do not have any grammatical function in either clause. (See also pp. 137 ff. For diagrams see pp. 391 ff.)

You meet me at six unless I notify you to the contrary. [The sole function of *unless* is to join the subordinate clause to *meet,* the verb in the main clause which the subordinate clause modifies.

The simple conjunction *unless* makes evident the subordinate character of the clause that it introduces.]

b. Functional connectives.   Often words that introduce subordinate clauses (and make evident their subordinate nature) and join them to other clauses also have a grammatical function to perform in the subordinate clause. We may, for convenience, call them functional connectives. A pronoun, an adjective, or an adverb may have its regular substantive or modifying function in a subordinate clause and at the same time relate this subordinate clause to some other element in the sentence. In this functioning-connective use, such pronouns, adjectives, and adverbs may be classified as definite relatives (or for convenience simply as relatives), indefinite relatives, and interrogatives.

1. Relative pronoun.   A relative pronoun (*a*) acts as a substantive in the subordinate clause; (*b*) acts as a reference word, looking back to a substantive, called its antecedent, in another clause; and (*c*) through this reference joins the subordinate clause that it introduces to the other clause. (See also pp. 170 f.)

I have an uncle who used to make wood engravings. [The relative pronoun *who* functions as the subject of the verb *used to make* in the subordinate clause; refers to *uncle*, its antecedent, in the main clause; and through this reference joins the subordinate clause (an adjectival modifier of *uncle*) to the main clause.]

2. Indefinite relative pronoun.   An indefinite relative pronoun (*a*) acts as a substantive in the subordinate clause; (*b*) has no antecedent expressed in its sentence, sometimes being said to contain in itself its own antecedent; and (*c*) joins its own clause to another clause. (See also pp. 162 f. and 235, Note.)

He took what he wanted. [The indefinite relative pronoun *what* functions as the object of *wanted* in the subordinate clause; it has no antecedent expressed in its sentence; it joins its own clause (as the object of *took*) to the main clause.]

I always accept whatever is offered to me. [The indefinite relative pronoun *whatever* functions as the subject of *is offered* in the subordinate clause; it has no antecedent expressed in its sentence; it joins its clause (as the object of *accept*) to the main clause.]

NOTE. There is a difference in grammatical construction between a definite relative pronoun and an indefinite relative pronoun. First, a definite relative pronoun has an antecedent expressed in its sentence, whereas an indefinite relative pronoun does not have an antecedent expressed in its sentence. Second, a definite relative pronoun introduces an adjectival clause (see p. 170), whereas an indefinite relative pronoun introduces a noun clause. Similarly, the presence or absence of a substantive in the sentence to refer to constitutes the essential difference between the definite relative adjectives and adverbs (see below) and the indefinite relative adjectives and adverbs.

A man who works will prosper. [*Who*, a definite relative pronoun, with *man* as its antecedent, introduces an adjectival clause that modifies *man*.]

Who enters here leaves hope behind. [*Who*, an indefinite relative pronoun, has no antecedent expressed in its sentence. *Who* introduces a noun clause, the subject of the main verb *leaves*.]

I know what I need. [*What*, an indefinite relative pronoun, has no antecedent expressed in its sentence. *What* (the object of *need*) introduces a noun clause, the direct object of the main verb *know*.]

Whoever walks on the grass will be reported. [*Whoever*, an indefinite relative pronoun, has no antecedent expressed in its sentence. *Whoever* (the subject of *walks*) introduces a noun clause, the subject of the main verb *will be reported*.]

3. Interrogative pronoun. An interrogative pronoun introducing a subordinate clause (*a*) acts as a substantive in its own clause and (*b*) introduces an indirect question that depends on a verb or verbal in another clause.

We wish to know who spread the rumor. [The interrogative pronoun *who* introduces the subordinate clause *who spread the rumor* (asking an indirect question) and functions as the subject of *spread*, the subordinate clause functioning as the object of the infinitive *to know*.]

NOTE. An interrogative (pronoun, adjective, or adverb) introducing a subordinate clause is actually a special kind of indefinite relative. There is no difference in grammatical construction (although usually a slight difference in meaning) between, for example, an indefinite relative pronoun and an interrogative pronoun introducing a subordinate clause.

Both introduce noun clauses (see pp. 162 ff. and 223 ff.). The difference in meaning lies in the fact that an interrogative pronoun introducing a subordinate clause asks or implies an indirect question. But this difference in meaning — especially in the case of the pronoun *what* — often is very slight indeed.

> I know what I want. [*What* is probably an indefinite relative pronoun.]
> I wonder what he wants. [*What* is here an interrogative pronoun, for an indirect question ("What does he want?") is clearly implied.]

4. Relative adjective.   The relative adjective (*a*) acts as an adjectival modifier in its own clause; (*b*) acts as a reference word looking back to a substantive, called its antecedent, in another clause; and (*c*) through this reference joins its own, the subordinate clause, to the other clause. (See also p. 172.)

> I know a man whose name is Launcelot Smith. [The relative adjective *whose* functions as a modifier of *name* in the subordinate clause; it refers to *man*, its antecedent, in the main clause; and through this reference it joins its own, the subordinate clause, to the main clause as an adjectival modifier of *man*, the object of the verb *know*.]

5. Indefinite relative adjective.   An indefinite relative adjective (*a*) acts as an adjectival modifier of a substantive in its own clause; (*b*) has no antecedent expressed in its sentence (sometimes being said to contain in itself its own antecedent; see p. 235, Note); and (*c*) joins the subordinate clause to another clause.

> I shall take whatever wage is offered me. [The indefinite relative adjective *whatever* functions as a modifier of *wage* in its own clause; it has no antecedent expressed in its sentence; and it joins the subordinate clause (as the direct object of *shall take*) to the main clause.]

6. Interrogative adjective.   An interrogative adjective introducing a subordinate clause (*a*) functions as an adjectival modifier of a substantive in its own clauses and (*b*) introduces an indirect question that depends on a verb or verbal in another

clause. An interrogative adjective does not have an antecedent expressed in its sentence.

We asked which road we should take. [The interrogative adjective *which* introduces the subordinate clause *which road we should take* (asking an indirect question) and functions as an adjectival modifier of *road*, the subordinate clause functioning as the object of the main verb *asked*.]

7. Relative adverb.[33] A relative adverb (*a*) acts as an adverbial modifier (usually of the verb) in its own clause; (*b*) looks back to a substantive in another clause as its antecedent; and (*c*) through this reference joins the subordinate clause, as an adjectival modifier of the substantive, to the other clause. (See also pp. 172 f.)

A time will come when you will regret your action. [The relative adverb *when* functions as an adverbial modifier of *will regret* in its own clause; it has *time* in the main clause as its antecedent; and it joins the subordinate clause, as an adjectival modifier of *time*, to the main clause.]

8. Indefinite relative adverb. An indefinite relative adverb (*a*) acts as an adverbial modifier (usually of the verb) in its own clause; (*b*) has no substantive in the sentence to refer to; and (*c*) joins the subordinate clause (a noun clause or an adverbial clause) to another clause. (See also pp. 164 f. and 180 f.)

I know where I can find a hammer. [The relative adverb *where* functions as an adverbial modifier of *can find* in its own clause; it has no antecedent expressed in its sentence; it joins the subordinate clause, which is the object of *know*, to the main clause.]

We play tennis whenever the weather favors it. [The relative adverb *whenever* functions as an adverbial modifier of *favors* in its own clause; it has no antecedent expressed in its sentence; it joins the subordinate clause, which is an adverbial modifier of the verb *play*, to the main clause.]

9. Interrogative adverb. An interrogative adverb introducing a subordinate clause (*a*) functions as an adverbial modifier

[33] On discarding the term "conjunctive adverb" see footnote, p. 105.

(usually of the verb) in its own clause and (*b*) introduces an indirect question that depends on a verb or verbal in another clause. An interrogative adverb does not have an antecedent expressed in its sentence. (See also pp. 165 f.)

> You ask where we may find the janitor. [The interrogative adverb *where* introduces the subordinate clause *where we may find the janitor* (asking an indirect question) and functions as an adverbial modifier of *may find*, the subordinate clause functioning as the object of the main verb *ask*.]

10. Correlative adverbs. For correlative adverbs acting as connectives see pp. 102 and 185. For diagrams of correlative adverbs see pp. 395 f. and 410.

EXERCISES

Conjunctions

Classify the conjunctions you find in the following sentences as coordinating, subordinating, correlative.

If a conjunction introduces a subordinate clause, indicate whether the conjunction is a simple conjunction or a functioning connective. If the conjunction is a functioning connective, explain what function it performs in the subordinate clause.

1. The pitcher and catcher gamble their judgment against the skill and knowledge of the batter.
2. An appeal was taken, and the executive committee ruled that the student had not had a chance to present all the facts and must have another.
3. He then approached the boy and suggested that he hadn't been doing a good job.
4. Then and then only did I realize that I had been the victim of the most successful joke that Hollywood loves to pull.
5. I saw him as I pulled my weary body toward the locker room and demanded why I should be burdened with such an impossible creature.
6. I am no longer so eager to find fault as you evidently are.

7. Not only England and America but also France and Holland have a stake in the settlement.

8. Although we proceeded to make a camp in the little valley where boughs could be cut for beds and running water was at hand, yet I felt all the time that we should have trudged on to higher ground.

9. I am not so sure as you seem to be that he is speaking the truth.

10. Willamette is the college that Dr. Doney was president of for so many years.

11. She does not seem to know precisely what she wants.

12. Whatever newspapers and weekly magazines publish becomes for some folks the gospel truth.

13. Who pays his bills promptly will never be in debt.

14. Are we expected to accept whoever applies?

15. Let's locate a man whose specialty is making keys.

16. I do not remember what he said.

17. Whatever action the committee takes will be all right with me.

18. This is one time when I must disagree with you.

19. Whenever I could find the time I used to call on him.

20. She seems to know what side her bread is buttered on.

21. I wonder where he hides himself all the time.

22. Find out who put in the call.

23. We need to know what demands are actually being made upon us today.

24. Maybe we should find out whose fault it really was.

25. The hotter it gets the better I like it.

26. In order that we might all have the same chance, the storekeeper gave us checks with serial numbers on them.

27. I would rather walk than wait for the bus.

28. When the bell rings, then is the time to start.

29. Although he has every advantage that wealth can give, still he fails to make any headway.

30. Where you go, there I go too.

CHAPTER 3

Shifts, Absolute Constructions, Expletives, Ellipsis, and Inverted Order

There are five matters of grammar that one needs to understand if grammatical analysis is to become relatively simple. They are shifts (of expressions from one part of speech to another), absolute constructions, expletives, ellipsis, and inverted order. They have all been mentioned before; but they are brought together here for ready reference.

A. *Shifts*

The functions that words perform in a sentence—subject, verb, complement, adjectival modifiers, adverbial modifiers, connectives — are fixed. But individual words are not in themselves nouns, verbs, adjectives, or adverbs. They become nouns, verbs, and so on, only in connection with the particular function they perform in a particular sentence. One of the marked characteristics of English is the fact that a word may perform one function in one sentence and an entirely different function in another. That is, a given expression may be used at one time as one part of speech and at another time as another part of speech. It is this tendency of an expression to shift from one function to another that accounts for the great variety of locutions that a writer or speaker may find at his disposal. Such shifts are especially common in colloquial discourse; and out of such shifts, often inelegant, has arisen much slang.

We may, for example, speak of a "person's foot." We may talk about a "foot ruler" or say that the ruler is a "foot long." We may also speak of "footing a bill," of "footing it to town," or of "footing up a column of figures."

An element should, then, be classed, not on the basis of its usual function, but on the basis of its function in a given sentence.

Some of the more common shifts are listed below.

For diagrams of shifts see p. 411.

1.   NOUNS AS VERBS AND VERBS AS NOUNS

One of the commonest shifts is that of a word normally a noun to the function of a verb; another is a verb shifting so as to perform the function of a noun. (See also p. 36.) These shifts are especially common in colloquial discourse.

Don't forget to hose off the porch. [*Hose,* normally a noun, here functions as a verb.]

The two of us are going to garden this spring. [*Garden,* normally a noun, here functions as a verb.]

We had to breakfast the stranded passengers. [*Breakfast,* normally a noun, here functions as a verb.]

He tried to make a run for it. [*Run,* normally a verb, here functions as a noun.]

The new play was a sellout. [*Sell,* normally a verb, combined with the adverb *out,* here functions as a noun.]

He made a clean sweep the first day he was in office. [*Sweep,* normally a verb, here functions as a noun modified by the adjective *clean.*]

2.   ADJECTIVES AS NOUNS AND NOUNS AS ADJECTIVES

Adjectives readily function as nouns; and nouns just as readily function as adjectives. (See also pp. 94 ff.)

The incapacitated were taken to the rest station. [*Incapacitated,* normally an adjective (a participle), preceded by the article *the,* here functions as a noun.]

All the perishables must be delivered without delay. [*Perishable,* normally an adjective, pluralized, here functions as a noun.]

Several population experts attended the summit meeting. [*Population* and *summit,* normally nouns, here function respectively as adjectival modifiers of *experts* and *meeting.*]

There is a New York train at ten o'clock. [*New York,* normally a noun, here functions as an adjectival modifier of *train.*]

3.   ADVERBS AS NOUNS AND NOUNS AS ADVERBS

Adverbs often function as nouns; and nouns function as adverbs.

It is exactly sixty miles from here to there. [*Here* and *there,* normally adverbs, here function as nouns, one the object of the preposition *from* and the other as the object of the preposition *to.*]

I do not know all the ins and outs about it. [*In* and *out,* normally adverbs (or prepositions), pluralized, here function as nouns, the direct objects of *do know.*]

I am going home. [*Home,* normally a noun, here functions as an adverbial modifier of *am going.*]

My father has to work nights. [*Night,* normally a noun, pluralized, here functions as an adverbial modifier of *to work.*]

Will he make the grade? I think so. [*So,* normally an adverb, here functions as a substantive, roughly the equivalent of a clause — that is, the meaning is "I think that he will make the grade."]

4.   OTHER SHIFTS

Many other shifts take place, especially in colloquial discourse.

There is no if, and, or but about it. [*If, and,* and *but,* normally conjunctions, here function as nouns.]

There is a downward tendency. [*Downward,* normally an adverb, here functions as an adjectival modifier of *tendency.*]

The would-be lady-charmer disgusted me. [*Would-be,* normally a verb, here functions as an adjectival modifier of *lady-charmer.*]

But me no buts. [*But,* normally a conjunction, here functions first as a verb and then, pluralized, as a noun.]

We are in the midst of an in-between season. [*In* and *between,* normally prepositions (or adverbs), here function as an adjectival modifier of *season.*]

I downed the bitter medicine. [*Down,* normally an adverb (or preposition), here functions as a verb.]

He bested his opponent. [*Best,* normally an adjective, functions as a verb.]

My job here is to see that everybody is happy. [*Here,* normally an adverb, here functions as an adjectival modifier of the noun *job.*]

Lincoln was six feet four inches tall. [*Feet* and *inches,* normally nouns, here function as adverbial modifiers of the adjective *tall* (which is a subjective complement of *was*).]

The water is scalding hot. [*Scalding,* normally a gerund, here functions as an adverbial modifier of the adjective *hot* (which is the subjective complement of *is*).] (See p. 314.)

The room above is my study. [*Above,* normally a preposition ("above this room"), here functions as an adjectival modifier of *room.*]

She looks like her sister. [*Like,* originally an adjective, here resembles a preposition taking *sister* as an object.]

EXERCISES

Shifts

In the following sentences point out instances in which nouns function as other parts of speech, other parts of speech function as nouns; adjectives function as other parts of speech, other parts of speech function as adjectives; adverbs function as other parts of speech, other parts of speech function as adverbs; prepositions function as other parts of speech, other parts of speech function as prepositions.

1. You tend to use too many ineffectual *ands* and *buts.*
2. The wounded were taken to the hospital.

3. From here to Chicago is a distance of two hundred miles.
4. We have work day and night; but they work only nights.
5. Mr. Meek is a first-class typewriter mechanic.
6. A walking stick seems to be an indispensable part of a Britisher's attire.
7. The rich are getting richer; the poor are getting poorer.
8. Till then there had been complete silence.
9. We had expected to have many ups and downs before now.
10. Tom will be home New Year's Day.
11. It is freezing cold this morning.
12. One store has already closed out its stock of dictionaries.
13. She chased the cat out at once.
14. The little boy is now six years old.
15. He went over there for a cigar.
16. The entrance below is for the sick and incapacitated.
17. Jim went skimming across the ice.
18. He left yesterday and plans to return tomorrow.
19. Washington, now the political capital of the world, is yet to be heard from.
20. Let's see if we can't iron out our difficulties without going to law.
21. He examined the to-and-fro movement of the pendulum.
22. When she attached the iron she blew out a fuse.
23. I expect to return home Wednesday next.
24. The report of the Senate committee differs a great deal from that of the House committee.
25. You will have to buttonhole him and get his answer.
26. He made a quick getaway and probably is now at his hide-out.
27. The young are full of energy and look to the future; the old have had their day and look to the past.
28. Why adopt that hang-your-clothes-on-a-hickory-limb-but-don't-go-near-the-water attitude?
29. That'll pin an accessory-after-the-fact charge on Mr. Perry Mason.
30. We had some hot words, and then he upped and smacked me.
31. He is one of those up-and-at-'em boys, you know.
32. Booted and spurred, she was all ready for the ride.
33. He was the victim of a freeze-out scheme.
34. Shall I book a passage to London for you?
35. Her *ifs* and *ands* and *maybes* were very disconcerting, to say the least.

B.   *Absolute Constructions*

An absolute construction is any expression (word, phrase, or clause) used independently — that is, so used that it has little or no *grammatical* function in the statement in which it appears. Such an expression will, of course, if rightly used, have a logical relation to its sentence.

Common among absolute constructions are (*a*) the nominative absolute (see pp. 61 f.); (*b*) the infinitive used absolutely (see p. 74); and (*c*) nouns and phrases used absolutely. Exclamations, interjections, nouns in direct address, expletives (see pp. 141 ff.), and certain expressions effecting rhetorical rather than grammatical transitions (see transitional adverbs, pp. 105 f.) may be regarded as absolute elements, serving as they do little or no grammatical function in the statements in which they appear.

For diagrams of absolute constructions see pp. 412 ff.

1. NOMINATIVE ABSOLUTE

A substantive without any grammatical function in the statement in which it appears, modified by a participle, constitutes a nominative absolute construction. It is so called because when the substantive shows case ending it reveals itself as in the nominative case. (See also pp. 61 f.)

The sun having set, the thermometer began to fall. [The phrase *the sun having set* is used absolutely; that is, it has no grammatical function in the statement *the therometer began to fall*.]

His mind burdened with many details, Bill forgot his appointment with her. [The phrase *his mind (being) burdened with many details* is used absolutely; that is, it has no grammatical function in the statement *Bill forgot his appointment with her*.]

He being out of town, can I sign for him? [The phrase *he being out of town* is used absolutely; that is, it has no grammatical function in the statement *can I sign for him*.]

The conference started late, the chairman having been delayed by traffic. [The phrase *the chairman having been delayed by traffic* is used absolutely; that is, it has no grammatical function in the statement *The conference started late*.]

2. INFINITIVE PHRASE OR INFINITIVE CLAUSE

Frequently an infinitive phrase is used absolutely. Less frequently an infinitive clause is so used. (See also pp. 74 f.)

To tell the truth, Henry doesn't seem to know his own mind. [The infinitive phrase *to tell the truth* is used absolutely; that is, it has no grammatical function in the statement *Henry doesn't seem to know his own mind.*]

We shall assemble at ten forty-five, the procession to start moving at precisely eleven. [The infinitive clause *the procession to start moving at precisely eleven* is used absolutely; that is, it has no grammatical function in the statement *We shall assemble at ten forty-five.*]

3.   CLAUSES — MAIN AND SUBORDINATE

Clauses, both main and subordinate, may be used absolutely; that is, they may appear in statements without having any grammatical function in the statements in which they appear. Clauses adverbial in appearance are very commonly so used. Main clauses are frequently thrust parenthetically into statements in which they serve no grammatical function. All such clauses may be said to be used absolutely.

As I said before, he is certainly not a handsome dog. [The subordinate clause *as I said before* (adverbial in appearance) is used absolutely; that is, it has no grammatical function in the statement *he is certainly not a handsome dog.*]

She is, if I may be so bold, somewhat portly. [The subordinate clause *if I may be so bold* (adverbial in appearance) is used absolutely; that is, it has no grammatical function in the statement *She is somewhat portly.*]

It is hotter today than it was yesterday, whether you believe it or not. [The subordinate clause *whether you believe it or not* is used absolutely; it has no grammatical function in the statement *It is hotter today than it was yesterday.*]

Mary will, I feel confident, prove herself a competent secretary. [The main clause *I feel confident* (inserted parenthetically) is used absolutely; it has no grammatical function in the statement *Mary will prove herself a competent secretary.*]

Jack — did you ever see such a man? — never stops to pick up anything. [The main clause *did you ever see such a man* (inserted parenthetically) is used absolutely; it has no grammatical function in the statement *Jack never stops to pick up anything.*]

One institution — its name will readily come to mind — boldly abandoned intercollegiate athletics. [The main clause *its name will readily come to mind* (inserted parenthetically) is used absolutely; it has no grammatical function in the statement *One institution boldly abandoned intercollegiate athletics.*]

4. EXCLAMATIONS, INTERJECTIONS, NOUNS IN DIRECT ADDRESS

Such elements as exclamations, interjections, and nouns in direct address may be regarded as elements used absolutely; for they serve no grammatical function in the statements in which they appear.

Oh, oh, oh, what shall I do? [The exclamation *oh*, repeated, may be regarded as used absolutely, for it serves no grammatical function in the statement *what shall I do.*]

That, good heavens, is the last thing I want to do. [The interjection *good heavens* may be regarded as used absolutely, for it serves no grammatical function in the statement *That is the last thing I want to do.*]

Bess, will you do an errand for me? [*Bess*, a noun in direct address, may be regarded as used absolutely, for it serves no grammatical function in the statement *will you do an errand for me.*]

John, close the door. [*John*, a noun in direct address, may be regarded as used absolutely, for it serves no grammatical function in the statement *(you) close the door.* Note that *you* understood, not *John*, is the subject of the imperative verb *close.*]

5. TRANSITIONAL ELEMENTS

Various transitional elements (words, prepositional phrases, transitional adverbs) such as *indeed, too, further, in fact, at any rate, in brief, hence, therefore, nevertheless,* may be regarded as absolute elements; for they usually have little or no grammatical function in the statements in which they appear. They effect rhetorical rather than grammatical transition. (See also pp. 105 f.)

Indeed, I never saw such a snowfall. [*Indeed* is used absolutely;

it has no grammatical function in the statement *I never saw such a snowfall.*]

That, at any rate, is how I feel about the matter. [The prepositional phrase *at any rate* is used absolutely; it has no grammatical function in the statement *That is how I feel about the matter.*]

There was a heavy frost last night; hence, we have no flowers this morning. [*Hence* is used absolutely; it has no grammatical function in the statement *we have no flowers this morning.* It effects a rhetorical, not a grammatical, transition between the two clauses.]

I have a dozen keys here. But not a single one of them will work. [*But* may be regarded as a transitional adverb (used absolutely); for it has no grammatical function in the statement in which it appears. It effects a rhetorical, not a grammatical, transition between two sentences. (See p. 124, Note.)]

6.   PARENTHETICAL ELEMENTS

All sorts of expressions — all the way from single words to independent clauses — may be wedged into statements in which they serve no grammatical function. They may be called parenthetical elements. Such words, phrases, and clauses are usually set off, as additive elements, with commas, dashes, or parentheses (see p. 176, footnote) and may be disregarded when analyzing the grammatical structure of the sentences in which they appear.

He was, I thought, a very powerful advocate. [The parenthetical clause *I thought* may be disregarded when analyzing the statement *He was a very powerful advocate.*]

We have discovered — we might just as well be frank about it — no satisfactory solution. [The parenthetical clause *we might just as well be frank about it* may be disregarded when analyzing the statement *We have discovered no satisfactory solution.*]

You might try the new drugstore — if I may be so bold as to offer a suggestion. [The parenthetical clause *if I may be so bold as to offer a suggestion* may be disregarded when analyzing the statement *You might try the new drugstore.*]

"You have until six o'clock tonight to make up your mind," he said brusquely. [The parenthetical quoting expression *he said brusquely* may be disregarded in analyzing the statement *You have until six o'clock tonight to make up your mind.*]

NOTE. A parenthetical clause does not change the grammatical nature of the sentence in which it appears. All four of the illustrative sentences printed above are, therefore, to be regarded as simple sentences.

EXERCISES

Absolute constructions

Explain all the absolute constructions in the following sentences.

1. Our first attempt having failed, we will make another.
2. To come to the point, just what do you want?
3. England has, if we come right down to it, the best reason of all.
4. Helen, do you really want to go? Maybe, though, you'd rather stay here and rest.
5. Gracious, what can he want of me?
6. Freshman grades are due tomorrow, all other grades to be in not later than day after tomorrow.
7. It being out of the question for us to expect any help from that source, we must do the next best thing.
8. Eliot is, when all is done and said, a philosopher rather than a novelist.
9. He is — may I say parenthetically? — exactly the kind of man we need in this emergency.
10. Gosh, I hate to go now.
11. That, my fine friend, is what I have been trying to tell you.
12. He is, in other words, our chief contender.
13. Such is, in the last analysis, our difficulty.
14. I'll give you an extension of time, our understanding being that you will hand in your paper on next Monday morning.
15. The sun having set, a gentle breeze started blowing down from the hill.
16. O my, O me! What a man!
17. There is no coordinating conjunction between the two clauses; hence, a semicolon must be used.
18. He was a stern taskmaster; nevertheless, I learned more from him than from any other teacher I ever had.

19. Issuing a stern warning having failed of its purpose, he proceeded to more energetic measures.
20. To be conservative, let's say two-thirds of a bushel.
21. These are the required readings, the supplementary readings to be done for any extra credit you may desire.
22. We are, whether you believe it or not, down finally to our last sheet of carbon paper.
23. The other bus having waited five minutes for our bus, which was late, we managed to get home that night.
24. This firm is thoroughly reliable in every way; at any rate, I have found it reliable in all of my dealings with them.
25. Oh, that was a narrow escape!
26. In a word, everything, tangible and intangible, is a "tool" with which the artist in life may produce thought or emotion.
27. Here, to quote an actual case, is a woman who announced herself as a member of the local school committee.
28. Mulkey — his usual nickname is "Cap"— announced the line-up.
29. Whether radio announcers know it or not, there is a difference in meaning between *infer* and *imply*.
30. He is a right guy, if you know what I mean.
31. Mrs. Gaskell — she is the most distinctly feminine of the Victorian novelists — manifested a keen sense of humor.
32. Why is it, if one wishes to press the point, that women are better masters of ironic comedy than men?
33. As far as I am concerned, infinity begins where infinity ends.
34. Honesty is the best policy, as Ben Franklin once remarked.
35. Whether we like it or not, the economic doctrine of let dog eat dog is dead.
36. Roosevelt — I refer to Theodore Roosevelt — never thought out any clear international policy.
37. When all is done and said, you taught me all that I know about photography.
38. An old injury to his spine — Anthony had heard that it was from a thrown marlinspike — made itself felt more and more as the captain grew older.
39. His conduct is, to say the least, a bit peculiar.
40. He is, when you come to think of it, just the man we have been looking for.

C.   EXPLETIVES

An expletive is merely a special kind of absolute construction. For an expletive is an expression that serves no real grammatical function in the statement in which it appears, although it does serve a very important rhetorical purpose, as we shall see. An expletive might be likened to a catalyst in chemistry — a substance that brings about a chemical reaction without itself entering into the reaction it brings about. Hence, expletives may be regarded as expressions used absolutely.

There follow here some of the common instances of expletives in ordinary sentences.

For diagrams of expletives see pp. 415 ff.

1. "IT" AS AN EXPLETIVE

It as an expletive serves merely to mark time until the true grammatical subject of a sentence appears. Thus the *it*-expletive performs a valuable rhetorical purpose: it permits the placing of a grammatical subject after its verb without any confusion in meaning. (See also p. 67.)

It may be noted that the *it*-expletive (unlike the *there*-expletive; see below) can be used only with a singular verb; that is, the construction will read "It is" or "It was," never "It are," "It were."

It as an expletive must not be confused with other uses of *it*. (See pp. 219 ff.)

It is hard to understand Mac's reasoning. [The sentence for analysis reads "To understand Mac's reasoning is hard." Thus the infinitive phrase *to understand Mac's reasoning* is the true subject of *is*; *it*, being grammatically (but not rhetorically) superfluous, is an expletive.[1]]

It is a fact that he possesses the necessary evidence. [The sentence for analysis reads "That he possesses the necessary evidence is a fact." Thus the subordinate clause *that he possesses the neces-*

[1] Some grammarians prefer to call *it* in such sentences the true grammatical subject (or object) of the verb and then regard what we call the true grammatical subject (or object) as the logical subject in apposition with *it*. But such an explanation does not fit the similar *there*-expletive (see pp. 146 f.). It would seem simpler to use one explanation that will fit both constructions rather than to insist upon two separate explanations. But this second explanation, for those who may prefer it, follows:
It is hard to understand Mac's reasoning. [*It* is the subject of the verb *is*, and the infinitive phrase *to understand Mac's reasoning*, the logical subject, is in apposition with *it*.]

sary evidence is the true subject of *is; fact* is a subjective complement; *it*, being grammatically (but not rhetorically) superfluous,
is an expletive.]

It seems to me that you have overlooked one important item.
[The sentence for analysis reads "That you have overlooked one
important item seems to me."]

It would appear certain that we can expect a good price for
wheat this year. [The sentence for analysis reads "That we can
expect a good price for wheat this year would appear certain."]

He believes it to be important to be able to put two and two
together. [The sentence for analysis reads "He believes to be able
to put two and two together to be important."]

I have it in mind to build a two-car garage. [The sentence for
analysis reads "I have in mind to build a two-car garage."]

I think it unlikely that the river will rise much higher. [The
sentence for analysis reads "I think that the river will rise much
higher unlikely."]

2.   "THERE" AS AN EXPLETIVE

a. With a finite verb. Like the *it*-expletive, the *there*-ex-
pletive may serve a valuable rhetorical purpose: it permits placing a subject after its verb without any confusion in meaning.
It may serve to mark time until the true subject of the verb
appears. The verb *be* used in connection with *there* is a notional
verb (see pp. 39 f.). It usually functions as a complete verb
(see pp. 41 f.); that is, it is used as a verb of complete predication, in the sense of "exist," and so has no subjective complement.[2] Variations of the *there* expletive sentence pattern make
use of such verbs as *seem, appear, happen* plus the infinitive
to be.

There is always one right way to do a thing. [The sentence for
analysis reads "One right way to do a thing always is" (*is* =
"exists"). Thus *way* is the true grammatical subject of *is; there*,
being grammatically (but not rhetorically) superfluous, is an
expletive.]

[2] Occasionally the *be* in this expletive sentence will be followed by a subjective complement: "There is available at the present time only one usable
textbook."

I believe there is to be an excursion. [The sentence for analysis reads "I believe an excursion is to be." Thus *excursion* is the true subject of the verb *is; to be* (used as a complete verb) is a complementary infinitive (see pp. 69 f.); *there*, being grammatically (but not rhetorically) superfluous, is an expletive.]

There seems to be no other course for us. [The sentence for analysis reads "No other course for us seems to be." Thus *course* is the true subject of the verb *seems*[3]; *there* is an expletive.]

NOTE. The use of *there* as an expletive must not be confused with the use of *there* as a regular adverb.

There he goes. [*There* is an adverbial modifier of *goes*.]

The library is over there. [*There* is an adverb used as a noun (see p. 108) functioning as the object of the preposition *over*, the prepositional phrase *over there* being an adverbial modifier of *is*.]

b. With a participle. The expletive is sometimes used in participial constructions.

There being no objection, we stand adjourned. [The phrase for analysis reads "no objection being (= existing)." The noun *objection* modified by the participle *being* constitutes a nominative absolute construction(see pp. 61f.). *There*, being grammatically (but not rhetorically) superfluous, is an expletive.]

No question of there being any need for assistance has yet arisen. [The sentence for analysis reads "No question of any need for assistance being (= existing) has yet arisen."]

He complained without there being any good reason for his complaints. [The sentence for analysis reads "He complained without any good reason for his complaints being (= existing)."]

NOTE. The use of *there* as an expletive with a participle must not be confused with the use of the possessive pronoun *their* functioning as an adjectival modifier of a gerund.

He had to take his chance on their being late. [The gerund *being*, with its subjective complement *late*, is modified by the possessive pronoun *their* (the gerund phrase *their being late* functioning as the object of the preposition *on*).]

---

[3] *Seems* can be called the notional verb in such a use, with the infinitive phrase used as a subjective complement. An equally logical interpretation would have *seems to be* the entire verb, with the *to be* used as a complementary infinitive.

c. Proper agreement.   The use of *there* as an expletive offers a problem of agreement in number between the true subject and the verb. For the expletive *there* does not determine the number of the verb; the number is actually determined by the number of the true grammatical subject of the verb, which, of course, follows the verb when the expletive *there* is used.

There is one good road to St. Louis. [The true subject of the verb *is* is *road*, a noun in the singular; hence *is* is correct.]

There are three poor roads to St. Louis. [The true subject of the verb *are* is *roads*, a noun in the plural; hence *are* is correct.]

There seems to be a difference of opinion. [*Difference*, a noun in the singular, is the true subject of *seems*; hence the singular is correct.]

There seem to be several opinions about the matter. [*Opinions*, a noun in the plural, is the true subject of *seem*; hence the plural is correct.]

3.   "FOR" AS AN EXPLETIVE

For is very commonly used as an expletive to introduce an infinitive clause.[4] (See also pp. 72 f.)

For me to go now is impossible. [The infinitive clause *me to go now*, functioning as the subject of *is*, is introduced by the expletive *for*.]

It is difficult for us to trust his word. [The infinitive clause *us to trust his word*, functioning as the true subject of *is*, is introduced by the expletive *for*.]

The best plan is for me to go to the mayor. [The infinitive clause *me to go to the mayor*, functioning as the subjective complement of *is*, is introduced by the expletive *for*.]

I have a new proposition for you to consider. [The infinitive clause *you to consider*, functioning as an adjectival modifier of *proposition*, is introduced by the expletive *for*.]

We are waiting for you to make up your mind. [Here *for* is the true preposition, for it is not grammatically superfluous. *For* takes the infinitive clause as its object; and the whole prepositional

---

[4] Some grammarians prefer to treat *for* at all times as a preposition with the following infinitive clause as its object. See Note, p. 73.

phrase *for you to make up your mind* functions as an adverbial modifier of *are waiting.*]

4. "AS" AS AN EXPLETIVE

As often functions as an expletive to introduce an appositional item, such as a noun used as an objective complement.[5]

We chose Edward as our leader. [*As* serves to introduce *leader*, an objective complement. Being grammatically (but not rhetorically) superfluous, *as* functions as an expletive.]

5. "OR" AS AN EXPLETIVE

Sometimes *or* is used as an expletive to introduce an item in apposition. (Note that *or* in such cases has no function that a conjunction is supposed to have.)

New York, or Bagdad-on-the-Subway, was O. Henry's favorite locale for stories. [*Or* functions as an expletive to introduce *Bagdad-on-the-Subway*, which is in apposition with *New York*.]

6. "OF" AS AN EXPLETIVE

Sometimes *of* is used to introduce an appositional item and may rightly be regarded as an expletive. (Note that *of* in such cases has no function that a preposition is supposed to have.)

The city of Cincinnati is located on the Ohio River. [The substantive *Cincinnati*, introduced by the expletive *of*, is in apposition with *city*. Having no grammatical function in the sentence, *of* may be regarded as an expletive.[6]]

[5] Some grammarians prefer to regard *as* as a preposition governing the following substantive as its object rather than as an expletive introducing the appositional item.

[6] Some grammarians prefer to regard *of* as a preposition governing the following substantive and call the *of*-phrase *of Cincinnati* an appositional item.

EXERCISES

Expletives

Point out all the expletives that you find in the following sentences.

1. It is important that we do something at once.
2. There is just one of three things that we can do in the circumstances.
3. It is necessary for us to take into consideration the greatest good to the greatest number.
4. Let's select *Per angusta ad augusta* as our motto.
5. Laissez-faire, or the doctrine of letting things alone, is not talked about these days.
6. It is a fact that many people are very superstitious.
7. We always turned to Father as a court of last resort.
8. There's a saying that if you want a thing done well you must do it yourself.
9. It is hard for some people to handle fractions.
10. It is a nice day; but I don't wish to start footing it to town.
11. There are several ways to make a perfect five-pointed star.
12. James or Mary will give you one; or, if you prefer, you can buy one at the dime store.
13. Chicago, or the Windy City as it is sometimes called, ranks second in population.
14. It is difficult to speak calmly of such an outrage.
15. For him to become our scoutmaster is exactly what we have in mind.
16. This is the book we wish to use as our textbook.
17. There are three answers that might be given; but there is only one right answer.
18. We waited all night for him to call up; but it was late in the morning before the call finally came through.
19. There are many things for us to do if we are to have permanent peace.
20. It is very necessary to take good care of a typewriter nowadays.
21. We regarded the little boy as a sort of mascot.
22. That is a fact well worth remembering.
23. It is a fact well worth remembering that the square of the hypotenuse

of a right-angle triangle is equal to the sum of the squares of the other two sides.

24. The right thing for us to do now is to wait for further instructions.
25. Richardson wrote *Pamela, or Virtue Rewarded*.
26. It is necessary for us to take every precaution to prevent any premature leak of what we are planning.
27. It is evident that the individual has got to decide what are the abiding values in life.
28. There's one fact that you have overlooked.
29. It now being clear that you can expect no help from him, you might consider the help we offer you.
30. We regarded the old man as a sort of Jack-of-all-trades.
31. The city of New York always overwhelms the foreigner.
32. She has it in mind to live in California for a while.
33. Samuel Clemens, or Mark Twain, created the immortal Huck Finn.
34. I have selected trade unionism as the topic for my paper.
35. I believe it to be best for us to take the lead.
36. It seems that John has left for the country.
37. Wait for me to catch up with you.
38. He had it in mind to withdraw from the race.
39. I believe it to be a general principle that possession is nine-tenths of the law.
40. Unaware of what it might mean to him later, he boldly plunged ahead with his stock buying.

D.   *Ellipsis*

Ellipsis is the omission of a word or words that are necessary to the grammatical analysis of the sentence but not necessary to its meaning. Ellipsis arises from the tendency of language toward brevity and conciseness. Thought is swifter than words; consequently, in order to hold the attention of the reader or listener, the writer or speaker speeds up his sentences by omitting words or phrases easily supplied. Out of such omissions, undoubtedly, have arisen many constructions that defy satisfactory grammatical analysis; hence, we call them idioms.

The analysis of many constructions that at first appear baffling yields a simple explanation when an ellipsis is supplied. Sometimes, to be sure, the original ellipsis is no longer felt; the construction has become an established idiom. In such cases it is better to accept the construction as an idiom than to try to supply the missing parts.

But one word of caution about "supplying." There is nothing that so quickly reduces grammatical analysis to hopeless confusion as the needless supplying of elements. There is just one safe rule to follow: Never supply anything that is not absolutely demanded for *grammatical* completeness. For a true ellipsis never alters a sentence. When it is supplied it merely furnishes the missing parts to make the syntax of the sentence complete.

For instance, to supply a needless *he* as the subject of the second verb in "He went up the steps and knocked at the door" is to turn a simple sentence into a compound sentence, one that the author of the sentence never intended. There is no *he* understood or to be supplied as the subject of *knocked*. For there is no ellipsis in the original sentence, which is a simple sentence with a compound predicate.

But in the sentence "He is a man I am acquainted with" a relative pronoun as the object of the preposition *with* must be supplied, so that the subordinate clause is related grammatically to the main clause. The sentence for analysis then reads "He is a man [whom] I am acquainted with." Hence, if grammatical analysis is to be simple and meaningful, no ellipsis should be manufactured where none exists.

For diagrams of elliptical constructions see pp. 420 ff.

Among the commoner instances of ellipsis are the following.

1.   OMISSION OF A SUBJECT OF A VERB OR A VERB OR BOTH

Come here. [That is, "You come here."]

Yes, thank you. [That is, "Yes, I thank you."]

Why not write at once? [That is, "Why do you not write at once?"]

Please close the door. [That is, "You please (to) close the door."]

2.   OMISSION IN QUESTIONS AND ANSWERS

"Did you hear that noise?"

"What noise?" [That is, "Did I hear what noise?"]

"Who took you to the dance?"
"Jim." [That is, "Jim took me to the dance."]

3. OMISSION OF FORMS OF "TO BE"

"Why so early?" [That is, "Why are you so early?"]

His job done, he went home. [That is, "His job being done, he went home."]

Some are lazy; some just stupid. [That is, "Some are lazy; some are just stupid."]

4. OMISSION OF NOUN EASILY SUPPLIED

I spent Christmas at my mother's. [That is, "I spent Christmas at my mother's home."]

I bought my shoes at Marshall Field's. [That is, "I bought my shoes at Marshall Field's store."]

I dislike Henry's practical jokes and his brother's too. [That is, "I dislike Henry's practical jokes and his brother's practical jokes too."]

5. OMISSION OF A PART OF A SUBORDINATE CLAUSE

We are going, rain or shine. [That is, "We are going whether it rain or shine."]

Once started, there is no end. [That is, "If it is once started there is no end."]

However stormy, he always makes his rounds. [That is, "However stormy it may be, he always makes his rounds."]

Though hot-tempered, he is a likable fellow. [That is, "Though he is hot-tempered, he is a likable fellow."]

6. OMISSION OF A RELATIVE PRONOUN

He bought the basket I wanted. [That is, "He bought the basket which I wanted."]

He is the kind of boy a father can be proud of. [That is, "He is the kind of boy whom a father can be proud of."]

I do not know the girl he seems to be crazy about. [That is, "I do not know the girl whom he seems to be crazy about."]

Laissez-faire is a doctrine I don't believe in. [That is, "Laissez-faire is a doctrine which I don't believe in."]

7.   OMISSION OF VARIOUS CONNECTIVES

I see you are ready to come to terms. [That is, "I see that you are ready to come to terms."]

Had I been there, this might not have happened. [That is, "If I had been there, this might not have happened."]

Granted your first statement, what is your conclusion? [That is, "If you are granted your first statement, what is your conclusion?"]

8.   OMISSION IN PARALLEL CONSTRUCTIONS

I will go my way; you yours. [That is, "I will go my way; you will go your way."]

If you have the goods in stock, ship them; if not, notify us. [That is, "If you have the goods in stock, ship them; if you do not have the goods in stock, notify us."]

9.   OMISSION IN A COMPARISON

He likes her better than me. [That is, "He likes her better than he likes me."]

He likes her better than I. [That is, "He likes her better than I like her."]

He likes her as well as I. [That is, "He likes her as well as I like her."]

He likes her as well as me. [That is, "He likes her as well as he likes me."]

It is just as easy to do the thing right as wrong. [That is, "It is just as easy to do the thing right as it would be easy to do the thing wrong."]

Strawberries are sweeter now than earlier in the season. [That is, "Strawberries are sweeter now than they were earlier in the season."]

10.   OMISSION AFTER *such as*

That a nominative case is demanded in a pronoun following *such as* is evident when the ellipsis is filled out. (See also p. 242.)

We must respect such a girl as she. [That is, "We must respect such a girl as she is."]

For such persons as we your advice is sound. [That is, "For such persons as we are your advice is sound."]

11.   OTHER OMISSIONS

The sooner he goes the better. [That is, "In which degree he goes sooner in that degree it will be better." (See pp. 103 f. for an explanation of the adverb form *the*.)]

EXERCISES

Ellipsis

Fill in any ellipsis you find in the following, placing supplied material in brackets.

1. Come in. But please close the door.
2. Did you bring your book with you? What book?
3. Why so happy?
4. Some are hesitant; others just shy.
5. I am going to my parents' for their wedding anniversary next Sunday.
6. I think you can find a suitable garment at Wanamaker's.
7. Though a bit disappointed, I'll make the best of it.
8. I like tea whether hot or iced.
9. However outmaneuvered, he generally manages to win in the end.
10. That's the kind of novel I like.
11. He is the kind of friend you can depend on.
12. She is the girl I'm going to the dance with.
13. We have several friends here we must call on.
14. Had you spoken you might have had the chance.
15. Granted you are half-way right, what then?
16. Take care of the dimes, and the dollars will take care of themselves.
17. I have my work to do; you yours.
18. If you have a pen use it; if not, use a pencil.
19. When in Rome do as the Romans do.
20. I like Trollope better than Thackeray.
21. I like Trollope better than you do.
22. I hope you are as well satisfied as I.

23. "Now, miss," began the policeman, bringing out his notebook again, "Your name? Age? You live here with your grandmother?"
24. "Janet West Carter," she said. "Twenty-three. With my mother's cousin. Just temporarily."
25. The more he ranted the funnier he became.
26. He believes he has a first edition of *The Scarlet Letter*.
27. That's a name to conjure with.
28. He manifests a kind of conduct I can't put up with.
29. She looked as if ready to cry.
30. Granted you are right, what hope is there for us?

E.   *Inverted Order*

One final matter that sometimes confuses the student is inverted order. Inverted order — or inversion, as it is sometimes called — is the placing of an element out of its usual order. Because English is so largely an uninflected language — that is, a language without many changes to show grammatical function — meaning very often resides in the order in which words come in a sentence. Thus "John laughed at Mary" means one thing; "Mary laughed at John" means another. The words in the two statements are identical; the difference in meaning comes from the difference in their order.

Although word order is usually very definitely fixed, certain departures from a natural word order may appear without any real confusion in meaning.

For diagrams of inverted sentences see pp. 425 f.

1.   EXPLETIVES

We have already seen under Expletives (see pp. 144 ff.) that the *it*-expletive and the *there*-expletive make it possible to throw the grammatical subject of a verb after the verb without any confusion in meaning.

It is obvious that you are right. [The normal order with subject first, would be "That you are right is obvious."]
There is one subject that is taboo. [The normal order, with subject first, would be "One subject that is taboo is (that is, exists)."]

2. PREPOSITIONAL AND INFINITIVE PHRASES

Prepositional and infinitive phrases that are adverbial modifiers may be placed out of their natural order without any resulting confusion.

From the mountains, valleys, and plains they come in great droves. [The normal order would be "They come from the mountains, valleys, and plains in great droves."]

To get good government we must periodically throw the "ins" out. [The normal order would be "We must throw the 'ins' out to get good government."]

3. INVERTED COMPLEMENTS

A very common form of inversion appears when a direct object or a subjective complement is placed before its verb.

A whole apple pie he devoured at one sitting. [The normal order would be "He devoured a whole apple pie at one sitting."]

To be pitied is the man who has lost his will to live. [The normal order would be "The man who has lost his will to live is to be pitied."]

A grand book *David Copperfield* is. [The normal order would be "*David Copperfield* is a grand book."]

A grand book is *David Copperfield*. [There is a question here whether this is a normal order with *book* as the subject and *David Copperfield* as the subjective complement or inverted order with *David Copperfield* the real subject and *book* the subjective complement.]

4. QUESTIONS AND SUBORDINATE CLAUSES

Interrogative pronouns and relative pronouns often appear out of their normal order when they function as complements or as objects of prepositions.

Whom do you wish to speak to? [The normal order for analysis is "You do wish to speak to whom?"]

She does not know which hat she should buy. [The normal order for analysis is "She does not know she should buy which hat."]

He is the boy whom she has been having dates with. [The normal order for analysis is "He is the boy she has been having dates with whom."]

In explaining the grammar of a sentence it is necessary, therefore, to first turn any inverted order into the natural order for analysis; then the analysis usually becomes very simple.

EXERCISES

Inverted Order

Rearrange into proper order for grammatical analysis any sentence that seems to show inversion.

1. Where did that dog come from?
2. I wonder what he has in mind.
3. In the morning I do my work; in the afternoon I like to play.
4. It is to be expected that you will have some problems to face.
5. There are three recent books on Charles Dickens that are excellent.
6. If a large number of voters turn out, Jones will be elected.
7. Can you give me a list of those whom I am supposed to call?
8. A mystery story is the thing to read when you are tired.
9. Mr. Maxwell is the man whom my father is in partnership with.
10. I wonder what cause Jim is promoting now.
11. Which course of action we should now take I don't know.
12. Who she is I haven't the faintest idea.
13. I believe it to be true that a stitch in time saves nine.
14. I have it in mind to ask for a wage increase.
15. I have my doubts about there being any good reason for the delay.
16. I am wondering whom we should try to confer with.
17. What Mother has in mind is anybody's guess.
18. What we are going to do with such a large box is what is bothering me.
19. Which coat I shall finally decide to buy only the future will tell.
20. I have often wondered just what you do believe in.
21. That there is only one right course is my firm conviction.
22. It is my belief that there is only one right course of action.
23. Whether we ought to vote for Minton I just don't know.

24. That he has an income of over a thousand dollars a month I know for a fact.
25. I wonder what he meant.
26. That his intentions are good I don't for a minute doubt.
27. From Leonard I finally learned the truth.
28. Untrustworthy is the man who says one thing and means another.
29. A most remarkable man was Benjamin Franklin.
30. From one source and then from another he gathers his facts patiently and painstakingly.
31. Carefree and happy as larks were the children on their holiday.
32. Evident it is that he has a perverted sense of humor.
33. Whom she laughed at she really respected.
34. With such conduct we can't put up any longer.
35. Lucky is he who has no worries.
36. Spinach I have always regarded as proper food for a rabbit.
37. Poetry he can spout by the hour.
38. What he wants to do now I cannot fathom.
39. Whom he prefers he has never revealed.
40. Which edition of Shakespeare he expects to use I have no way of knowing.

CHAPTER 4

The Grammar of Subordinate Clauses

If the student will rid himself of two erroneous notions that he may have and will hold fast one right notion, he will find that the interpretation of subordinate clauses will be greatly simplified.

First, it is not the meaning of the connective itself introducing the subordinate clause that establishes the grammatical function of the subordinate clause.

Second, it is not the grammatical function of the connective in the subordinate clause (if it should happen to have a function) that establishes the grammatical function of the subordinate clause.

But it *is* the grammatical relationship that a subordinate clause bears to the main clause (or the element on which it depends) that determines the grammatical function of the subordinate clause. That is, as we shall see later, if a subordinate clause functions as a subject or a complement of a verb or is the object of a preposition, the subordinate clause is by that fact a noun (substantive) clause, no matter how it is introduced and no matter what function the connective itself may happen to perform in the subordinate clause. If a subordinate clause modifies a noun (substantive), it is by that fact an adjectival clause, no matter how it is introduced and no matter what function the connective itself may happen to perform in the subordinate clause. If a clause modifies a verb, an adjective, or an adverb, it is by that fact an adverbial clause, no matter how it is introduced and no matter what function the connective itself may happen to perform in the subordinate clause.

The problems of subordinate clauses, therefore, reduce themselves to two: (*a*) what function, if any, the connective performs in its own clause, the subordinate clause; and (*b*) to what in the main clause does this connective join the subordinate clause.[1]

From this survey it should be clear that there are just three kinds of subordinate clauses — noun (substantive) clauses, adjectival clauses, and adverbial clauses. (For main and subordinate clauses used absolutely see pp. 140 f.)

For diagrams of subordinate clauses see pp. 397 ff.

A.   *Noun (Substantive) Clauses*

A noun (or substantive) clause may be introduced by (*a*) a subordinating conjunction (see pp. 127 f.), an expression whose sole duty is to connect the two clauses; or (*b*) an expression that connects the subordinate clause to the main clause and at the same time has a grammatical function of its own in the subordinate clause, called a functioning connective (see pp. 128 ff.).

For diagrams of noun clauses see pp. 397 ff.

1.   **INTRODUCED BY A SUBORDINATING CONJUNCTION**

A noun clause may be introduced by a subordinating conjunction — such as *that, if, whether* — an expression whose sole duty is to join the subordinate clause to the main clause (see also p. 127). That is, the subordinating conjunction has no grammatical function in the subordinate clause itself.

---

[1] The student will find very helpful as a review Functions of Connectives in Clauses, pp. 127 ff.

I hope that tickets are still available. [The noun clause *that tickets are still available,* functioning as the direct object of the main verb *hope,* is introduced by the subordinating conjunction *that.*]

I wonder whether he caught his train. [The noun clause *whether he caught his train,* functioning as the direct object of the main verb *wonder,* is introduced by the subordinating conjunction *whether.*]

He asked me if I knew the president. [The noun clause *if I knew the president,* functioning as one of the double objects after the main verb *asked,* is introduced by the subordinating conjunction *if.*]

NOTE. The subordinating conjunction *that* introducing a noun clause is often omitted by ellipsis (see p. 154). But it is easily supplied.

I think I passed my examination. [That is, "I think that I passed my examination." The subordinating conjunction *that,* introducing the subordinate clause *I passed my examination,* has been supplied.]

2. INTRODUCED BY A FUNCTIONING CONNECTIVE

A noun clause may be introduced by an expression that not only serves to connect the two clauses but also has a grammatical function of its own in the subordinate clause — such as *(a)* an indefinite relative pronoun, *(b)* an interrogative pronoun, *(c)* an indefinite relative adjective, *(d)* an interrogative adjective, *(e)* an indefinite relative adverb, or *(f)* an interrogative adverb. (See also pp. 128 ff.)

a. Indefinite relative pronoun. A noun clause may be introduced by an indefinite relative pronoun — such as *what, whatever, whichever, whoever, whosoever.* Occasionally *who* may be used as an indefinite relative pronoun. An indefinite relative pronoun is one that has no antecedent expressed in its sentence, sometimes being said to contain in itself its own antecedent. (See also pp. 234 f.)

That is not what I meant. [The noun clause *what I meant,* functioning as a subjective complement of *is,* is introduced by the indefinite relative pronoun *what* (the object of *meant*). *What* has no antecedent expressed in its sentence.]

make change in word order – clause
SVO ≠ OVS

You may choose whichever you please. [The noun clause *whichever you please*, functioning as the direct object of the main verb *may choose*, is introduced by the indefinite relative pronoun *whichever* (the object of *to choose* understood). *Whichever* has no antecedent expressed in its sentence.]

We talked about whatever came into our minds. [The noun clause *whatever came into our minds*, functioning as the object of the preposition *about*, is introduced by the indefinite relative pronoun *whatever* (the subject of *came*). *Whatever* has no antecedent expressed in its sentence.]

Who enters here leaves hope behind. [The noun clause *who enters here*, functioning as the subject of the main verb *leaves*, is introduced by *who* (the subject of *enters*), which is used here as an indefinite relative pronoun, with no antecedent expressed in its sentence.]

NOTE.   When relative pronouns, relative adjectives, and relative adverbs have no antecedents expressed in their sentences, they are conveniently called indefinite relatives. That is, they may be thought of as containing in themselves their own antecedents. Thus the indefinite relative pronoun *what* is roughly equivalent in meaning (but not in grammar) to "that which"; *whoever* to "any one who"; *whichever* to "any one which"; *whatever* to "anything which"; *who* to "anyone who." But if the antecedents are expressed, then the relatives are no longer indefinite and the grammatical nature of the clauses in which the relatives appear is changed.

Who steals my purse steals trash. [*Who* is an indefinite relative pronoun introducing a noun clause that functions as the subject of the main verb *steals*.]

He who steals my purse steals trash. [*Who* is a definite relative pronoun, having *he* in the main clause as its antecedent; and the clause introduced by *who* is now an adjectival clause modifying *he* in the main clause.]

b. *Interrogative pronoun.*   A noun clause may be introduced by an interrogative pronoun — such as *who, which,* and *what* — which asks or implies an indirect question. The interrogative pronoun functions as a substantive in its own clause; it has no antecedent in its sentence. (See also pp. 235 f.)

We wondered who he might be. [The noun clause *who he might be*, functioning as the direct object of the main verb *wondered,* is introduced by the interrogative pronoun *who,* which functions as a subjective complement with *might be* ("he might be who"). The direct question was, "Who may he be?"]

I forgot to ask what he wanted. [The noun clause *what he wanted,* functioning as the direct object of the infinitive *to ask,* is introduced by the interrogative pronoun *what,* which functions as the object of *wanted* ("he wanted what"). The direct question was "What do you want?"]

c. Indefinite relative adjective.   A noun clause may be introduced by an indefinite relative adjective — such as *which, whichever, what, whatever.* An indefinite relative adjective functions as an adjectival modifier in its own clause and has no antecedent expressed in its sentence, sometimes being said to contain in itself its own antecedent. (See also p. 130.)

Leave the package at whichever office is handiest. [The noun clause *whichever office is handiest,* functioning as the object of the preposition *at,* is introduced by the indefinite relative adjective *whichever* (which in turn is an adjectival modifier of *office*). *Whichever* has no antecedent expressed in its sentence. (See Note, p. 163.)]

d. Interrogative adjective.   A noun clause may be introduced by an interrogative adjective — such as *which, what,* and *whose* — which asks or implies an indirect question. An interrogative adjective functions as an adjectival modifier in its own clause; it has no antecedent in its sentence. (See also pp. 130 f.)

He wanted to know which course he should take and whose textbook he might buy. [The noun clauses *which course he should take* and *whose textbook he might buy,* functioning as the compound direct object of the infinitive *to know,* are introduced by the interrogative adjectives *which* and *whose.* *Which* functions as an adjectival modifier of *course,* and *whose* functions as an adjectival modifier of *textbook.* Neither *which* nor *whose* has an antecedent in its sentence.]

e. Indefinite relative adverb.   A noun clause may be introduced by an indefinite relative adverb — such as *when, where, why, how.* An indefinite relative adverb has no expressed antecedent in its sentence.[2]

> I know where he keeps his scythe. [The noun clause *where he keeps his scythe,* functioning as the direct object of the main verb *know,* is introduced by the indefinite relative adverb *where* (which in turn functions as an adverbial modifier of *keeps*). Note that *where* has no antecedent expressed in its sentence.]
>
> I am making no mystery about when I am leaving. [The noun clause *when I am leaving,* functioning as the object of the preposition *about,* is introduced by the indefinite relative adverb *when* (which in turn functions as an adverbial modifier of *am leaving*).]
>
> Why he left is no business of mine. [The noun clause *why he left,* functioning as the subject of the main verb *is,* is introduced by the indefinite relative adverb *why* (which in turn functions as an adverbial modifier of *left*).]

f. Interrogative adverb. A noun clause may be introduced by an interrogative adverb — such as *when, where, why,* and *how* — which asks or implies an indirect question. An interrogative adverb functions as an adverb (usually modifying the verb) in its own clause; it has no antecedent in its sentence. (See also p. 101 and pp. 131 f.)

> Where we can meet is the next question. [The noun clause *where we can meet,* functioning as the subject of the main verb *is,* is introduced by the interrogative adverb *where,* which functions as an adverbial modifier of *can meet* ("we can meet where"). The direct question was "Where can we meet?"]
>
> The boy inquired how he might qualify for the race. [The noun clause *how he might qualify for the race,* functioning as the direct object of *inquired,* is introduced by the interrogative adverb *how,* which functions as an adverbial modifier of *might qualify* ("he might qualify how"). The direct question was "How may I qualify?"]

[2] An indefinite relative adverb, like an indefinite relative pronoun and an indefinite relative adjective, is sometimes said to contain in itself its own antecedent. Thus the indefinite relative adverb *where* is roughly equivalent in meaning (but not in grammar) to "the place in which"; *when* to "the time at which"; *why* to "the reason for which," etc.

3. FUNCTIONS OF NOUN CLAUSES

A noun clause may function as *(a)* a subject of a finite verb or of an infinitive, *(b)* a direct object, *(c)* an indirect object, *(d)* a subjective complement, *(e)* an objective complement, *(f)* one of double objects, *(g)* a retained object, *(h)* an object of a preposition, or *(i)* an appositive.

a. Subject

That we shall have no serious trouble has become evident. [The subordinate clause *that we shall have no serious trouble* functions as a noun clause, the subject of the main verb *has become.*]

He declared what had been alleged to be untrue. [The noun clause *what had been alleged* functions as the subject of the infinitive *to be.*]

It is certain that we have become lost. [The noun clause *that we have become lost* functions as the true subject of the main verb *is.* (*It* is an expletive; see pp. 145 f.)]

b. Direct object

I heard that Tom had enlisted in the Marine Corps. [The noun clause *that Tom had enlisted in the Marine Corps* functions as the direct object of the main verb *heard.*]

Having learned why he resigned, I refused to vote for him. [The noun clause *why he resigned* functions as the direct object of the participle *having heard.*]

I think it entirely possible that the judges had been bribed. [The noun clause *that the judges had been bribed* functions as the direct object. (*It* is an expletive.)]

c. Indirect object

We will make whoever asks for it a quotation for the whole job. [The noun clause *whoever asks for it* functions as an indirect object of the main verb *will make.*]

d. Subjective complement

The trouble is that we do not know her address. [The noun clause *that we do not know her address* functions as a subjective complement of the main verb *is.*]

He was made by his wife what he is today. [The noun clause *what he is today* (that is, "he is what") functions as a subjective complement after the passive verb *was made*.]

e. Objective complement

She made him what he is today. [The noun clause *what he is today* (that is, "he is what") functions as an objective complement.]

f. Double object

Ask him what his name is. [The noun clause *what his name is* functions as one of the double objects after the verb *ask* (the other one of the double objects being *him*).]

g. Retained object   *always passive*

We were not told which route we should take. [The noun clause *which route we should take* functions as a retained object after the passive verb *were told*.]

I was taught that haste makes waste. [The noun clause *that haste makes waste* functions as a retained object after the passive verb *was taught*.]

h. Object of a preposition

I know nothing about him except that he is a brilliant conversationalist. [The noun clause *that he is a brilliant conversationalist* functions as the object of the preposition *except*.]   *takes form by function*

Dr. Hale has good advice for whoever is in need of help. [The noun clause *whoever is in need of help* functions as the object of the preposition *for*.]

i. Appositive

The fact (that she is a pleasing speaker) is important. [The noun clause *that she is a pleasing speaker* functions as a clause in apposition with *fact*.]

NOTE. A clause introduced by the subordinating conjunction *that* and functioning as a noun clause used in apposition with a substantive must not be confused with a clause introduced by the relative pronoun *that* and functioning as an adjectival clause modifying a substantive.

The fact that we must recognize is the gradual disappearance of Greek from our curricula. [The subordinate clause *that we must recognize* is introduced by the relative pronoun *that* (which is the direct object of *must recognize*) and functions as an adjectival modifier of *fact*, which is the antecedent of *that*.]

If a clause is in apposition, the clause may be substituted for the preceding substantive without impairing the logic of the sentence. (See also p. 175.)

EXERCISES

Noun (substantive) clauses

Make clear how any noun clause in the following sentences functions and how it is attached to the element on which it depends.

1. We believe that democracy is ultimately the salvation of the world.
2. He soon discovered that all is not gold that glitters.
3. She was left to wonder who he might be.
4. Which car we should buy has upset my whole family.
5. Ask the agent when the next train leaves for Chicago.
6. You know very well what I expect of you.
7. She wondered which dictionary she ought to buy.
8. He always does well in whatever role he is cast in.
9. I think we shall have some rain this afternoon.
10. You may choose whichever you prefer.
11. The future of our country is what we must ever keep in mind now.
12. I think I gave him what he wanted most of all.
13. We were told that we had just fifteen minutes.
14. The fact that our country and Canada have an unfortified boundary line is something to be proud of.
15. They objected to what we proposed to do.
16. That we have come so far unscathed does not justify us in relaxing our vigilance.
17. His proposal — that we give the boy another chance — failed to appeal to us very strongly.
18. I suspect that the influence of women on our national development is not fully realized.
19. It is surely more than a coincidence that the increase in women's control of education has gone on in a fairly direct ratio to the increase in their purchasing power.

20. We had great hopes that the League of Nations would prevent war.
21. We know now that there was a defect in von Moltke's system.
22. But the sequel showed how Lincoln had understood the situation.
23. Lincoln thought of nothing but what was the right military policy.
24. A corresponding account of how things are managed at Oxford might be obtained.
25. In Alaska one might see how Old Vulcan himself threw a huge heat-welded dam across the doughty Yukon at the confluence of the Pelly and note how the gallant river tore down this formidable barrier in its efforts to free itself from the lake holding it captive.
26. The idea that a list of two would exhaust the number of reputable citizens is a reflection upon the whole community.
27. We had better make up our minds about what price we are willing to pay for permanent peace.
28. The question seems to be whether we are willing to pay the price.
29. That we shall have to make some compromises is now evident to us all.
30. What those compromises must be is anybody's guess.
31. Whose the responsibility is is a matter of debate.
32. I question what right he has to interfere in what does not concern him.
33. The fact that his intentions are good is all in his favor.
34. We shall have to make some decision about whether we wish all our savings in one enterprise or not.
35. I believe it will be feasible for us to make the trip tomorrow.
36. Children must be shown how closely related careful pronunciation and correct spelling are.
37. My roommate will argue with whoever has definite ideas on any subject.
38. No one took the time to explain to me why my phone had been moved to Johnson's desk.
39. My chief concern is that our chairman will not remember how many of us have already voted.
40. Have the police determined whose car was used in the robbery?

B. *Adjectival Clauses*

An adjectival clause may modify any kind of substantive — such as a subject, a complement, and the object of a preposition.

For diagrams of adjectival clauses see page 402.

concern here with connecting line

1.   INTRODUCED BY

An adjectival clause may be introduced by (*a*) a relative pronoun (see p. 128); (*b*) an understood relative pronoun easily supplied; (*c*) a relative adjective; or (*d*) a relative adverb (see p. 131).

a. Relative pronoun.   An adjectival clause may be introduced by a relative pronoun,[3] such as *who, which, that, as,* which functions as a substantive in its own clause and has a substantive in the main clause as its antecedent.

He who pays his debts is to be respected. [The adjectival clause *who pays his debts,* functioning as a modifier of *he,* is introduced by the relative pronoun *who. Who* functions as the subject of *pays* in its own clause and has *he,* in the main clause, as its antecedent.]

I know a man whom we can trust. [The adjectival clause *whom we can trust,* functioning as a modifier of *man,* is introduced by the relative pronoun *whom. Whom* functions as the object of *can trust* in its own clause and has *man,* in the main clause, as its antecedent.]

Is this the book which you referred to? [The adjectival clause *which you referred to,* functioning as a modifier of *book,* is introduced by the relative pronoun *which. Which* functions as the object of the preposition *to* in its own clause and has *book,* in the main clause, as its antecedent.]

She is a person that one can admire. [The adjectival clause *that one can admire,* functioning as a modifier of *person,* is introduced by the relative pronoun *that. That* functions in its own clause as the object of *can admire* and has *person,* in the main clause, as its antecedent.]

Appoint someone who you know is trustworthy. [The adjectival clause *who you know is trustworthy,* functioning as a modifier of *someone,* is introduced by the relative pronoun *who. Who* functions as the subject of *is* in its own clause and has *someone,* in the

---

[3] For the differences in grammatical construction and in meaning among definite relative pronouns, indefinite relative pronouns, and interrogative pronouns see pp. 129 f.

main clause, as its antecedent. (For the case problem with parenthetical expressions such as "you know," see p. 244).]

Appoint someone whom you know to be trustworthy. [The adjectival clause *whom you know to be trustworthy*, functioning as a modifier of *someone*, is introduced by the relative pronoun *whom. Whom* functions as the subject of the infinitive *to be* in its own clause and has *someone*, in the main clause, as its antecedent.]

He has the same grin as his father had. [The adjectival clause *as his father had*, functioning as a modifier of *grin*, is introduced by the relative pronoun *as* (= "which"). *As* functions in its own clause as the direct object of *had* and has *grin*, in the main clause, as its antecedent.]

NOTE. A relative pronoun introducing an adjective clause will be used within its own clause as a substantive, nearly always as a subject, a direct object, or an object of a preposition, and rarely, as a subject of an infinitive. The relative pronoun *that*, however, has one use in which it functions in its own clause as the equivalent of an adverbial prepositional phrase such as "in which," "at which," or "during which." In this use the adjectival clause will usually modify the noun *time* (or another noun denoting time) or the noun *way*.

I remember the first time that I saw you. [The adjectival clause *that I saw you* functions as a modifier of the noun *time*.]

I'll never forget the way that he looked when he received the message. [The adjectival clause *that he looked when he received the message* functions as a modifier of the noun *way*.]

In this type of adjectival clause the relative pronoun *that*, since it is the equivalent of an adverbial prepositional phrase, can be construed as a substantive used adverbially. (See Adverbial Noun, p. 106.) The relative pronoun in this kind of clause is often not expressed—"the first time (that) I saw him"; "the way (that) he explained the problem."

b. Relative pronoun understood. An adjectival clause may be introduced by a relative pronoun that has been omitted by ellipsis (see p. 153) but that may be easily supplied.

Steinbeck is the writer I meant. [The relative pronoun *whom* (or *that*) is understood as the object of *meant* and has *writer* as its antecedent. The sentence may be expanded to read "Steinbeck is the writer whom (or that) I meant."]

That is a doctrine I don't believe in. [The relative pronoun *which* (or *that*) is understood as the object of the preposition *in* and has as its antecedent *doctrine*. The sentence may be expanded to read "That is a doctrine which I don't believe in."]

 c. Relative adjective.   An adjectival clause may be introduced by the relative adjective *whose*, which functions as an adjectival modifier of a substantive in its own clause and has a substantive in the main clause as its antecedent. (See also p. 130.)

Harrison is a man whose integrity is unquestioned. [The adjectival clause *whose integrity is unquestioned*, functioning as a modifier of *man*, is introduced by the relative adjective *whose*. *Whose* functions as an adjectival modifier of *integrity* in its own clause and has *man*, in the main clause, as its antecedent.]

Which may be used as a relative adjective. In this use the modifying function of *which* in its own clause is somewhat different from that of *whose*, which shows possession.

He was elected chairman, in which capacity he served for two years. [The adjective clause *in which capacity he served for two years*, functioning as a modifier of *chairman*, is introduced by the relative adjective *which*, an adjectival modifier of *capacity* in its own clause. In this use *which* is roughly the equivalent of a demonstrative ("he served for two years in that capacity").]

 d. Relative adverb.   An adjectival clause may be introduced by a relative adverb — such as *when, where, why* (less commonly, *before* or *after*). The relative adverb functions as an adverbial modifier (usually of the verb) in its own clause and has some substantive, in the main clause, as its antecedent. (See p. 131) (For adverbial clauses introduced by indefinite relative adverbs see pp. 180 f.)

I know a place where we can have a quiet talk. [The adjectival clause *where we can have a quiet talk*, functioning as a modifier of *place*, is introduced by the relative adverb *where*. *Where* functions as an adverbial modifier of *can have* ("we can have a quiet talk where") in its own clause and has *place*, in the main clause, as its antecedent.]

We moved here in 1947, when Molly was in kindergarten. [The adjectival clause *when Molly was in kindergarten,* functioning as a modifier of the noun 1947, is introduced by the relative adverb *when.* *When* functions as an adverbial modifier of *was* ("Molly was in kindergarten when") in its own clause and has 1947, in the main clause, as its antecedent.]

We found the reason why the lights went out. [The adjectival clause *why the lights went out,* functioning as a modifier of *reason,* is introduced by the relative adverb *why.* *Why* functions as an adverbial modifier of *went* "the lights went out why") in its own clause and has *reason,* in the main clause, as its antecedent.]

He resigned the day after the company went bankrupt. [The adjectival clause *after the company went bankrupt,* functioning as a modifier of the noun *day,* is introduced by the relative adverb *after.* *After* functions as an adverbial modifier of *went* ("the company went bankrupt after") in its own clause and has *day* (functioning as an adverbial noun in the main clause) as its antecedent.]

2.   FUNCTIONS OF ADJECTIVAL CLAUSES

An adjectival clause may modify any substantive. Adjectival clauses commonly modify subjects, complements, and objects of prepositions.

a. Modifying the subject of a verb

I, who have nothing to gain, will go to see him. [The clause *who have nothing to gain* functions as an adjectival modifier of *I,* subject of the main verb.]

b. Modifying a complement

He is not a man I am acquainted with. [The sentence for analysis reads "He is not a man whom (or that) I am acquainted with." (For ellipsis see pp. 151 f.) The clause (*whom*) *I am acquainted with* (that is, "with whom I am acquainted") functions as an adjectival modifier of *man,* the subjective complement of *is.*]

We climbed a tower, from the top of which we could see for many miles. [The clause *from the top of which we could see for many miles* functions as an adjectival modifier of *tower,* the direct object of the main verb *climbed.*]

c. Modifying the object of a preposition

He returned to the town where he had spent his childhood. [The clause *where he had spent his childhood* functions as an adjectival modifier of *town*, which is the object of the preposition *to* in the main clause.]

d. "Which" with no single-word antecedent.

An adjectival clause introduced by *which* may sometimes be used to modify the whole idea expressed in a preceding clause rather than one substantive in the clause.

Several students giggled, which annoyed the speaker. [The adjectival clause *which annoyed the speaker* is introduced by the relative pronoun *which*. The antecedent of *which* is the whole preceding clause: "Several students giggled, (a fact) which annoyed the speaker."]

3.   NOUN CLAUSES AND ADJECTIVAL CLAUSES

It is not always easy to distinguish sharply between a noun function and an adjective function of a subordinate clause; but, fortunately, the distinction is not an important one. An appositive clause may represent a noun in apposition to a preceding noun or may be an appositive modifier of the preceding noun. A subordinate clause functioning as a subjective complement may represent either a noun or an adjective.

either one

Mr. James, who is a lawyer, can advise us. [The subordinate clause *who is a lawyer* may be interpreted as a noun clause in apposition with *Mr. James*. Compare "Mr. James, a lawyer, can advise us." Or, the *who*-clause may be interpreted as an appositive adjectival modifier of *Mr. James*. Compare "Lawyer James can advise us." Since the *who* is a definite relative pronoun, with *Mr. James* as its antecedent, it is probably more logical to call the clause an adjectival clause.]

The details are what are bothering me. [The subordinate clause *what are bothering me* may be interpreted as a noun clause functioning as a subjective complement — in a sense meaning the same thing as *details*. Or, the *what*-clause may be interpreted as an adjectival clause functioning as a subjective complement, looking back to and qualifying the noun *details* and at the same time completing the predication begun by the verb *are*. Compare "bothersome details." But since the function of the clause is more noticeably to rename the substantive rather than to describe it, and since *what* is an indefinite relative pronoun, the clause should probably be considered a noun clause.]

The construction in which the subordinating conjunction *that* introduces an appositional clause can be easily distinguished from the construction in which the relative pronoun *that* introduces an adjectival clause. *That* introducing a noun clause is a nonfunctioning connective; but *that* introducing an adjective clause is a relative pronoun, which is a functioning connective. If *which* (which may function as a relative pronoun but not as a conjunction) can be substituted for the *that*, the clause will be an adjectival clause.

which
for
that

The fact that we have not had sufficient training should not discourage us. [The subordinate clause *that we have not had sufficient training* is introduced by the subordinating conjunction *that* and functions as a noun clause in apposition with *fact*. Notice that *which* is not a usable substitute for *that* in this sentence.]

The fact that we have not taken into consideration is our lack of sufficient training. [The subordinate clause *that we have not taken into consideration* is introduced by the relative pronoun *that* (which is the direct object of the verb *have taken*) and functions as an adjectival modifier of *fact*. Notice that *which* could be substituted for *that* in this sentence.]

4. ATTRIBUTE AND APPOSITIVE CLAUSES

Most adjectival clauses are attributive in meaning (that is, restrictive) even though such clauses follow the nouns they modify. But some adjectival clauses are appositive in meaning. (See pp. 89 ff. for a discussion of the difference in meaning between attribute and appositive modifiers.) There is no difference between clauses functioning as attribute modifiers and those functioning as appositive modifiers as far as their grammar is concerned. But there is a difference in meaning and a corresponding difference in punctuation to show this difference in meaning. Clauses that function as attribute modifiers are called restrictive clauses. Such clauses, narrowing or restricting the meaning of the substantives on which they depend, could not be dropped without changing the meaning of the substantives they modify. A restrictive clause is never set off with commas.

Clauses that function as appositive modifiers are called nonrestrictive (or additive) clauses. Such clauses merely add thoughts without restricting the substantives on which they depend; that is, they could be dropped without changing the meaning of the substantives that they modify. An additive (or nonrestrictive) clause is always set off with commas.[4]

Relative clauses introduced by *who* or *which* seem to give the most trouble in punctuation, because the relatives *who* and *which* may introduce either restrictive or nonrestrictive adjectival clauses. But the relative pronoun *that* normally introduces restrictive clauses only. Hence, a simple test to determine whether a given *who-* or *which*-clause is restrictive or nonrestrictive is to see whether the *who* or *which* can be replaced with *that* without changing the meaning. If the change can be made, the clause is restrictive and should not be set off with commas; if it cannot be made, the clause is nonrestrictive and demands commas.

---

[4] "Set off" means "commas on both sides" or something stronger than commas, as distinguished from one comma used to "separate." That is, an item to be set off will be enclosed with commas. Possibly one of the commas will be replaced by a stronger mark, such as a semicolon, a dash, a colon, or a period. Or it may be that a capital at the beginning of a sentence will take the place of the first comma. In any case the item that is to be set off will have commas on both sides or something stronger that absorbs the function of one or the other of the two commas. Thus:

> Noisy and boisterous, the children rushed into the house. [The initial capital and the comma after *boisterous* set off the appositive modifier *noisy and boisterous*.]
> The children, noisy and boisterous, rushed into the house. [The two commas set off the appositive modifier *noisy and boisterous*.]
> The children rushed into the house, noisy and boisterous. [The comma before *noisy* and the period after *boisterous* set off the appositive modifier *noisy and boisterous*.]

The plan that I have in mind is simple. [The *that*-clause is an attribute modifier of *plan*. It is restrictive; hence, it is not set off with commas.]

My plan, which I have used many times, is very simple. [The *which*-clause is an appositive modifier of *plan*. It is nonrestrictive; hence, it is set off with commas. Note that the substitution of *that* for *which* would change its meaning.]

All who plan to go hold up their hands. [*That* may be substituted for *who*, showing that the relative clause is restrictive in meaning and so should not be set off with commas.]

EXERCISES

Adjectival clauses

Make clear how any adjectival clause in the following sentences is introduced and what it modifies.

1. Will the gentleman who held up his hand come forward?
2. I am sure St. Louis is the city he referred to.
3. That is one toast that we all can drink to.
4. He has the same privileges as you and I.
5. Mme. Curie was a woman whose supreme passion in life was scientific research.
6. I have always wished to visit the spot where Custer made his last stand.
7. I don't know any good reason why you can't be admitted to this class.
8. Backslapping is a usage that may be said to be an integral part of a pecuniary civilization.
9. This brings us to that growing army of "publicity men and women" who sometimes give the best of their vitality to pushing causes in which they have no faith.
10. Perhaps the independent storekeeper, surviving in those few remote neighborhoods where chain stores have not rendered his life a burden, takes second place.
11. There was a time when this class topped the whole list.
12. I spent the afternoon trying to locate a friend of mine who I knew was to be in New York at the same time as I was.

13. A car whose battery has run down can't help us now.
14. Mr. Bradford makes for himself another difficulty which Mr. Strachey has shed with a shrug of his shoulders.
15. There is the gentleman I wish to be introduced to.
16. He lived at a time when tallow candles were made in every home.
17. And we cannot hold our leaders responsible for conditions they did not create.
18. I can present three poor reasons why I was late this morning.
19. He is saying the same things as you have said on many occasions.
20. Mr. Gamaliel Bradford, who developed what he liked to call psychography, practiced what he preached.
21. But the artist in life is confronted by an almost infinite number of "tools" which for him consist of all those things by which thought and emotion can be brought into being.
22. This life was a preparation for an eternal one, entrance to the happiness of which was possible only by following certain rules of conduct.
23. The question we wish to raise is one of fair play.
24. What will happen to this seemingly new movement that began with the depression the years ahead must decide.
25. There is a kind of simple openness in talks with men which I find it difficult to attain in the case of women.
26. The fact that we must give careful consideration to is Henderson's failure to meet his appointment.
27. The building whose tower you see through the trees is the Williams Hotel.
28. These are the times that try men's souls.
29. All such arguments as have been advanced are childish.
30. At the moment when we thought we had everything in order, Lumley went over to the other side.
31. I see no reason why we should delay longer.
32. We have found that the statement that we sent you last week is wrong.
33. I confess to a blunder for which there is no adequate excuse.
34. It is a university from which any man would be proud to hold a degree.
35. This is the day for whose coming we have waited patiently.
36. The song that the orchestra is now playing is one of my favorites, "The Last Time I Saw Paris."
37. The auditorium may not be available for our meeting next Tuesday, in which case we shall meet in Alden Hall.
38. Fortunately for me, I finished high school in 1932, when young

people did not have to be compulsively concerned with getting into the college of their choice.

39. Your grades in mathematics are low, which might be looked on unfavorably by the admissions board.

40. The delay is explained by the fact that your report reached me the day before I sailed for Europe.

c.   *Adverbial Clauses*

An adverbial clause may modify a verb, an adjective, or an adverb.

For diagrams of adverbial clauses see pp. 407 ff.

1.   INTRODUCED BY

An adverbial clause may be introduced by (*a*) a simple subordinating conjunction (see p. 127), by (*b*) an indefinite relative adverb (see p. 131), or by (*c*) one of a pair of correlative adverbs (see pp. 102 f.).   *functional connective*

a. Subordinating conjunction. An adverbial clause may be introduced by a subordinating conjunction — such as *if, although, unless, because, that, in order that, so that,* etc. — an expression whose sole function is to join the subordinate clause to the element in the main clause on which it depends. That is, the subordinating conjunction has no grammatical function in the clause that it introduces. (See also p. 127.)

People will not buy goods if prices are too high. [The adverbial clause *if prices are too high*, functioning as a modifier of *will buy*, is introduced by the subordinating conjunction *if*, which has no other function than to join the subordinate clause to the main clause.]

I'll give you this note so that you will not have any trouble at the gate. [The adverbial clause *so that you will not have any trouble at the gate*, functioning as an adverbial modifier of *'ll give*, is introduced by the subordinating conjunction *so that*, which has no other function than to join the subordinate clause to the main clause.]

She seems confident that she will be chosen. [The adverbial

clause *that she will be chosen*, functioning as an adverbial modifier of the adjective *confident*, is introduced by the subordinating conjunction *that*,[5] which has no other function than to join the subordinate clause to the main clause.]

b. Indefinite relative adverb.   An adverbial clause may be introduced by an indefinite relative adverb, such as *when, where, whenever, wherever,* etc. The indefinite relative adverb functions as an adverbial modifier (usually of the verb) in the subordinate clause that it introduces and connects this clause to the verb, adjective, or adverb in the main clause that it modifies. An indefinite relative adverb introducing an adverbial clause has no antecedent expressed in its sentence. (See also p. 131.)

I came when I heard your call. [The adverbial clause *when I heard your call*, functioning as a modifier of the main verb *came*, is introduced by the indefinite relative adverb *when*. *When* functions in its own clause as an adverbial modifier of *heard*; it has no antecedent expressed in its sentence. (*When* may, of course, be expanded to mean "at the moment at which.")]

We like to go where the crowd goes. [The adverbial clause *where the crowd goes*, functioning as a modifier of the infinitive *to go*, is introduced by the indefinite relative adverb *where*. *Where* functions in its own clause as an adverbial modifier of *goes*; it has no antecedent expressed in its sentence. (*Where* may, of course, be expanded to mean "to the place to which.")]

They collected old rubber wherever they could find it. [The adverbial clause *wherever they could find it*, functioning as a modifier of *collected*, is introduced by the indefinite relative adverb *wherever*. *Wherever* functions in its own clause as an adverbial modifier of *could find*; it has no antecedent expressed in its sentence. (*Wherever* may, of course, be expanded to mean "in any place in which.")]

[5] Some grammarians prefer to regard such *that*-clauses following adjectives like *certain, sure,* etc., as noun clauses functioning as adverbial objectives — that is, as adverbs. Inasmuch as anything modifying an adjective is by that fact adverbial in function, it seems simpler to call such clauses adverbial clauses in the first place. .

NOTE. Some confusion may arise from the fact that such words as *when* and *where* may be *(a)* interrogative adverbs, *(b)* relative adverbs, *(c)* indefinite relative adverbs. The confusion may be resolved by remembering that an interrogative adverb can introduce only a noun clause (or an independent clause, asking a direct question); that a relative adverb (an adverb with an expressed antecedent) can introduce only an adjectival clause; and that an indefinite relative adverb (a relative adverb without an expressed antecedent) can introduce either a noun clause or an adverbial clause. These basic differences are evident in the examples given below.

He wondered when he might call. [The interrogative adverb *when* introduces an indirect question, *when he might call,* a noun clause, the direct object of the main verb *wondered.* The direct question was "When may I call?"]

There comes a time when a man must fight. [The relative adverb *when* introduces the adjectival clause *when a man must fight* and modifies *must fight* in its own clause. The expressed antecedent of *when* is *time;* therefore the subordinate clause functions as an adjectival modifier of *time.*]

Come when I call. [The indefinite relative adverb *when,* modifying *call* in its own clause, introduces the adverbial clause *when I call,* which functions as an adverbial modifier of *come.* *When* has no antecedent in its own clause.]

c. Correlative adverbs. An adverbial clause may be introduced by one of a pair of correlative adverbs, such as *as . . . as, so . . . as, when . . . then, where . . . there, the . . . the,* etc. (see also pp. 102 f.). One of the correlatives serves as a simple adverbial modifier in the main clause; the other correlative serves as an indefinite relative adverb, functioning as an adverbial modifier in the subordinate clause and connecting its clause, as an adverbial modifier of the simple adverb, to the main clause.

Paired Sub. Conj.

He is as ambitious as his father. [That is "He is as ambitious as his father is ambitious." The first *as* functions as a simple adverbial modifier of *ambitious;* the second *as* functions as an indefinite relative adverb modifying *ambitious* understood in the subordinate clause. The second *as* attaches its clause to the main clause as an adverbial modifier of the first *as,* a simple adverb.]

The longer he waits the more he frets. [That is, "To which

degree he waits longer to that degree he frets more." The first *the* functions as an indefinite relative adverb modifying *longer* (which modifies *waits*); the second *the* functions as a simple adverbial modifier of *more* (which modifies *frets*). The first *the* attaches its subordinate clause to the main clause as an adverbial modifier of the second *the*, a simple adverb.

2.   FUNCTIONS OF ADVERBIAL CLAUSES

An adverbial clause may modify (*a*) a verb, (*b*) an adjective, or (*c*) an adverb. It may also be used absolutely.

a. Modifying a verb

Wait until you are summoned. [The adverbial clause *until you are summoned* functions as an adverbial modifier of the main verb *wait*.]

Stopping quickly when the light changed, Jim avoided a collision. [The adverbial clause *when the light changed* functions as an adverbial modifier of the participle *stopping*.]

Playing as if everything depended on it can make any sport attractive. [The adverbial clause *as if everything depended on it* functions as an adverbial modifier of the gerund *playing*.]

b. Modifying an adjective

You are younger than I am. [The adverbial clause *than I am* (*young*) functions as an adverbial modifier of the adjective *younger* (which is a subjective complement of *are*.)]

She has such confidence in herself that she can meet any situation. [The adverbial clause *that she can meet any situation* functions as an adverbial modifier of the adjective *such* (which in turn modifies *confidence*).]

We are sorry that we have to leave. [The adverbial clause *that we have to leave* functions as an adverbial modifier of the adjective *sorry* (which in turn is a subjective complement of *are*).]

I am sure that he will come. [The adverbial clause *that he will come* functions as an adverbial modifier of the adjective *sure* (which in turn is a subjective complement of *am*).]

That is a true, though hackneyed, statement. [The adverbial

cause *though* (*it is a*) *hackneyed* (*statement*) functions as a modifier of the adjective *true*.]

c. Modifying an adverb

Grandfather is not so active as he used to be. [The adverbial clause *as he used to be* functions as a modifier of the adverb *so*, which in turn is an adverbial modifier of the adjective *active* (a subjective complement of *is*).]

It is snowing harder than it did yesterday. [The adverbial clause *than it did* (*snow*) *yesterday* functions as a modifier of *harder*, which in turn is an adverbial modifier of *is snowing*.]

I work so hard that I have no time to play. [The adverbial clause *that I have no time to play* functions as a modifier of *so*, which in turn is an adverbial modifier of *hard* (an adverbial modifier of *work*).]

d. Used absolutely.
Clauses adverbial in appearance but having no actual grammatical function in the statement in which they appear may be regarded as subordinate clauses used absolutely.[6] (See also p. 140.)

Whether we like it or not, Jane has been selected for the leading role. [The adverbial-like clause *whether we like it or not* performs no grammatical function in the main clause *Jane has been selected for the leading role*.]

3. IDEAS EXPRESSED BY ADVERBIAL CLAUSES

An adverbial clause may express an idea of (*a*) time, (*b*) place, (*c*) manner, (*d*) degree, (*e*) condition, (*f*) concession, (*g*) cause (or reason), (*h*) purpose, and (*i*) result.

NOTE. Although adverbial clauses express such ideas as time and place, this does not mean that all subordinate clauses of time and place are by that fact adverbial. As was seen above, some time and place clauses are noun clauses (see pp. 165 f.), and some time and place clauses are adjectival (see pp. 172 f.). It is not, therefore, the idea that the sub-

---

[6] Some grammarians regard such clauses as "loose" modifiers of the main statement in which they appear. But inasmuch as the relation that such a clause bears to the main clause is a logical, not a grammatical, relation, they are here classed with other expressions used absolutely.

ordinate clause conveys, or even the introductory word, that determines the grammatical function of the clause; its grammatical function is determined by its grammatical relationship to the element on which it depends. (See pp. 160 f.)

Where we go is immaterial to me. [The subordinate *where*-clause is a noun clause functioning as the subject of the main verb *is*. (The same would be true with "When we go. . . .")]

We found a good place where we could camp for the night. [The subordinate *where*-clause is an adjectival clause modifying the noun *place*. (The same would be true of "We found a time when we all could meet.")]

I shall go where I please. [The subordinate *where*-clause is an adverbial clause functioning as a modifier of *shall go*. (The same would be true of "I shall go when. . . .")]

a. Time. An adverbial clause of time may be introduced by such indefinite relative adverbs as *when, whenever,* and by such subordinating conjunctions as *as, just as, since, before, after, until.*

She will find our note when she returns. [The adverbial clause *when she returns* is introduced by the indefinite relative adverb *when* (which modifies *returns*) and functions as a modifier of *will find.*]

He stopped her just as she was turning the corner. [The adverbial clause *just as she was turning the corner* is introduced by the subordinating conjunction *as* and functions as a modifier of *stopped*. (For *just* see p. 101.)]

He goes to his grandfather whenever he needs money. [The adverbial clause *whenever he needs money* is introduced by the indefinite relative adverb *whenever* (which modifies *needs*) and functions as a modifier of *goes.*]

b. Place. An adverbial clause of place may be introduced by such indefinite relative adverbs as *where, wherever.* (See p. 131.)

I go where my fancy leads me. [The adverbial clause *where my fancy leads me* is introduced by the indefinite relative adverb *where* (which modifies *leads*) and functions as a modifier of *go.*]

He works wherever he can find a job. [The adverbial clause

wherever he can find a job is introduced by the indefinite relative adverb *wherever* (which modifies *can find*) and functions as a modifier of *works*.]

c. *Manner.* An adverbial clause of manner may be introduced by the particle *as*, which for convenience may be regarded as an indefinite relative adverb (equivalent in meaning to "in the manner in which"), or by such a subordinating conjunction as *as though, as if*.

He does not talk as he did yesterday. [The adverbial clause *as he did* (*talk*) *yesterday* is introduced by the indefinite relative adverb *as*, which modifies *did* (*talk*), and functions as an adverbial modifier of *does talk*. (The sentence may be expanded to mean "He does not talk in the manner in which he did talk yesterday.")]

As a man soweth, so shall he reap. [The adverbial clause *as a man soweth* is introduced by the indefinite relative adverb *as* (which modifies *soweth*) and functions as a modifier of *so* (which in turn is an adverbial modifier of *shall reap*). (The sentence may be expanded to mean "In the manner in which a man soweth in that manner shall he reap.")]

He walks as if he were lame. [The adverbial clause *as if he were lame* is introduced by the subordinating conjunction *as if* and functions as a modifier of *walks*.]

d. *Degree.*[7] An adverbial clause of degree may be introduced by one of a pair of correlative adverbs such as *as . . . as* or *not so . . . as, the . . . the* (see pp. 102 f.), one of which functions as a simple adverb in the main clause and the other as an indefinite relative adverb in the subordinate clause; or it may be introduced by the subordinating conjunction *than*.

He is as honest as he is homely. [The adverbial clause *as he is homely* is introduced by the indefinite relative adverb *as* (= "to which degree"), which modifies *homely*, and functions as an adverbial modifier of the first *as*, which in turn is an adverbial

[7] The term "degree" as used here includes those adverbial clauses introduced by *than* and *as* — "He is taller than I (am)"; "Today is as cold as yesterday (was)" — which are sometimes grouped under a separate classification called "clauses of comparison."

modifier of *honest*. (The sentence may be expanded to mean "He is honest to that degree to which degree he is homely.")]

She is not so ambitious as her sister. [The adverbial clause *as her sister* (*is ambitious*) is introduced by the indefinite relative adverb *as* (= "to the degree to which"), which modifies the second *ambitious* understood, and functions as a modifier of *so*, which in turn is an adverbial modifier of *ambitious*. (The sentence may be expanded to mean "She is not ambitious to the degree to which degree her sister is ambitious.")]

He was so mad that he could not say a word. [The adverbial clause *that he could not say a word* is introduced by the subordinating conjunction *that* and functions as a modifier of *so*, which in turn is an adverbial modifier of *mad*.]

I am older than my brother. [The adverbial clause *than my brother* (*is old*) is introduced by the subordinating conjunction *than* and functions as a modifier of *older*, a subjective complement of *am*.]

You came sooner than I expected. [The adverbial clause *than I expected* is introduced by the subordinating conjunction *than* and functions as a modifier of *sooner*, which is an adverbial modifier of *came*.]

The more he tried the more he failed. [The adverbial clause *the more he tried* is introduced by the correlative adverb *the* and functions as an adverbial modifier of the second correlative adverb *the* (which in turn is a simple adverbial modifier of *more*). The correlative adverbs *the . . . the*, expressing the idea of degree, mean "to which degree . . . to that degree"; hence, the sentence may be expanded to mean "To which degree he tried more to that degree he failed."]

The sooner you come to your senses the better. [The adverbial clause *the sooner you come to your senses* is introduced by the correlative adverb *the* and functions as an adverbial modifier of the second *the* (which in turn is a simple adverbial modifier of *better*). *Better*, an adjective, is a subjective complement in the main clause (*it will be*) *better*. (The sentence may be expanded to mean "To which degree you come to your senses sooner to that degree it will be better.")]

e. Condition. An adverbial clause of condition may be introduced by the subordinating conjunction *if* or any equivalent of *if* — such as *unless, provided, supposing, in case.* The conjunction *if* is omitted when the auxiliary *should* or *had* comes first in the clause.

If I were you I should consult a doctor. [The adverbial clause *if I were you* is introduced by the subordinating conjunction *if* and functions as a modifier of *should consult.*]

Supposing we report the matter, what do we gain? [The adverbial clause *supposing we report the matter* is introduced by *supposing,* used as the equivalent of *if,* and functions as a modifier of *do gain.*]

Call me immediately in case my mother arrives. [The adverbial clause *in case my mother arrives* is introduced by *in case,* used as the equivalent of *if,* and functions as a modifier of *call.*]

Should I be late, don't wait for me. [The adverbial clause *should I be late,* with the auxiliary *should* coming first and the subordinating conjunction *if* being implied, functions as a modifier of *do wait.*]

Had I been notified in time, I would have attended the meeting. [The adverbial clause *had I been notified in time,* with the auxiliary *had* coming first and the subordinating conjunction *if* being implied, functions as a modifier of *would have attended.*]

I will pay the full sum provided you will give me a cash discount. [The adverbial clause *provided you will give me a cash discount* is introduced by *provided,* used as the equivalent of *if,* and functions as a modifier of *will pay.*]

f. Concession. An adverbial clause of concession may be introduced by a subordinating conjunction such as *though* or *although, while* used in the sense of *though,* or *even if.*

He agreed to file suit, although it was against his better judgment. [The adverbial clause *although it was against his better judgment* is introduced by the subordinating conjunction *although* and functions as a modifier of *agreed.*]

While I am terribly sorry for her, I can do nothing for him. [The adverbial clause *while I am terribly sorry for her* is introduced by the subordinating conjunction *while* and functions as a modifier of *can do.*]

However hard he tried, he always failed. [The adverbial clause *however hard he tried* is introduced by *however* (an adverbial modifier of the adverb *hard*) and functions as a modifier of *failed*. (*However hard he tried* = "although he tried ever so hard.")]

Whichever course we take we lose. [The adverbial clause *whichever course we take* is introduced by the indefinite relative adjective *whichever* (a modifier of *course*) and functions as a modifier of *lose*. (*Whichever course we take* = "though we take any course we please to take.")]

g. *Cause* (*or reason*). An adverbial clause of cause (or reason) may be introduced by such subordinating conjunctions as *because, since, as* (in the sense of "because"), *that, inasmuch as*.

I read detective stories because I enjoy them. [The adverbial clause *because I enjoy them* is introduced by the subordinating conjunction *because* and functions as a modifier of *read*.]

Since you object, we will strike off his name. [The adverbial clause *since you object* is introduced by the subordinating conjunction *since* and functions as a modifier of *will strike*.]

I cannot do what you ask, as that would be against my principles. [The adverbial clause *as that would be against my principles* is introduced by the subordinating conjunction *as* and functions as a modifier of *can do*.]

Inasmuch as you made the motion, you can act as the chairman of the new committee. [The adverbial clause *inasmuch as you made the motion* is introduced by the subordinating conjunction *inasmuch as* and functions as a modifier of *can act*.]

h. *Purpose*. An adverbial clause of purpose may be introduced by such subordinating conjunctions as *that, so that, in order that,* and *lest* (= "that not").

He opened the window so that we might enjoy the breeze. [The adverbial clause *so that we might enjoy the breeze* is introduced by the subordinating conjunction *so that* and functions as a modifier of *opened*.]

He died that we might have life. [The adverbial clause *that we might have life* is introduced by the subordinating conjunction *that* and functions as a modifier of *died*.]

The speaker raised his voice in order that all might hear his message. [The adverbial clause *in order that all might hear his message* is introduced by the conjunction *in order that* and functions as a modifier of *raised*.]

Speak softly lest you wake the baby. [The adverbial clause *lest you wake the baby* is introduced by the subordinating conjunction *lest* (= "that not") and functions as a modifier of *speak*.]

i. Result. An adverbial clause of result may be introduced by the subordinating conjunction *so that.*

Our bus line has been discontinued, so that now I have to walk. [The adverbial clause *so that now I have to walk* is introduced by the subordinating conjunction *so that* and functions as a modifier of *has been discontinued*.]

NOTE. Although there is no difference so far as grammatical construction is concerned, clauses of result are to be distinguished from clauses of purpose and clauses of degree as far as meaning is concerned. Notice that a clause of degree often expresses also an idea of result.

He ran so that he might catch his train. [Purpose]
He ran, so that he caught his train. [Result]
He ran so fast that he got out of breath. [Both degree and result]

4. ABRIDGED ADVERBIAL CLAUSES

Certain types of adverbial clauses lend themselves to ellipsis (see pp. 151 f.).

When in New York, I stay at the Excelsior Hotel. [The adverbial clause in its complete form is "when I am staying in New York."]

Replacements will be made wherever necessary. [The adverbial clause in its complete form is "wherever they are necessary."]

While driving to school, Linda saw a strange sight. ["While she was driving to school. . . ."]

Although unable to attend, I appreciate the invitation. ["Although I am unable to attend. . . ."]

If possible, plan to arrive before noon. ["If it is possible. . . ."]

NOTE. The abridged adverbial clause is standard English at both spoken and written levels. However, if the clause in its abridged form contains a prominent participle or adjective, the clause can "dangle" (see pp. 306 f.) if it is carelessly constructed.

While mowing my lawn, I was frightened by a large snake.

[*Not:* While mowing my lawn, a large snake frightened me.]

Although weary from the strenuous weekend, I cleaned the trout.

[*Not:* Although weary from the strenuous weekend, the trout were cleaned.]

EXERCISES

Adverbial clauses

Make clear how any adverbial clause in the following sentences is introduced and what the adverbial clause modifies.

1. We left when the speaking started.
2. I picked berries where I found them ripest.
3. I always go whenever there is a circus in town.
4. Wouldn't it be fun to travel wherever your fancy led you?
5. She is as kind as she is beautiful.
6. Father is not so energetic as he used to be.
7. The longer he waited the more impatient he became.
8. I am so angry that I can't control my tongue.
9. We are certain the other nations will follow our lead.
10. When I entered college forty years ago, the chief purpose in acquiring an education was to fit oneself to enter a profession.
11. As with our fellow creatures in life, so it is with our fellow creatures in Shakespeare.
12. There will be as many Hamlets or Macbeths or Othellos as there are readers or spectators.
13. Until there is a marked rise in the tone and standards of our public life this bad custom will continue.
14. If a sceptical scientist in the sixteenth century could have been so bold as to find the goat had not become a man, the faith in the hearts of countless believers would have proved him conclusively wrong.
15. He was so insistent that I could not turn him away.
16. We reached the crest of the hill just as the sun came up.
17. My teacher acts as if she were monarch of all she surveyed.
18. Business revived sooner than anyone had expected.
19. I'll visit the museum with you provided you will visit the art gallery with me.

20. Although we have had a very late spring, crops have grown to full maturity well before we may expect any frosts.
21. However tough the going became, he never whimpered.
22. Since you insist upon a particular brand, I can't help you out this time.
23. As the late Frederick J. Turner discovered the West, so in his historical narratives John Bach McMaster discovered the plain American people.
24. You can't do what you have in mind, as that would mean eating your cake and having it too.
25. He retired from newspaper work so that he might have time for creative writing.
26. We are insistent that you be our guest on this trip.
27. Read poetry lest the soul thirst.
28. Three plants closed down so that more than six thousand men were laid off work.
29. Other members have criticized it because it has never dared to adopt the principle that any individual could be expelled for dishonorable conduct.
30. Even the most jaundiced observer must admit that business is ethically better than it used to be.
31. Better hide those Christmas packages well lest the children find them.
32. The more I read of Jane Austen the more I am convinced that she is one of our greatest masters of social comedy.
33. I am very eager that you see my mother and give her a message.
34. I do not know whence he came or whither he went.
35. Will you move your chair so that we can make a place for this girl?
36. I'm afraid your case is hopeless.
37. Your recommendations, though impressive, did not offset the fact that your competitor had more experience than you.
38. Since the notice of the meeting arrived after I had left home, I am not prepared to vote on the proposals.
39. While vacationing in Florence, she became so interested in architecture that she decided to finish work on her degree.
40. That kind of shot troubles players who have been playing golf much longer than you.

Sentences for analysis

Explain fully the syntax of the following sentences. Make clear how any subordinate clause is introduced and how it functions in the statement in which it appears.

1. The worst phase of nepotism is when the relative draws half the pay and does nothing while the real secretary gets the other half for long hours of labor.

2. One of the fundamental differences between a work of art and a machine product is that the former is unique.

3. The only standard is what we consider a worthwhile life for each of us.

4. The Englishman makes a bad impression on strangers because he doesn't care what impression he makes.

5. Libraries have been written about baseball players, but mostly they are so crammed with figures, tables, and tabulations that the human side of the player is lost in a mass of digits and too big a percentage of zeros.

6. It is most refreshing to renew acquaintances with old friends and meet, face to face, as it were, stars of yore who carved their niche in the Hall of Fame or left a lasting imprint on the pages of baseball history.

7. Along the Embankment the fog was even worse than it had been in the Strand.

8. You will have noticed that when people are inquisitive they nearly always have bad memories and are stupid.

9. A man who begins by asking you how many brothers and sisters you have is never a sympathetic character, and if you meet him in a year's time he will probably ask you how many brothers and sisters you have, his mouth again sagging open and his eyes still bulging from his head.

10. But down the Embankment, though his advance was still slow and uncertain, he had more room to feel his way, and to breathe freely, for that road was as silent and deserted as a Scottish village on a Sunday afternoon.

11. We seek to introduce speed into realms where it does not belong.

12. Fossil river valleys that trench the continental shelves out to the very edge of the abysmal ocean and fossil marine shells that star the soil and stone of the highest mountains tell of eras when portions of the beds of the sea were high and dry and when the summits of our mountains lay beneath the ocean's waves.

13. I took a personal interest in him; I loaned him money, patched up a quarrel between himself and his wife, gave him books to read, tried to help him slide a little more easily along his white-collar groove.

14. That he was grateful, that he really respected and liked me, I do not doubt to this day.

15. At first I thought the poor boy had really come to the end of his rope; that this was the last desperate gesture before the routine of his job doomed him altogether.
16. In the custody and handling of transferable property Americans grow ever more dependable; but in that more subtle definition of integrity which bids a man to play fair with his own soul never has the Republic sunk to lower levels.
17. From the cultural mulch in which we are reared — compounded of the influences of parents, school, church, folkways, literature — our personalities are formed.
18. The psychological effect of continually pretending to agree with that with which one does not agree is disastrous.
19. It was only too plain that there was a tragic breach between his standard of workmanship and the work that he had to do.
20. There may be more deplorable human behavior than the violation of hospitality practiced daily by uncounted thousands of house-to-house canvassers, but I am at a loss to know what it is.
21. There is no better way to encourage a child to do something than to forbid him to do it.
22. We advocate speed laws for motor cars, and we break them when opportunity presents; but we are insistent that others should obey them, and we are secretly glad when we see a policeman handing a summons to a reckless motorist.
23. We pride ourselves grossly and turbulently on what we have done; we experience a glow of satisfaction when we have succeeded in defeating an adversary; and we are loud in our self-praise and laudation.
24. Children never remain long at one thing; they tire of it as soon as it has yielded its first glamor of novelty, and their attention and interest are directed toward the next thing until that, too, loses its savor.
25. We display an anxiety about the physical welfare of our children which would be justified were they made of sugar, salt, or tobacco.
26. When you come right down to it, this ship's on the high seas, and no one's got any authority here except a representative of the United States Marshal's office.
27. Jimmie, the bartender, his white apron removed, a gold-braided cap pulled low on his forehead, said in the soothing voice of a man who has learned his diplomacy dealing with drunks across a mahogany bar, "It won't be long now."
28. Employment at his trade was not so easily found as he had imagined; but while he waited he did such odd jobs as offered, carrying parcels and the like, until he found work in a printer's office.

29. It is necessary to coin a word properly to describe my grandfather's diligence as a reader; he was the readingest person I have ever known.
30. Now of course there's no objection to taking sides when you know what you mean and the cause is worth fighting for.
31. I have to get to the office, because I'm working for a slave driver who insists on my being there by nine-thirty every morning and who prefers to have me there to open the mail at nine o'clock.
32. Broadly speaking, his philosophy has been a refusal to think in terms of principle.
33. The condition upon which he maintained his supremacy was simple enough.
34. The truth of the matter is that the Englishman demands of a law not only that it shall be a good law in itself but that it shall command general assent.
35. The older I grow the less I become interested in reports of supermen, in flares of precociousness and genius.
36. I am not concerned with what he said when the policeman queried him.
37. We discovered the place whence he came; but we have been unable to learn whither he went.
38. It must have finally dawned on Bulgaria that it hitched its wagon to a falling star.
39. In urging people not to visit New York until the war was over Mayor LaGuardia had the full cooperation of the local baseball teams, which seemed to be doing everything in their power to keep the city free of strangers in October.
40. We dropped into the Paramount one morning last week, looking for a cool place to sit between a business appointment and a luncheon date in the neighborhood, and we aren't likely to forget it for a long time.
41. Tell us whom you meant when you said that, if we are to obtain a fair measure of justice, we must select as our leader a man whom the politicians can't control when he is once in office.
42. It is not hard to guess why he hurried away so fast.
43. There was the knowledge that one of the oldest nightmares had been fulfilled when into man's hands came the power to destroy his civilization and himself at a single stroke.
44. When you give men who do not like to be bossed but whom you have been bossing industrially the power to boss you politically, and when they realize that they can get very definite material advantage by bossing you politically, you have set the stage for a contest that

will not be stopped by any instrument or policy of mere opportunism.

45. Employees not only have political power but they outnumber the employers so far that employees can get by political means most of the things that they are unable to get by industrial means.

46. Although the war brought increased employment and new capital equipment to the West and stimulated the region to renewed activity, Western leadership has remained shortsighted and proud of its outdated conservatism.

47. I am sick and tired of people who know all the answers and want to regiment me into joining their party.

48. I should like, while there is yet time, to strike a small blow for that objectivity which has been the basis of the American free press and for every publication that still has question marks on its typewriter keyboard and uses them.

49. They believe they know what is mechanically good for us and practical.

50. Not only have the modern architects failed to understand the limits of our zeal for mechanical efficiency; they have also, thus far, tended to take a somewhat arbitrary view of what we need in our daily life.

PART Two

FORM AND USAGES

CHAPTER 5

Nouns[1]

A. Classes of Nouns

1. COMMON AND PROPER

A common noun is the name of every member of a class; that is, it is the name common to all members of the class. A proper noun is the name of a particular member of a class; that is, it is the name that is the "property" of that member. The initial letter of a proper noun, or a name derived from a proper noun, is capitalized.

man, city, mountain, college [Common nouns]
Henry, New Orleans, Rocky Mountains, Amherst College [Proper nouns]

a. Noun personified. A common noun may become a proper noun when it is personified — that is, when something without life is given the attributes of life — or when it becomes as individual name.

Little round hats seem to be the *fashion* this season. [Common noun]
Madam worships at the shrine of *Fashion.* [Proper noun]

b. Title or word of relationship. A common noun indicating rank or office or relationship may become a proper noun when it is used as the equivalent of a personal name.

[1] For definition of nouns and their constructions in sentences see pp. 33 ff.

He is the new *dean* of the college. [Common noun]
You have, *Dean*, an ingenious line of reasoning. [Proper noun]
My *mother* and *father* will be here Saturday. [Common nouns]
I am expecting *Mother* and *Father* on Saturday. [Proper nouns]

c. *Proper noun derived from a proper name.* A noun, although a common noun in meaning, because it is derived from a proper name is regarded as a proper noun and so is capitalized.

a Republican [any member of the Republic Party]
a Baptist [any member of the Baptist denomination]

a Frenchman [any native of France]
a Rotarian [any member of the Rotary Club]

NOTE. Ordinarily an article used with a proper noun is not a part of the proper noun and so is not capitalized, unless it is a part of the legal name.
the Rockies   the Atlantic   the West Indies   the Louisville *Courier-Journal*   the University of Michigan
But: The Dalles [legal name]   The Hague [legal name]   The Ohio State University [legal name]   *The Nation* [legal name of a magazine]

2.   ABSTRACT AND CONCRETE NOUNS

An abstract noun is one that names a quality, state, or activity apart from any particular subject. A concrete noun is one that names a physical or material thing.

goodness, hope, progress, candor, mercy [Abstract nouns]
house, John, sun, cloth, iron, book [Concrete nouns]

3.   COLLECTIVE NOUNS

A collective noun is one that in the singular denotes a group of similar members. A collective noun is sometimes used to designate a group as a unit, in which case accompanying verbs and reference words are in the singular. At other times it may be used to designate the members of the group taken separately, in which case accompanying verbs and reference words are in the plural. (See also pp. 253 f.)

The *committee* has held its first meeting.
The *crowd* conducted itself in an orderly manner.
The *class* is to have its picture taken tomorrow.
The *committee* have disagreed among themselves.
The *crowd* are now releasing their toy balloons.
The *class* are to bring their notebooks tomorrow.

NOTE. Such collective nouns may, of course, be used in the plural to designate two or more groups.

Three new *committees* have been appointed.
The *crowds* varied in number.
The four *classes* are to elect their new officers next week.

B. *Properties of Nouns*

1. GENDER

Gender is that property of a noun which usually makes evident the sex of the object represented by the noun. As far as grammar is concerned we may recognize four genders of nouns.

a. Kinds of gender

1. Masculine. A noun referring to a being of the male sex or thought of as of the male sex is said to be in the masculine gender: *boy, man, father, James, rooster, bull, brother, uncle.*

2. Feminine. A noun referring to a being of the female sex or thought of as of the female sex is said to be in the feminine gender: *girl, woman, mother, Janice, hen, cow, sister, aunt.*

3. Neuter. A noun referring to an object without life is said to be in neuter gender: *sky, loveliness, pencil, amiability, metabolism, gold.*

NOTE. Through personification many nouns of neuter gender may become either masculine or feminine in gender: *sun* (masculine); *moon* (feminine); *ship* (feminine); *war* (masculine).

4. Common. A noun referring to a being which may be either male or female is said to be in common gender: *child, parent, person, relative, mouse, an American, a Methodist.*

b. Methods of indicating gender.   Gender may be indicated in several ways.

1. By adding or changing an ending.   Common feminine endings are *-ess* and *-ix.*

Masculine	*Feminine*
actor	actress
administrator	administratrix
duke	duchess
executor	executrix
hero	heroine
waiter	waitress
widower	widow

2. By changing the word:

Masculine	*Feminine*
bachelor	spinster
boy	girl
brother	sister
father	mother
husband	wife
uncle	aunt
wizard	witch

3. By placing a word before or after:

Masculine	*Feminine*
boy friend	girl friend
bridegroom	bride
he-devil	she-devil
landlord	landlady
manservant	woman servant
salesman	saleswoman

c. Nothing to show gender.   Sometimes gender is not indicated.

baby	parent
chairman	person
child	relative
citizen	servant
neighbor	teacher

NOTE. The presence of a pronoun (which shows gender) may indicate the gender of a noun of common gender or of a noun personified.

My neighbor likes to work among *his* flowers.

Death does not stop to debate whom *he* shall take.

2. NUMBER

Number is that property of a noun which indicates whether the noun names one person or thing or more than one. (For agreement with a verb see under Agreement, pp. 250 ff.)

a. Singular and plural. Singular number represents one person or thing: *man, boy, child, favor, cloud, church.* Plural number represents two or more persons or things: *men, boys, children, favors, clouds, churches.*

b. Spelling the plural

1. Some nouns add *s* to the singular to form the plural. (When the singular ends in *ce* or *se*, the addition of *s* forms an extra syllable, which is pronounced as such.)

Singular	Plural
boy	boys
dance	dances
desk	desks
fence	fences
kitten	kittens
sense	senses
zebra	zebras

2. Nouns ending in a sibilant (*s, ss, sh, x, z*), or in *ch* soft, add *es* to form the plural. (This plural is pronounced with an extra syllable.)

Singular	Plural
box	boxes
bus	buses (*also* busses)
kiss	kisses
march	marches
match	matches
waltz	waltzes

3. Nouns in the singular ending in *y* preceded by a consonant change the *y* to *i* and add *es*.

Singular	Plural
ally	allies
army	armies
baby	babies
city	cities
country	countries
duty	duties
fly	flies
lady	ladies
party	parties
salary	salaries
sky	skies

NOTE. For the plural of proper names see pp. 209 f.

4. Nouns in the singular ending in *y* preceded by a vowel retain the *y* and add *s* to form the plural.

Singular	Plural
alley	alleys
alloy	alloys
bay	bays
journey	journeys
joy	joys
turkey	turkeys
valley	valleys

5. Nouns ending in *o* preceded by a vowel add *s* to form the plural: *cameos, folios*. With nouns ending in *o* preceded by a consonant, a few form their plurals by adding *es*: *echoes, heroes, Negroes, noes, potatoes, tomatoes, torpedoes*. For most other nouns of this type — *banjo, buffalo, calico, cargo, halo, lasso, mosquito, motto, tobacco, tornado, volcano, zero* — present-day dictionaries record two plurals, *es* and *s*.

6. Some nouns ending in *f* or *fe* change the *f* or *fe* to *v* and add *es* to form the plural.

Singular	Plural
calf	calves
half	halves
knife	knives
leaf	leaves
life	lives
loaf	loaves
self	selves
sheaf	sheaves
shelf	shelves
thief	thieves
wife	wives
wolf	wolves

NOTE. Many words ending in f form their plurals in the regular way—that is, by adding s to the singular.

Singular	Plural
beef	beefs (*also* beeves)
belief	beliefs
chief	chiefs
grief	griefs
gulf	gulfs
handkerchief	handkerchiefs
hoof	hoofs (*also* hooves)
roof	roofs
safe	safes
scarf	scarfs (*also* scarves)
staff	staffs (*also* staves)
waif	waifs
wharf	wharfs (*also* wharves)

7. Some nouns have plural endings in *en*.

Singular	Plural
brother	brethren (in a special sense)
child	children
ox	oxen

8. Some nouns undergo an internal change in making the plural.

Singular	Plural
foot	feet
goose	geese
louse	lice
man	men
mouse	mice
tooth	teeth
woman	women

9. Some nouns have the same form in the plural as in the singular.

Singular	Plural
one bellows	two bellows
one corps	two corps
(pronounced kōr)	(pronounced kōrz)
one deer	two deer
one fish	two fish
one gross	two gross
one grouse	two grouse
one quail	two quail
one salmon	two salmon
one series	two series
one sheep	two sheep
one species	two species

NOTE. Such proper names as *Chinese, Japanese, Portuguese, Sioux,* have the same form in the singular and the plural.

I met two Chinese, three Japanese, and four Portuguese.

10. Some nouns are nearly always plural.

alms	mumps
annals	oats
archives	obsequies
ashes	pants
billiards	pincers
clothes	pliers
dregs	proceeds
entrails	remains
gallows	scales (for weighing)
goods	scissors
measles	shears

smallpox ("small pocks")
spectacles
suds
thanks
tidings

tongs
trousers
tweezers
victuals

NOTE. For such words as *wages, odds, means,* and words ending in *ics* (*physics, athletics, politics*) see under Agreement, pp. 255 f.

11. Some adjectives when preceded by *the* are used as plural nouns. (See also p. 95.)

the rich
the poor
the sick

the needy
the helpless
the weary

12. Some adjectives are pluralized and become plural nouns with no corresponding singular forms. (See also p. 95.)

betters
odds
nuptials
particulars

riches
valuables
vespers
vitals

13. Names of numbers, quantities, and measurements frequently permit a singular form in a plural sense, even though they may have regular plural forms.

Singular	*Plural*
a dozen eggs	five dozen eggs
a gross of bolts	six gross of bolts
a score of years	three score (of) years
a hundred men	six hundred men
a thousand planes	thirty thousand planes
a ton of coal	six ton [*or* tons] of coal

NOTE. This use of a singular form in a plural sense is very common in the case of compounds.

a gallon jug	a two-gallon jug
a mile race	a two-mile race
a foot ruler	a two-foot ruler
a ninety-acre farm	a two-quart jar
a two-by-six inch plank	an eight-pound baby
a two-ton truck	three three-inch bolts

14. The plural of a compound noun is formed in various ways.

a) The plural may be formed by forming the plural of the principal word of the compound.

Singular	Plural
bystander	bystanders
court martial	courts martial
editor in chief	editors in chief
hanger-on	hangers-on
maid of honor	maids of honor
man-of-war	men-of-war

b) When the expression has ceased to be felt as a compound, it is pluralized in the regular way, by adding s (or es) at the end.

Singular	Plural
basketful	basketfuls
cupful	cupfuls
handful	handfuls
mouthful	mouthfuls
tablespoonful	tablespoonfuls
teaspoonful	teaspoonfuls
holdup	holdups
touchdown	touchdowns

NOTE.   When individual containers are thought of, the name of the container itself is pluralized and *full* is written as a separate word.

three baskets full [that is, three separate baskets that are full]
six cups full [that is, six cups that are full]
two teaspoons full [that is, two teaspoons that are full]

c) The final part is pluralized when none of the words making up the compound is dominant.

Singular	Plural
forget-me-not	forget-me-nots
Jack-in-the-pulpit	Jack-in-the-pulpits
Johnny-jump-up	Johnny-jump-ups
touch-me-not	touch-me-nots

NOTE.   Many extemporized compounds are pluralized in the regular way.

Singular	Plural
down-and-outer	down-and-outers
go-between	go-betweens
in-and-outer	in-and-outers

d) Sometimes both parts of a compound noun are pluralized.

Singular	Plural
Knight Templar	Knights Templars
Lord Justice	Lords Justices
man doctor	men doctors
manservant	menservants
woman doctor	women doctors
woman servant	women servants

e) The word *man* is used in forming such compounds as *Englishman, Frenchman, Dutchman*; consequently, the plural is *Englishmen, Frenchmen, Dutchmen*.

But such words as *German, Mussulman, Norman, talisman, Brahman, pullman*, are not compounds of *man*; consequently, the plural forms are *Germans, Mussulmans, Normans, talismans, Brahmans, pullmans*.

15. The plural of a proper name is formed by adding *s* unless the plural is pronounced with an extra syllable, in which case *es* is added. (Note that the rule about changing a final *y* preceded by a consonant to *i* before adding *es* does not apply to proper names.)

the three Roberts [the singular being *Robert*]
the three Robertses [the singular being *Roberts*]
the two Edwards [the singular being *Edward*]
the two Edwardses [the singular being *Edwards*]
the two Burnses [the singular being *Burns*]

the six Joneses   the three Charleses
the two Marys   the two Kansas Citys

NOTE. For *Englishmen* and *Germans* see above. For *Chinese* and *Japanese* see p. 206, Note.

16. Titles are pluralized in various ways.

a) The plural for *Miss* is *Misses*; for *Mr.* is *Messrs.*; for

Madam is *Mesdames*. *Mrs.* has no plural. *Mesdames* is sometimes used as a plural for *Mrs.*

Either the title itself may be pluralized or the surname may be pluralized, the former method usually being preferred. But inasmuch as there is no plural form for *Mrs.* the surname in this case must be pluralized.

Miss Jones, (the) Miss Joneses [or] (the) Misses Jones
Mr. Brown, (the) Messrs. Brown [or] (the) Mr. Browns
Madam Moisson, Mesdames Moisson; Mrs. Griffith, (the) Mrs. Griffiths

b) When one title is used with two or more names, the title is pluralized.

Dr. Parker and Dr. McGaughey	Drs. Parker and McGaughey
Professor Martin and Professor James	Professors Martin and James
Governor Schricker and Governor Bricker	Governors Schricker and Bricker
General MacArthur and General Eisenhower	Generals MacArthur and Eisenhower
Mrs. Gibson and Mrs. Whalen	[Or] Mesdames Gibson and Whalen

17. The plural of numbers, letters, and symbols used as such and not as names of ideas is formed by adding *'s*. The plural of words used as such is usually formed by adding *s*. But unusual words, words that might be momentarily misread, and extemporized foreign words are written with the apostrophe.

Your *8's* and *9's* look alike.
He does not know his *ABC's*.
Dot your *i's* and cross your *t's* and don't use so many *ands* and *buts* and *&'s* in your manuscripts.
Use fewer *so's*; try more *hences* and *therefores*.
We certainly could use some *n'est-ce pas's* or *nicht wahr's* if we only had them.

18. The plural of some foreign nouns is the plural of that language.

Singular	Plural
addendum	addenda
administratrix	administratices
	agenda (used only in the plural)
alumnus [masculine]	alumni
alumna [feminine]	alumnae
analysis	analyses
antithesis	antitheses
axis	axes
bacillus	bacilli
bacterium	bacteria
basis	bases
corps [see p. 206]	corps
crisis	crises[2]
datum	data
desideratum	desiderata
ellipsis	ellipses
erratum	errata
hypothesis	hypotheses
larva	larvae[3]
locus	loci[4]
madam(e)	mesdames [see p. 209 f.]
minutia	minutiae
oasis	oases
opus	opera[5]
ovum	ova
parenthesis	parentheses
stimulus	stimuli
synopsis	synopses
synthesis	syntheses
thesis	theses

NOTE. There is a tendency to anglicize the plural of many foreign nouns.

(The form in first position in this list should not necessarily be considered the "preferred" form. The order of listing used here follows that found in most present-day dictionaries, among which, understandably, there is not always complete agreement.)

[2] Also *crises* in *Webster's Third New International Dictionary* (1961).
[3] Also *larvas* in *Webster's Third New International Dictionary*.
[4] Also *loca* in *Webster's Third New International Dictionary* and *Webster's New Collegiate Dictionary* (1956).
[5] Also *opuses* in *Webster's Third New International Dictionary* and *Webster's New World Dictionary of the American Language* (1957).

Singular	Plural
antenna	antennas [radio]
	antennae [zoological]
apparatus	apparatus or apparatuses
appendix	appendixes or appendices
aquarium	aquariums or aquaria
automaton	automatons or automata
beau	beaus or beaux
bureau	bureaus or bureaux
cactus	cacti or cactuses
candelabrum	candelabra or candelabrums
criterion	criteria or criterions
crux	cruxes or cruces
curriculum	curriculums or curricula
dilettante	dilettantes or dilettanti
focus	focuses or foci
formula	formulas or formulae
fungus	fungi or funguses
genus	genera or genuses
gymnasium	gymnasiums or gymnasia
index	indexes or indices
matrix	matrices or matrixes
maximum	maxima or maximums
medium	mediums or media
memorandum	memorandums or memoranda
minimum	minima or minimums
nebula	nebulae or nebulas
nucleus	nuclei or nucleuses
octopus	octopuses or octopi
phenomenon	phenomena or phenomenons[6]
plateau	plateaus or plateaux
radius	radii or radiuses
referendum	referendums or referenda
stratum	strata or stratums
syllabus	syllabuses or syllabi
symposium	symposiums or symposia
tableau	tableaus or tableaux
terminus	terminuses or termini
vertebra	vertebrae or vertebras
vertex	vertexes or vertices
virtuoso	virtuosos or virtuosi

[6] For the meanings "an exceptional, unusual, or abnormal thing or occurrence; an extraordinary or remarkable person," *phenomenons* is listed as an alternate plural in *Webster's Third New International Dictionary, Webster's New World Dictionary of the American Language, Webster's New Collegiate Dictionary,* and *Thorndike-Barnhart Comprehensive Desk Dictionary* (1957).

3. *Case*

Case is that property of a noun (or pronoun) that helps make evident the relationship of the noun to other words in the sentence. As the only case forms of nouns that remain in English are those of the possessive case, case forms of nouns present few problems of usage. But nouns are said to have three cases.

a. Nominative. Nominative is the case of a noun that functions as the subject of a finite verb, as the subjective complement of a finite verb, as the subjective complement of an infinitive that has no grammatical subject of its own (see pp. 319 f.), or that is used absolutely (see pp. 61 f.).

The window is open. [*Window,* as the subject of the verb *is,* is in the nominative case.]

My brother became a lawyer. [*Lawyer,* as a subjective complement of the finite verb *became,* is in the nominative case.]

The dog was thought to be a pet. [*Pet,* as a subjective complement of the infinitive *to be,* is in the nominative case.]

My watch having stopped, I don't know the time. [*Watch,* as a nominative absolute, is in the nominative case.]

b. Objective. Objective is the case of a noun that functions as (1) any kind of complement of a finite verb except a subjective complement; (2) the subject of an infinitive (see p. 70); (3) the subjective complement of an infinitive in an infinitive clause (see pp. 319 f.); or (4) the object of a preposition. (For complements of verbs see pp. 45 ff.)

Grandmother gave my brother a new bicycle. [*Brother,* as the indirect object of the verb *gave,* and *bicycle,* as the direct object of the verb *gave,* are in the objective case.]

I was given a full report of the transaction. [*Report,* as the retained object of the verb *was given,* and *transaction,* as the object of the preposition *of,* are in the objective case.]

The court ordered the landlord to pay the costs. [*Landlord,* as the subject, and *costs,* as the object, of the infinitive *to pay,* are in the objective case.]

We thought next Sunday to be the right time. [*Time*, as a subjective complement after *to be* in the infinitive clause, and *Sunday*, as the subject of *to be*, are in the objective case.]

He left his entire fortune to his wife. [*Wife*, as the object of the preposition *to*, is in the objective case.]

c. Possessive.   Possessive is the case of a noun used to indicate possession. Possession, in a grammatical sense, may include something more than mere physical possession.[7] (See pp. 312 ff. for the possessive as it relates to verbal constructions.)

I am wearing my brother's hat. [Actual possession is indicated.]

I thoroughly enjoy Shakespeare's plays. [Authorship rather than actual possession is indicated.]

Lincoln's portrait hangs on the wall. [Here it is a portrait of Lincoln, not a portrait that Lincoln possessed, that is meant.]

I keep my account at the Merchants and Manufacturers Bank. [As all idea of physical possession is absent, the proper name is spelled without the apostrophe. See also p. 216.]

1. Spelling the possessive.   There are many complicated and conflicting rules for spelling the possessive. (See *Webster's Collegiate Dictionary*, fifth edition, under "possession," for a series of highly detailed rules.) Probably the most confusion has arisen from a not too successful attempt to make the spelling of the possessive correspond to the pronunciation of it. The sensible thing would seem to be to spell the possessive in the simplest manner possible to indicate possession and then to pronounce the resultant form with an extra syllable or not as euphony dictates.

a) The possessive case of a singular or plural noun not ending in *s* is formed by adding an apostrophe and *s*; the possessive

[7] Some grammarians use the term "genitive case" to include what we have included under the possessive case and the following *of*-relationships as well:
Genitive of possession — that old hat of mine.
Genitive of connection — a miracle of love (cf. love's miracle).
Subjective genitive — the decline of Rome (cf. Rome's decline).
Objective genitive — the salvation of man (cf. man's salvation — that is, something that saves man).

case of a singular or plural noun ending in *s* is formed by an apostrophe only.[8]

boy, boy's	Dumas, Dumas'
boys, boys'	Buz, Buz's
man, man's	prince, prince's
men, men's	princes, princes'
lady, lady's	princess, princess'
ladies, ladies'	princesses, princesses'
child, child's	horse, horse's
children, children's	Essex, Essex's
Burns, Burns'	Moses, Moses'
Dickens, Dickens'	Xerxes, Xerxes'
Jones, Jones'	Venus, Venus'
Jesus, Jesus'	Achilles, Achilles'

b) If joint possession is intended, the apostrophe is placed on the last element of a series. Individual possession requires the apostrophe with each element of a series.

> Moore and Johnson's store. [Joint]
> Moore's and Johnson's stores. [Individual]
> America and England's problem. [Joint]
> America's and England's problems. [Individual]

c) Where one noun is in apposition with another, or where one group of words is used as one idea, the sign of the possessive is added to the last word of the expression.

> Basil the blacksmith's shop
> the King of England's throne
> King George VI's proclamation

d) For the possessive of such expressions as *anybody else, anyone else, nobody else, no one else, who else,* see p. 232.

I'll not take anybody else's word for it.
We should respect everyone else's opinions.

[8] This is the practice recommended by the Government *Style Manual* (1959 edition). Some other style books prefer the addition of the apostrophe and *s* to nouns ending in *s*, especially those of one syllable, when the possessive form adds a syllable in pronunciation: *Burns'* [or] *Burns's* poems; Mr. *Jones'* [or] *Jones's* house; the *class'* [or] *class's* attendance record; for *conscience'* [or] *conscience's* sake.

If that is no one else's umbrella, I'll borrow it.
This one is nobody else's; but that one is somebody else's.
Who else's can it be?

NOTE.   Present-day usage favors *who else's*, made by analogy with *anybody else's*. But *whose else* is also in good standing. Of course, "Who's else" is wrong.
Who else's can it be? [*Or*] Whose else can it be? [*Not:* Who's else can it be?]

e) Some proper names use the apostrophe and some do not. The form officially established should be followed in every case. The tendency is away from the apostrophe where actual ownership is not indicated.

Harpers Ferry	Turners Falls
Merchants and Manufacturers Bank	Teachers College
Bricklayers Union	Pikes Peak
But: St. James's Court	*But:* Grant's Tomb

NOTE.   The names of magazines usually retain the apostrophe: *Writer's Digest, Geyer's Topics, Woman's Home Companion. Harper's Magazine,* which used to appear without the apostrophe, now appears with it.

f) Either the singular or plural possessives may be used in such expressions as the following:

> printer's ink *or* printers' ink
> child's disease *or* children's disease
> writer's cramp *or* writers' cramp
> author's alterations *or* authors' alterations

g) The possessive is not ordinarily used for anything without life, except for certain forms that have become established. (For *its* and *whose* see Note, p. 221.)

> the roof of the house   [*Not:* the house's roof]
> the steeple of the church   [*Not:* the church's steeple]
> the blue of the sea and sky.   [*Not:* the sea and sky's blue]

But such possessive forms as the following have become established in good use.

a day's work   two years' delay
the sun's rays   at death's door
a week's pay   the earth's orbit
two weeks' pay   the world's troubles
a year's delay   the country's destiny
a stone's throw   goodness' sake

2. Possessive as an adjective and a substantive.   The possessive case of a noun may function as an adjectival modifier or as
a substantive the equivalent of an understood substantive modified by a possessive. (See also under posessive pronouns, p. 221.
For the "double possessive" — *a hat of John's* — see pp. 345 f.)

I have Edward's pencil. [The possessive noun *Edward's* functions as an adjectival modifier of *pencil.*]

This pencil is Edward's. [The possessive noun *Edward's* functions as a subjective complement of *is.* This is equivalent to, but
not the same grammatically as, "This pencil is Edward's pencil."]

I have lost my pencil. May I take Edward's? [The possessive
noun *Edward's* functions as the direct object of *may take.*]

I have last my pencil. I'm going to borrow one of Edward's.
[The possessive noun *Edward's* functions as the object of the
preposition *of.*]

CHAPTER 6

Pronouns[1]

A. Classes of Pronouns

Pronouns may be classed as personal (including compound personal), relative (including compound relative), interrogative, demonstrative, and indefinite.

1. PERSONAL PRONOUNS

A personal pronoun is one that makes evident by its forms whether reference is made to the speaker, to the person or thing spoken to, or to the person or thing spoken of — known respectively as first person, second person, and third person.

a. Forms. Personal pronouns show the following forms for number, gender, and case.

FIRST PERSON

	Singular	Plural
Nominative	I	we
Objective	me	us
Possessive	my, mine	our, ours

SECOND PERSON[2]

	Singular	Plural
Nominative	you, thou	you, ye
Objective	you, thee	you, ye
Possessive	your, yours	your, yours
	thy, thine	

[1] For definition and constructions in sentences see pp. 33 ff.
[2] The forms *thou, thee, thine,* and *ye* are now used only in poetry and in

THIRD PERSON

	Singular	Plural
Nominative	he, she, it	they
Objective	him, her, it	them
Possessive	his, her, hers, it, its	their, theirs

b. Usages

1. Editorial *we*.   The personal pronoun *we* is used in journalism as representative of the whole staff. Hence, this *we* is often called the editorial *we*. A business firm often uses *we* in communications.

> We decline to debate the question with our esteemed rival. [From a newspaper editorial]
> Thanks for your expression of confidence in this firm. We aim to make every transaction satisfactory. [From a business communication]

2. *We, you, they*.   *We, you,* and *they* are often used indefinitely without antecedents, in the sense of "persons," "one," "people in general." (For the lack of a satisfactory indefinite reference word in English see p. 306.)

> We may take Thackeray as an example of a master of genial satire.
> You never know when an emergency may arise.
> They say that there is a skeleton in his closet.

3. *Your* used indefinitely.   *Your* is sometimes used indefinitely in the sense of "a" (or "an").

> Take your modern novelist, for example.

4. *It* used indefinitely.   The personal pronoun *it* is often used indefinitely — that is, without any definite antecedent being in the mind of the writer or speaker. (See also p. 58.)

---

addressing the Diety. The Society of Friends (Quakers) sometimes use *thee* in the nominative and objective and *thy* and *thine* in the possessive in addressing one another.

a) As the grammatical subject in expressions having to do with the weather or with time.

> It is raining now, but I think it will clear up later.
> It is now after six o'clock.
> It is time to take stock of things.

b) As the grammatical subject of the verb *be* without regard for the person or number of the subjective complement.

> It is the President who must take complete charge in time of war. [This impersonal *it* is the true subject of *is*; the subordinate clause *who must take charge in time of war* functions as an adjectival modifier of *President*, which is the subjective complement after *is*.]
> It was night before last that it happened. [For *that* see p. 225, Note.]
> It is such advantages that we value.

NOTE. A relative pronoun in such a construction agrees in number and person with the noun or pronoun that follows the main verb.
> It is I who am disappointed.   [*Not:* It is I who is disappointed.]
> It is you who are not satisfied.   [*Not:* It is you who is not satisfied.]

c) As an object in a general sense — especially common in colloquial discourse.

> We must keep at it everlastingly.
> He footed it to town.
> Mark Twain wrote *Roughing It*.

d) As a general reference word referring to a preceding phrase or clause. (See also p. 227.)

> I asked him to return my dollar. It seemed to make him angry.

e) As an expletive, a "filling-in" expression, that anticipates the true grammatical subject or object. (See Expletives, pp. 144 ff.)

> It is true that we have no definite objective. [*That we have no definite objective* is the true grammatical subject of the verb *is*. The sentence for analysis reads "That we have no definite objective is true."]

I find it difficult to believe your story. [*To believe your story* is the true grammatical direct object of the verb *find*. The sentence for analysis reads "I find to believe your story difficult."]

NOTE. The difference between *it* used impersonally and *it* used as an expletive lies in the fact that *it* used impersonally is a true subject of the verb (and so this use might be called the noun use of *it*), whereas *it* used as an expletive does not enter into the grammar of the statement in which it appears; it merely marks time until the true grammatical subject or object of the clause appears.

5. No apostrophe with a possessive personal pronoun. Possessive personal pronouns do not take an apostrophe. But the possessive indefinite pronouns (see p. 232), such as *one, one another, each other,* do take the apostrophe and *s*.

his hand	one's integrity
her book	each other's wishes
their car	someone else's overcoat
its tires	one another's anxieties

NOTE. The possessive pronoun *its* and the relative pronoun *whose* (see p. 226) are freely used to refer to nonhuman things, whereas the possessive case of nouns is, in general, not so used (see p. 216).
Its leaves are falling.   [*Not:* The tree's leaves are falling.]
The tree whose leaves are falling is an elm.

6. Possessive pronoun as an adjective and as a substantive. The possessive forms *my, your, his, her, its, our,* and *their* are used before nouns and function as regular attribute adjectives (see pp. 89 f.). They may be called possessive adjectives. The forms *mine, yours, his, hers, its, ours,* and *theirs* are used as substantives and function exactly as do nouns in the possessive case (see p. 217) — that is, they are used as substitutes for an understood noun and a possessive modifier. *His* may be either a possessive adjective or a possessive pronoun functioning as a substantive. (For the "double possessive" — *a hat of his* — see pp. 345 f.)

My book and her pencil lie on the table. [The pronouns *my* and *her*, in the possessive case, function as attribute adjectival modifiers of *book* and *pencil* respectively.]

The book is mine; the pencil is hers. [The personal pronouns *mine* and *hers*, in the possessive case, function as substantives, the subjective complements of *is*. That is, *mine* and *hers* are equivalent in meaning, but not in grammar, to "my book" and "her pencil." Compare "The book is Ben's; the pencil is Helen's." See also p. 217.]

NOTE.   A pronoun should not, as a rule, refer to a noun used as a possessive modifier.

In his public addresses Winston Churchill has given the world some memorable phrases.   [*Not:* In Winston Churchill's public addresses he has given the world some memorable phrases.]

The use of a pronoun to refer to a possessive pronoun used as a substantive, however, is standard English.

Of the two cars, mine is older, but it uses less oil than yours.

7. Prospective reference.   A personal pronoun may be used as a prospective reference word — that is, may precede its antecedent — when the antecedent follows so closely that there is no resulting confusion.

In their respective spheres Shakespeare and Chaucer reign supreme. [Here the pronoun *their* actually precedes its antecedents *Shakespeare* and *Chaucer*; but there is no resultant confusion.]

8. For agreement see pp. 234 ff.; for case usages see pp. 239 ff.

2.   COMPOUND PERSONAL PRONOUNS

a. Forms.   Compound personal pronouns are made by adding *self* (plural *selves*) to the possessive case of personal pronouns in the first and second persons (*myself, ourselves, yourself, yourselves*) and to the objective case of personal pronouns in the third person (*himself, herself, itself, themselves*). The case to which *self* (*selves*) is added has nothing to do with the case function of the compound personal pronoun itself. (See pp. 239 ff.)

b. Usages.   The compound personal pronouns may be used as reflexive or as emphatic pronouns.

1. Reflexive.   In its reflexive use a compound personal pro-

noun "reflects" (that is, "bends back") the action described by the verb.

> Perry hit himself. [*Himself* is a direct object of *hit* but renames *Perry*. The reflexive is the only exception to the rule that a direct object never renames the subject.]

NOTE 1.   Simple personal pronouns are not, as a rule, used as reflexives.
   I made myself a good pruning fork.   [*Not:* I made me a good pruning fork.]
   He got himself a new muffler.   [*Not:* He got him a new muffler.]
   But we do say "I looked behind me"; "We looked behind us"; "Look behind you."

NOTE 2.   *Yourself* is used when referring to one person; *yourselves* when referring to more than one.
   Mary, did you see the snapshot of yourself?
   You boys must not deceive yourselves.

2. Emphatic.   In its emphatic use a compound personal pronoun gives emphasis to a substantive already named. It may follow the substantive immediately, or it may appear at the end of a statement. In either case it is in apposition with the substantive.

> Even John himself became suspicious.
> Mary made the blouse herself.
> His words, of themselves, are not important. [The prepositional phrase *of themselves* stands in apposition with *words*.]

NOTE.   Except occasionally at the colloquial level of usage, the compound personal pronouns are used only to show the reflexive or emphatic function; in other words, they are not used in sentence positions in which personal pronouns are normally used.
   Pat and I made the discovery.   [*Not:* Pat and myself made the discovery.]
   Mr. Jones made the arrangements with Mrs. Harris and me.   [*Not:* Mr. Jones made the arrangements with Mrs. Harris and myself.]

3.   RELATIVE PRONOUNS (SIMPLE AND COMPOUND)

The relative pronouns *who, which, that,* and *what* are called simple relative pronouns. (*As* and *but* may also function as simple relative pronouns; see pp. 226 f.) (For relative pronouns and indefinite relative pronouns see p. 129, Note. For *what* see p. 228.)

Combinations of *who, which,* and *what* with *-ever* or *-soever* (such as *whoever, whosoever*) are called compound relative pronouns.

a. Forms.   *Who* is the only simple and *whoever* (*whosoever*) the only compound relative pronoun that change forms for the objective and possessive cases. The forms for the singular and the plural are the same.

SIMPLE RELATIVES

Singular and Plural

Nominative	who	which	that	what
Objective	whom	which	that	what
Possessive	whose			

COMPOUND RELATIVES

Singular and Plural

Nominative	whoever	whosoever
Objective	whomever	whomsoever
Possessive	whosever	whosesoever

The relative pronouns *which, that,* and *what* have no possessive forms; hence, a possessive idea can be expressed by an *of which* phrase. (For the use of *whose* see p. 226; for the problem of *which* and *that* with verbals see pp. 312 ff.)

There is one book the first chapter of which [*or* whose first chapter] I shall never forget.

b. Usages

1. Relative pronoun omitted by ellipsis.   The relative pronoun is sometimes omitted by ellipsis (see pp. 151 ff.)

You have the book I want. [That is, "You have the book which I want."]

She is the girl we chose. [That is, "She is the girl whom we chose."]

It is your help I am in need of. [That is, "It is your help which (*or* that) I am in need of."]

He is the proper official to appeal to. [That is, "He is the proper official whom to appeal to."]

2. *Who, which, that* distinctions. The following distinctions in the use of *who, which,* and *that* are generally observed.

a) *Who* is used when the antecedent is a person.

Jim is one who never leaves a friend in the lurch.
She is a girl whom I have never seen.

b) *Which* is used when the antecedent is anything but a person.

The book which I need badly has disappeared.
The dog which you see was given to me.
I do not like the excuse which he presented.

c) *That* is used to refer to either persons or things.[3]

He is a person that needs to be encouraged. [*Or*] He is a person who needs to be encouraged.

There are people that believe anything they see in print. [*Or*] There are people who believe anything they see in print.

The book which I need badly has disappeared.
The dog which you see was given to me.
I do not like the excuse which he presented.

NOTE. The relative pronoun *that* is often used in its adjective clause as an adverbial modifier in the sense of "at which," "in which," or "on which," after the noun *time* (or some other noun denoting time) or the noun *way*. (See also p. 171.)

I remember the time that you fell out of the apple tree. [*That* functions as an adverbial modifier of *fell*. That is, "I remember the time at which you fell out of the apple tree."]

[3] A persistent but erroneous notion exists that there is something wrong with using *that* as a pronoun referring to persons. Not only may *that* be used freely to refer to persons, but there are times when it is actually preferable. In view of the fact that *who* may be used for either restrictive or additive clauses, whereas *that* may be used only for restrictive clauses, some prefer to use *that* for all restrictive clauses as an aid to correct punctuation. (See pp. 175 f.)

The very day that I came you left.   [That is, "The very day on which
I came you left."]

I objected to the way that he dismissed our complaint.   [That is, "I
objected to the way in which he dismissed our complaint."]

3. *Whose.*   The relative pronoun *whose* functions as an adjectival modifier in its own clause and so becomes what may be
called a relative adjective.

Inasmuch as *which* (and *that*) has no possessive form, *whose*
is now often used as the possessive of *which* to avoid the awkward prepositional phrase *of which.*

The church whose steeple you see through those trees belongs
to the Baptists. [*Rather than:* The church the steeple of which you
see through those trees belongs to the Baptists.]

NOTE.   The possessive *whose* is used much oftener than a corresponding
noun in the possessive case for inanimate objects. Thus we say "the door
whose lock is broken" rather than "the door the lock of which is
broken." But we say "The lock of the door is broken" rather than "The
door's lock is broken." (See also pp. 216 f.)

4. *As* as a relative pronoun.   *As* used after *such* and *same* may
for convenience be regarded as a relative pronoun, roughly the
equivalent of *who* or *which.* (For case after *as* see p. 241; for
omission after *such as* see p. 242.)

I do not have such patience as you have. [*As*, the equivalent of
which and functioning as the object of *have*, introduces the relative clause *as you have* (which modifies *patience*). The sentence
is equivalent to "I do not have the patience which you have."]

He has the same faults as his brother has. [That is, "He has the
same faults which his brother has."]

Such as are able to pay should pay the taxes. [*Such*, an adjective
functioning as a noun, is the subject of *should pay* and is modified
by the relative clause *as* (= *who*) *are able to pay.*]

· Your schedule is not the same as mine. [*Same*, an adjective functioning as a noun, is a subjective complement of *is* and is modified
by the elliptical clause *as* (= *which*) *mine* (*is*).]

As is also used occasionally as a relative pronoun in a construction in which the *as* is the equivalent of *a fact which.*

He was a procrastinator, as we soon learned. [*As*, the equivalent of *a fact which*, is a relative pronoun used as the direct object of *learned* and introducing an adjective clause. As in the use of *which* referring to a whole clause (see below), we can say that the antecedent of *as* is the preceding clause. Or we can say that the relative pronoun contains within it its own antecedent.]

5. *But* as a relative pronoun. *But* is rarely used as a relative pronoun, the equivalent of *who* (*that* or *which*) . . . *not*.

There is no one but respected Jim. [That is, "There is no one who did not respect Jim."]

There are no regulations but work hardships at times. [That is, "There are no regulations which do not work hardships at times."]

There is not a family but has been touched by the war. [That is, "There is not a family which has not been touched by the war."][4]

6. *Which* referring to a whole clause. *Which* may be used to introduce an adjective clause modifying the preceding clause. This construction is an alternate to the usually cumbersome construction in which some such summarizing expression as *a thing, a fact, a notion* is inserted to provide a single-word antecedent for *which*. (See also p. 221.)

We are going to move quickly, which is just what our opponents do not expect. [*Or*] We are going to move quickly, a thing which our opponents do not expect.

This type of reference to the idea of the preceding clause is also common with *which* used as a relative adjective.

The directors may vote against us, in which case we shall devise new tactics. [The antecedent of the relative adjective *which* is the preceding clause.]

[4] There are other, less satisfactory, explanations of this construction, which does not occur very often. One interpretation makes *but* a preposition, the equivalent of *except* (see pp. 351 f.). With this interpretation the first sentence above might be expanded to read "There is no one except him who respected Jim"; that is, "There is no one who did not respect Jim." The third sentence might be expanded to read "There is not a family except a family which has been touched by the war."

NOTE. The objection that some people have to this use of a *which* clause is warranted when the construction could lead to ambiguity.

The housemother objected to Linda's costume, which surprised us.
[The ambiguity here results from the two possible referents for *which: costume* or *the fact that the housemother objected.*]

7. *What.* Inasmuch as the relative pronoun *what* has the meaning of "that which" (that is, is sometimes said to contain in itself its own antecedent; see p. 235, Note), *what* should normally be used without an expressed antecedent.

There is a bus which leaves at ten. [*Not:* There is a bus what leaves at ten.]
I try to do what is right. [That is, "I try to do that which is right."]

NOTE. Occasionally *what* is used with an expressed antecedent.
What they admired that they copied.

8. *Which, what, whichever, whatever,* as adjectives. *Which, what, whichever, whatever,* may be used as indefinite relative adjectives (see p. 130). As such they are sometimes called pronominal adjectives (see p. 326). *Which* and *what* may introduce infinitive phrases as well as subordinate clauses (see p. 66.)

I do not know which course I should take.
I do not know which course to take.
I do not know what course I should take.
I do not know what course to take.
You may take whichever course you prefer.
You may take whatever course you prefer.

4.   INTERROGATIVE PRONOUNS

The interrogative pronouns *who, which, what* are used to introduce direct and indirect questions. A direct question gives the actual words of the speaker and is followed by a question mark. An indirect question rephrases a direct question in words other than the exact words of the speaker and usually appears in a noun clause functioning as the direct object of such a verb as *ask, wonder, tell.* An indirect question is never followed by a question mark.

Who is the tall man? [Direct]
She asked who the tall man was. [Indirect]
Which shall I select? [Direct]
I wondered which I should select. He wondered which I should
select. I wondered which he should select. [Indirect]
I can't tell what I should do. He can't tell what I should do.
I can't tell what he should do. [Indirect]

a. Forms. The interrogative pronoun *who* has the same
forms as the relative pronoun *who* — namely, *who*, nominative;
whom, objective; and *whose*, possessive.

Which and *what* have the same forms for the nominative
and the objective. Neither *which* nor *what* has a possessive form;
hence a possessive idea has to be expressed by an *of which* or *of
what* phrase. The interrogative *whose* is rarely used in place of
which. (Cf. p. 226.)

You have tried all three typewriters. The action of which do you
like best? [*Not:* Which's action do you like best? *Not:* Whose
action do you like best?]
I am trying to find out the ingredients. The ingredients of what?
[*Not:* What's ingredients? *Not:* Whose ingredients?]

b. Usages
1. *Whose, which, what.* When *whose*, *which*, and *what*
precede nouns, they function as adjectives and are sometimes
called pronominal adjectives (see p. 326).

Which hat should I buy?
I wish to know *which* hat I should buy.
What means do you propose?
They asked *what* means we proposed.
Whose coat are you wearing?
I asked him *whose* coat he was wearing.

2. *Whoever, whatever*, introducing a direct question. Occasionally the compound forms *whoever, whomever, whichever,
whatever* introduce direct questions.

Whoever could so such a thing?
Whomever could he have had in mind?
Whatever can have happened to him?

NOTE. It is not important grammatically to try to distinguish between compound pronouns functioning as relative pronouns and as interrogative pronouns when they introduce a subordinate clause. For convenience we have treated them as relative pronouns used indefinitely unless the subordinate clause is obviously an indirect question. (See also pp. 129 f.)

5. DEMONSTRATIVE PRONOUNS

The pronouns *this* and *that* (with their plurals *these* and *those*) are called demonstrative pronouns, because they point out persons or things with special definiteness. In spoken discourse they are often accompanied by a gesture.

a. Forms. The demonstratives *this* and *that* (*these* and *those*) have the same form for the nominative and the objective. They have no possessive form. A possessive idea must be expressed by the preposition *of* plus the demonstrative as it object.

This is my coat. That is your hat. [*This* and *that* are demonstrative pronouns functioning as subjects of verbs.]
These I bought; those were sent to me. [*These* is the object of *bought*; those is the subject of *were sent.*]
That is what I meant. [*That* is the subject of *is.*]
I like the taste of this; but I don't like the taste of that. [Possessive ideas presented by *of*-phrases.]

So and *such* have acquired substantive uses that have a demonstrative effect.

Mr. Sanders has asked me to recommend him, and I am happy to do so. [*So*, used as the direct object of the infinitive *to do*, is the equivalent of *that* and can thus be considered a demonstrative pronoun.]
We had hoped for clear weather, but such was not the case. [*Such*, used as the subject of the verb *was*, is the equivalent of *that* and can thus be considered a demonstrative pronoun.]

b. Usages

1. As an adjective. The demonstrative pronoun when it precedes a noun or a modifier of a noun functions as an adjective and is sometimes called a pronominal adjective (see p. 326).

This book is authoritative.

I am suspicious of *that* heavy-set man.

Those clothes do not become you.

There is a difference of opinion about the good intentions of *those* people.

NOTE. Some grammarians, objecting to calling a demonstrative a pronoun ·when it functions as an adjectival modifier, prefer the term "pronominal adjective."

2. The demonstrative *that* not to be confused with the relative *that*. The demonstrative *that* must not be confused with the relative pronoun *that*. The demonstrative pronoun *that* points out and is often accompanied by a gesture; the relative pronoun *that* refers back to a definite antecedent.expressed in its sentence. If the demonstrative has an antecedent, this antecedent usually appears in a previous sentence. (For the subordinating conjunction *that* see pp. 161 f.)

The book that is lying on the desk is yours. [*That* is a relative pronoun; *book* is its antecedent.]

That book lying on the table is yours. [*That* is a demonstrative pronoun modifying *book*.]

That is something that I cannot do. [The first *that* is the demonstrative pronoun *that*; the second *that* is the relative pronoun, having *something* as its antecedent.]

3. The demonstrative *that* used as the subject of *is*. The demonstrative pronoun *that* is sometimes used as the subject of *is* to introduce a correction or modification of a previous statement.

He is just the man for us; that is, I think he is.

6. **INDEFINITE PRONOUNS**

Certain pronouns are called indefinite pronouns because they do not refer to definite persons or things. Some of the common indefinite pronouns are the following:

any, another, anyone, anybody, anything
some, someone, somebody, something

one, none, no one, nobody, nothing, many, few, much
each, each one, several, all, both, either, neither
everyone, everybody, everything

One another and *each other* are sometimes called reciprocal pronouns or compound indefinite pronouns.

a. Forms.   The forms of the indefinite pronouns are the same for the nominative and objective cases.

1. *One, other.*   The indefinite pronouns *one* and *other* have plural forms — *ones* and *others* — although the plural form *ones* is not used very often.

The singular *one* and *other* have possessive forms — *one's, other's.* The plural *others* has a possessive form — *others'* — although it is seldom used.

> These are the ones I picked for myself; the others I do not care for.
> One's binding is of full leather; the other's binding is of cloth.
> I try not to meddle in others' affairs.

One has the reflexive form *oneself* or *one's self.*

> One should try to restrain oneself [*or* one's self].

2. *One's, other's, somebody's.*   One, other, and compounds of *one* and *body* have possessives in *'s — one's, other's, another's, anyone's, anybody's, someone's, somebody's, each one's, each other's, one another's.*

> We should be interested in one another's problems.

3. *Else.*   *Else* used after an indefinite pronoun may be regarded as a part of the pronoun; hence the apostrophe and *s* are added to *else* to make the possessive case.[5]

> I'll not take anybody else's word for it.
> We must respect everyone else's opinions.
> If that is no one else's umbrella, I'll borrow it.

[5] Some still cling to the awkward forms *anybody's else, no one's else,* on the basis of the fact that *else* is an adjective modifying the preceding substantive — which, of course, is true. But present-day usage overwhelmingly favors the more euphonious *anybody else's, no one else's.*

This one must be somebody else's.
Who else's can it be?

NOTE. Present-day usage favors *who else's*, made by analogy with *anybody else's*. But *whose else* is also in good standing. Of course, "who's else" is incorrect.

Who else's can it be? [*Or*] Whose else can it be? [*Not:* Who's else can it be?]

b. Usages

1. *Any, some, each,* as an adjective. When such a word as *any, some,* or *each* is followed by a substantive or a modifier of a substantive, the word functions as a regular adjective, not as an indefinite pronoun.

I do not desire *any*. [Indefinite pronoun]
I do not have *any* fear on that score. [Adjective]
Each has its advantages. [Indefinite pronoun]
Each person must hold his own ticket. [Adjective]
Only a *few* were chosen. [Indefinite pronoun]
Few persons can resist a good cantaloupe. [Adjective]

2. *Each other* and *one another*. The indefinite pronouns *each other* and *one another* (sometimes called reciprocal pronouns) are used only in the objective case. *Each other* is used of two persons or things; *one another* is used of more than two.

My brother and I always help each other with the garden and the lawn.
My three sisters usually help one another with the housework.

3. *He, we, you,* and *they*. *He, we, you,* and *they* may be used in a general sense without reference to a definite person and so may be called indefinite pronouns in such cases. (See also p. 219.)

He who fights and runs away may live to fight another day. [*He* means "any person."]
We tend to forget some things all too quickly. [*We* means "people in general" or "everybody."]
You learn by doing. [*You* means "any one."]

They say the best comes last. [*They* means "people in general."]

B.   Agreement

1.   ANTECEDENT

The substantive for which a pronoun stands is called the antecedent (Latin, *ante,* meaning "before," and *cedens,* meaning "going") of the pronoun.

a. Antecedent expressed.   An antecedent of a pronoun usually precedes the pronoun and is usually expressed or is easily supplied by the reader or the listener.

Mason wrote his sister that he would be home in time for her party. [*Mason* is the antecedent of *his* and *he; sister* is the antecedent of *her.*]

In many of his novels Dickens shows his genius for humor. [*Dickens,* the antecedent of the pronoun *his,* here follows rather than precedes the pronoun.]

They who came late must take what they find. [Here the pronoun *who* has another pronoun, *they,* as its antecedent.]

Here is a fact that we must consider. [*That* has *fact* as its antecedent.]

All that believe such a tale are fools. [*That* has *all* (an indefinite pronoun; see p. 231) as its antecedent.]

b. Antecedent not expressed

1. Relative pronouns.   *Who* and *which* may be used without an antecedent expressed in their sentences, in which case they are called indefinite relative pronouns. *What* as a relative pronoun is nearly always used indefinitely.

The compound relative pronouns *whoever, whatever, whichever, whosoever,* ordinarily do not have antecedents expressed in their sentences and so may be called indefinite relative pronouns.

Who steals my purse steals trash. [*Who* has no antecedent expressed in its sentence and so may be called an indefinite relative pronoun.]

I know which she prefers. [*Which* has no antecedent expressed in its sentence and so may be called an indefinite relative pronoun.]

Whoever arrives first is to turn on the lights. [*Whoever* has no antecedent expressed in its sentence.]

Take whichever you please. [*Whichever* has no antecedent expressed in its sentence.]

Forget whatever seems to be bothering you. [*Whatever* has no antecedent expressed in its sentence.]

I have forgotten what I came to ask. [*What* has no antecedent expressed in its sentence.]

Appoint whomever you know to be best equipped for the task. [*Whomever* has no antecedent expressed in its sentence.]

NOTE. Indefinite relative pronouns are sometimes said to contain within themselves their own antecedents. That is, *who* used as an indefinite relative pronoun is equivalent in meaning (but not in grammar) to "he who"; *which* to "that which"; *what* to "that which"; *whoever* to "anyone who"; *whichever* to "anything which"; *whatever* to "anything which." See also p. 163 and p. 228.

For the grammatical construction of definite and indefinite relative pronouns see pp. 128 f.

For the difference between indefinite relative pronouns and interrogative pronouns introducing subordinate clauses see p. 129, Note.

2. Interrogative pronouns. An interrogative pronoun whether introducing a direct or an indirect question has no antecedent expressed in its sentence.

Who will go? [Direct question. *Who*, an interrogative pronoun, has no antecedent expressed in its sentence.]

She asked who would go. [Indirect question. *Who*, an interrogative pronoun, has no antecedent expressed in its sentence.]

What is the matter? [Direct question]

We asked what was the matter. [Indirect question]

NOTE. There is no difference in grammatical structure (although a difference in meaning) between an interrogative pronoun introducing a subordinate clause and an indefinite relative pronoun introducing a subordinate clause. And often the difference in meaning is slight. See p. 129, Note.

> I wonder who made this bench. [The statement implies the direct question "Who made this bench?" Hence, *who* is an interrogative pronoun.]
>
> Choose whom you please. [That is, "Choose anyone whom you please." No indirect question is asked. Yet *whom* has no antecedent expressed in its sentence. Hence, *whom* may be called an indefinite relative pronoun.]

3. Demonstrative pronouns.   The antecedent of a demonstrative pronoun may be expressed in its sentence; more often than not the antecedent is merely implied. Frequently *this* and *that* are used as correlatives, corresponding in meaning to "the former," "the latter."

> This will suffice, I think.
>
> The sweet corn I raise is quite unlike that you buy on the market.
>
> This is our station, I think.
>
> That is all for today.
>
> These you can have for the asking; those you must work for.

Sometimes a phrase or a clause may function as the antecedent of the demonstrative pronoun *this* or *that*.

> They grabbed everything in sight; and that made me furious.
>
> To set off items of a date or an address, to set off parenthetical items, to set off additive phrases and clauses — these are among the most important uses of the comma.

4. Indefinite pronouns.   Because they do not refer to definite persons or things indefinite pronouns do not have antecedents in the statements in which they appear.

> Everyone must determine his own course of action for himself. [The indefinite pronoun *everyone* has no antecedent expressed in its statement.]
>
> All who wish leaflets hold up their hands. [The indefinite pronoun *all* has no antecedent expressed in its statement.]

2.   NUMBER, GENDER, AND PERSON

A pronoun agrees with its antecedent in number and gender and person. But its case depends on its own function in the statement in which it appears. (See below, pp. 239 ff.)

a. Personal pronouns

Jim brought his sister and Mary brought her brother. [*His* agrees with its antecedent *Jim* in number and gender and person; *her* agrees with its antecedent *Mary* in number and gender and person.]

b. Relative pronouns.   There is no change in form of a relative pronoun to show gender, number, or person. But a relative agrees with its antecedent in gender, number, and person and so determines gender, number, and person in its own clause.

We love to watch a little girl whose plaything is a tattered doll.

We love to watch little boys whose playthings are trains and airplanes. [The form *whose* remains the same whether its antecedent is masculine or feminine, singular or plural.]

They referred the matter to me, who am no expert. [*Who* agrees with *me*, its antecedent, and determines the form of its own verb *am*.]

They should have referred the matter to you, who are an expert.

They should have referred the matter to Jack, who is an expert.

We love to watch a little girl whose plaything, a tattered doll, is her pride and joy. [*Whose* refers to *girl*, its antecedent, and determines the form of the reference pronoun *her*.]

c. Interrogative pronouns.   Interrogative pronouns do not change form to show gender, number, or person.

Who is that man? Who is that girl? Who are those people? Who am I? Who are you?

d. Indefinite pronouns

1. Indefinite pronouns either singular or plural.   The indefinite pronouns may take singular or plural verbs in accordance with the sense. *Each, each one, everyone,* and *everybody* take singular verbs. The other indefinite pronouns, including

none, may take either singular or plural verbs, depending on the sense. (See also p. 252.)

> Some [of the profit] has disappeared.
> Some [of the guests] have gone home.
> Is there any left?
> Are there any left?
> Each has his task to perform.
> Each one knows his own heart.
> Everybody was there.
> None of the ice cream is left.
> None of those pears are [*or* is] ripe.

NOTE.   Although grammar would seem to demand a singular verb with *none* at all times, because *none* seems to be the equivalent of "no one," the fact is that usage has thoroughly established as an idiom "none are" when a number of members are involved, as in such a sentence as "None of these people are familiar with the new tune." Although "none is" is perfectly correct it would sound a bit pedantic to some ears.

  2. *Each, every,* with pronoun in reference.   The indefinite pronouns *each, each one, everyone,* and *everybody* are singular; therefore a pronoun referring to one of these words is normally a singular form. Exact usage would also require that a pronoun referring to one of these indefinite pronouns be without gender, as the indefinite pronouns do not indicate gender. But we have in English no such pronoun; therefore we have to choose among *he, she,* and *it* in the singular. In trying to resolve this difficulty one may be led into the questionable use of the plural *their* (which of course does not show gender). Or he may resort to an awkward "his or her" in reference. There is no way out of the difficulty; hence, it has become a convention of usage to employ the masculine personal pronoun *he* (*him, his*) in reference to one of these indefinite pronouns, it being understood that the masculine personal pronoun in such instances includes both male and female.

  Each must bring his registration card with him tomorrow. [*Not:* Each must bring their registration card with them tomorrow. *Preferably not:* Each must bring his or her registration card with him or her tomorrow.]

Everybody must make up his mind that he has many sacrifices to make if his country is to achieve final victory. [*Not:* Everybody must make up their mind that they have many sacrifices to make if their country is to achieve final victory. *Not:* Everybody must make up his or her mind that he or she has many sacrifices to make if his or her country is to achieve final victory.]

Each one of the women drives her own car once a week. [A feminine reference word is used, of course, if the context demands it.]

3. *One* and the problem of reference. *One*, being singular, demands that pronouns referring to it be singular. Exact usage would also require that a pronoun referring to *one* be without gender, inasmuch as *one* is without gender. But we have no such pronoun. British usage meets the difficulty by using *one* and *one's* in reference. But American usage prefers the less exact *he* (*him, she, her*).[6]

One may make his plans most carefully only to discover that plans have a way of making him their slave. [American usage]
One may make one's plans most carefully only to discover that plans have a way of making one their slave. [British usage]

NOTE 1. The indefinite pronoun *one* must not be confused with the numeral *one* (used as an adjective or as a noun), which takes *he* (*she, it*), of course, in reference.
One man brought his whole family.
One of the women arose and expressed herself most vigorously.
One of these hats has apparently lost its owner.

NOTE 2. The indefinite *one* may be used in the plural.
Which ones do you prefer?

3. CASE

The case of a pronoun is determined not by the case of its antecedent but by the demands of the statement in which the pronoun appears. The proper case forms for pronouns that

---

[6] This difficulty explains why we often resort to an unsatisfactory indefinite "they" or "you" in place of *one*. The fact is, as is pointed out on p. 306, English lacks a satisfactory indefinite pronoun like the French *on* or the German *man*. And it is this lack and resultant attempts to meet the problem that account for many of the dangling constructions in English.

are inflected require particular attention in the following situations.

a. Personal pronouns

1. Subjective complement.   The case of a subjective complement is always the same as the case of the substantive to which the subjective complement refers.

a) With a finite verb.   The subjective complement of a finite verb will be in the nominative case inasmuch as the subject of the finite verb is in the nominative case.

> It was he who ran. [*Not:* It was him who ran.]
> It was they that the President had in mind. [*Not:* It was them that the President had in mind.]
> I thought the tall girl was she. [*Not:* I thought the tall girl was her.]
> Hackett thought that the person was I. [*Not:* Hackett thought that the person was me.]

NOTE.   The propriety of the "It's me" locution seems to be, unfortunately, a matter of great moment to those who worry unduly about inconsequential niceties of language. For the informal language situations which are the only occasions for which the construction is ever needed, it is, of course, completely established in the language.

b) With an infinitive that has no subject.   The subjective complement after an infinitive that has no grammatical subject of its own is in the nominative case; for the subjective complement refers to the subject of the main verb, which is, of course, in the nominative case. (See also pp. 319 f.)

> The person was thought to be I. [*I,* a subjective complement of *to be* (which has no grammatical subject of its own), refers to *person,* the subject of the finite verb *was thought,* which is in the nominative case, of course. *Not:* The person was thought to be me.]
> The tall girl was believed to be she. [*She,* a subjective complement of *to be* (which has no grammatical subject of its own), refers to *girl,* the subject of the finite verb *was believed,* which is in the nominative case, of course. *Not:* The tall girl was thought to be her.]

c) With an infinitive that has a subject. Inasmuch as the subject of an infinitive is in the objective case, a subjective complement referring to this grammatical subject of the infinitive is in the objective case. (See also pp. 319 f.)

I thought the tall girl to be her. [*Girl*, as the subject of the infinitive *to be*, is in the objective case; hence, *her*, a subjective complement referring to *girl*, is in the objective case. *Not:* I thought the tall girl to be she.]

Hackett thought him to be me. [*Him*, as the subject of the infinitive *to be*, is in the objective case; hence, *me*, a subjective complement referring to *him*, is in the objective case. *Not:* Hackett thought him to be I.]

NOTE. A simple test will assure the proper case form for a pronoun functioning as a subjective complement. If a subjective complement is correctly used it can always change places with the substantive to which it refers.

They thought the boy to be me. [*Test:* They thought me to be the boy. Hence, *me* is correct.]

The boy was thought to be me. [*Test:* Me was thought to be the boy. Hence, *me* is incorrect. *But:* The boy was thought to be I. *Test:* I was thought to be the boy. Hence, *I* is correct.]

2. Pronoun compounded with a substantive. The case of a pronoun compounded with a substantive is in the same case as the case of the substantive with which it is compounded.

They invited Mary and me. [*Not:* They invited Mary and I.]

This is a present from Bert and me. [*Not:* This is a present from Bert and I.]

Mother made my brother and me a coconut cake. [*Not:* Mother made my brother and I a coconut cake.]

Father does not know which to take with him, you or me. [*Not:* Father does not know which to take with him, you or I.]

Father does not know which loves him more, you or I. [*Not:* Father does not know which loves him more, you or me.]

3. After *as well as.* The case of a pronoun after *as well as* may be determined by filling out the ellipsis. (See pp. 151 ff. for Ellipsis.)

You can do this as well as I. [That is, "You can do this as well as I can do this."]

You know him as well as I. [That is, "You know him as well as I know him."]

You know him as well as me. [That is, "You know him as well as you know me."]

You, as well as I, have a duty. [As *well as* = *and*. That is, "You and I have a duty."]

He meant you as well as me. [As *well as* = *and*. That is, "He meant you and me."]

4. After *such as*. That a pronoun following *such as* should be in the nominative case may be seen by filling out the ellipsis. (See pp. 151 ff. for Ellipsis.)

The arrangement is not suited to such persons as we. [That is, "The arrangement is not suited to such persons as we are."]

For such a one as I to offer a solution is presumptuous. [That is, "For such a one as I am. . . ."]

b. Relative pronouns. The case of a relative pronoun is determined by its use in its own clause, never by the case of its antecedent (whether expressed or unexpressed) and never by its position in its own clause. Inasmuch as a relative pronoun normally introduces the clause in which it stands and so perhaps may not have the position in its clause that a noun of similar function might have, the function of a relative pronoun may be mistaken. Note especially the case demands of (*a*) subjects and complements of finite verbs, (*b*) subjects and subjective complements of infinitives, (*c*) objects of prepositions, and (*d*) constructions in which appear such expressions as *we believe, he thought.*

1. Subjects and complements of finite verbs

I know a man who will help us. [*Who* is the subject of *will help.*]

I know a man whom we can trust. [*Whom* is the direct object of *can trust.*]

Notify whoever is available. [*Whoever* is the subject of *is*, not the object of *notify.*]

Notify whomever you meet. [*Whomever* is the object of *meet*.]

Ned does not care who he becomes in the play. [*Who* is a subjective complement of *becomes*.]

I hope they punish whomever they catch. [*Whomever* is the object of *catch*.]

We will be satisfied with whomever we are given as our guide. [*Whomever* is a retained object of *are given*. The whole clause *whomever we are given as our guide* is the object of the preposition *with*.]

The man proved not to be who he pretended he was. [*Who* is the subjective complement of *was* ("he pretended he was who").]

2. Subjects and subjective complements of infinitives.   (For the case of subjects and subjective complements of infinitives see above, pp. 240 f.)

She is the girl whom they thought to be the right choice. [*Whom* is the subject of *to be* ("whom to be the right choice"). The whole infinitive clause *whom to be the right choice* is the direct object of the finite verb *thought*.]

He is not the trustworthy manager whom we expected him to be. [*Whom* is the subjective complement of *to be* ("we expected him to be whom"). The whole infinitive clause *him to be whom* is the direct object of the finite verb *expected*.]

I know a boy whom people think to be a genius.[*Whom* is the subject of the infinitive *to be* ("people think whom to be a genius"). The whole infinitive clause *whom to be a genius* is the direct object of the finite verb *think*.]

I cannot imagine whom they believe me to be. [*Whom* is the subjective complement of the infinitive *to be* ("they believe me to be whom"). The whole infinitive clause *me to be whom* is the direct object of the finite verb *believe*.]

3. Object of a preposition (see also p. 345)

I know a man whom we can put our trust in. [*Whom* is the object of the preposition *in*. Not: I know a man who we can put our trust in.]

That is the man whom my sister is engaged to. [*Whom* is the object of the preposition *to*. *Not:* That is the man who my sister is engaged to.]

She is the woman whom I received the news from. [*Whom* is the object of the preposition *from*. *Not:* She is the woman who I received the news from.]

I am not interested, whomever you may be talking about. [*Whomever* is the object of the preposition *about*. *Not:* I am not interested, whoever you may be talking about.]

4. Inserted *they thought, we believe,* and so on.   Care needs to be exercised not to permit a parenthetical expression to influence the case of a relative pronoun.

She is the girl who they said should have been chosen. [*Who* is the subject of *should have been chosen*, not the object of *said*.]

She is the girl whom they said we should have chosen. [*Whom* is the object of *should have chosen*, not the object of *said*.]

We selected whomever we thought to be worthy. [*Whomever* is the subject of *to be* ("they thought whomever to be worthy"). The whole infinitive clause *whomever to be worthy* is the object of *thought*.]

The police listed the names of whoever they believed might know something about the matter. [*Whoever* is the subject of *might know*. *Whoever they believed might know something about the matter* is the object of the preposition *of*.]

c. Interrogative pronouns.   The case uses of interrogative pronouns are the same as those of nouns and pronouns generally. But inasmuch as an interrogative pronoun normally introduces a clause and so may not have the position that a noun of like function would have, the function of an interrogative pronoun may be easily mistaken. Care needs to be exercised (1) when the interrogative pronoun functions as a complement of a finite or nonfinite verb, (2) when the pronoun functions as the object of a preposition, and (3) when the pronoun precedes such an inserted expression as *they thought, we believe.*

1. Complement

Whom do you mean? [*Whom* is the object of *do mean.*]

Who is this speaking? [*Who* is the subjective complement of *is.*]

We wish to ask whom you had in mind. [*Whom* is the direct object of *had*. The sentence rephrased for analysis reads "We wish to ask you had in mind whom."]

Ask him who he is. [*Who* is the subjective complement of *is*. The sentence rephrased for analysis reads "(You) ask him he is who."]

I wonder who the man is that she is engaged to. [*Who* is the subjective complement of *is*. The sentence rephrased for analysis reads "I wonder the man that she is engaged to is who."]

I asked who I was supposed to be in the skit. [*Who* is the subjective complement of *to be*. The sentence rephrased for analysis reads "I asked I was supposed to be who in the skit." (For the case of the subjective complement of an infinitive that has no grammatical subject of its own, see p. 319.)]

I inquired whom they thought me to be. [*Whom* is the subjective complement of *to be*. The sentence rephrased for analysis reads "I inquired they thought me to be whom." (For the subjective complement of an infinitive that has a grammatical subject of its own, see p. 319. Cf. Relative Pronouns, pp. 240 f.)]

2. Object of a preposition (see also p. 345).

Whom were you with last night? [*Whom* is the object of the preposition *with*. *Not:* Who were you with last night?]

I do not know whom you are talking about. [*Whom* is the object of the preposition *about*. *Not:* I do not know who you are talking about.]

I wonder whom she is engaged to. [*Whom* is the object of the preposition *to*. *Not:* I wonder who she is engaged to.]

3. Inserted *they thought, we believe,* etc.

Who do you think will be appointed? [*Who* is the subject of *will be appointed*. The sentence rephrased for analysis reads "You do think who will be appointed."]

Whom do you think we should appoint? [*Whom* is the direct object of *should appoint.*]

Who do you believe is the logical appointee? [*Who* is the subject of *is*.]

Whom do you believe to be the logical appointee? [*Whom* is the subject of the infinitive *to be*.]

NOTE. In spoken discourse, in which we never consciously plan our sentence before we start to utter it nor revise it once it is uttered, the nominative case for the interrogative *who* is very commonly heard when the pronoun precedes the verb or the preposition that governs it. This use of the nominative in informal spoken discourse is regarded by some as acceptable, although the fastidious person will probably look upon it as sloppy speech. But in written discourse, in which we both plan and revise our sentence, there is certainly not much justification for this nominative use when the construction would normally demand the objective.

Who are you looking for? [Accepted by some in spoken discourse]
I don't know who she is writing to.
I wonder who they are talking about now.
Who should we designate as our spokesman?

In formal speech and certainly in written discourse these will be "*Whom* are you looking for?" "I don't know *whom* she is writing to." "I wonder *whom* they are talking about now." "*Whom* should we designate as our spokesman?" [See also NOTE, p. 345.]

4. *Whose* as a nominative or objective. *Whose*, although possessive in form, is sometimes used as a nominative or an objective (for other possessive pronouns functioning as substantives, see p. 221).[7]

I didn't ask whose the responsibility was supposed to be. [*Whose* here has a nominative use, functioning as the subjective complement of the infinitive *to be*. The sentence rephrased for analysis reads "I didn't ask the responsibility was supposed to be whose."]

I wonder whose they believe the fault to be. [*Whose* here has an objective use, functioning as the subjective complement in an infinitive clause (see p. 241). The sentence rephrased for analysis reads "I wonder they believe the fault to be whose."]

Whose are you taking? [*Whose* is the object of *are taking*.]

Whose is available? [*Whose* is the subject of *is*.]

---

[7] A less desirable explanation is to say that *whose* modifies an understood substantive.

CHAPTER 7

Verbs[1]

A. Definitions

For verb and verb phrases see p. 39; for finite and non-finite verbs, p. 40; for transitive and intransitive verbs, p. 42; for verbs of complete and of incomplete predication, p. 41; for complements of transitive verbs, pp. 45 ff.; for complements of intransitive verbs, pp. 51 ff.; for various kinds of verbs — absolute, cognate, causative, complete and link, impersonal, notional, auxiliary, defective, redundant — see pp. 56 ff.

B. Properties of Verbs

A verb may vary in form to show five so-called "properties" — namely, (1) voice, (2) person, (3) number, (4) mood, and (5) tense.

1. VOICE

Voice is that property of a verb which shows whether the subject of the verb performs the action or receives the action described by the verb (see p. 42). If the subject performs the action (or is in the state or condition) described by the verb, the verb is in the active voice. If the subject receives the action described by the verb, the verb is in the passive voice. A transitive verb (see p. 42) may be turned into the passive voice, in

[1] For constructions of verbs in sentences see pp. 39 ff.

which case it functions, of course, as an intransitive verb. But an intransitive verb in the active voice as a rule cannot be turned into the passive voice. (See pp. 55 f. for exceptions.)

A small girl *opened* the door. [Active voice (transitive)]

The door *was opened* by a small girl. [Passive voice (intransitive)]

It *rained* hard last night. [Active voice (intransitive)]

The ground *feels* wet. [Active voice (intransitive)]

This peach *is* not ripe. [Active voice (intransitive)]

(For complements that may be used with verbs see pp. 45 ff.)

The common forms of the passive voice consist of the auxiliary verb *be* combined with the past participle of the notional verb. (See pp. 296 ff.) Another less common form of the passive makes use of the auxiliary *get* plus the past participle: "Be careful; you might *get* killed." This form, commonly encountered at colloquial levels of usage, is now established as standard English. The *get* form is useful in focusing emphasis upon the actual action of the passive verb rather than upon the resultant state or condition: "He *was* injured sometime during the early morning hours, but no one has determined exactly when he *got* injured." This passive also lends itself to future progressive and perfect progressive forms, which are not possible with the *be* passive: "Tomorrow at this time I shall be *getting* sworn in as president"; "During the past week many of our group have been *getting* inoculated for typhus."

2.   PERSON

Person is that property of a verb which makes evident whether the subject names the person(s) speaking (first person), the person(s) or thing(s) spoken to (second person), or the person(s) or thing(s) spoken of (third person).

3.   NUMBER

Number is that property of a verb which makes evident whether the subject denotes one (singular) or more than one (plural).

a. Forms.   In modern English only a few forms survive that indicate person and number. The verb *be* shows the greatest number of variations. The verb *have* has the form *has* in the third person singular. All other verbs, except the auxiliaries (see p. 39), have *(e)s* in the third person singular number of the present indicative. (See also pp. 275 ff.)

Be

PRESENT TENSE INDICATIVE

Singular	*Plural*
First person: I am	We are
Second person: You are (thou art)	You are
Third person: He[2] is	They are

PAST TENSE INDICATIVE

First person: I was	We were
Second person: You were (thou wert)	You were
Third person: He was	They were

Have

PRESENT TENSE INDICATIVE

Singular	*Plural*
First person: I have	We have
Second person: You have (thou hast)	You have
Third person: He has	They have

Do

PRESENT TENSE INDICATIVE

Singular	*Plural*
First person: I do	We do
Second person: You do (thou doest)	You do
Third person: He does	They do

Walk (and all other verbs except the auxiliaries)

PRESENT TENSE INDICATIVE

Singular	*Plural*
First person: I walk	We walk
Second person: You walk (thou walkest)	You walk
Third person: He walks	They walk

[2] Or *she* or *it* throughout.

b. Usages in agreement. A verb agrees with its subject in person and number.

1. A phrase or clause standing between the subject and the verb does not influence the number of the verb.

The behavior of our company's representatives in foreign countries is being investigated. [*Not:* The behavior of our company's representatives in foreign countries are being investigated. For *behavior* is the subject and requires a singular verb.]

The price of the last shipment of radio sets was incorrectly quoted. [*Not:* The price of the last shipment of radio sets were incorrectly quoted. For *price* is the subject and requires a singular verb.]

2. A singular subject followed by such an expression as *with, together with, including, as well as, in addition to,* plus a substantive, usually takes a singular verb.

Mrs. Adams, together with her two children, has taken up residence here.

Chapter Twelve, including the paragraphs in fine print, is the subject of tomorrow's discussion.

Ohio, in addition to several other states, has a sales tax.

The United States, as well as England and Russia, has a stake in the Orient.

3. A verb agrees with its subject, not with a subjective complement.

The art theories of the Greeks are my major interest. [*Or*] My major interest is the art theories of the Greeks. [*Not:* The art theories of the Greeks is my major interest. *Not:* My major interest are the art theories of the Greeks.]

4. A verb agrees with its subject even when the subject follows the verb. (For inverted order see pp. 156 ff.) Care needs to be exercised to obtain proper agreement when a statement is introduced by the expletive *there* (see also pp. 146 f.).

Most formidable were his posture, his voice, and his mustache. [*Not:* Most formidable was his posture, his voice, and his mustache.]

Here were to be found the many results of years of investigation. [*Not:* Here was to be found the many results of years of investigation.]

There happen to be available four volumes of his short stories. [*Not:* There happens to be available four volumes of his short stories.]

5. Singular nouns joined by *and* usually take a plural verb.

Bert and Mabel are brother and sister.
A college and a university have one aim in common.

6. When nouns joined by *and* are thought of as a unit, the verb is normally singular.

The ebb and flow of the sea is one thing we can always depend on.
The sum and substance of it is easily comprehended.
The Stars and Stripes flies overhead today.

7. When singular subjects joined by *and* are introduced by *many a, such a, no, every, each,* the verb is singular.

Many a town and village is rejoicing tonight.
No dog and no cat is to run at large.
Every man, woman, and child is to be included.
Each window and each door has been weather-stripped.

8. When one of two subjects is introduced by such an expression as *and not, not, not only,* the verb agrees with the other subject.

Action, and not words, is demanded now.
Words, not action, are all we have from him.
Not words, but action is demanded now.
Not only words but action is demanded now.

9. When two nouns in the singular are joined by an alternative conjunction (*or, nor, either . . . or, neither . . . nor*), the verb is normally singular.

Neither husband nor wife has the right to dispose of property without the consent of the other.
Either pen or pencil is satisfactory.

10. When two nouns are of different number or of different person, the verb should agree with the one nearer it.

Neither the men nor the boy was responsible.
Neither the boy nor the men were responsible.
Either you or I am to be delegated to the job.

NOTE.   As such constructions are awkward at best, it is normally preferable to recast a sentence so that the verb has a form suitable to both.
Neither the men were responsible, nor was the boy. [Or] Neither the
men nor the boy could be held responsible.

11. *No one, nobody, everyone, everybody, anyone, anybody, someone, somebody* take singular verbs.

No one [or nobody] is aware of the secret.
Somebody surely has the key.
Everybody is to be admitted before ten o'clock.

12. The pronouns *either, neither*, and *each*, and substantives modified by the adjectives *either, neither*, and *each*, take singular verbs.

Either is right. [Or] Either construction is right.
Neither is right. [Or] Neither construction is right.
Each is to be questioned. [Or] Each person is to be questioned.

13. *None* may take either a singular or a plural verb.   When a plural idea is implicit, *none* regularly takes a plural verb. (See also p. 238.)

None of this fruit is for sale. [Or] None is for sale.
None of these apples are ripe. [Or] None are ripe.
None of these gowns have [or has] ever been on display before.

14. The antecedent of *who, which*, or *that* as the subject of a subordinate clause determines the number and the person of the verb in the subordinate clause.

A man who laughs at the right time will make friends.
Men who laugh at the right time will make friends.
She is one of those women who love to gossip. [Not: She is one
of those women who loves to gossip. For *women*, not *one*, is the

antecedent of *who*. The meaning is this, "Of all the women who love to gossip she is one." *But:* She is one who loves to gossip.]

This is one of those times that try men's souls. [*Not:* This is one of those times that tries men's souls. For *times*, not *one*, is the antecedent of *that*. The meaning is this, "Of all the times that try men's souls this is one."]

I who am most vitally concerned have not been consulted. [The antecedent of *who* (namely, *I*) governs the number and person of the verb in the *who*-clause; hence, *am* is used.]

You who are most vitally concerned have not been consulted. [The antecedent of *who* (namely, *you*) governs the number of the verb in the *who*-clause.]

He who is most vitally concerned has not been consulted. [The antecedent of *who* (namely, *he*) governs the number and person of the verb in the *who*-clause.]

It is I who am to blame. It is you who are to blame. It is he who is to blame. It is we who are to blame. It is they who are to blame. (For *it* see pp. 219 ff.)

15. Collective nouns may be either singular or plural, depending on their meaning. If the subject is regarded as naming the group as a unit, it takes a singular verb; if the subject is regarded as naming the individuals of the group, the verb is plural. (See also pp. 200 f.)

The class has been dismissed. [*Class* expresses a unit idea; hence the verb is singular.]

The class were divided on the question. [*Class* here names the individuals of the group; hence the verb is plural.]

The committee has filed its report.

The committee have been unable to agree on a place for their meetings.

A large squad of men was out for football practice last night.

The football squad are all eating their meals at a training table.

The enemy by the weakness of his counterattacks demonstrates that he has little effectiveness left.

The enemy have been repulsed on all fronts.

NOTE.   *Data,* originally the plural of a rarely used singular, *datum,* usually preserves its exact meaning ("facts," "figures") in professional and technical writing ("These data are. . . ."). In general use the word has acquired a collective meaning ("information") which governs singular forms ("This data is. . . ."). Similarly, *agenda,* originally plural, is often encountered as a singular in the sense of "a list of items to be considered."

16. A plural noun of weight, extent, quantity, when considered as a unit takes a singular verb.

> Five dollars is too much for me to pay.
> Ten miles seems a very long distance when you have to walk it.
> One hundred and ninety pounds is a good weight for a six-footer.

17. Abstract numbers in addition, multiplication, subtraction, and division preferably take the singular. (But usage is evenly divided here.)

> Two times two is four. [*Or*] Two times two are four.
> Three from six leaves three. [*Or*] Three from six leave three.
> Twelve divided by three makes four. [*Or*] Twelve divided by three make four.
> Nine is a third of twenty-seven. [*Or*] Nine are a third of twenty-seven.

18. The number of the verb used with such expressions as *all, half, quarter, more, most, some, such, percentage, all of,* and *half of* depends on the sense.

> All were present today.
> All is in order.
> Some [of my friends] are in Government service.
> Some [of the ice cream] is left.
> Half are to sit here; half are to sit there.
> Half of the cake is left.
> Half of the boys have left.
> Part of the guests have arrived.
> Part of the roof was blown off.
> Three-fourths of his books are works of fiction.
> Three-fourths of his library is fiction.

19. *Number* preceded by *a* takes a plural verb; *number* preceded by *the* takes a singular verb.

A number of persons have asked the same question.
The number of entering freshmen has been limited.

20. Some nouns like *measles, molasses, mumps, news, small-pox, summons*, although plural in form, are singular in meaning and take singular verbs.

Measles is a children's disease, and mumps is too.
The news today is most encouraging.
A summons has been issued for his appearance in court.

21. Such words as *wages, odds, pains, tidings, whereabouts, headquarters, pants, trousers, pincers, scissors, shears*, and *victuals* are now generally plural and take plural verbs. *Means* may be either singular or plural. *United States* is singular unless the individual states are thought of. *Wages* is now generally plural; but *wage* is, of course, singular.

His wages have increased rapidly.
His weekly wage is fifty dollars.
The odds are now with us.
His good tidings are most welcome.
His whereabouts have not been discovered.
His headquarters have been established in London.
The one means of escape left to him is the Supreme Court; all other means have been exhausted.
The United States now has the greatest navy in the world.
We take justifiable pride in the achievements which these United States of ours have to their credit.

NOTE. There is an increasing tendency to treat *headquarters* as a singular noun.
His headquarters is now in Chicago.

22. Nouns in *-ics* when denoting a branch of knowledge (*civics, mathematics, physics*) take singular verbs. Nouns in *-ics* when denoting practices, activities, and qualities (*gymnastics, tactics, athletics, acoustics*) take plural verbs. In informal discourse *politics* is generally plural; in formal discourse *politics* is generally singular.

Physics was hard for me, although mathematics was always easy.

Their tactics were faulty in many places.

Athletics at one college I know of are conducted on the same plane as the academic subjects.

The acoustics of the new building are very good.

Statistics is an indispensable science in the field of life insurance.

I feel that your statistics are very unreliable.

Politics is a great field for the ambitious young man just out of college.

My politics, like my religion, are my own private affair.

4.   MOOD

Mood (or Mode as it is also called) is that property of a verb which indicates how the verbal idea is to be regarded — whether as a statement of fact; a command; a supposition, a doubt, or impossibility. The three moods generally recognized are the indicative, the imperative, and the subjunctive.[3] But neither in form nor in meaning are these three moods sharply distinguished from one another in modern English.

a. Indicative mood.   The indicative mood is used primarily to state a fact or to ask a question. (A question anticipates a statement of fact as an answer.) For forms of the indicative mood see pp. 296 ff.

He is a person of some distinction.

Is he a person of some distinction, did you ask?

b. Imperative mood.   The imperative mood expresses a request or a command. It is used almost exclusively in the second person present tense. The subject *you* is generally understood, although it may be expressed for emphasis. Occasionally the imperative is used in the third person.

Come here. You come here.

Don't do that. Don't you do that.

[3] Verb forms made by the use of the auxiliaries *can* and *may* are sometimes said to constitute the potential mood.

Be on time tonight. You be on time tonight.
Somebody open a window.

NOTE. It should be noted that in such a sentence as "Mary, bring in the coffee," *you* understood, not *Mary*, is the subject of *bring*. *Mary* is a noun used absolutely in direct address. (See also p. 141.)

1. Usages in the imperative

a) Used with *and* to express a condition

Be good and you will be happy. [That is, "If you are good you will be happy."]

Take care of your health and your health will take care of you. [That is, "If you take care of your health your health will take care of you."]

b) Used almost as an interjection

Come, you must control yourself.
Hark, isn't that the bell?
Confound it, where's my hat?

NOTE. The indicative in both declarative and interrogative sentences is used at times with the effect of an imperative.

May we have your remittance by return mail. [Note the absence of a question mark.]

You are to be here promptly at seven-thirty this evening.

Radioman Pollard will dispatch this message at once.

c. Subjunctive mood. The subjunctive mood expresses an idea that is a supposition, a wish, or an idea that is doubtful or uncertain.

If I were you, I should not think of accepting.
Would that you were in my place.
Had I been in your place I should have laughed.

NOTE. The subjunctive is sometimes said to be the *mood* of futurity. This explains why most grammarians do not recognize the existence of a true future tense of the subjunctive.

1. Forms

a) *Be.* The largest number of forms that are distinctly subjunctive forms occurs in the verb *be* in the present and past tenses.

PRESENT SUBJUNCTIVE		PAST SUBJUNCTIVE	
Singular	*Plural*	*Singular*	*Plural*
1. [If⁴] I be	[If] we be	[If] I were	[If] we were
2. [If] you be	[If] you be	[If] you were	[If] you were
3. [If] he⁵ be	[If] they be	[If] he were	[If] they were

b) The third person singular present tense of verbs other than *be* and *have* simply leaves off the final (*e*)*s* of the indicative.

SUBJUNCTIVE	INDICATIVE
[If] he go	He goes

c) The third person singular present of the verb *have* has the form *have* instead of *has*.

SUBJUNCTIVE	INDICATIVE
[If] he have	He has

d) The third person singular present perfect tense (not often used) of the verb *have* has the form *have* instead of *has*.

SUBJUNCTIVE	INDICATIVE
[If] he have lost his chance	He has lost his chance

2. Usages in the subjunctive.   Some of the commoner uses of the distinctively subjunctive forms are listed below. (For the use of auxiliaries in place of the subjunctive, see pp. 260 f. and p. 284.

a) In a main clause (usually in certain set expressions) to express a wish or prayer.

Heaven help us.
God be with you.
Long live the King.
Blest be the tie that binds.

⁴ *If* is not a part of the subjunctive mood. But inasmuch as *if* frequently introduces a group of words containing a subjunctive, it is used here so that the forms may be more readily felt as subjunctive forms.
⁵ Or *she* or *it* throughout.

b) In a subordinate clause after a main clause expressing a wish, command, preference, or necessity.

I ask that he be cross-examined.
The law requires that there be a delay of three days.
I wish I were home.
They prefer that she be placed in charge.
I would that John were here.
It is imperative that I be excused at two o'clock.

c) In a subordinate clause expressing a condition that is contrary to fact (as distinguished from a condition in which nothing is implied as to reality or nonreality).

If I were you I would remain here. [The use of the subjunctive *were* suggests that the condition is contrary to fact, for I am not you. Note that the past tense form *were* represents actual present time.]

Were he here, Father would know what to do. [The use of the subjunctive *were* suggests that Father is not here. Note that the past tense form *were* represents actual present time. The past perfect is used for actual past time: "Had Father been here yesterday he would have known what to do."]

If there was a letter for you, I did not see it. [The use of the indicative *was* suggests that nothing is to be implied as to whether there was a letter or not.]

If Max was at home, he did not answer the doorbell. [The use of the indicative *was* suggests that nothing is to be implied as to whether Max was home or not.]

d) In a subordinate clause expressing a condition suggesting doubt as to its being true to fact, although the indicative is also used.

If that be true, then I have nothing further to say. [The use of the subjunctive *be* carries a suggestion that "that" is not true.]

If that is true, then I have nothing further to say. [The use of the indicative *is* carries no suggestion as to whether "that" is true or not.]

But if he hesitate a second, he loses everything. [There is here a suggestion that he will not hesitate.]

But if he hesitates a second, he loses everything. [There is here no implication as to whether he will hesitate or not.]

NOTE. Inasmuch as the subjunctive implies strong doubt or uncertainty, one may, in such instances of the use of the present tense, be guided by this principle: If the emphasis is on the *if*, the subjunctive is to be preferred; if the emphasis is on the statement that follows *if*, the indicative is to be preferred.

If he be sincere, he will accept your suggestion. [The subjunctive *be* adds to the emphasis of "if."]

If he is sincere, he will accept your suggestion. [In spoken discourse, a stressed "if" used with the indicative form of the verb suggests doubt as to the truth of the conditional statement.]

If he is sincere, he will accept your suggestion. [The use of the indicative (with normal stress in spoken discourse) carries no particular implication as to the truth of the conditional statement.]

e) In a subordinate clause expressing a doubtful or contrary-to-fact supposition.

Suppose I be chosen, what can I accomplish?
Suppose I were chosen, what could I accomplish?

f) In a subordinate clause after *as if* or *as though*.

He acts as if he were the boss.
She looks as though she were ill.

g) In a subordinate clause expressing an ideal concession (as distinguished from a concession of fact).

Though he stand alone, he will never yield. [The implication is that he will not stand alone. The subjunctive *stand* expresses an "ideal" concession.]

h) In a subordinate clause expressing a parliamentary motion.

I move that his request be granted.
I make a motion that this meeting be adjourned.

i) Distinctively subjunctive forms are often displaced in modern usage by the auxiliaries *may, might, shall, should, will,* and *would.* (See also p. 284.)

Even if she were to object, that would not change matters. [Or]
Even if she should object, that would not change matters.

It were better to stop this nonsense. [Or] It would be better to
stop this nonsense. [Or] We had better stop this nonsense.

Be this his epitaph. [Or] May this be his epitaph.

Peace be to you. [Or] May you have peace.

Though he be as honest as the day is long, he doesn't win
people's confidence. [Or] Though he may be as honest as the day
is long, he doesn't win people's confidence.

Custom requires that there be a short period of silence. [Or]
Custom requires that there should be a short period of silence.

If that be his motive, he is courting trouble. [Or] If that should
be his motive, he is courting trouble.

5. TENSE

Tense is that property of a verb that makes clear the
time of the action expressed by the verb. Although grammatical
tense, in general, represents actual time, nevertheless there are
occasions when grammatical tense and actual time do not agree
— when, for example, a past tense represents present time and a
present tense represents future time.

There are six tenses in English — three of them simple (present, past, and future) and three of them perfect (present perfect, past perfect, and future perfect). Past tense is sometimes
called preterit. Present perfect is sometimes called simply the
perfect tense. The past perfect is sometimes called the pluperfect.

a. Present tense[6]

1. Forms. The forms of the present tense of the indicative
and of the subjunctive are the same as that of the first of the
three principal parts of a verb (see pp. 284 ff.) — with the following exceptions:

a) The addition of s or es in the indicative third person singular: he sees, he catches, he does.

---

[6] The following statements about tense have to do with the tenses of finite
verbs. For tenses of the participle, the gerund, and the infinitive see pp. 269 ff.

b) The irregular forms of the verb *be* (see pp. 249 ff.).

c) The form *has* for the third person singular of *have*.

d) The old forms, surviving in some poetry and solemn prose, with *-est*, *-eth*, and *-th* in the indicative second and third person singular: Thou *sayest*, he *doeth*, she *maketh*.

The progressive form (see pp. 301 f.) of the present tense is made by the use of the present tense forms of *be* plus the present participle of the given verb.

> I am coming.
> He is coming.

The emphatic form (see p. 302) of the present tense is made by the use of the present tense forms of *do* plus the simple infinitive of the given verb.

> But I do enjoy talking with you.
> Do you see Bob very often?

2. Usages

a) Present time. The present tense in general represents present time. In the simple form of the verb — "The man *works*" — the time may actually be very indefinite. For instance, the sentence "The man works when he can find work" may imply that the man is not working at the time the sentence is formed. In other words, the present tense may represent merely a customary or habitual action. The progressive form — "The man *is working*" — generally represents an action as actually going on at the time the sentence is formed. (But see below.)

b) Future time. The present tense is often used, generally with an adverbial expression, to suggest future action — "My lease expires tomorrow." Other present tense forms — the present progressive, *be* plus *about* plus an infinitive, *be* plus *going* plus an infinitive — are also common methods of expressing the future. (See p. 277.)

> I am leaving on the seven-o'clock plane tonight.
> We are to be invited, I understand.
> I am about to show you a clever trick.
> They are going to regret their action.

c) Historical present. The so-called historical present is sometimes used to increase vividness in narrating something that actually happened in the past.[7]

I nose down and start earthward in a steep, wide spiral. I've got to get down. I feel as though I shall cave in at any moment. Not too fast! A too-rapid change in atmospheric pressure wouldn't improve my strange ailment. I trim the elevator tabs so the spiraling ship will require but little control effort, watch the instruments, and feel sorry for myself. I reduce the oxygen pressure now, but I must continue to smoke oxygen until I get down round 12,000; though on the way up I didn't start until I reached 15,000.

My head throbs! Mouth, throat, and lungs are raw and irritated — and cold. . . .

— James L. Peck, "579 Miles an Hour Vertically."

A corresponding use of the present for a fact or an idea of the past is seen in such sentences as the following:

I see you arrived here all right last night.
We learn as children that it is best to keep away from a hot radiator.
Shakespeare tells us that all the world's a stage.

d) In critical writings. The present tense is used for statements of present-day convictions about artists, even though the normal past tense is used in narrating the facts of their lives.

Jane Austen uses ironic comment with devastating effect. But it is irony in a distinctly feminine key. For, after all, we must not forget that she knew women far better than she knew men.

e) Universal truths. Universal truths and generally accepted facts are put into the present tense even when they follow quoting verbs in the past tense. (See p. 275, Note.)

[7] Note how Damon Runyon's persistent use of the historical present in his short stories has become virtually his trademark.
He opens the package and what is in it but a baby's nursing bottle full of milk. Moreover, there is a little stew pan, and Butch hands the pan to me and whispers to me to find a water tap somewhere in the joint and fill the pan with water. So I go stumbling around in the dark in a room behind the office and bark my shins several times before I find a tap and fill the pan. . . .

He believed that nothing succeeds like success.
He learned that all is not gold that glitters.

b. Past tense

1. Forms.   The second of the principal parts of a verb (see pp. 284 ff.) gives the form for the past tense of the indicative and of the subjunctive. The exceptions are found in the verb *be* (see pp. 296 ff.).

The progressive form of the past tense is made by the use of the past tense forms of *be* plus the present participle of the given verb.

I was coming.
They were coming.

The emphatic form of the past tense is made by the use of the past tense form of *do* plus the simple infinitive of the given verb. (Emphatic forms occur in only the present tense and the past tense.)

I did not see the accident.
Did you believe his story?

2. Usages.   The past tense represents, in general, actual past time. The simple form of the verb — The man *worked* — may represent indefinite time, any time prior to the time at which the sentence is formed. The simple form of the past tense may represent merely a customary or habitual action — The man *worked* whenever he could get work. Either the simple form or the progressive form may represent an action located at a particular time in the past by means of an added phrase or clause — The man *worked* six hours yesterday; the man *was working* when I came by an hour ago.

The past tense of the subjunctive is used to express present time in a contrary-to-fact condition (see p. 259).

If I were you I should decline the invitation.
If it were possible to grant your request I should be very glad to grant it. [*Were* in both cases refers to time that is actually present.]

c. Future tense

1. Forms.   As English has no real future tense, a future tense is made by the use of *shall* or *will* plus the infinitive of the verb in question without the sign *to. Shall* and *will* were originally notional verbs; but we now regard them as auxiliaries used to form the future tense; and the infinitive we now regard as the notional verb. Hence, we now say that *shall go* in "He shall go" is simply the future tense of the verb *go.*

> I shall see you in the morning.
> I hope you will be here tomorrow night.
> John will start his new job sometime next week.

The progressive form of the future tense is made by the use of the auxiliary *shall* or *will* followed by the auxiliary *be* plus the present participle of the given verb.

> I shall be coming.
> He will be coming.

2. Usages. For usages in *shall* and *will* and *should* and *would* see under Auxiliaries, pp. 281 ff.

For the use of the present tense to suggest future action or condition, see pp. 277 f.

d. Present perfect tense

1. Forms.   The present perfect tense is made by the use of the present tense forms of *have* plus the past participle of the given verb.

> I have come.
> He has come.

The progressive form of the present perfect tense is made by the use of the present tense forms of *have* plus the auxiliary *been* plus the present participle of the given verb.

> I have been coming.
> He has been coming.

2. Usages. The present perfect tense represents an action as having been completed at some indefinite time up to the present or an action continuing in the present.

Mac has completed his diagram.
The girl has been playing the piano for the past thirty minutes.
Mr. Heck has been teaching in the local high school for the past five years.

e. Past perfect tense

1. Forms. The past perfect tense is made by the use of *had* followed by the past participle of the given verb.

I had come.
He had come.

The progressive form of the past perfect tense is made by the use of *had* plus the auxiliary *been* plus the present participle of the given verb.

I had been coming.
He had been coming.

2. Usages. The past perfect tense represents an action as completed at some definite time in the past — completed prior to some other action that may be indicated by an adverbial word, phrase, or clause.

Mac had completed his diagram before we noticed the mistake.
The girl had been playing the piano an hour before she realized how late it was.
By that time the thief had disappeared.

f. Future perfect tense

1. Forms. The future perfect tense is made by the use of the auxiliaries *shall* and *will* followed by the auxiliary *have* plus the past participle of the given verb.

I shall have come.
He will have gone.

The progressive form of the future perfect tense is made by the use of the auxiliaries *shall* and *will* followed by the auxiliary *have* plus the auxiliary *been* plus the present participle of the given verb. (The future perfect progressive form is used very rarely.)

> I shall have been coming.
> He will have been coming.

2. Usages. The future perfect tense represents an action that will be completed at some definite time in the future.

> He will have completed his third year in high school next June.
> I shall have had four examinations this week by the time I take my English exam next Friday.

NOTE. Occasionally the future perfect tense represents an action as completed before the present – "He will have made his decision before now."

g. *Special tense forms.* For tense forms of the irregular verb *be* see pp. 296 ff.

For the tense forms of the passive voice see pp. 300 f.

For the tense forms of the progressive conjugation see pp. 301 f.

For the tense forms of the emphatic conjugation see pp. 302 f.

h. *Tenses of verbals (participle, gerund, infinitive)*

1. Forms of verbals

a) Forms of the participle. There are two tense forms of the participle – the present and the perfect. Normally only verbs that can be used transitively have participles in the passive voice.

The present participle, active voice, is made by adding *ing* to the first of the principal parts of a verb – *seeing*. The present participle, passive voice, is made by the auxiliary *being* plus the past participle – *being seen*. The perfect participle, active voice, is made by the auxiliary *having* plus the past participle – *having seen*. The perfect participle, passive voice, is made by the auxiliary *having been* plus the past participle – *having been seen*.

The so-called past participle of a transitive verb is always passive — *seen*.[8] The past participle of an intransitive verb is very seldom used as a separate element in a sentence; instead it is combined with the auxiliary *have (has, had)* to make perfect tenses of the indicative, the subjunctive, or the infinitive — "The letter has *disappeared*"; "Had I *been* there"; "My father seems to have *gone* to his office."

There is a rarely used present perfect progressive form made by the auxiliary *having been* plus the present participle: *having been seeing*.

Forms of the Participle

ACTIVE VOICE

Present	Past	Present Perfect	Present Perfect Progressive
seeing	———	having seen	having been seeing

PASSIVE VOICE

being seen	seen	having been seen	———

b) Forms of the gerund. There are two tense forms of the gerund, the present and the present perfect, active and passive voice, which are identical with the corresponding forms of the participle. (Of course there is no gerund form to correspond with the past participle.) Normally only verbs that can be used transitively have gerunds in the passive voice.

c) Forms of the infinitive. There are two tense forms of the infinitive, the present and the present perfect, and the active and passive voice. In the active voice the present infinitive is the first of the three principal parts of a verb, the form by which the verb is known — *to see*. The present perfect active is made with the auxiliary *have* and the past participle — *to have seen*. In the passive voice (normally only verbs that can be used transitively have infinitives in the passive voice) the present infinitive is made with the auxiliary *be* plus the past participle

---

[8] A past participle form used as an adjective is often an ellipsis for the perfect passive participle. "Once seen, he will never be forgotten" may stand for "Once having been seen, he will. . . ."

— *to be seen*. The present perfect passive infinitive is made with the auxiliary *have been* plus the past participle — *to have been seen*. There are also the present progressive, made with the auxiliary *be* plus the present participle — *to be seeing*; and the present perfect progressive, made with the auxiliary *have been* plus the present participle — *to have been seeing*.

Forms of the Infinitive

ACTIVE VOICE

Present	Present Progressive	Present Perfect	Present Perfect Progressive
to see	to be seeing	to have seen	to have been seeing

PASSIVE VOICE

to be seen	————	to have been seen	————

2. Usages. The tenses of the verbals do not express absolute time but rather what is known as relative time. That is, they express a time that is relative to that of the principal verb (a finite verb) of the statement in which they appear. A so-called present tense of a verbal expresses a time that is contemporaneous (or roughly contemporaneous) with that of the principal verb, which usually expresses absolute time. The perfect tense represents a time that is antecedent to that of the principal verb.

a) Relative time of a participle

Seeing the ocean for the first time, the child is thrilled. [As the time of the main verb *is thrilled* is present time, the present participle *seeing* expresses here actual present time.]

Seeing the ocean for the first time, the child will be thrilled. [As the time of the main verb *will be thrilled* is future time, the present participle *seeing* expresses here actual future time.]

Seeing the ocean for the first time yesterday, the child was certainly thrilled. [As the time of the main verb *was thrilled* is past time, the present participle *seeing* expresses here actual past time.]

Not having studied very hard, I was not ready for yesterday's exam. [The perfect participle *having studied* represents time that is antecedent to that expressed by the main verb *was*.]

Having studied hard, I shall have no fear of tomorrow's exam. [The perfect participle *having studied* expresses time that is antecedent to that expressed by the main verb *shall have*.]

NOTE.   When the times expressed by the participle and by the principal verb are practically but not actually contemporaneous, the present tense is generally used instead of the perfect.

Leaping to his feet, he demanded a roll call. [*Rather than:* Having leaped to his feet, he demanded a roll call.]

Stumbling against a hidden root, I fell flat on my face. [*Rather than:* Having stumbled against a hidden root, I fell flat on my face.]

Completing their business, the committee voted to adjourn. [*Or:* Having completed their business, the committee voted to adjourn.]

Having worked in every capacity from janitor to vice president, the new president is the best trained man the company ever had in that office. [*Not:* Working in every capacity from janitor to vice president, the new president is the best trained man the company ever had in that office. For here the participle should be in the perfect tense to represent time that is antecedent to that of the main verb *is*.]

b) Relative time of a gerund

Opening the door at seven o'clock every morning is my job. [As the time of the main verb *is* is present time, the present gerund *opening* expresses here actual present time.]

Opening the door at seven o'clock every morning was my job last week. [As the time of the main verb *was* is past time, the present gerund *opening* expresses here actual past time.]

Opening the door at seven o'clock every morning has been my job for the last year. [As the time of the main verb *has been* is past time up to the present (the perfect tense), the present gerund *opening* expresses here actual past time that runs up to the present.]

Opening the door at seven o'clock every morning will be my job next month. [As the time of the main verb *will be* is future time, the present gerund *opening* expresses here actual future time.]

Having lost one job is not a good recommendation for another. [The perfect gerund *having lost* represents time that is antecedent to that of the main verb *is*.]

Having lost one job was not a good recommendation for another when I applied yesterday. [The perfect gerund *having lost* represents time that is antecedent to that of the main verb *was*.]

·Having lost one job will not be a good recommendation when I apply for another tomorrow. [The perfect gerund *having lost* represents time that is antecedent to that of the main verb *will be*.]

c) Relative time of an infinitive

I like to skate. [As the time of the main verb *like* is present time, the present infinitive *to skate* expresses here actual present time.]

I liked to skate when I was a boy. [As the time of the main verb *liked* is past time, the present infinitive *to skate* expresses here actual past time.]

I shall always like to skate. [As the time of the main verb *shall like* is future time, the present infinitive *to skate* expresses here actual future time.]

I am glad to have seen him. [The perfect infinitive *to have seen* represents time that is antecedent to that of the main verb *was*.]

I was glad to have seen him. [The perfect infinitive *to have seen* represents time that is antecedent to that of the main verb *was*.]

Some day I shall be glad to have seen him. [The perfect infinitive *to have seen* represents time that is antecedent to that of the main verb *shall be*.]

I was sorry to miss you. ["I was sorry to have missed you" could only mean that I was sorry yesterday (let us say) for having missed you the day before, a meaning one would rarely want to convey.]

I should like to go. [As the time of the main verb *should like* is future, the present infinitive *to go* expresses here actual future time.]

I should have liked to go. [The present infinitive *to go* expresses time that is contemporaneous with that of the main verb *should have liked*. That is, "liking" was yesterday (let us say) and the "going" was yesterday.]

I should like to have gone. [The perfect infinitive *to have gone* expresses time that is antecedent to that of the main verb *should like*. That is, the "liking" is today (let us say) and the "going" was yesterday. "I should have liked to have gone" could mean only that the "liking" was yesterday (let us say) and the "going" the day before yesterday, a meaning one would rarely intend to convey.]

I intend to go tomorrow. [As there is no future tense of the infinitive, the present tense is often used to express time that is subsequent to that of the main verb.]

I am planning to catch the morning train. [The present infinitive has to be used to express time that is subsequent to that of the main verb.]

I am going to leave in the morning. [The present infinitive *to leave* is used to express time that is subsequent to that of the main verb.]

I had to go yesterday. [The present infinitive is used to express time that is contemporaneous with that of the main verb. (The obligation was yesterday and the "going" was yesterday. The construction, incidentally, makes up for the lack of a past tense of *must*. See also p. 278.)]

When you arrived I was just about to leave. [Some of the so-called "complementary" infinitive uses can show a time relation not possible with "shall" and "will" forms: a future projection from the past time indicated in the main verb.]

i. Tenses of auxiliaries. The actual time suggested by such auxiliaries as *may, might, can, could, must, ought, will, would, shall,* and *should* (see p. 39 and pp. 275 ff.) does not necessarily correspond to the form. That is, the so-called past forms, *might, could, would,* and *should,* may actually be used to suggest present or even future time. The present forms, such as *may* and *can,* may often be used to suggest future time.

I may own a copy of *Alcestis.* [Present]
I may not go tomorrow. [Future]
I might let you have a dollar. [Present]
I might meet your somewhere tomorrow. [Future]
I can repair the tube right now. [Present]
I can repair it better late this afternoon. [Future]
I could give a good reason, but I won't. [Present]
I could be there tomorrow morning. [Future]
I must leave now. [Present]
I must leave tomorrow. [Future]

NOTE. *Must* cannot be used of the past. A past idea may be phrased "I had to leave yesterday." (See p. 278.)

> I ought to go now. [Present]
> I ought to go tomorrow. [Future]

NOTE. *Ought* has no past tense. A past idea may be phrased "I should have gone yesterday." (See also p. 278.)

> He would go in spite of everything. [Past]
> He would arise at exactly six o'clock every morning. [Past]
> I would go now, if I could. [Present]
> I would go tomorrow if circumstances demanded it. [Future]
> I should know better. [Present]
> I should know him if I were to meet him. [Future]

The perfect tenses of the auxiliaries represent actual past time.

> I may have overlooked something.
> I might have known that this would happen.
> He cannot have discovered his error by this time.
> He could not have discovered his error by this time.
> He must have left some time ago.
> I should have gone yesterday.
> He would have declined if he had used his better judgment.

j. Sequence of tenses. Sequence of tenses has to do with the relationship of time as expressed by verbs, especially by verbs in subordinate clauses in relationship to verbs in main clauses.

1. Natural sequence. When verbs indicate a logical time relationship they are in what is called natural sequence. That is, the tense of the verb in the subordinate clause may be anything that the sense demands without reference to the time of the main verb.

> I go alone, because I prefer solitude.
> I went alone, because I preferred solitude. [*Or*] I went alone, because I prefer solitude. [Note the slight difference in meaning.]
> I shall go alone, because I prefer solitude. [*Or*] I shall go alone, because I know I shall prefer solitude. [Note slight difference in meaning.]

I am deeply mortified, because I had intended to have the manuscript ready for you before you should ask for it again.

2. Attracted sequence. There are two situations in which the tense in the subordinate clause is "attracted" into a form demanded by the tense of the verb in the main clause; that is, the tense of the verb in the subordinate clause does not necessarily represent actual time. The tenses are in idiomatic rather than natural sequence. In these two situations listed below — in subordinate clauses in indirect discourse and in subordinate clauses expressing purpose — the so-called law of sequence by attraction prevails. In accordance with this law primary tenses (present, perfect, future, and future perfect) are followed by primary tenses, and historical tenses (past and past perfect) are followed by historical tenses.

a) In indirect discourse[9] or in statements following such verbs as *expect, suppose, know,* and such predicate adjectives as *certain, sure, evident,* a present tense in the main clause will dictate natural sequence in the subordinate clause; that is, a present tense in the main clause may be followed by any tense in the subordinate clause that the sense demands.

He says that he makes (is making, made, was making, has made, will be making, will have made, will have been making, can make, may make) a hundred dollars a week. [The direct form was "I make, am making, made, etc. . . ."]

I am sure that he makes (is making, made, etc.) a hundred dollars a week.

But a past tense in the main clause of such statements is normally followed by a past tense or a past perfect tense.

He said that he made (was making, had made, had been making, would make, would be making, would have made, would have been making, could make, might make) a hundred dollars a

---

[9] Indirect discourse is a form of statement in which the words or thoughts of a person are repeated in a form other than that of the original utterance or thought.

He said, "I am going tomorrow." [Direct discourse]
He said that he was going tomorrow. [Indirect discourse]

week. [The direct form was "I make (am making, have made, etc. . . .) a hundred dollars a week."]

I was certain that he was (would be, had been) in his office. [The direct thought was "He is (was, will be, has been) in his office."]

She supposed that her sister had taken the car. [The direct thought was "My sister has taken the car."]

NOTE. But if the subordinate clause expresses a universal truth—something that is true at all times—a past tense in the main clause is followed by a present tense in the subordinate clause. (See also p. 263.)

Our forefathers declared that all men are born free and equal.

Many people believed that the world was flat. But Columbus knew that it is round.

b) In a statement expressing purpose a present, perfect, or future tense in the main clause will be followed by a present tense in the subordinate clause.

He comes (is coming, has come, will come) that he may be of assistance.

But a past or past perfect tense in the main clause will be followed by a past tense in the subordinate clause.

He came (was coming, had come, had been coming) that he might be of assistance.

c. *Auxiliaries*

A verb that helps another verb to make various tenses, moods, and voices is called an auxiliary. (For tense see pp. 272 f.)

The principal auxiliaries are *have, do, be, may, can, must, ought, shall,* and *will.* The verbs *have, do, will,* and *be* may also serve as notional verbs (see pp. 39 f.).

I have lost faith in my hunch. [*Have* is an auxiliary, here helping to make the perfect tense of the verb *lose.*]

I have a hunch. [*Have* is a notional verb.]

Did you see my father? [*Did* is an auxiliary, here helping to make the past tense of *see* for use in a question.]

We do intend to do our best. [The first *do* is an auxiliary, here helping to make the emphatic form of the verb *intend;* the second *do* is a notional verb.]

He is to be congratulated. [*Be* is an auxiliary, here helping to make the passive voice of the infinitive of the verb *congratulate.*]

Later there will be a reception. [*Be* is a notional verb.]

I will come. [*Will* is an auxiliary, here helping to make the future tense of the verb *come.*]

He willed me his library. [*Willed* is a notional verb.]

1.   USES OF AUXILIARIES

Auxiliaries have three principal uses.

a. To form tenses

I *am* walking. I *do* walk. I *have* walked. I *shall have* walked. I *shall be* walking.

b. To form moods

I *would* walk. I *should* walk. I *may* walk. I *might* walk.

c. To form the passive voice

She *was* made jealous. He *has been* defeated. The tires *should be* changed.

2.   FORMS

a. "Have."   The auxiliary *have* combines with the past participle of the notional verb to make the perfect tenses (the present perfect, the past perfect, the future perfect).

I *have* arrived. I *had* arrived. I *shall have* arrived.

Have also combines with the "to" form of the infinitive of the notional verb to show a required or compulsory action or condition (the equivalent of *should* or *must*).

I *have* to leave early. I *had* to repay the debt.
You will *have* to be more careful.
Lately I have been *having* to study harder.

b. "Do." The auxiliary *do* combines with the simple infinitive of the notional verb to make the emphatic forms of the verb.

(See p. 302.) This form is commonly used also in questions, in answers to questions, and in negative statements.

I *do* intend to go. I *did* intend to go.
Did you go? Yes, I *did*. I *did* not go.

c. "Be"

1. The auxiliary *be* combines with the past participle of the notional verb to make the passive voice of the notional verb (see pp. 300 f.).

The door *was* closed. The door has *been* closed. The door had *been* closed. The door will have *been* closed.

2. The auxiliary *be* combines with the present participle of the notional verb to make the progressive forms of the notional verb (see pp. 301 f.).

I *am* walking today. He seems to *be* laughing. I have *been* hesitating. I had *been* hesitating. I shall *be* studying.

3. The auxiliary *be* combines with the "to" infinitive of the notional verb to indicate an impending action.

He *is* to take his examination tomorrow.
We *were* to meet some friends here.

4. The auxiliary *be* combines with *about* plus the "to" infinitive of the notional verb to denote an impending action.

He seems *to be* about to jump off.
She *was* about to drive away.

5. The auxiliary *be* combines with *going* plus the "to" infinitive of the notional verb to denote future action.

I *am* going to see him today. He seems *to be* going to laugh.

NOTE. The infinitive in such closely welded expressions as *is to walk, going to walk, about to walk, have to walk* is often called a "complementary infinitive." See pp. 69 f.

d. "May," "might"; "can," "could."

The auxiliaries *may* and *can* have the past tense forms *might* and *could*, although these past tense forms do not necessarily represent actual past time. (For tense see pp. 272 f.) These auxiliaries combine with infinitives without *to* to form what are sometimes called potential verb phrases or the potential mood.

> He may go tonight. [*May*, an auxiliary, combines with the infinitive *go* to form a potential verb phrase.]
> He might go tomorrow. [Note that the past form *might* actually represents an action that is a possibility in the future.]

e. "*Must.*"   *Must* has only the present tense. Past time is indicated by the expression *had to* followed by an infinitive.

> I *must* go now. He *must* go tomorrow.
> He *had to* go yesterday.

NOTE. *Must* may be added to a present perfect tense form but with a meaning different from *had to*.

He must have gone yesterday.

f. "*Ought.*"   *Ought*, originally a past form of *owe*, is usually regarded as an auxiliary: it has no past tense of its own and, like *may*, *can*, etc., does not have the distinctive *s* ending for the third person singular of the present tense. *Ought* combines with a following "to" infinitive to make a verb phrase, although in negative statements the *to* is often omitted.

> I ought to close the office today.
> I ought to have closed the office yesterday.
> He ought not (to) leave everything to the last moment.

g. "*Dare*" *and* "*need.*"   *Dare* was originally an auxiliary verb; it had no participial forms and no *s* form for the third person singular of the present tense. In present-day English, however, it has acquired the forms of a notional verb, with resultant divided usage. It is used with or without the third person singular present tense *s*, and the infinitive used with it may be the "to" form or the simple form, although in negative statements the form without the *to* is the one commonly used.

I dared to question the foreman.
I would not dare question the foreman.
Sometimes he dares to question the foreman.
He dare not question the foreman.
He dares not question the foreman.

Need, in the sense of "to lack," "to require," is a notional verb with the full conjugation of a regular verb.

He needs ten dollars. He needs to study harder.
For three years I have needed a new typewriter.
You will be needing warmer clothing.

Need, as the equivalent of the auxiliaries *should* and *must,* has acquired some of the characteristics of a modal auxiliary: it is sometimes used without the *s* added to the third person singular of the present tense, and, especially in negative statements and in questions, it is followed by the simple form of the infinitive.

My roommate need never worry about finances.
You need not concern yourself with my problems.
Need I say more?

h. "Shall" and "will." The auxiliaries *shall* and *will* combine with the simple infinitive to make future tense forms. They have past tense forms *should* and *would,* although these past tense forms do not necessarily represent actual past time. (For special uses of *should* and *would,* see pp. 283 f.)

I shall be there. [*Shall* combines with the infinitive *be* to make the future tense of the verb *be.*]
They will represent us at the conference. [*Will* combines with the infinitive *represent* to make the future tense of the verb *represent.*]

3. USAGES IN AUXILIARIES

a. "May" and "can." *Can* is used to denote ability of the subject to do something or to have something done to it. *May* is used to denote permission, possibility, or wish. Strict usage requires *may* rather than *can* to denote permission; but the line

is not sharply drawn, especially in negative statements in which
can is more usual than *may.*

> It can't be done, they say.
> I think I can untie that rope.
> Why could not the rope have been cut?
> You may go now.
> I may not be able to be present.
> May you have all the happiness in the world.
> May I have your attention? [*Not:* Can I have your attention?]
> You may have another piece of cake. [*Not:* You can have an-
> other piece of cake.]
> You cannot have another piece. [*Or*] You may not have another
> piece.]

NOTE.   *Cannot* is the usual form in negative statements unless *not* is
emphatic, in which case *not* is written separately.

> I cannot see what he has in mind. [Usual form.]
> I can not accept his explanation. [*Not* is emphasized.]

b. "Ought."   As *ought* has no past tense, past time is de-
noted by the perfect tense of the following infinitive. (See also
p. 273.)

> I ought to go now.
> I ought to have gone yesterday.
> She ought to be congratulated.
> She ought to have been met at the train last night.

Had ought is not considered standard English. The expression
tends to creep in, especially in negative statements and in
elliptical negative questions tacked on to affirmatives.

> He ought to be more careful. [*Not:* He had ought to be more
> careful.]
> She oughtn't be so selfish, ought she? [*Not:* She oughtn't be so
> selfish, had she? (*Had she* is here elliptical for *had she ought.*)]
> He oughtn't to have acted as he did, ought he? [*Not:* He
> oughtn't to have acted as he did, had he?]

NOTE.   *Should* is very often used in the sense of *ought.* The problem
mentioned above then disappears.

She shouldn't be so selfish, should she?
He shouldn't have acted as he did, should he?

c. "Shall" and "will"

A careful examination of modern American discourse, both oral and written, shows that most of the traditional "rules" for the use of *shall* and *will* have broken down. Nearly every statement that can be made about the current use of these two auxiliaries must be extensively qualified, and the matter is further complicated by the noticeable variance between American and British practice. It is safe to say that many Americans habitually use *will* (or *'ll*) for all future forms, paying attention neither to the person of the subject nor to any such modal implication as volition, willingness, promise, or the like.

In spite of the fact that the complexity of the problem makes concise and satisfying statements about *shall* and *will* nearly impossible,[10] it is important to note the "rules" concerning their uses. Any serious student of the language studies them as they reflect regional, social, and historical variations in usage. Equally important is the fact that many present-day American speakers and writers, with varying degrees of success and consistency, do attempt on occasion to add precision and formality to their language by observing the traditional distinctions.

1. To express simple futurity or expectation, *shall* is used with the first person and *will* with the second and third persons.

I don't think I shall have the money.
You will be invited, I am sure.
He will be given a free ticket.

[10] The student who wishes to study the *shall-will* problem in more detail can find much written on the subject. He would do well to start his study by looking into the following:

Stuart Robertson, *The Development of Modern English* (second edition, revised by Frederic G. Cassidy). Englewood Cliffs, N. J.: Prentice-Hall, Inc., 1954, pages 309-313.

Charles C. Fries, "The Periphrastic Future with *Shall* and *Will* in Modern English," *Publications of the Modern Language Association of America*, (December, 1925) pp. 963-1024.

Robert C. Pooley, *Teaching English Usage*. New York: Appleton-Century-Crofts, 1946, pp. 49-55.

NOTE. Although, as noted above, the use of *shall* has declined, *shall* with a first-person subject is often used as an auxiliary with verbs of wishing, wanting, or caring, or with *be* followed by *glad, sorry, happy,* etc.

I shall wish to learn more about your offer.
I shall want to keep track of you.
I shall be glad to help.
I shall be sorry to see him go.

2. To express determination, command, willingness, or promise, *will* is used with the first person and *shall* with the second and third persons.

I will go in spite of everything,
You shall go whether you wish to or not.
They shall pay for the damage they have done.
I will not be forced to sign any agreement. If I sign at all, I shall sign of my own free will.
You shall have my answer in the morning.
He shall have any assistance that I can give him.

NOTE. Although these distinctions, codified by eighteenth-century grammarians, are still reflected in present-day usage, variations are common. Military convention, for example, employs *will* in the second and third persons with direct or implied commands.

Sergeant James will report to Baer Field.
Mr. Smith, you will meet with the disciplinary committee.

And in spoken English, placing heavy stress on the auxiliary has become a common way of showing strong feeling or determination. Thus such expressions as the following, although contrary to the "rule," would for many people be the most emphatic method of expressing determination:

I most certainly *shall* see the manager about this.
You have no choice; you *will* apologize to the class.

3. In asking questions, *shall* (or *should*) is the common auxiliary with the first person; the auxiliary expected in the reply often determines the auxiliary used in a second- or third-person question.

Shall I call you when I am ready?
Shall we go to the theater tonight?
Will you read your theme, please?

Shall he be made to obey?
Will it be convenient?

NOTE. *Will* in a first-person question is a set expression with a distinct meaning. To native users of English, the difference between "Shall we see a movie?" and "Will we see a movie?" is instantly clear: the first is an invitation, and the second is an inquiry of the possibility of an occurrence.

With second-person questions, "Shall you . . ." is rarely encountered. To most present-day Americans, in fact, the combination is a curiosity that would call attention to itself. *Should, would, will,* or some other expression of the future (e.g., "Are you going to . . .") would be the usual form.

4. The form used in an indirect quotation is the form that would be used if the quotation were direct.

We insist that you shall stay.
I insist I will have my own way.
We demand that he shall be reprimanded.

NOTE. *Should* and *would* often replace *shall* and *will* in indirect discourse.

d. *"Should" and "would"*

1. *Should* and *would* have a few present-day uses based on the conventional distinctions between *shall* and *will*.

I should not go, if I were you.
You would not leave now, would you?
He would not expect any concession, would he?
I would go now if I thought I were needed.

2. *Should* is used in all persons as the equivalent of *ought to* to express obligation.

I should try to be more charitable.
You should try to be more charitable.
I think they should try to be more charitable.

3. *Should* is used in all persons to express likelihood.

I should be hearing from him this week.
At this very moment John should be leaving the factory.

4. *Would* is used in all persons to express a customary action.

Every evening I would go to his room and read to him for an hour.
Every autumn you would put in a supply of popcorn.
Every day after dinner he would light up his pipe and smoke exactly fifteen minutes by the clock.

5. In conditional clauses introduced by *if, should* is used in all persons to express contingency or simple futurity and *would* in all persons to express determination or willingness.

If I should decide to go, should I notify you first?
If you should decide to go, let me know.
If he should come today, please call me up.
If I would work hard, I could make good grades.
If you would only make up your mind once and for all, there would be no further delay.
If he would take me into his confidence, I might be of some real help to him.

6. *Should* is frequently used in modern English instead of the present tense of the subjunctive. (See pp. 258 ff.)

If he should fail to arrive in time, get somebody else to serve. [Or] If he fail to arrive in time, get somebody else to serve.
His request was that his lawyer should be notified. [Or] His request was that his lawyer be notified.
It is necessary that he should have the fullest information. [Or] It is necessary that he have the fullest information.
We urge that she should be given an opportunity to qualify. [Or] We urge that she be given an opportunity to qualify.
If I should be detained, start the program without me. [Or] If I be detained, start the program without me.

D. *Inflections*

The variations in form of a verb to indicate the different meanings of tense, mood, number, person, and voice are called the inflections of the verb. A complete list of all the forms of a verb is called its conjugation (see pp. 295 ff.).

1.   PRINCIPAL PARTS OF A VERB

The three principal parts of a verb are the present infinitive, the past indicative (first person singular), and the past participle. From these basic forms of the verb are derived all other forms (except in the case of the verb *be* and the defective verbs *may, can, must, ought, will,* and *shall;* see pp. 281 ff.). All forms of every verb (with the exceptions just noted) are made from these principal parts plus such auxiliaries as may be needed. The present infinitive, active voice, is the form by which the verb is ordinarily known — *come, talk, walk, sing, be.* Sometimes a verb is referred to by its "to" infinitive form — *to come, to talk, to walk, to sing, to be.*

On the basis of the way in which the past indicative and the past participle are formed, all verbs may be grouped in two classes known as regular and irregular verbs.[11]

a. Regular and irregular verbs.   A regular verb is one that forms its past tense and past participle by adding *-ed* to the present. (If the present ends in *e, -d* instead of *-ed* is added.)

Present	Past	Past Participle
defeat	defeated	defeated
close	closed	closed

Any verb that does not form its past and past participle by adding *-ed* (or *d*) to the present is an irregular verb.

Present	Past	Past Participle
do	did	done
am	was	been
set	set	set
eat	ate	eaten

Regular verbs are far more numerous than irregular ones, for to this group belong verbs that have come into the language since it lost the power of changing a root vowel to show

---

[11] Since it is difficult to classify verbs in modern English as "strong" or "weak" without a knowledge of their earlier forms, it seems best to discard these terms and to classify all the verbs as "regular" and "irregular."

inflection. Nearly all verbs derived from other parts of speech, verbs of foreign origin, and newly coined or improvised verbs belong to this regular class.

Derived from nouns:

> box, boxed, boxed
> fence, fenced, fenced
> tree, treed, treed

Derived from adjectives:

> cool, cooled, cooled
> warm, warmed, warmed

Derived from nouns or adjectives by adding -en:

> soften, softened, softened
> weaken, weakened, weakened
> strengthen, strengthened, strengthened
> frighten, frightened, frightened
> lengthen, lengthened, lengthened

Derived from foreign terms or newly coined expressions:

> camouflage, camouflaged, camouflaged
> x-ray, x-rayed, x-rayed
> radio, radioed, radioed
> televise, televised, televised

Derived from proper names:

> pasteurize, pasteurized, pasteurized
> Americanize, Americanized, Americanized

Because of the tendency for verbs to become regular, many verbs originally irregular are now regular in modern usage. They are starred (*) in the following list, even though some of them still retain irregular forms, especially in spoken discourse and in poetry. An irregular form in -en (or -n) in the past participle often becomes a pure adjective instead of functioning as a past participle — as noted in the list printed below. Thus we speak of a "hand-hewn (not hewed) log," "new-mown (not mowed) hay," a "badly swollen (not swelled) finger."

b. Principal parts of some common verbs. Except in the case of the verb *be*, the most irregular verb in English, the principal parts of any verb (present infinitive, past indicative, and past participle) may be seen in the first person singular present indicative, first person singular past indicative, and the first person singular present perfect indicative. These are the forms that are shown in the following list.

Present	Past	Present Perfect
I abide	I abode *or* abided	I have abode *or* abided
I am[12]	I was	I have been
I arise	I arose	I have arisen
I awake	I awoke *or* awaked	I have awaked *or* awoke
*I bake	I baked	I have baked
*I bark	I barked	I have barked
I bear	I bore	I have borne[13]
I beat	I beat	I have beaten
I become	I became	I have become
I beget	I begot	I have begotten
I begin	I began	I have begun
I behold	I beheld	I have beheld
I bend	I bent	I have bent
I bereave	I bereaved *or* bereft	I have bereaved *or* bereft
I bet	I bet	I have bet
I bid (at auction)	I bid	I have bid
I bid (command)	I bade[14] *or* bid	I have bidden *or* bid
I bide (my time)	I bode *or* bided	I have bided
I bind	I bound	I have bound
I bite	I bit	I have bitten
I bleed	I bled	I have bled
I blend	I blended *or* blent[15]	I have blended *or* blent[15]
I bless	I blessed *or* blest[15]	I have blessed *or* blest[15]
I blow	I blew	I have blown

[12] The principal parts of *be* are the present infinitive *be*, the past indicative *was*, and the past participle *been*.

[13] But *born* in the sense of coming into this world — "Poe *was born* in 1809."

[14] Pronounced "băd."

[15] Used especially in spoken discourse.

Present	Past	Present Perfect
*I bow	I bowed	I have bowed
I break	I broke	I have broken
I breed	I bred	I have bred
*I brew	I brewed	I have brewed
I bring	I brought	I have brought
I broadcast	I broadcast *or* broadcasted[16]	I have broadcast *or* broadcasted[16]
I build	I built	I have built
*I burn	I burned *or* burnt[17]	I have burned *or* burnt[17]
I burst	I burst	I have burst
I buy	I bought	I have bought
I can	I could	
I cast	I cast	I have cast
I catch	I caught	I have caught
*I chew	I chewed	I have chewed
I chide	I chided *or* chid	I have chided or chid or chidden
I choose	I chose	I have chosen
I cleave (split)	I cleft *or* clove *or* cleaved	I have cleft *or* cleaved[18]
I cleave (adhere)	I cleaved	I have cleaved
I cling	I clung	I have clung
I clothe	I clothed *or* clad	I have clothed *or* clad
I come	I came	I have come
I cost	I cost	I have cost
I creep	I crept	I have crept
*I crow	I crowded *or* crew	I have crowed
I cut	I cut	I have cut
*I dare	I dared	I have dared
I deal	I dealt	I have dealt
I dig	I dug	I have dug
I dive	I dived *or* dove[17]	I have dived
I do	I did	I have done
I draw	I drew	I have drawn
*I dread	I dreaded	I have dreaded
I dream	I dreamed *or* dreamt[17]	I have dreamed *or* dreamt[17]

[16] Common in radio.
[17] Common in spoken discourse.
[18] The adjective is *cloven* — *a cloven hoof;* but *a cleft palate.*

Present	Past	Present Perfect
I drink	I drank	I have drunk[19]
I drive	I drove	I have driven
I dwell	I dwelt *or* dwelled	I have dwelt *or* dwelled
I eat	I ate	I have eaten
*I engrave	I engraved	I have engraved
I fall	I fell	I have fallen
*I fare	I fared	I have fared
I feed	I fed	I have fed
I feel	I felt	I have felt
I fight	I fought	I have fought
I find	I found	I have found
I fit	I fitted	I have fitted
I flee	I fled	I have fled
I fling	I flung	I have flung
*I flow	I flowed	I have flowed
I fly[20]	I flew	I have flown
I forbear	I forbore	I have forborne
I forbid	I forbade[21] *or* forbad	I have forbidden
I forecast	I forecast *or* forecasted[22]	I have forecast *or* forecasted[22]
I forget	I forgot	I have forgotten *or* forgot
I for(e)go	I for(e)went	I have for(e)gone
I forsake	I forsook	I have forsaken
I forswear	I forswore	I have forsworn
I freeze	I froze	I have frozen
I get	I got	I have got *or* gotten[23]
I gild	I gilded *or* gilt[24]	I have gilded *or* gilt[24]
I gird	I girt *or* girded	I have girt *or* girded
I give	I gave	I have given
*I gnaw	I gnawed	I have gnawed
I go	I went	I have gone
I grind	I ground	I have ground
I grow	I grew	I have grown
I hang	I hung *or* hanged[25]	I have hung *or* hanged[25]
I have	I had	I have had

[19] The adjective is *drunken* — *a drunken man.*
[20] In baseball the verb is *fly, flyed, flyed,* — *I fly out; I flyed out; I have flyed out three times in succession.*
[21] Pronounced "forbăd."
[22] From the influence of *broadcasted*; see above.
[23] Used especially as an adjective — *ill-gotten gains.*
[24] Common in spoken discourse.
[25] Used only of execution by hanging.

Present	Past	Present Perfect
I hear	I heard	I have heard
I heave	I heaved *or* hove	I have heaved *or* hove
*I hew	I hewed	I have hewed *or* hewn[26]
I hide	I hid	I have hidden
I hit	I hit	I have hit
I hold	I held	I have held
I hurt	I hurt	I have hurt
I keep	I kept	I have kept
*I knead	I kneaded	I have kneaded
I kneel	I knelt *or* kneeled	I have knelt *or* kneeled
I knit	I knitted *or* knit	I have knitted *or* knit
I know	I knew	I have known
*I laugh	I laughed	I have laughed
I lay	I laid	I have laid
(see p. 294)		
I lead	I led	I have led
I leap	I leaped *or* leapt	I have leaped *or* leapt
I learn	I learned *or* learnt	I have learned *or* learnt
I leave	I left	I have left
I lend	I lent	I have lent
I let	I let	I have let
I lie	I lay	I have lain
(see p. 294)		
I lie (to	I lied	I have lied
prevaricate;		
see p. 294)		
I light	I lighted *or* lit	I have lighted *or* lit
I lose[27]	I lost	I have lost
I make	I made	I have made
I may	I might	
I mean	I meant	I have meant
I meet	I met	I have met
*I melt	I melted	I have melted[28]
*I mow	I mowed	I have mowed *or* mown[29]
I must		
I ought[30]		

[26] Used especially as an adjective — *a hand-hewn log.*

[27] Not to be confused with *loose* (*loose, loosed, loosed*) meaning "to release" — *I loose the rope now; I loosed the rope yesterday; I have loosed the rope every day for the last week.*

[28] The adjective is *molten* — *molten lead;* but *melted snow.*

[29] Used especially as an adjective — *new-mown hay.*

[30] Originally the past tense and later past participle of *owe.*

Present	Past	Present Perfect
I pay	I paid[31]	I have paid[31]
I plead	I pleaded	I have pleaded
I prove	I proved	I have proved or proven[32]
I put	I put	I have put
I quit	I quit or quitted	I have quit or quitted
I raise	I raised	I have raised
(see p. 294)		
I read	I read	I have read
*I reek	I reeked	I have reeked
I rend	I rent	I have rent
I rent	I rented	I have rented
I rid	I rid or ridded	I have rid or ridded
I ride	I rode	I have ridden
I ring	I rang	I have rung
I rise	I rose	I have risen
(see p. 294)		
I rot	I rotted	I have rotted[33]
*I row	I rowed	I have rowed
I run	I ran	I have run
I saw	I sawed	I have sawed or sawn[34]
I say	I said	I have said
I see	I saw	I have seen
I seek	I sought	I have sought
I seethe	I seethed	I have seethed or sodden[35]
I sell	I sold	I have sold
I send	I sent	I have sent
I set	I set	I have set
(see p. 295)		
*I sew	I sewed	I have sewed or sewn[36]
I shake	I shook	I have shaken
*I shape	I shaped	I have shaped[37]
I shave	I shaved	I have shaved or shaven[38]
I shear	I sheared	I have sheared or shorn[39]

[31] In the meaning "to let out," as a rope, cable, etc., the past tense and the past participle are spelled *payed.*

[32] Used especially as an adjective — *an unproven statement.*

[33] There is an adjective, *rotten* — *a rotten apple;* but *well-rotted straw.*

[34] Used especially as an adjective — *a roughly sawn board.*

[35] Used as an adjective — *a sodden mass of debris.*

[36] Used especially as an adjective — *a neatly sewn seam.*

[37] There is an adjective, *shapen* — *an ill-shapen bowl.*

[38] Used especially as an adjective — *a freshly shaven face.*

[39] Used especially as an adjective — *a newly shorn lamb.*

Present	Past	Present Perfect
I shed	I shed	I have shed
I shine	I shone or shined[40]	I have shone or shined[40]
I shoe	I shod	I have shod
I shoot	I shot	I have shot
*I shove	I shoved	I have shoved
I show	I showed	I have shown
I shred	I shredded or shred	I have shredded or shred
I shrink	I shrank	I have shrunk or shrunken[41]
I shut	I shut	I have shut
I sing	I sang	I have sung
I sink	I sank or sunk	I have sunk or sunken[42]
I sit	I sat	I have sat
(see p. 295)		
I slay	I slew	I have slain
I sleep	I slept	I have slept
I slide	I slid	I have slid or slidden
I sling	I slung	I have slung
I slink	I slunk	I have slunk
I slit	I slit	I have slit
I smell	I smelled or smelt[43]	I have smelled or smelt[43]
I smite	I smote	I have smitten or smit or smote
*I sow	I sowed	I have sowed or sown[44]
I speak	I spoke	I have spoken
I speed	I sped or speeded	I have sped or speeded
I spell	I spelled or spelt[43]	I have spelled or spelt[43]
I spend	I spent	I have spent
I spill	I spilled or spilt[43]	I have spilled or spilt[43]
I spin	I spun	I have spun
I spit	I spat or spit	I have spat or spit
I split	I split	I have split
I spoil	I spoiled or spoilt[45]	I have spoiled or spoilt[45]
I spread	I spread	I have spread
I spring	I sprang or sprung	I have sprung

[40] Used especially in the sense of "cause to shine" — *I shined the silver; I have shined the silver.*

[41] Used especially as an adjective — *a badly shrunken shirt.*

[42] Used especially as an adjective — *a sunken boat.*

[43] Common in spoken discourse.

[44] Used especially as an adjective — *newly sown grass seed.*

[45] Common in spoken discourse.

Present	Past	Present Perfect
*I sprout	I sprouted	I have sprouted
I stand	I stood	I have stood
*I starve	I starved	I have starved
I stay	I stayed	I have stayed[46]
I steal	I stole	I have stolen
I stick	I stuck	I have stuck
I sting	I stung	I have stung
I stink	I stank *or* stunk	I have stunk
I strew	I strewed	I have strewed *or* strewn[47]
I stride	I strode	I have stridden
I strike	I struck	I have struck *or* stricken[48]
I string	I strung	I have strung
I strive	I strove	I have striven *or* strived
I swear	I swore	I have sworn
I sweat	I sweat *or* sweated	I have sweat *or* sweated
I sweep	I swept	I have swept
*I swell	I swelled	I have swelled *or* swollen[49]
I swim	I swam	I have swum
I swing	I swung	I have swung
I take	I took	I have taken
I teach	I taught	I have taught
I tear	I tore	I have torn
I tell	I told	I have told
I think	I thought	I have thought
*I thrash	I thrashed	I have thrashed
*I thresh	I threshed	I have threshed
I thrive	I throve *or* thrived	I have thrived *or* thriven
I throw	I threw	I have thrown
I thrust	I thrust	I have thrust
I tread	I trod	I have trodden[50] *or* trod
*I wake	I waked *or* woke	I have waked
*I warp	I warped	I have warped
*I wax	I waxed	I have waxed[51]
I wear	I wore	I have worn
I weave	I wove	I have woven

[46] An old form *staid* is now used only as an adjective – *a staid old gentleman.*
[47] Used especially as an adjective – *the carelessly strewn flowers.*
[48] Used in a figurative sense – *I have stricken his name from the list.* Also used as an adjective – *the stricken man.*
[49] Used as an adjective—*a badly swollen wrist.*
[50] Used especially as an adjective – *downtrodden people.*
[51] There is an adjective *waxen* – *a waxen image.*

Present	Past	Present Perfect
I wed	I wedded	I have wedded or wed[52]
I weep	I wept	I have wept
*I weigh	I weighed	I have weighed
I wet	I wet[52] or wetted	I have wet[52] or wetted
I whet	I whetted	I have whetted
I win	I won	I have won
I wind	I wound	I have wound
I work	I worked	I have worked or wrought[53]
I wring	I wrung	I have wrung
I write	I wrote	I have written
*I yelp	I yelped	I have yelped
*I yield	I yielded	I have yielded

c. *Lay, lie; raise, rise; set, sit.* These six verbs—three usually transitive and three usually intransitive—are frequently confused.[54]

1. *Lay, lie.* *Lay* (principal parts *lay, laid, laid*) is usually transitive. *Lie* (principal parts *lie, lay, lain*) is usually intransitive.

I lay [or am laying] the book on the table now. I laid the book on the table yesterday. I have laid the book on the table every morning for the last week.

The hen lays an egg every day. The hen laid an egg yesterday. The hen has laid an egg every day for the last week.

I have a laying hen. [That is, "I have a hen that lays eggs."]

I lie [or am lying] down for a rest. I lay down for a rest yesterday. I have lain down for a rest each afternoon for the last week.

NOTE. The verb *lie* meaning "to prevaricate" (principal parts *lie, lied, lied*) is usually intransitive.

I lie [or am lying] to you. I lied to you yesterday. I have lied to you every day for the last week.

2. *Raise, rise.* *Raise* (principal parts *raise, raised, raised*) is usually transitive. *Rise* (principal parts *rise, rose, risen*) is usually intransitive.

[52] Common in spoken discourse.
[53] Used especially as an adjective — *wrought iron.*
[54] *Lay, raise,* and *set* are sometimes said to be the causative verbs of *lie, rise,* and *sit;* that is, *lay*="to cause to lie"; *raise*="to cause to rise"; and *set*="to cause to sit." For causative verbs see p. 57.

I raise [or am raising] the window now. I raised the window yesterday. I have raised the window every morning for the past week.

The curtain rises [or is rising] now. The curtain rose at eight-fifteen last night. The curtain has risen at eight-fifteen each night for the last week.

Bread rises. The sun rises. Prices rise.

NOTE. *Raise* is used in this country as a noun to mean a salary increase; but in England it is *rise* that is used as a noun in this sense.
I had a raise in salary. [American usage]
I had a rise in salary. [English usage]

3. *Set, sit.* Set (principal parts *set, set, set*) is usually transitive. *Sit* (principal parts *sit, sat, sat*) is usually intransitive.

I set [or am setting] the clock. I set the clock yesterday morning. I have set the clock every morning for the last week.

I set the hen this morning. I have set six hens this spring.[55]

I sit [or am sitting] on the porch. I sat on the porch yesterday. I have sat on the porch every morning for the last week.

NOTE. The verb *set* is also used intransitively.
The sun sets at about seven o'clock. It set somewhat earlier last week.
It has been setting later every day for the last month.
This new concrete sets within twenty-four hours.

2. CONJUGATIONS

The systematic arrangement of all the inflections of a verb is called its conjugation. Some of these inflections come through a change in the verb itself — I *walk*; he *walks*; he is *walking*. Others come through the addition of auxiliaries (see pp. 275 ff.) to the verb—I *proved* my point; my point *has been* proved; my point *shall be* proved.

There are three possible conjugations of a verb: simple, progressive, and emphatic.

a. Simple conjugation

1. Simple conjugation of *be*. Principal parts: *be* (infinitive), *was* (past); *been* (past participle).

[55] As used here *to set* means "to put (a fowl) on eggs to hatch them." Although logically she ought to become a "sitting hen," a hen that sits, actual linguistic practice has made her a "setting hen."

Conjugation of TO BE

Indicative Mood

PRESENT TENSE

Singular	Plural
1. I am	We are
2. You are (thou art)	You are
3. He[56] is	They are

PAST TENSE

1. I was	We were
2. You were (thou wast)	You were
3. He was	They were

FUTURE TENSE

1. I shall[57] be	We shall be
2. You will be (thou wilt be)	You will be
3. He will be	They will be

PRESENT PERFECT (PERFECT) TENSE

1. I have been	We have been
2. You have been (thou hast been)	You have been
3. He has been	They have been

PAST PERFECT TENSE

1. I had been	We had been
2. You had been (thou hadst been)	You had been
3. He had been	They had been

FUTURE PERFECT TENSE

1. I shall have been	We shall have been
2. You will have been (thou wilt have been)	You will have been
3. He will have been	They will have been

Subjunctive Mood

PRESENT TENSE

1. If[58] I be	If we be
2. If you be (thou be or be'st)	If you be
3. If he be	If they be

[56] Or *she* or *it* throughout.
[57] For *shall* and *will* see pp. 281 ff.
[58] "If" is not an actual part of the subjunctive mood but is printed here because of its very common use in subjunctive clauses.

Subjunctive Mood

PAST TENSE

1. If I were   If we were
2. If you were (thou wert)   If you were
3. If he were   If they were

FUTURE TENSE[59]

1. If I should (would, shall, will) be   If we should (etc.) be
2. If you should be (thou shouldst be)   If you should be
3. If he should be   If they should be

PRESENT PERFECT TENSE

1. If I have been   If we have been
2. If you have been (thou have been)   If you have been
3. If he have been   If they have been

PAST PERFECT TENSE

1. If I had been   If we had been
2. If you had been (thou hadst been)   If you had been
3. If he had been   If they had been

FUTURE PERFECT TENSE

1. If I should have been   If we should have been
2. If you should have been (thou should   If you should
   have been)   have been
3. If he should have been   If they should have been

Imperative Mood

Singular   *Plural*

PRESENT TENSE

2. Be (you *or* thou)   Be (you *or* ye)

INFINITIVES

Present   *Perfect*
to be   to have been

[59] Some grammarians hold—and rightly too—that there are no true future and future perfect tenses of the subjunctive, maintaining that the subjunctive is itself a kind of future mood. But the forms that some regard as future and future perfect tense subjunctive forms have been printed here for those who may feel the need of them.

PARTICIPLES

Present	Past	Perfect
being	been	having been

GERUNDS

Present	Perfect
being	having been

There are no emphatic forms for the verb *be*. Progressive forms of *be* occur in the present and past tenses: *The child is (was) being obstreperous.*

2. Simple conjugation of the active voice of *see* (principal parts *see, saw, seen*).

Indicative Mood

PRESENT TENSE

Singular	Plural
1. I see	We see
2. You see (thou seest)	You see
3. He[60] sees	They see

PAST TENSE

1. I saw	We saw
2. You saw (thou sawest)	You saw
3. He saw	They saw

FUTURE TENSE

1. I shall[61] see	We shall see
2. You will see (thou wilt see)	You will see
3. He will see	They will see

PRESENT PERFECT TENSE

1. I have seen	We have seen
2. You have seen (thou hast seen)	You have seen
3. He has seen	They have seen

PAST PERFECT TENSE

1. I had seen	We had seen
2. You had seen (thou hadst seen)	You had seen
3. He had seen	They had seen

[60] Or *she* or *it* throughout.
[61] For *shall* and *will* see pp. 281 ff.

FUTURE PERFECT TENSE

Singular	*Plural*
1. I shall have seen	We shall have seen
2. You will have seen (thou wilt have seen)	You will have seen
3. He will have seen	They will have seen

Subjunctive Mood

PRESENT TENSE

1. If[62] I see	If we see
2. If you see (thou seest)	If you see
3. If he see	If they see

PAST TENSE

1. If I saw	If we saw
2. If you saw (thou sawest)	If you saw
3. If he saw	If they saw

FUTURE TENSE[63]

1. If I should see	If we should see
2. If you should see (thou shouldst see)	If you should see
3. If he should see	If they should see

PRESENT PERFECT TENSE

1. If I have seen	If we have seen
2. If you have seen (thou hast seen)	If you have seen
3. If he have seen	If they have seen

PAST PERFECT TENSE

1. If I had seen	If we had seen
2. If you had seen (thou hadst seen)	If you had seen
3. If he had seen	If they had seen

FUTURE PERFECT TENSE

1. If I should have seen	If we should have seen·
2. If you should have seen (thou shouldst have seen)	If you should have seen
3. If he should have seen	If they should have seen

Imperative Mood

2. See (you *or* thou)	See (you *or* ye)

[62] Not a part of the subjunctive mood but printed here because it frequently introduces a subjunctive clause.

INFINITIVES

Present	*Perfect*
to see	to have seen

PARTICIPLES

Present	*Past*	*Perfect*
seeing	seen	having seen

GERUNDS

Present	*Perfect*
seeing	having seen

3. Synopsis of the simple conjugation of the passive voice of *see*. The systematic conjugation of a verb through one person and one number (usually first person singular) is called a synopsis. On the basis of the complete conjugations which appear above, it becomes a simple matter to use a synopsis as a guide for deriving all the other forms for person and number. The conjugations of the passive voice, of the progressive form, and of the emphatic form are given by synopsis in the following outlines:

Synopsis of the Passive Voice of *see*

INDICATIVE MOOD

Present tense—I am seen
Past tense—I was seen
Future tense—I shall[63] be seen
Present perfect tense—I have been. seen
Past perfect tense—I had been seen
Future perfect tense—I shall have been seen

SUBJUNCTIVE MOOD[64]

Present tense—If I be seen
Past tense—If I were seen
Future tense—If I should be seen
Present perfect tense—If I have been seen
Past perfect tense—If I had been seen
Future perfect tense—If I should have been seen

[63] See page 281 ff.
[64] See footnote, p. 299.

IMPERATIVE MOOD

Singular–Be (you *or* thou) seen
Plural–Be (you *or* ye) seen

INFINITIVES

Present	*Perfect*
to be seen	to have been seen

PARTICIPLES

Present	*Past*	*Perfect*
being seen	seen	having been seen

GERUNDS

Present	*Perfect*
being seen	having been seen

b. Progressive conjugation.   The active voice of the progressive form is made by combining the auxiliary *be* and the present participle of the notional verb. (For the simple conjugation of *be*, see pp. 296 ff.) The passive voice of the progressive form, which occurs in only the present and past tenses, is made by combining the progressive forms of *be* and the past participle of the notional verb — *I am being punished, I was being punished*, etc.

Synopsis of the Active Voice, Progressive
Conjugation of *See*

INDICATIVE MOOD

Present tense–I am seeing
Past tense–I was seeing
Future tense–I shall be seeing
Present perfect tense–I have been seeing
Past perfect tense–I had been seeing
Future perfect tense–I shall have been seeing

SUBJUNCTIVE MOOD[65]

Present tense–[If] I be seeing
Past tense–[If] I were seeing
Future tense–[If] I should be seeing

[65] See footnote, p. 299.

Present perfect tense—[If] I have been seeing
Past perfect tense—[If] I had been seeing
Future perfect tense—[If] I should have been seeing

IMPERATIVE MOOD

Singular—Be (you *or* thou) seeing
Plural—Be (you *or* ye) seeing

INFINITIVES

Present	*Perfect*
to be seeing	to have been seeing

PARTICIPLES (rarely used)

Present	*Past*	*Perfect*
being seeing	been seeing	having been seeing

GERUNDS (rarely used)

Present	*Perfect*
being seeing	having been seeing

c. Emphatic conjugation. The emphatic form exists only in the active voice and in the present and past indicative and the imperative. It is made by combining the auxiliary *do* and the simple infinitive of the notional verb.

Synopsis of the Emphatic Conjugation of *See*

INDICATIVE MOOD

Present tense—I do see
Past tense—I did see

IMPERATIVE MOOD

Singular—Do (you *or* thou) see
Plural—Do (you *or* ye) see

NOTE. The auxiliary *do* plus infinitive is commonly used, without emphasis, with the negative *not*, in questions, and in answers to questions.

I *do* not think it is likely to rain.
Do you think it is likely to rain?
I *did* not find what I was looking for.
Did you find what you were looking for?
Yes, I *did*.

E. *Verbals*

There are three nonfinite forms of the verb, commonly called verbals — the participle, the gerund, and the infinitive. They are nonfinite because they merely indicate an action without limiting it as to number, person, and actual time. In "He did the assigned work" the verb *did* is finite; it represents third person, singular number, and past time. But in "doing the assigned work" and "to do the assigned work" there is no such limitation.

These three verbals may be called hybrids of speech; for they may serve the functions of two parts of speech at the same time.

1. PARTICIPLE

The participle, a verbal (or nonfinite verb form), is incapable of making an assertion. Combined with auxiliaries, it makes certain verb phrases (see below) and so in such cases ceases to be thought of as a separate participle. But it retains its character as a participle when it functions as a verbal adjective; that is, when it is used as a verb and as an adjective at the same time (see pp. 59 ff; for forms see p. 268).

a. Uses of the participle. The participle has two major uses: (*a*) it may, as was stated above, help make various verb phrases; and (*b*) it may attach itself to a noun as an adjectival modifier.[66]

1. To make verb phrases. The participle is used to make forms of the progressive conjugation (see pp. 301 f.), forms of the passive voice (see pp. 300 f.), and forms of the perfect tenses (see pp. 265 ff.).

a) The present participle combines with forms of the verb *be* to make the progressive conjugation — "I am *seeing*"; "I was *seeing*"; "to be *seeing*"; "to have been *seeing*."

b) The past participle combines with forms of the verb *be* to make the passive voice — "I am *seen*"; "I was *seen*"; "to be *seen*"; "to have been *seen*."

[66] For the adverbial force of many participial phrases, see p. 61.

c) The past participle combines with the auxiliary *have* to make the present perfect, the past perfect, and the future perfect tenses (see pp. 265 ff.) — "I have *seen*"; "I had *seen*"; "I shall have *seen*"; "to have *seen*"; "I have been *seen*"; "I had been *seen*"; I shall have been *seen*"; "to have been *seen*."

2. As an adjectival modifier attached to a noun. As was pointed out earlier, the participle is a hybrid, taking on the functions of two parts of speech at the same time—the function of a verb and the function of an adjective.

The mob, shouting insults, pressed closer. [The participle *shouting* takes *insults* as a direct object and at the same time modifies the noun *mob*.]

3. The past participle may have lost so much of its original force that it has become a regular adjective: "the wind-*swept* plains"; "a clean-*shaven* face"; "the *molten* iron." (See notes to some of the past participle forms listed on pp. 287 ff.) The past participle may, of course, be used as a subjective complement (that is, as an adjective) after a link verb.

He became discouraged.
She seems interested.

This use of the past participle as a subjective complement resembles closely the past participle used as a part of a verb phrase in the passive voice. But they differ in the fact that the past participle as a subjective complement expresses merely a condition, whereas the past participle as a part of a passive verb phrase implies a notion of a person or thing as the doer or sufferer of an action.

John can't go, for his back is injured. [*Injured*, a subjective complement, merely describes the condition of *back*.]
John's back is injured every time he plays football. [*Injured* is here a part of the passive verb *is injured*, which represents a definite action in the passive voice.]

But the distinction is not often very important. Other things being equal, it is well to consider the participle a part of a verb phrase when a distinction cannot be made readily.

4. With a negative prefix *un-*. The negative prefix *un-* is often attached to a participle in such a way that the participle loses all verbal force and becomes a regular adjective.

We found the child unharmed. [*Unharmed* is an adjective rather than a participle (functioning here as an objective complement). There is no finite verb "to unharm."]

The letter remained unopened. [*Unopened* is an adjective rather than a participle (functioning here as a subjective complement). There is no finite verb "to unopen."]

He appeared at rehearsal unshaven. [*Unshaven* is an adjective rather than a participle (functioning as a subjective complement). There is no finite verb "to unshave."]

But this does not mean that there are not times when a participle with the prefix *un-* remains a true participle.

The package became unwrapped. [*Unwrapped* is a participle (functioning here as a subjective complement). For there is a finite verb "to unwrap."]

5. Compounded. Participles are frequently compounded with (*a*) adjectives, (*b*) adverbs, or (*c*) nouns to form adjectival modifiers.

a) With adjectives

a bitter-tasting orange; a triangular-shaped pattern; an easy-running machine.

b) With adverbs

a well-kept lawn; a far-reaching program; a forward-looking leader.

c) With nouns

an epoch-making treaty; an ice-covered road; a heart-broken child.

NOTE.   By analogy many compound adjectival expressions are made by adding *d* or *ed* to a noun: *a broken-hearted child; a good-natured man; a full-blooded Scotch collie.* These are simply compound adjectives, not participles. There are no such verb forms as *hearted, natured, blooded.*

6. As a substantive. As an adjective may become a noun in function (see pp. 95 f.), it is natural that a participle may be used as a noun.

All the wounded were removed to Station A; the dying were carried on to Station B. [The past participle *wounded* and the present participle *dying* function as nouns, *wounded* as the subject of *were removed* and *dying* as the subject of *were carried*. Or, we may regard them as adjectives modifying some word like *persons* understood. (For the use of *the* see p. 95.)]

7. As a preposition. Certain words, originally participles — such as *concerning, regarding, excepting* — have come to function for all practical purposes as prepositions. (See also p. 121.)

He will say nothing concerning his part in the affair. [*Concerning* = "about" and may be interpreted as a preposition governing *part*.]
All the chairmen excepting one have reported. [*Excepting* = "except" and may be interpreted as a preposition governing *one*.]
Regarding the coming election one important fact must be kept in mind. [*Regarding* = "about" and may be interpreted as a preposition governing *election*.]

b. Usages in participles. 1. Dangling participle. When the agency of a participle is demanded (as it is when the participle in its adjectival capacity modifies a substantive) and this agency is not readily apparent, the participle is said to dangle. In other words, a participle ought to attach itself immediately and unerringly to a substantive that indicates its agency.

Probably the main reason participles dangle is the fact that we lack in English a satisfactory indefinite expression corresponding to the German *man* or the French *on*. "One" is not entirely satisfactory; "you" is not satisfactory; nor does the indefinite "we" entirely meet the demand. Hence, the inexpert writer, or speaker, in trying to avoid an unsatisfactory "one," "you," or "we," resorts to the passive voice and unwittingly uses a participle without a suitable noun for the participle to modify.

A similar situation develops in the case of dangling gerunds (see pp. 310 f.) and dangling infinitives (see pp. 318 f.). In the following examples it will be seen that a dangling participle is usually found in connection with a passive voice. When the passive voice is changed to the active, the dangling construction disappears.

Holding the rope in the left hand in this manner, you make two loops with the portion held in the right hand. [Not: Holding the rope in the left hand, two loops are made with the portion held in the right hand. For the participle *holding* modifies *loops*, which is nonsense; *loops* did not do the holding. Thus the participle, because it does not immediately relate itself to the noun with which it has a logical association, is said to dangle.]

Coming into the room, we saw that the center table had been moved to one side. [Not: Coming into the room, the center table had been moved to one side. For the participle *coming* modifies *table*, which is nonsense; *table* did not do the coming. Thus the participle is said to dangle.]

Dismissing the class, the instructor erased the exercises on the board. [Not: Dismissing the class, the exercises on the board were erased by the instructor. For the participle *dismissing* does not immediately attach itself to *instructor*, which is in a subordinate construction (the object of the preposition *by*).]

The class having been dismissed, the instructor erased the exercises on the board. [Here the participle *having been dismissed* has the noun *class* to modify. (Inasmuch as *class* has no grammatical function in the statement in which it appears—namely, *the instructor erased the exercises on the board*—the noun *class* and its participial modifier constitute what is known as a nominative absolute construction.) (See pp. 61 f.)]

The train wreck was caused by a washout. [Or] The train was wrecked as the result of a washout. [Not: The train was wrecked, caused by a washout. For the participle *caused* has no noun that it can logically and grammatically attach itself to.]

Having been late three times in one week, the janitor was discharged. [Not: Having been late three times in one week, they discharged the janitor. For here the participle erroneously attaches itself to *they*.]

NOTE 1. A dangling participle was very common in what is now regarded as an old-fashioned complimentary close to a letter, such as "hoping to receive your order, yours very truly"; "trusting that this finds you well, yours very sincerely." Something like "I am," "We are," to which the participle might attach itself ("hoping to receive your order, we are yours very truly"; "trusting that this finds you well, I am yours very sincerely") has been omitted.

NOTE 2. A few participles, through usage, are allowed to stand as "absolute participles," that is, without any nouns to modify, even though strictly speaking they are dangling participles. (*Strictly speaking* here is an example.) They are acceptable because there is no specific agency involved to cause confusion. Among such participles used absolutely are *allowing, concerning, owing, speaking, talking*. Some of these may well be regarded now as prepositions (see p. 306).

Generally speaking, a selfish man is an unhappy man. [The participle *speaking*, with its adverbial modifier *generally*, may be regarded as a participle used absolutely.]

Considering the trouble he has been to, no more should be asked of him. [*Considering the trouble he has been to* may be regarded as a participial phrase used absolutely.]

Speaking of baseball, where is Woody English now? [*Speaking of baseball* may be regarded as a participial phrase used absolutely.]

2. For the nominative absolute, sometimes confused with the dangling participle, see pp. 61 f.

3. Subjective complement with a participle. A subjective complement after a participle will be in the same case as the noun that the participle modifies. It is, of course, very seldom that this problem arises; for the substantive modified by a participle rarely is one that shows case endings.

I not being she, the question you ask is ridiculous. [*She*, a subjective complement after the participle *being*, is in the same case as *I*, the pronoun which the participle modifies — namely, the nominative case.]

A doubt about me being him did not seem to occur to them. [*Him*, a subjective complement after the participle *being*, is in the same case as *me*, the pronoun which the participle modifies — namely, the objective case.]

4. Erroneous use of *very* with a participle. *Very* is an adverb of degree and may modify an adjective or an adverb, but not

a verb. Hence, *very* should never modify a present or past participle unless the participle has lost all verbal force and has become an ordinary adjective. But *very much, very greatly,* and *very well* may be used to modify a participle, for *very* now modifies an adverb like *much, greatly, well.*

Very much hesitating to take the final plunge, he looked about for a way of escape. [*Not:* Very hesitating to take the final plunge, he looked about for a way of escape.]
Being very greatly angered, he did not trust himself to speak. [*Not:* Being very angered, he did not trust himself to speak.]
The author inserted in the first chapter a very well-concealed clue. [*Not:* The author inserted in the first chapter a very concealed clue.]
That was a very exciting play we saw last night. [The force of *exciting* is primarily adjectival rather than participial; hence, *very* is correctly used.]

I am a very tired man tonight. [*Tired* has lost all participial force and has become a regular adjective; hence, *very* is correctly used.]

5. For the relative time expressed by a participle see under Tense, pp. 269 f.

2. GERUND

The gerund, like the participle and the infinitive a verbal (or nonfinite verb form), is incapable of making an assertion. It functions as a noun and a verb at the same time (see pp. 63 f.) and so is called a verbal noun, just as the participle is called a verbal adjective. (For forms see p. 268).

a. Uses of the gerund. As was pointed out earlier (p. 63 f.), the gerund, like the participle and the infinitive, is a hybrid; for it performs the functions of two parts of speech at the same time — the function of a verb and the function of a noun.

She likes giving violin lessons to children. [The gerund *giving* as a verb takes *lessons* as a direct object and *to children* as an adverbial modifier; as a noun the gerund (with its object and adverbial modifier) functions as the direct object of the finite verb *likes.*]

Some grammarians prefer to make a distinction between true gerunds and -*ing* words that, though originally gerunds, have lost most of their verbal content and so have become much like ordinary nouns. This distinction is exemplified below.

1. True gerund. The true gerund takes or·may take complements and adverbial modifiers.

> *Misspelling* my name three times was inexcusable.
> *Writing* one's signature legibly is very important.
> His mission is *preaching* the gospel to the heathen.

2. Ordinary noun. When the -*ing* word has lost its power to take complements and adverbial modifiers, when it may be modified by an adjective, or when it may be pluralized, it has ceased to be a true gerund and has become an ordinary noun.

> His inexcusable *misspelling* of my name irritated me.
> A legible *writing* of one's signature is important.
> His eloquent *preaching* of the gospel made him a bishop.
> Her *writings* have usually been in a satiric vein.
> His grotesque *misspellings* were something to marvel at.
> His earnest *preachings* do not coincide with his devious practices.
> I no longer pay any attention to his *comings* and *goings*.

But it is usually sufficient to regard as a gerund any -*ing* word derived from a verb and functioning as a noun. But, of course, pluralized -*ing* words must be classed as ordinary nouns.

b. Usages in gerunds.

1. Dangling gerund. When the agency of a gerund is demanded and is not readily apparent, the gerund is said to dangle. This situation usually develops when the gerund functions as the object of a preposition and the agency is not apparent in the grammatical subject of the main verb—that is, in what would be the subject of the gerund if the gerund were to take a subject. Sometimes, of course, the agency is apparent in a possessive modifier of the gerund; and sometimes the agency of the gerund is so general that expression of it is not demanded.

The main reason why dangling gerunds occur is the same as in the case of dangling participles and dangling infinitives (see p. 306).

In the following examples it will be seen that a dangling gerund is usually found in connection with a main verb in the passive voice. When the passive voice is changed to the active, the dangling construction disappears.

In tying a "diamond hitch" one [or you or we] must hold the rope in this manner [Not: In tying a "diamond hitch" the rope must be held in this manner. For the agency of the gerund *tying* is not apparent in *rope*, the subject of the main verb *must be held*. But in the correct sentence the agency of *tying* is apparent in *one* (or *you* or *we*), the subject of the main verb *must hold*. Note that, although the agency of the gerund is apparent in the subject of the main verb, the prepositional phrase in which the gerund functions as the object of the preposition *in* functions as an adverbial modifier of the main verb *must hold*. Compare with an adverbial clause "when one ties. . . ."]

The Government lost six precious weeks in trying to find the right man for the job. [Not: Six precious weeks were lost in trying to find the right man for the job. For the agency of the gerund *trying* is not apparent in *weeks*, the subject of the main verb *were lost*. But in the correct sentence the agency of *trying* is apparent in *Government*, the subject of the main verb *lost*. Note that the prepositional phrase *in trying to find the right man for the job* is an adverbial modifier of *lost*.]

After swimming steadily for an hour the boys found a good rest most welcome. [The agency of *swimming* is apparent in *boys*, the subject of the main verb *found*. The prepositional phrase *after swimming steadily for an hour* modifies *found*.]

A satisfactory belt was achieved by our splicing the two pieces of rope. [Here the agency of the gerund *splicing* is evident in the possessive modifier *our*.]

For his confusing of our names there is no excuse. [The agency of the gerund *confusing* is evident in the possessive modifier *his*.]

The head should be held high in walking. [Here the gerund *walking* represents a general action; hence, its agency is not demanded.]

2. For the gerund used absolutely see pp. 64 f.

3. Subjective complement with a gerund. A subjective complement used in connection with a gerund should be in the same case as the gerund. That is, if the gerund functions as a noun in the nominative case, a subjective complement used with it will be in the nominative case; if the gerund functions as a noun in the objective case, a subjective complement used with it will be in the objective case.[67]

> Its being he did not deter us. [The gerund *being* as the subject of the main verb *did deter* is in the nominative case; hence, *he*, a subjective complement after *being*, is in the nominative case.]
>
> We never thought of its being him. [The gerund *being* as the object of the preposition *of* is in the objective case; hence, *him*, a subjective complement after *being*, is in the objective case.]

4. Gerund versus participial construction. There are times when either a gerund or a participle is correct grammatically, although the two have slightly different meanings. There are times when a participial construction is not only to be preferred but actually is the only construction that the language will permit.

A guiding principle, other things being equal, is this: inasmuch as a noun notion is always more emphatic than an adjective notion modifying the noun, place the more important notion in a noun construction, modifying the noun with the lesser notion. This may mean either a noun modified by a participle or a gerund modified by an adjective (such as a possessive).

> It is a question of Henry going or of Burt going. [Here the emphasis is on the substantives *Henry* and *Burt* rather than on the "going." Hence, the substantive modified by the participle is the neater construction.]

[67] Fortunately, a situation involving this principle seldom arises. For at best the construction has little to commend it. Again, we see that the fact that a construction is grammatically possible does not assure acceptance of it from the point of view of style.

It is a question of Henry's going and of Burt's remaining. [Here the emphasis is on the ideas expressed by the gerunds *going* and *remaining*. Hence, the gerunds modified by the substantives in the possessive case is the neater construction.]

But when a phrase or a clause intervenes between the substantive and the verbal, or when the substantive happens to have no possessive form, the participial construction is the only construction possible.

The likelihood of a man with his reputation taking the risk is excellent. [*Not:* The likelihood of a man's with his reputation taking the risk is excellent.]

I am hoping for someone who is to be away renting us his house for the summer. [*Not:* I am hoping for someone's who is to be away renting us his house for the summer.]

The chances of that being true are few. [Here only the participial construction is possible (the participle *being* modifying the substantive *that*), for the pronoun *that* has no possessive form.]

Now he must pay the cost, the possibility of which being necessary never having entered his head before. [Here only the participial construction is possible (the participle *being* modifying the pronoun *which*), for the pronoun *which* has no possessive form.]

Let's talk about you and me forming a partnership. [Here the participial construction (the participle *forming* modifying the pronouns *you* and *me*, which in turn are the objects of the preposition *about*) certainly is preferable to the gerund construction "Let's talk about your and my forming a partnership."]

Hence, the question of whether to use a participial or a gerund construction will depend on the emphasis desired and sometimes will actually depend on the limitations of the language itself. But other things being equal, usually a gerund modified by a possessive will express an idea more neatly than a participle modifying a substantive.

They did not object to my writing my answers in longhand. [*Rather than:* They did not object to me writing my answers in longhand.]

The crowd seemed to admire his dodging this way and that across the field. [*Rather than:* The crowd seemed to admire him dodging this way and that across the field.]

I had a glimpse of him dodging this way and that. [*Or*] I had a glimpse of his dodging this way and that. [Both are equally good. But the first emphasizes the person concerned; the second emphasizes the "dodging."]

5. Special constructions of the gerund.

a) A gerund is sometimes used as the object of *a* (originally the preposition *on*). Although the *a* is infrequently encountered in modern English (see first two examples below), the pattern survives in the construction illustrated in the last two sentences given below.[68]

> I have spent
> Long time a-wondering when I shall be
> As happy as Cliff Klingenhagen is.
> (E. A. Robinson, "Cliff Klingenhagen")

. . . bulldozers chewed the frozen earth, and riveters set steel beams arattling. (*Time*, February 9, 1962)

My mother has gone calling.

I spent the afternoon studying geometry.

b) Just as an ordinary noun may function as an adverb (see p. 106), so may a gerund.

He is fighting mad. [*Fighting,* a gerund, functions as an adverbial modifier of the adjective *mad*, which is the subjective complement after *is*.]

Anything worth doing is worth doing well. [The first *doing*, a gerund, functions as an adverbial modifier of the adjective *worth* (which modifies the substantive *anything*). The second *doing* is another gerund, modifying the adjective *worth*, which is a subjective complement after *is*.]

---

[68] When the *a* is dropped the verbal is now often regarded as a participle rather than as a gerund. In "Let's go fishing" *fishing* may be regarded as a gerund the object of an understood *a* or as a participle modifying *'s* (*us*). (See p. 352.)

c) Just as an ordinary noun may function as an adjective (see p. 94), so may a gerund. But such a use of the gerund must not be confused with a participle in *-ing* modifying a noun. In the gerund construction the gerund shows what the noun is used for; in the participial construction the participle qualifies or limits the noun like any adjective modifier.

A Pullman is a sleeping car. [*Sleeping* is a gerund functioning as a modifier of *car*. *Sleeping car* means, not a "car that sleeps," but a "car for sleeping."]

We looked at the sleeping child. [*Sleeping* is a participle that functions as an adjectival modifier of *child*. *Sleeping child* means a "child that sleeps."]

A sliding board means a "board for sliding." [That is, *sliding* is a gerund. But a *sliding scale* means a "scale that slides"; that is, *sliding* is a participle.]

A dining room means a "room for dining." [That is, *dining* is a gerund. But a *dining patron* means a "patron who dines"; that is, *dining* is a participle.]

In such expressions as "walking stick," "fishing rod," "swimming suit," *walking, fishing,* and *swimming* are gerunds functioning as modifiers of nouns.

6. For the relative time that a gerund represents see under Tense, pp. 270 f.

3. INFINITIVE

The infinitive, like the participle and the gerund a verbal (nonfinite verb form), is incapable of making an assertion. The infinitive may function as a noun, an adjective, and an adverb. And in a construction known as the infinitive clause it may take a grammatical subject of its own, in which case it tends to function somewhat like a finite verb. (See pp. 70 f. For forms see p. 269.)

a. Simple infinitive. When *to,* the so-called sign of the infinitive, is omitted, the infinitive is called the simple infinitive. The simple infinitive is found in several present-day uses:

1. After verbs of feeling, hearing, seeing

> I felt the ground shake. [That is, "I felt the ground to shake."]
> Did you see him run away? [That is, "Did you see him to run away?"]
> We heard him whistle a song. [That is, "We heard him to whistle a song."]

2. After such verbs as *bid, dare, help, let, make, need,* and *please*

> They bade us leave. [That is, "They bade us to leave."]
> Help me lift this log. [That is, "Help me to lift this log."]
> He made me take another examination. [That is, "He made me to take another examination."]
> I did not let him help me. [That is, "I did not let him to help me."]
> Please close the door. [That is, "Please to close the door."]
> I dare not oppose him. [That is, "I dare not to oppose him."]
> You need not do it at once. [That is, "You need not to do it at once."]
> You ought not hesitate now. [That is, "You ought not to hesitate now."]

NOTE.   For the special problem of *need* and *dare* as auxiliary verbs and as notional verbs, see pp. 278 f.

3. As objects of certain prepositions

> She does nothing but spend money. [That is "She does nothing but to spend money." The infinitive phrase (*to*) *spend money* is the object of the preposition *but*; and the whole prepositional phrase *but* (*to*) *spend money* functions as an adjectival modifier of *nothing*.]

> He does everything except wash the dishes. [That is, "He does everything except to wash the dishes." The infinitive (*to*) *wash the dishes* is the object of the preposition *except*; and the prepositional phrase *except* (*to*) *wash the dishes* functions as an adjectival modifier of *everything*.]

NOTE.   Formerly the infinitive could become the object of the preposition *for* to express purpose: "He came for to see me." But such a use is now considered dialectic. Yet an infinitive clause may function as the object of the preposition *for*: "He left his car for me to use." See p. 73, Note.

4. In a series of infinitives when *to* appears only with the first and is understood with the others.

I don't know whether to walk or ride. [That is, "I don't know whether to walk or to ride."]
The Board asked me to go to San Francisco, make an investigation, and draw up a complete report. [That is, "The Board asked me to go to San Francisco, to make an investigation, and to draw up a complete report."]

5. In appositional expressions, and occasionally as a renaming subjective complement.

There is just one thing to do—get out as quickly as possible. [That is, "There is just one thing to do—to get out as quickly as possible."]
All he ever wants to do is watch television. [That is, "All he ever wants to do is to watch television."]

6. After *better, had better, would rather, had rather,* and after the conjunction *than*

You had better go now. [That is, "You had better to go now."]
I would rather play baseball than eat. [That is, "I would rather to play baseball than to eat."]

7. After certain auxiliaries to form finite verb phrases. (See pp. 276 ff.)
b. Uses. The infinitive has two major uses: it may combine with other verb forms to make tenses and moods; and it may be used as a part of speech, such as a noun, adjective, adverb, or with a subject of its own in the infinitive clause (see pp. 70 f.).
1. Used as part of a finite verb phrase. The infinitive may combine with auxiliaries (*may, might, must, can, could, will, would, shall, should, do, have, ought*) to show tense or mood.

I shall go. [The infinitive (*to*) *go* combines with the auxiliary *shall* to make the future tense of the verb *go*.]

I do go. [The infinitive (*to*) *go* combines with the auxiliary *do* to make the emphatic conjugation of the verb *go*.]

I can go. [The infinitive (*to*) *go* combines with the auxiliary *can* to make the so-called potential mood of the verb *go*.]

I have to go soon. [The infinitive *to go* combines with the auxiliary *have* to form a verb which is the equivalent of *must go* or *should go*.]

I ought to go soon. [The infinitive *to go* combines with the auxiliary *ought* to form a verb which is the equivalent of *should go*.]

2. Used as a part of speech. The infinitive may have the sense of a verb and the function of a part of speech — such as a noun, an adjective, an adverb.

To retreat to a new position is sometimes the better part of valor. [The infinitive *to retreat*, with its adverbial modifier *to a new position*, functions as a noun, the subject of the main verb *is*.]

I have a story to tell you. [The infinitive *to tell*, with its indirect object *you*, functions as an adjectival modifier of *story*.]

Your mother has come to see you. [The infinitive *to see*, with its direct object *you*, functions as an adverbial modifier of *has come*.]

They ordered him to report immediately. [The infinitive *to report* takes *him* as its grammatical subject and *immediately* as an adverbial modifier, the whole (*him to report immediately*) constituting an infinitive clause (see pp. 70 ff.) that functions as the direct object of the main verb *ordered*.]

c. *Usages in infinitives.*

1. Dangling infinitive. When the agency of an infinitive is demanded and is not readily apparent, the infinitive is said to dangle. This situation usually develops when an infinitive expresses purpose and its agency is not apparent in the grammatical subject of the main verb. Sometimes, of course, the agency of an infinitive expressing purpose is so general that it is not demanded in the interest of clearness.

The main reason why dangling infinitives occur is the same as in the case of dangling participles and dangling gerunds (see pp. 306 f.).

In the following examples it will be seen that a dangling infinitive is usually found in connection with a passive voice in the main verb. When the passive voice is changed to the active, the dangling construction disappears.

To tie a "diamond hitch" one [or you or we]́must hold the rope in this manner. [Not: To tie a "diamond hitch" the rope must be held in this manner. For the agency of the infinitive *to tie* is not apparent in *rope*, the subject of the main verb *must be held*. But in the correct sentence the agency of *to tie* is apparent in *one* (or *you* or *we*), the subject of the main verb *must hold*. But note that, although the agency of the infinitive is apparent in the subject of the main verb, the infinitive phrase *to tie a "diamond hitch"* functions as an adverbial modifier of the main verb *must hold*. Compare an equivalent adverbial clause "when one ties a 'diamond hitch.' . . ."]

We broke a window to get into the garage. [Not: A window was broken to get into the garage. For the agency of the infinitive *to get* is not apparent in *window*, the subject of the main verb *was broken*.]

One must save a little money every day to have something for the future. [Not: A little money must be saved every day to have something for the future. For the agency of the infinitive *to have* is not apparent in *money*, the subject of the main verb *must be saved*.]

Alcohol can be used to soften a typewriter platen. [Here the infinitive *to soften* represents a general action; hence, its agency is not demanded.]

2. For the infinitive used absolutely see p. 74.

3. Subjective complement. A subjective complement after an infinitive refers to the subject of the infinitive if the infinitive has a grammatical subject of its own; otherwise it refers back to the subject of the finite verb. As the subject of an infinitive is always in the objective case, a subjective complement referring to this subject will also be in the objective case. But if the infinitive has no grammatical subject of its own, then a subjective complement after the infinitive will refer back to the subject of the finite verb; and, inasmuch as this subject of the

finite verb will, of course, be in the nominative case, a subjective complement referring to it will also be in the nominative
case. (For a simple test for the proper case form of any subjective complement see p. 241, Note.)

> They thought me to be him. [*Not:* They thought me to be he.
> For the subjective complement refers to *me*, the grammatical sub-
> ject of the infinitive *to be*.]
> I was thought to be he. [*Not:* I was thought to be him. For the
> subjective complement refers back to *I*, the subject of the main
> verb *was thought*, inasmuch as the infinitive *to be* has no gram-
> matical subject of its own.]

4. For the relative time that an infinitive represents see under
Tense, pp. 271 f.

5. The split infinitive. Two observations may be made about
the much discussed and greatly misunderstood split-infinitive
construction.

First, many people are confused over what actually constitutes a split infinitive. The true split infinitive results when an
adverbial modifier is placed between *to* and the infinitive. Thus
"to truly appreciate the view" and "a view that is to truly be
appreciated" are split infinitives. But "to be truly appreciated"
and "to have been truly appreciated" are *not* split infinitives.
Indeed, the majority of expressions thought by some to be split
infinitives turn out, on examination, not to be split infinitives
at all.[69]

Second, the fact is that the problem of the split infinitive is a
problem of rhetoric, not of grammar. Often a split infinitive is
a needlessly ungraceful way of saying a thing. There is not much
excuse for writing "to adequately within the limits of a paragraph explain the subject is impossible." But one might well
wish to write "to adequately explain the subject within the

---

[69] Because of their misconception as to what a split infinitive really is, some
have reached the erroneous conclusion that an adverbial modifier must never
be placed between parts of a compound verb phrase, with the result that they
write in such an eccentric stvle as "I greatly have been disappointed" instead
of writing naturally "I have been greatly disappointed."

limits of a paragraph is impossible," in which case the infinitive
has been split deliberately.[70]

[70] It is a curious fact that some people will remember odd bits of misinformation about English usage—such as, that it is wrong to split an infinitive, it is wrong to end a sentence with a preposition (see pp. 352 f.), it is wrong to refer to persons with the relative pronoun *that* (see p. 225), and it is wrong to begin a sentence with *and, but,* or *for*—long after they have forgotten many of the really important matters of English grammar and rhetoric. Here is a problem the psychologist might try his hand at.

CHAPTER 8

Adjectives[1]

An adjective is a word that describes or modifies a noun. Any expression — single word, phrase, or clause — that modifies a noun may be said to be adjectival in function.

blue sky   *bad* weather   *unforeseen* events
the man *with the green tie* [Phrase]
the man *who is wearing a green tie* [Clause]

A.   *Classes of Adjectives*

Adjectives may be divided into two general classes: descriptive adjectives and definitive adjectives.

1.   DESCRIPTIVE ADJECTIVES

A descriptive adjective names a quality or characteristic of the substantive modified.

ripe apples   *tall* man   *ample* food

a. Proper adjectives. A proper adjective is a proper noun used as an adjective or a descriptive adjective derived from a proper noun.

Greek architecture   *Grecian* urn   a *Christmas* holiday
a *Fourth of July* celebration

[1] For the use of adjectives in sentences see pp. 87 ff.

2.   DEFINITIVE ADJECTIVES

A definitive adjective specifies which or how many. Definitive adjectives may be classed as follows:

a. Demonstrative adjectives

that boy   *those* apples   *this* church   *these* children

b. Indefinite adjectives

any man   *some* good   *which* book   *what* course   *many* nations   *much* competition   *either* door

c. Numerical adjectives.   Numerical adjectives are of two classes:

1. Cardinal numerals. Cardinal numerals answer the question "How many?" The cardinals are *one, two, three,* etc.

six men   *two* cars   *seven* dogs

2. Ordinal numerals. Ordinal numerals answer the question "In which order?" The ordinals are *first, second, third,* etc.

d. Articles.   The definite article *the* and the indefinite articles *a* and *an* are regarded as adjectival in function.

the house   *a* unit   *an* hour

1. *The.* In its ordinary use the definite article *the* designates an object as distinguished from other objects of the same class.

This is not *the* book that I meant.
I did not give you *the* reason.
The tree in the front yard is a hard maple.

NOTE 1.   The spelling *ye* for *the* in archaic expressions—"Ye Olde Gift Shoppe" — arose from the fact that the Old English character thorn (þ) for the sound *th* was mistaken for the letter *y*, which it resembles. *Ye* is, then, in such expressions exactly the same thing as *the* and should be pronounced exactly like *the* — not "yee."
NOTE 2.   *The* in such expressions as "the more the merrier" is not the article *the* but an old adverb form. See pp. 103 f.

324 A GRAMMAR OF PRESENT-DAY ENGLISH

a) The definite article may be used with a strong demonstrative effect.

Do you mean *the* Robert Frost?

b) The definite article is often used in an indefinite sense — in the sense of "any" or "every" — to designate a whole class.

The beginner needs to be conservative.
The dog and the cat seem to have a natural antipathy toward each other.

c) *The* is sometimes a part of a proper name.

The Dalles   *The* Hague   *The* Honorable Nelson Rockefeller

d) The article *the* is sometimes used with an adjective to form a plural noun. (See also p. 95.)

The rich are getting richer and *the* poor are getting poorer.
The dead are at peace; *the* living have many sorrows to bear.

2. A (*an*). In ordinary use the indefinite article *a* (*an*) designates an object as merely one among other objects of the same class.

A book may be *a* great comfort at times.
I should like *an* apple, please.
I have *an* uncle who is *an* architect.

a) A or *an*. The article *a* is used before a consonant sound: *a* broom, *a* bag, *a* cat; before a sounded *h*: *a* history book, *a* helpmate, *a* hopeful outlook; and before any other word having an initial consonantal sound: *a* union, *a* one-man god, *a* ewe.

NOTE. Some prefer to write *an* before an *h*-sound in an unaccented syllable: *an* historical fact (but: *a* history of England).

The article *an* is used before a vowel sound: *an* apple, *an* epoch, *an* island; and before an unsounded *h*: *an* hour, *an* heir, *an* herb (pronounced ûrb) or *a* herb (pronounced hûrb).

b) Sometimes the article *a* (*an*) is placed immediately before a noun that is modified by an adjective or an adjective that in turn is modified by an adverb.

many a man   such an expression   too sweeping a statement
what a notion   so great an ordeal   how great a menace

c) Although *a* (*an*) means "one," it may modify a plural noun used as a unit, even though the plural noun may require a plural verb. In such expressions as *a few books, a dozen eggs, a great many persons,* an original preposition (*of*) has dropped out, the original expression being "a few of books," "a dozen of eggs," "a great many of persons."

> Only a few books are needed to start a private library.
> A dozen eggs cost fifty cents in those days.
> A great many persons have joined the organization.
> A dozen pencils have to be sharpened.

d) In such expressions as *once a week, twice an hour,* the article *a* (*an*) has the meaning of "each" or "every": "once each (*or* every) week," "twice each (*or* every) hour."

e) In such expressions as *a-fishing, a-swimming, a-hunting,* the *a* is not the article but a weakened form of the preposition *on,* the original form being "on fishing," "on swimming," "on hunting." (See also p. 352.)

In some cases the *a* has become an actual part of the word: *asleep, aboard.* (Compare "*aboard* the vessel" and "on board the vessel.")

B.   *Expressions Used as Adjectives*

1.   NOUN USED AS ADJECTIVE

Words that have the form of nouns may modify nouns and thus become adjectival in function.

a. Possessive noun

> John's hat. [*John's* is an adjectival modifier of *hat.*]
> the King of England's throne. [*King of England's* is an adjectival modifier of *throne.*]
> the parents' responsibility. [*Parents'* is an adjectival modifier of *responsibility.*]

b. Noun modifier of another noun[2]

a bird fancier [The noun *bird* is an adjectival modifier of *fancier*.]
the language laboratory. [The noun *language* is an adjectival modifier of *laboratory*.]

2.   PRONOUN USED AS ADJECTIVE

Words that have the form of pronouns may modify nouns and thus become adjectival in function. They are sometimes called pronominal adjectives.

a. Personal pronoun

my friend	your house
our country	their ingenuity

NOTE.   *Mine* and *thine* are used as adjectives in poetry.
Mine eyes have seen the glory . . .
(For *mine, ours, yours, theirs*, used as substantives see pp. 221 f.)

b. Relative pronoun

I know a man whose name is Reginald. [*Whose* is an adjectival modifier of *name*.]
Choose whichever basket you prefer. [*Whichever* is an adjectival modifier of *basket*.]

c. Interrogative pronoun

What alternative do you suggest? [*What* is an adjectival modifier of *alternative*.]
I wonder which door he will enter. [*Which* is an adjectival modifier of *door*.]

d. Demonstrative pronoun

This apple is ripe. [*This* is an adjectival modifier of *apple*.]
Those tomatoes look good. [*Those* is an adjectival modifier of *tomatoes*.]

---

[2] A noun in this use is sometimes called a noun adjunct.

e. Indefinite pronoun

Either book will do. [*Either* is an adjectival modifier of *book*.]
Some people always find fault. [*Some* is an adjectival modifier
of *people*.]
Do you have any money? [*Any* is an adjectival modifier of
money.]

3. OTHER PARTS OF SPEECH USED AS ADJECTIVES

See pp. 94 f.

4. PHRASES USED AS ADJECTIVES

See p. 88.

5. CLAUSES USED AS ADJECTIVES

See pp. 169 ff.

c. Comparison of Adjectives

1. THREE DEGREES OF COMPARISON

Comparison is the name given to the change in the form
of an adjective (or an adverb) to indicate degree. There are
three degrees of comparison — positive, comparative, and superlative. The positive degree is represented in the ordinary form
of the adjective without any suggestion of comparison. The
comparative degree represents an increase or diminution of that
which has been expressed in the positive degree. The superlative
degree represents the greatest or the least degree of that which
has been expressed in the positive degree.

Most descriptive adjectives are capable of being compared;
but definitive adjectives are not comparable.

a. Positive degree. The positive degree is used when there is
no suggestion of comparison between two or more items.

Mr. Simpson is a *tall* man.

328 A GRAMMAR OF PRESENT-DAY ENGLISH

b. Comparative degree. The comparative degree is used when a comparison is made between only two items.

Mr. Simpson is the *taller* of the two men.

c. Superlative degree. The superlative degree is used when a comparison is made among three or more items.

Mr. Simpson is the *tallest* of the three men.

2. USAGES IN COMPARISONS

Certain conventions are generally observed in the use of the comparative and superlative degrees.

a. Comparative degree between two items only. The comparative degree is used when the comparison is made between only two items. The second term of the comparison should exclude the first.

Jimmie is smarter than any other boy in his class. [Not: Jimmie is smarter than any boy in his class. This would mean that he was smarter than himself, which is nonsense.]

b. Superlative degree among three or more items. The superlative degree is used when the comparison is made among three or more items. The second term of the comparison should include the first.

Jimmie is the smartest boy in his class. [Not: Jimmie is the smartest of any other boy in his class.]

NOTE. When the total in the class of items being compared does not exceed two, the superlative is frequently used, especially in spoken discourse, in place of the comparative demanded by the rule. We say "Get your best foot forward"—not "Get your better foot forward."

c. Adjectives incapable of comparison. Although many adjectives designating absolute qualities — *white, round, perfect, chief, unique* — are said to be incapable of comparison, many of them are compared in contemporary prose. That is, "more perfect" and "most perfect" are apparently thought of as stages in a progression toward absolute perfection. One sheet of paper may rightly be said to be "whiter" than another, even though the purist may insist that one should say that one piece of paper is "more nearly white" than another.

3.   METHODS OF FORMING COMPARISONS

There are two methods of making comparative and superlative forms. In accordance with one method a comparative is formed by adding -er to the positive degree and a superlative by adding -est to the positive degree. In accordance with the other method a comparative is formed by preceding the positive degree with *more* or *less* and a superlative by preceding the positive degree with *most* or *least*.

Although most adjectives of regular comparison admit theoretically of both methods, actual practice tends to favor one method, the method that produces the greater euphony. Certain general principles governing a choice between the two methods may be listed.

a. Adjectives of one syllable.   Adjectives of one syllable and many of two syllables usually have the -er and -est forms.

tall, taller, tallest   thick, thicker, thickest   handsome, handsomer, handsomest

b. Adjectives of two syllables.   Adjectives of two syllables and adjectives ending in *y* usually may have either form.

absurd, absurder, absurdest [or] absurd, more absurd, most absurd
happy, happier, happiest [or] happy, more happy, most happy

c. Adjectives of more than two syllables.   Adjectives of more than two syllables usually have the *more* and *most* forms, especially adjectives ending in -able, -al, -ful, -ic, -ile, -ious, -ose, and -ous.

beautiful, more beautiful, most beautiful
amiable, more amiable, most amiable
trivial, more trivial, most trivial
gracious, more gracious, most gracious

4.   IRREGULAR COMPARISONS

Some adjectives have irregular or defective comparisons, having lost some forms that have been replaced by other forms of similar meaning.

Positive	Comparative	Superlative
bad	worse	worst
far	farther, further	farthest, furthest
good,	better	best
	inner	inmost, innermost
late	later, latter	latest, last
little	less, lesser	least
many, much	more	most
near	nearer	nearest, next
old	older, elder	oldest, eldest
	outer	outermost, outmost
top		topmost
	upper	uppermost
well (relating to health)	better	

5.   LATIN COMPARATIVES

Certain Latin comparatives have neither positive nor superlative degree and are followed by *to* instead of *than* used with other comparatives: *anterior to, inferior to, posterior to, prior to, senior to, superior to.*

This fabric is inferior to that.
The bidder must file a bond prior to submitting a bid.

D.   Usages in Adjectives

1.   ADJECTIVE WITH A LINK VERB

An adjective to characterize the subject, not an adverb to designate manner of action of a verb, is demanded after a link verb (see pp. 43 ff.). For a link verb connects a subjective complement to a subject; and an adverb cannot normally function as a subjective complement.

Typical link verbs are *be, seem,* and *become.* Other verbs, such as *appear, come, go, grow,* may at times function as link verbs. Verbs having to do with the senses, such as *look, feel, taste,* may function as link verbs. Verbs having to do with health often function as link verbs. And verbs in the passive voice sometimes have a link function. All such verbs may, then, demand adjectives as subjective complements.

a. "Be," "seem," "become." Such verbs as *be, seem,* and *become* commonly function as link verbs and take adjectives as subjective complements. (For *be* as a notional verb see p. 43.)

Jim is certainly very happy. [*Happy,* an adjective, is used as a subjective complement to characterize *Jim,* the subject.]

He seemed hesitant. [*Hesitant,* an adjective, is used as a subjective complement to characterize *he,* the subject.]

The children became restless. [*Restless,* an adjective, is used as a subjective complement to characterize *children,* the subject.]

b. "Appear," "come," "get." Such verbs as *appear, come, go, get, grow, lie, prove, remain, stay, turn* may at times serve as link verbs and take adjective subjective complements.

Glenn always appears sure of himself. [*Sure,* an adjective, is used as a subjective complement to characterize *Glenn,* the subject.]

My locket clasp has come loose. [*Loose,* an adjective, is used as a subjective complement to characterize *clasp,* the subject.]

At times I get discouraged. [*Discouraged,* an adjective, is used as a subjective complement to characterize *I,* the subject.]

His horse went lame on the back stretch. [*Lame,* an adjective, is used to characterize *horse,* the subject.]

Our poplars have grown very tall.

The rumor proved false.

We must remain quiet.

The cream did not stay sweet.

She turned red with embarrassment.

c. "Smell," "taste," "feel." A verb — such as *smell, taste, feel, look, sound* — having to do with the senses often functions as a link verb and takes an adjective as a subjective complement to characterize the subject rather than an adverb to designate manner of action of a verb.

This apple tastes sour. [*Sour*, an adjective, is used as a subjective complement after *tastes*, here functioning as a link verb.]

I tasted the concoction cautiously. [*Cautiously*, an adverb, is used here to designate the manner in which the action of the verb takes place.]

His story does not sound very plausible. [*Plausible*, an adjective, is used as a subjective complement after *does sound*, here functioning as a link verb.]

The bell sounds loud. [*Loud*, an adjective, is used as a subjective complement after *sounds*, here functioning as a link verb.]

He sounded the bell loudly. [*Loudly*, an adverb, is used here to designate the manner in which the action of the verb takes place.]

Your dinner smells fine. [*Fine*, an adjective, is used as a subjective complement after *smells*, here functioning as a link verb.]

He smelled the flowers suspiciously. [*Suspiciously*, an adverb, is used here to designate the manner in which the action of the verb takes place.]

The child's hand felt soft. [*Soft*, an adjective, is used as a subjective complement after *felt*, here functioning as a link verb.]

He felt the lining of the coat carefully. [*Carefully*, an adverb, is used here to designate the manner in which the action of the verb takes place.]

That man looks suspicious. [*Suspicious*, an adjective, is used as a subjective complement after *looks*, here functioning as a link verb.]

He looked slyly about him. [*Slyly*, an adverb, is used here to designate the manner in which the action of the verb takes place.]

d. "Well," "ill," "good," "bad."   An adjective, such as *good, bad, ill, well,* is used as a subjective complement after a link verb in expressions concerning health to characterize the subject rather than an adverb to designate manner of action of a verb.[3]

[3] The reason such expressions may cause trouble is that there happen to be two words *well*. One is the regular adverb *well*, and the other is an adjective *well*. It is the adjective *well*, not the adverb, that is demanded in such an expression as "I feel well." But if one falsely assumes that this is an adverb, he might, by analogy, feel compelled to say "I feel badly." Since *badly* has the regular form and function of an adverb, there is no more justification, on the basis of grammatical analogy, for saying "I feel badly" than there is for saying "I feel happily," "I feel illy," or "The medicine tastes bitterly."
Of course, when other than a link verb is used, an adverbial form is called for: He acted badly; he behaved badly; he managed badly.

I feel good (*or* fine, splendid, excellent, miserable, fit, able, bad, ill) today. [*Not:* I feel finely (*or* splendidly, excellently, miserably, fitly, ably, badly, illy) today.]

She looked sick (*or* ill, miserable).

She appeared sickly. [*Sickly* is an adjective.]

e. Adjective after a passive verb used as a link verb. A verb in the passive voice may have a linking function, joining a subjective complement to a subject. (This complement represents what was an objective complement in the active construction. See pp. 49 ff.)

The rope was tied tight. [The passive verb *was tied* has a linking function, joining *tight* (an adjective), a subjective complement, to *rope*, the subject. (The active construction was "They tied the rope tight," in which *tight* is an objective complement.)]

The rope was tied tightly. [Here *tightly*, an adverb, designates the manner of the action of the verb.]

The rivet was heated red-hot. [The passive verb *was heated* has a linking function, joining *red-hot* (an adjective), a subjective complement, to *rivet*, the subject. (The active construction was "They heated the rivet red-hot.")]

The rivet was heated sufficiently. [Here *sufficiently*, an adverb, designates the manner of the action of the verb.]

2. ADJECTIVE AS AN OBJECTIVE COMPLEMENT

An adjective, not an adverb, is used as an objective complement. (Sometimes, of course, a situation demands an adverb as a modifier of the verb. And occasionally the two constructions are equally correct as far as good usage is concerned, but they do not mean the same thing and so are not to be thought of as interchangeable.)

Be sure to tie the rope tight. [*Tight*, an adjective, functioning as an objective complement, describes the condition of the direct object *rope* as the result of the action of the verb on it.]

Please tie my tie neatly. [*Neatly*, an adverb, functioning as a modifier of the verb *tie*, designates the manner in which the action of the verb takes place.]

They have restored the Greek temple complete. [*Complete*, an adjective, functioning as an objective complement, describes the condition of the direct object *temple* as the result of the action of the verb on it.]

They have restored the Greek temple completely. [*Completely,* an adverb, functioning as a modifier of *have restored,* designates the manner in which the action of the verb takes place.]

3.   OTHER USAGES

a. *"This kind," "these kinds."* Note especially the need of the singular *this* or *that* with singular nouns like *kind* and *sort.*

I like this kind of day. [*Not:* I like these kind of days.]

That sort of examination irritates me. [*Not:* Those sort of examinations irritate me.]

Those kinds of marks are intelligible to a shipping clerk.

NOTE.   Do not insert a superfluous *a* after *kind of* or *sort of.*

You are the sort of friend that I prize. [*Not:* You are the sort of a friend that I prize.]

b. *"Few" and "little."* *Few* answers the question "How many?" *Little* answers the question "How much?"

He has few friends and little ambition to acquire more.

c. *Repetition of an adjective.* Clearness may demand the repetition of an adjective, especially an article. Sometimes the change will necessitate a change in the number of the noun modified.

I have a black and white coat. [*Or,* with a different meaning] I have a black and a white coat.

I know the secretary and treasurer. [*Or*] I know the secretary and the treasurer.

I want some ham and eggs. [*Or*] I want some ham and some eggs.

The Old and New Worlds have many problems to solve. [*Or*] The Old and the New World have many problems to solve.

The poet repeats his theme in the third, fifth, and seventh stanzas. [*Or*] The poet repeats his theme in the third, the fifth, and the seventh stanza.

The novel developed rapidly in the eighteenth and nineteenth centuries. [*Or*] The novel developed rapidly in the eighteenth and the nineteenth century.

d. "All" and "both."   *All* and *both* usually precede any other modifier of a noun that they modify; but they usually follow a pronoun that they modify. They may follow an auxiliary verb.

He piled all the books on the floor. [*All* modifies *books.*]
He spoke to both the disappointed boys. [*Both* modifies *boys.*]
I have not read them all. [*All* modifies *them.*]
She gently chided us both. [*Both* modifies *us.*]
We had all departed. [*All* modifies *we.*]
They had both consented to the agreement. [*Both* modifies *they.*]
We waited patiently all day long. [*All* modifies *day* (*long* also being a modifier of *day*).]

e. "Else."   *Else,* an adjective, follows the expression it modifies. *Else* may be regarded as a part of a phrase in such expressions as *anybody else, someone else, no one else, who else.* For the possessive in *'s* (*anybody else's, who else's*) see pp. 215 and 232.

I forgot all else. [*Else* modifies *all.*]
Does anybody else wish to ask a question? [*Else* modifies *anybody.*]
That is somebody else's overcoat.
That is nobody else's but John's.
Just who else's do you think it is?

f. "Half."   *Half* used as an adjective may precede a modifier (an article) of a noun that it modifies, or it may come between a modifier (an article) and the noun it modifies. (See also p. 254.)

He waited half an hour. [*Half,* an adjective, modifies *hour.*]
He waited for a full half hour. [*Half,* an adjective, modifies *hour.*]

NOTE.   Of course, *half* may be used as a noun.
Half of these apples are rotten. [*Half,* a noun, is the subject of *are.*]
I ate only half of the pie. [*Half,* a noun, is the direct object of *ate.*]

g. *"Either," "neither," "any."*   *Either* and *neither* are used when two items are involved; *any* is used when more than two items are involved.

You will find the expression in either dictionary. [Two dictionaries are involved.]
You will find the expression in any dictionary. [More than t vo dictionaries are involved.]
The expression is in neither dictionary. [Two dictionaries are involved.]
The expression is not in any dictionary. [More than two dictionaries are involved.]

h. *"Each" and "every."*   *Each* and *every* as adjectives qualify singular nouns, although the nouns may, of course, be used in a collective sense.

Each one of us is responsible to himself alone. [Not: Each one of us are responsible to ourselves alone.]
Every committee has its chairman. [Not: Every committee have their chairmen.]

i. *Usages in comparisons.*   See pp. 328 ff.

4.   **DISTINCTIONS BETWEEN ADJECTIVES AND ADVERBS**

See pp. 330 f. and 333 f.

CHAPTER 9

Adverbs[1]

A. **Kinds of Adverbs**

Adverbs may be classified on the basis of the grammatical functions they perform.

For interrogative adverbs see pp. 101 f.; for relative adverbs, p. 102; for correlative adverbs, pp. 102 f.; for independent adverbs, p. 104; for transitional adverbs, pp. 105 f.

B. **Meanings of Adverbs**

Adverbs may express various notions in relation to the element that the adverb modifies. (For meanings of adverbial clauses see pp. 183 ff.)

1. **TIME**

The adverb answers the question "When?" and usually modifies the verb.

I shall *soon* know the truth.
Let's go *now*.
I never knew that *before*.

2. **PLACE**

The adverb answers the question "Where?" and usually modifies a verb. (It may be noted that many adverbs of place may also function as prepositions; see p. 108.)

[1] For construction of adverbs in sentences see pp. 98 ff.

We went *inside*.
There is the book I have been looking for.
He struggled *forward*.

3.   MANNER

The adverb answers the question "How?" and usually modifies a verb.

She played the violin *beautifully*.
I could not do *better* myself.
He blundered *badly*.

4.   DEGREE

The adverb answers the question "To what extent?"

I am *very* tired.
That is *too* soon.
She is *quite* happy.

5.   MISCELLANEOUS

The adverb expresses various other notions. In this miscellaneous group may be placed expressions that seem to have little or no grammatical function in the statements in which they appear. Here may be included those adverb-like words — such as *however, therefore, nevertheless* — that effect a rhetorical transition rather than a grammatical connection between statements, expressions which this book has perferred to call transitional adverbs (see pp. 105 f.).

Also may be included here expressions that seem to modify a whole statement rather than any one item in the statement. Yet in the interest of simplicity such adverbs may be regarded as modifiers of the verb of the statement in which they appear.

I *scarcely* know what to say. [*Scarcely*, an adverb, may be said to modify the whole statement, or it may be regarded simply as a modifier of the verb *know*.]
She *never* fails to smile.
John has *not* arrived.
Evidently he missed the train.

c. *Forms of Adverbs*

Although *-ly* is often thought of as a characteristic adverbial ending, it is the function of the word, not its form, that determines whether it is an adverb or not. Note that (*a*) some words ending in *-ly* are both adjectives and adverbs; (*b*) not all adverbs end in *-ly*; (*c*) not all words ending in *-ly* are adverbs; and (*d*) some adverbs have two forms, not necessarily to be used interchangeably.

1. "ONLY," "LIKELY"

Such words as *only, likely, kindly, hourly, daily, yearly*, are both adjectives and adverbs.

This is the *only* copy I own. He is a *kindly* man. We have *daily* exercises. That is a *likely* story. [Adjectives]
He is *only* pretending. She *kindly* offered to help. I am paid *monthly*. He *likely* missed his train. [Adverbs]

2. "HERE," "THERE"

Such words as *here, there, far, near, soon, fast*, although they do not end in *-ly*, are adverbs.

Come *here*. I shall go *there*. He can throw a ball *far*. Walk *fast*.

3. "LOVELY," "SEEMLY"

Such words as *lovely, seemly, manly, friendly*, although they end in *-ly*, are actually adjectives.

Tex is a *friendly* dog. He is a *manly* boy. That is a *lovely* scene. His conduct became *unseemly*.

4. "SLOW," "SLOWLY"

Some adverbs have two forms: *slow, slowly; quick, quickly; cheap, cheaply; right, rightly; sharp, sharply*. The shorter form[2] is the one commonly used in short commands and in comparisons with *as . . . as* (or *not so . . . as*).

---

[2] The shorter form (sometimes miscalled the "clipped" form, although the shorter form existed before the *-ly* form evolved) must not be confused with a true adjective functioning as a subjective or objective complement. (See also pp. 330 ff.)

He closed the door *slowly*. He *quickly* leaped to one side. It does not pay to buy *cheaply* made goods. She is *rightly* concerned. He regarded the man *sharply*. [The shorter forms would be incorrect.] Drive slow [*or* slowly]. Come quick [*or* quickly.] Buy cheap [*or* cheaply.] Do right [*or* rightly]. Play fair [*or* fairly]. Look sharp [*or* sharply]. [Either form would be correct; but the shorter form is more common, especially in spoken discourse.]

Drive as slow [*or* slowly] as you can. Come as quick [*or* quickly] as you can. Play as fair [*or* fairly] as your opponent. You do not need to talk so loud [*or* loudly] as to wake people up.

5.   "HARD," "HARDLY"

In some cases the two adverbial forms have slightly different meanings and may not be used interchangeably; for instance, *hard* and *hardly*, *late* and *lately*.

I have worked *hard* all day. [*Not:* hardly]
She *hardly* knows what to say. [*Not:* hard]
Do not come *late*. [*Not:* lately]
It has not rained *lately*. [*Not:* late]

D.   Comparisons of Adverbs

1.   ADVERBS COMPARED AND NOT COMPARED

Many adverbs, like adjectives, may be compared: *neatly, more neatly, most neatly*. But many adverbs may not be compared: *here, there, now, then, when, where, why, how*.

2.   METHODS OF COMPARISON

As in the case of adjectives, there are two basic methods of forming the comparative and superlative degrees of adverbs.

a. Comparative in "more," superlative in "most." The comparative degree of most adverbs is formed by placing *more* (or

---

Tie the rope tight. [*Tight* is an adjective functioning as an objective complement.]
This coffee tastes bitter. [*Bitter* is an adjective functioning as a subjective complement.]
They arrived safe and sound. [*Safe* and *sound* are adjectives functioning as subjective complements.]

less) before the positive degree; and the superlative degree is formed by placing *most* (or *least*) before the positive degree.

Positive	Comparative	Superlative
gladly	more gladly	most gladly
hopefully	more hopefully	most hopefully
satisfactorily	more satisfactorily	most satisfactorily

b. Comparative in "-er," superlative in "-est." The comparative degree of a few adverbs is formed by adding *-er* to the positive degree; and the superlative degree is formed by adding *-est* to the positive degree. (All but *soon* may also be used as adjectives.)

Positive	Comparative	Superlative
near	nearer	nearest
early	earlier	earliest
slow	slower	slowest
soon	sooner	soonest
fast	faster	fastest
loud	louder	loudest
quick	quicker	quickest

c. Either method. A few adverbs may be compared in either way.

Positive	Comparative	Superlative
often	oftener *or* more often	oftenest *or* most often

d. Irregular comparisons. A number of adverbs have irregular comparisons.

Positive	Comparative	Superlative
ill, badly	worse	worst
far	farther, further	farthest, furthest
late	later	latest, last
little	less	least
much	more	most
well	better	best

E.   *Usages in Adverbs*

Adverbs and adjectives offer many problems of correct usage. A comparison between adjectives and adverbs will offer solutions to most of them.

1.   ADVERB TO DESIGNATE MANNER OF ACTION

The adverb is used to designate the manner in which an action of a verb is performed. An adverb, not an adjective, is used to modify an adjective or another adverb.

He combed his hair neatly. [*Not:* He combed his hair neat. The adverb *neatly* designates the manner of the action of the verb *combed.*]

We surely enjoyed your lecture. [*Not:* We sure enjoyed your lecture. The adverb *surely* is demanded to modify the verb *enjoyed.*]

Mr. Hammond is somewhat better today. [*Not:* Mr. Hammond is some better today. For the adverb *somewhat* is demanded to modify the adjective *better.*]

I feel really [*or* very] good. [*Not:* I feel real good. For the adverb *really* or *very* is demanded to modify the adjective *good.*]

2.   ADVERBS AND ADJECTIVES SOMETIMES CONFUSED

There are a few adjectives and adverbs that, because of their close resemblance, are sometimes confused.

a. "Near," "nearly."   *Near* may be used as an adverb of place. *Nearly* is used as an adverb of degree. They should not be confused. (*Near* may, of course, be used also as a preposition.)

The car drew near. [*Near* is an adverb of place.]

I nearly died of curiosity. [*Nearly* is an adverb of degree.]

The people came from near and far. [*Near* (as well as *far*) is an adverb functioning as a noun, the object of the preposition *from.*]

He came near falling. [That is, "He came close to falling." *Near* functions as a preposition governing the gerund *falling.*]

We live near a lake. [*Near* is a preposition governing *lake.*]

b. "Most" and "almost." *Most* may be used as an adverb in forming the superlative degree (see pp. 340 f.); otherwise *most* is usually an adjective. *Almost*, which means "nearly," regularly modifies verbs, adjectives, and adverbs. *Most* and *almost* should not be confused.

I am most certain of it. [*Most* here functions as an adverb to form the superlative degree of *certain* and modifies *certain*. The meaning is "I am certain to the greatest degree."]

I am almost certain of it. [*Almost* functions as a regular adverbial modifier of the adjective *certain*. The meaning is "I am nearly certain of it."]

I like most people. [*Most* is an adjective modifying *people*.]

The moon is almost full now. [*Almost* is an adverb modifying the adjective *full*.]

She almost collapsed at the last moment. [*Almost* is an adverb modifying the verb *collapsed*.]

He almost always goes to church. [*Not*: He most always goes to church. The adverb *almost* is demanded as an adverbial modifier of the adverb *always*.]

3. "HARDLY," "SCARCELY"

Inasmuch as such adverbs as *hardly* and *scarcely* imply a negative idea, they should not be used in negative statements.

I can scarcely [*or* hardly] believe my eyes. [*Not*: I can't hardly (*or* scarcely) believe my eyes.]

4. "VERY" WITH A PARTICIPLE

For the misuse of *very* with a participle see pp. 308 f.

5. ADJECTIVES FOR SUBJECTIVE AND OBJECTIVE COMPLEMENTS

See pp. 330 ff.

6. VERB + ADVERB COMBINATIONS

See p. 55.

CHAPTER 10

Prepositions[1]

A preposition is an expression governing a substantive in the objective case, called its object, and joining this substantive to some other element in the sentence. The preposition and its object and any modifiers of the substantive or of the preposition and the substantive constitute a prepositional phrase. (See also pp. 111 f.)

A. Kinds of Prepositions

1. SIMPLE PREPOSITION

A preposition may be a single word, in which case it is called a simple preposition.

about	before	by	into	outside	to
above	behind	down	like	over	under
across	below	except	near	past	until
after	beneath	for	of	since	up
against	beside	from	off	through	upon
around	between	in	on	throughout	with
at	beyond	inside	out	till	without

2. PHRASAL PREPOSITION

A preposition may consist of more than one word, in which case it is called a phrasal preposition.

[1] For constructions of prepositions in sentences see pp. 111 ff.

according to	by reason of	in spite of
as for	by way of	instead of *
as to	for the sake of	on account of
because of	in keeping with	out of
by means of	in regard to	with respect to

B. **Usages in Prepositions**

1. **SUBSTANTIVE IN THE OBJECTIVE CASE**

The object of a preposition is in the objective case. When a relative or an interrogative pronoun functioning as the object of a preposition comes first and so precedes its preposition, care needs to be taken that the proper form of the pronoun is used.[2] (See also p. 241 and p. 243.)

Whom were you with yesterday? [Not: Who were you with yesterday?]
I do not know whom you are thinking of. [Not: I do not know who you are thinking of.]
Between you and me there ought to be a cordial understanding. [Not: Between you and I there ought to be a cordial understanding.]
Everyone except George and me had gone home. [Not: Everyone except George and I had gone home.]

2. **DOUBLE POSSESSIVE**

By an old and well-established English idiom, sometimes called the double genitive, possession may be shown by two methods at the same time, by an *of*-phrase and by a possessive form of the substantive. (See also pp. 217 and 221.)

You are no friend of mine. [Possession is shown by the prepositional *of*-phrase and by the possessive form *mine*.]
I like very much that fountain pen of yours. [Possession is shown

---

[2] The nominative form of the interrogative pronoun *who* at the beginning of a sentence, notwithstanding its grammatical function as the object of a preposition, has found general acceptance in informal discourse. Although there are logical explanations for this use (position, emphasis, similarity to non-inflected forms like *what* and *which*), the objective form *whom* is the one usually found in formal discourse.

by the prepositional *of*-phrase and by the possessive form *yours*. Actually, possession is shown three times here: once by the *of*-phrase; again by the *r* in *your*; and finally by the *s* in *yours*.]

That must remain a responsibility of the President's. [Note the slight difference in meaning in "That must remain a responsibility of the President."]

Did you notice that curious portrait of Father's? [Note the difference in meaning in "Did you notice that curious portrait of Father?"]

3. APPOSITIVE "OF"-PHRASE

A common English idiom is seen in the use of an *of*-phrase in an appositive relationship to a substantive. *Of* in such a construction may be regarded as an expletive (see p. 149).

The state of New York has the greatest number of electoral votes. [*New York*, introduced by the expletive *of*, is in apposition with *state*. Or, *of* may be regarded as a preposition with the whole prepositional phrase *of New York* in apposition with *state*.]

He bears the title of Comptroller. [*Comptroller*, introduced by the expletive *of*, is in apposition with *title*. Or, *of* may be regarded as a preposition governing *Comptroller*, with the whole prepositional phrase *of Comptroller* in apposition with *title*.]

4. PREPOSITION DEMANDED BY IDIOM

Many perplexing problems in English usage have to do with prepositions. Consult the dictionary for shades of difference in meaning of the following.

abhorrence of
abhorrent to
abide by, with
absolve by, from
accommodate to, with
account for, to
adapted for, from, to
admit of, to
advantage of, over
adverse to
advise of, with
agree in, on, to, upon, with
agreeable to, with
alarmed at, by
amused at, by, with
analogous to, with
angry at, with
anxious about, for
appeal to, with
apply for, to
apposition to, with
apropos of

argue about, against, for, with
ask about, after, for, of
averse to
care about, for
careless about, of
cause for, of
center at, in, upon [not about]
compare to, with
concerned about, for, in
conducive to
confide in, to
conform to, with
connect by, with
consist in, of
contend against, for, with
contrast to, with
convenient for, to, with
correspond to, with
danger in, of
deal in, with
depend on or upon
desirous of
die from, of, with
differ about, from, with (see p. 350)
different from (see p. 350)
dispute about, over, with
dissent from
distinguish among, between, from
divide between, among
enter in, into, upon
entrust to, with
expert at, in
free from, of
frown at, upon
furnish by, to, with
give for, to
glad about, of or because of
grateful for, to
grieve at, for, over
guard against, from
happen on or upon, to
hinder from, in
in behalf of, on behalf of

independent of
indulge in, with
infer from
initiated into
inquire about, after, for, into, of
inseparable from
instill into
intercede for, with
interest in, with
interfere in, with
join in, to, with
jump at, to
liable for, to
live at, in, on
meddle in, with
necessity for, of
need for, of
overcome by, with
parallel between, to, with
part from, with
ponder on or upon, over
possessed by, of, with
prejudice against
preside at, over
prevail against, upon, over, with
provide against, for, with
quarrel about, over, with
reason about, with
reconcile to, with
rejoice at, in, with
relieve from, of
result from, in
retire from, into, upon
seek after, for, out
strive against, for, with
supply to, with
trade in, with
useful for, in
variance with
vary from, in, with
vexed at, by, with
view to, of
wait for, on

5.   **SUSPENDED PREPOSITIONAL CONSTRUCTION**

Care must be exercised to use the preposition that idiom demands in the so-called suspended prepositional construction, the construction in which one object must serve two different prepositions. (The construction is one that should be used sparingly by the inexperienced writer.)

He seems to have a deep interest in and a keen appreciation of effective writing. [*Not:* He seems to have a deep interest and a keen appreciation of effective writing.]

6.   **OMITTED PREPOSITIONS**

Idiom not only permits but often demands the omission of prepositions, especially in expressions having to do with measurements. The noun, originally the object of a preposition, is now thought of as functioning as an adverbial modifier and is sometimes called an adverbial objective (see p. 106).

He went home Sunday. [That is, "He went to home on Sunday." But *home* and *Sunday* are now regarded as nouns functioning as adverbial modifiers of *went*.]

He is six feet tall. [That is, "He is tall by six feet." But *feet* is now regarded as a noun functioning as an adverbial modifier of the adjective *tall*.]

That hat is not worth six dollars. [That is, "That hat is not worth to the extent of six dollars." But *dollars* is now regarded as a noun functioning as an adverbial modifier of the adjective *worth*.]

1.   **SUPERFLUOUS PREPOSITIONS**

Often one or the other preposition is superfluous in combinations like "at about" or "off of." Often *behind* is better than "in back of,"[3] *within* than "inside of," *without* than "outside of." "At" is superfluous when added to *where*, as is "up" when added to such verbs as *connect, divide, finish, settle.*

---

[3] It is curious that we regard "in front of" as standard yet frown on "in back of" for no good consistent reason. Here again is illustrated one of the vagaries of usage.

I'll be there at [or about] five-fifteen. [*Preferably not:* I'll be there at about five-fifteen.]

You will find the shovel behind the garage. [*Rather than, perhaps:* You will find the shovel in back of the garage.]

She got off the six o'clock train. [*Preferably not:* She got off of the six o'clock train.]

She got off on the six o'clock train. [Here *off* is an adverb modifying *got*, not a preposition.]

Where did you buy it? [*Not:* Where did you buy it at?]

When you finish the work we will settle our account. [*Preferably not:* When you finish up the work we will settle up our account.]

NOTE.   The preposition *of* is superfluous following such verbs as *smell, feel, taste,* used as transitive verbs.

Did you feel the ground to see if it was still wet? [*Not:* Did you feel of the ground to see if it was still wet?]

Taste this cream. [*Not:* Taste of this cream.]

Smell this camphor. [*Not:* Smell of this camphor.]

This milk tastes of milkweed. [*Tastes* here functions as an intransitive verb.]

That smells of carbolic acid. [*Smells* here functions as an intransitive verb.]

8.   "DUE TO"

Due to is avoided by many careful writers as a phrasal preposition equivalent to "because of" or "owing to." The traditional explanation for this usage distinction is that *due* is an adjective, not a preposition. Thus one thing may be "due to" another, in which case *due* has its established function as an adjective (a subjective complement.)[4]

Owing to [or because of] bad weather, our train was delayed more than an hour. [*Or*] The delay of our train for more than an hour was due to bad weather. [*Rather than:* Due to bad weather, our train was delayed more than an hour.]

---

[4] The use of *due to* as a phrasal preposition has grown so rapidly during the past few years that it seems destined to be accepted into good standing, a thing which has already happened to *owing to.* In fact, if *owing to* is acceptable there is no reason in logic why *due to* should not be accepted.

9.   "BECAUSE OF"

Because of is sometimes misused for *due* to.

His absence was due to illness. [*Not:* His absence was because of illness.]

10.   "FROM" AFTER "DIFFERENT" AND "DIFFERENTLY"

It is traditional American practice to use the preposition *from*, rather than the conjunction *than*, after *different* and *differently*. But *than* is so commonly used by careful speakers and writers, especially as an alternative to such cumbersome forms as *from that which*, *from what*, and *from the way that*, that it certainly should not be looked down on as substandard English. Of course, other prepositions, such as *about, in that, with*, are used according to the meaning intended.

My galoshes are different from yours.
I seem to feel somewhat differently from the way that you do in the matter. [Most people would probably use ". . . differently than you do. . . ." in this kind of sentence, certainly a more natural and graceful construction.]
I differ from [*or* with] you. We differ in minor details only.

NOTE.   The British very commonly use "different to."
New York is different to London. [British common usage]
New York is different than London. [American common usage]
New York is different from London. [American formal usage]

11.   "WITHOUT," "EXCEPT"

Without is used as a preposition (or as an adverb) but not as a conjunction. Similarly, the use of *except* (a preposition) as a conjunction is archaic. (But note that a noun clause may be used as the object of the preposition *except*.)

I shall have to go without my hat. [*Without* functions as a preposition, taking *hat* as its object.]
Within it was warm and cheery; without it was cold and uninviting. [Both *within* and *without* function here as adverbs, *within* modifying *was warm and cheery* and *without* modifying *was cold and uninviting*.]

You should never go hunting unless you have a hunting license. [*Not:* You should never go hunting without you have a hunting license. A conjunction like *unless* is demanded; and *without* cannot function as a conjunction. *Right:* You should never go hunting without a hunting license. For here *without* functions properly as a preposition.]

You will not be admitted unless you have a ticket. [*Not:* You will not be admitted except you have a ticket.]

I remember nothing except that the other car swerved toward us. [The object of the preposition *except* is the noun clause *that the other car swerved toward us.*]

12. "BUT" AS A PREPOSITION

But very commonly functions as a preposition in the sense of "except." (For the use of *but* as a pronoun see p. 227.)

We have questioned everybody but him. [That is, "We have questioned everybody except him."]

I did everything but preach. [The infinitive *(to) preach* is the object of the preposition *but;* and the whole prepositional phrase *but (to) preach* functions as an adjectival modifier of *everything.*]

I could not but wonder at his audacity. [That is, "I could not do anything except to wonder at his audacity," the infinitive *(to) wonder* being an object of the preposition *but.*]

NOTE 1. Present-day usage has established *but,* when it means *except,* as a preposition; and handbooks customarily advocate the objective case of a following pronoun. But because of the predominant conjunctive use of *but,* there has always been a strong feeling that it introduces a clause, even a severely elliptical clause. This variant (and perfectly logical) interpretation accounts for the occasional nominative pronoun found after *but;* e.g., the well-known line from Felicia Hemans' "Casabianca": "The boy stood on the burning deck, whence all but he had fled." [That is, "Whence all had fled, but he (had not fled)."]

NOTE 2. *Can but wonder, cannot but wonder,* and *cannot help wondering* are all equally correct; but they have slightly different meanings. *Can but wonder* means "can only wonder"; *cannot but wonder* means "cannot do anything but wonder"; *cannot help wondering* means "cannot avoid wondering." "Cannot help but wonder," although generally regarded as undesirable, is very common in present-day English, especially in spoken discourse.

> I can but wonder at his audacity. [That is, "I can only wonder at his audacity."]
> I cannot but wonder at his audacity. [That is, "I cannot do anything but wonder at his audacity."]
> I cannot help wondering at his audacity. [That is, "I cannot avoid wondering at his audacity."]

13. "BETWEEN," "AMONG"

Between is normally used of two items; *among* is used of more than two.

> Peace has been declared between the two nations.
> Peace now reigns among the three nations.

14. "A (ON)"

A shortened form of the preposition *on* is sometimes used with a gerund (sometimes attached to the gerund with a hyphen). (See also p. 314.)

> I am going a hunting [*or* a-hunting]. [That is, "I am going on hunting."]

15. PREPOSITION AT THE END OF A STATEMENT

It should be evident from the discussion of verb + preposition (and verb + adverb) combinations (see p. 55 and pp. 55 f.) that there are many times when a preposition, or a preposition-like adverb, comes naturally at the end of a statement and that consequently there is no real basis for the silly superstition that there is something grammatically wrong about ending a sentence with a preposition. Of course, there are times when, from the point of view of *effective* composition, a preposition becomes a poor word to end a sentence with. For the end of a sentence is very important as far as emphasis is concerned, whereas a preposition is obviously a weak part of speech. Hence, in a given situation it may often be poor strategy to waste the last position — this emphatic position — on a weak sentence element like a preposition. Instead of declaring, then, that it is grammatically wrong to end a sentence with a preposition, we may take the position that especially in written discourse a preposition may very well be a weak word with which to end a statement. For written discourse is the subject of both prevision and revision. That is, we can plan our written discourse and re-write it as many times as we choose.

But spoken discourse is the subject of neither prevision nor revision. We usually start framing a statement without much idea as to how it is going to turn out, trusting good fortune, as it were, to bring us out somehow. Hence, it is often far more natural to end a statement with a preposition than to plan deliberately to avoid such an ending. It is far more natural, for instance, to say "He is a man I am acquainted with" than to say "He is a man with whom I am acquainted"; to say "She is the girl my brother is engaged to" than to say "She is the girl to whom my brother is engaged." (For the problems of getting the right case form in such situations as "I do not know whom it is intended for" see pp. 243 ff.)

Further, it may be noted that the preposition-like word at the end of a statement often is not a preposition at all but an adverb (see p. 108).

> They are tearing the old building down. [*Down* is an adverb modifying *are tearing*.]
> The old building was torn down. [*Down* is an adverb modifying *was torn*.]
> I found the ticket office shut up. [*Up* is an adverb modifying *shut*.]
> First, we shall have to tear the old roof off. [*Off* is an adverb modifying *tear*, not a preposition governing *roof*, which is the direct object of *tear*.]

16. PREPOSITION + VERB COMBINATIONS

See pp. 55 f.

CHAPTER II

Conjunctions[1]

A. *Kinds*

There are two general classes of conjunctions — coordinating conjunctions that join words, phrases, or clauses of the same grammatical rank (see pp. 123 f.); and subordinating conjunctions that join a subordinate clause to a main clause (see pp. 124 f.). Conjunctions used in pairs are called correlative conjunctions or correlatives.

1. COORDINATING CONJUNCTIONS

The common coordinating conjunctions are *and, but, nor, or* and *for*.[2] *Yet* is now generally accepted as a coordinating conjunction, at least as far as punctuation is concerned; and *so* seems well on the road to acceptance as such.

2. SUBORDINATING CONJUNCTIONS

A simple subordinating conjunction is one whose sole function is to join a subordinate clause to a main clause (see pp. 124 f.). A functional or functioning connective is one that has a dual function: it joins a subordinate clause to a main clause and at the same time functions as a noun, an adjective, or an adverb in the subordinate clause.

---

[1] For constructions of conjunctions in sentences see pp. 123 ff.
[2] See footnote, p. 123, regarding classing *for* as a coordinating conjunction.

a. Simple conjunctions. The common simple conjunctions
are these:

after	inasmuch as	though
although	in order that	till
as	lest	unless
as if	since	until
because	so that	whether
before	than	while
if	that	

b. Functional connectives. Functional connectives include
relative and interrogative pronouns, adjectives, and adverbs.[3]
(See pp. 127 ff.).

who	whoever, whichever, whatever	when
which	whosoever, whichsoever, whatsoever	where
what		why
whose	whosever, whosesoever	how
that		whence
		whither

3. CORRELATIVES

Conjunctions may be used in pairs as coordinating conjunctions with items of equal grammatical importance and as
connectives between subordinate and main clauses. (See also p.
126. For correlative adverbs see pp. 102 f.)

a. Coordinating correlatives. The commonly used coordinating correlative conjunctions are *not only . . . but also, both . . .
and, neither . . . nor, either . . . or.*

b. Subordinating correlatives. The commonly used subordinating correlative conjunctions are *although . . . yet (still),
though . . . yet (still), if . . . then, since . . . therefore.*

[3] Anything — including relative and interrogative pronouns, adjectives, and
adverbs — that connects grammatically one clause to another is to that extent
a conjunction. Expressions that not only join clauses but function grammatically
within their own clauses are called "functional (or functioning) connectives,"
and are treated in this chapter with the regular conjunctions, which join clauses
but do not function as another part of speech within the subordinate clause.

c. Correlative adverbs. The commonly used correlative adverbs, which are called functional connectives, are *as . . . as, so . . . that, the . . . the, when . . . then, where . . . there.*

4. PHRASAL CONJUNCTIONS

The commonly used phrasal conjunctions (conjunctions composed of several words) are *in order that, so that, as if, inasmuch as, on condition that, in so far as.*

5. IDEAS EXPRESSED BY CONJUNCTIONS

Subordinating conjunctions (simple and functional) introducing adverbial, adjectival, and substantive clauses may express a variety of meanings in relating subordinate clauses to main clauses.

a. Adverbial. Conjunctions introducing adverbial clauses may express the following notions (see also pp. 183 ff.).
Cause or reason: *as, because, for, since, whereas.*
Comparison or degree: *as, than, so . . . that.*
Concession: *although, though, even if, even though, however.*
Condition: *if, provided, since, unless.*
Manner: *as, as if, as though.*
Place: *where, wherever, whence, whither.*
Time: *as, before, after, since, until, till, when, whenever, while, as soon as.*

b. Adjectival. Subordinating words introducing adjectival clauses are *which, that, who, as, but, when, where, why, before, after.*

c. Substantive. Subordinating words introducing noun clauses are *that, if, whether, how, when, where, why, who, what, which, whoever, whatever, whichever.*

B. *Meanings of Conjunctions*

1. CUMULATIVE OR COPULATIVE

A cumulative or copulative conjunction, such as *and*, is one that adds an item to another.

The boy *and* girl bought tickets to the movie.

2. ADVERSATIVE

An adversative conjunction, such as *but* or *yet*, opposes one item to another.

Harvard has a good team, *but* Yale has a better one.

3. ALTERNATIVE

An alternative (or disjunctive) conjunction, such as *or* or *else*, offers the choice of acceptance of one statement or another.

That man leaves, *or* I leave.

4. ILLATIVE

An illative conjunction, such as *for, because, since,* joins a reason or an inference to a statement. (For expressions like *hence, so, therefore, consequently,* see pp. 105 f.)

Jim can't go, *because* he has the measles.

C. *Usages in Conjunctions*

1. MISPLACED CONJUNCTIONS

Correlative conjunctions should be so placed that they correlate the elements intended.

I read not only technical magazines but many literary publications as well. [*Not:* I not only read technical magazines but many literary publications as well.]

Pomona is a college both well equipped and adequately financed. [*Not:* Pomona is both a college well equipped and adequately financed.]

Either you do it, or I must do it. [*Not:* You either do it, or I must do it.]

2.   INADVERTENT OMISSION IN A COMPARISON

A connective demanded by idiom in a comparison should not be inadvertently omitted. (See also p. 154.)

John is as tall as if not taller than his father. [*Or*] John is as tall as his father if not taller (than his father). [*Not:* John is as tall if not taller than his father.]

This hat is more attractive than that one and is just as cheap. [*Or*] This hat is just as cheap as that one and is more attractive. [*Not:* This hat is more attractive and just as cheap as that one.]

3.   "AND WHO"

And who, and which, and *but who* should be used only when there is a previous parallel item, or items, introduced by *who* or *which.*

Jack Ryan, who is our pitcher and who happens to be our best batter, will not play tomorrow. [*Not:* Jack Ryan, our pitcher and who happens to be our best batter, will not play tomorrow.]

A plan that is as simple as this and that allows such free play of individuality ought to commend itself to our general manager. [*Not:* A plan as simple as this and that allows such a free play of individuality ought to commend itself to our general manager.]

4.   "TRY AND"

It is usually better to follow *try* with an infinitive rather than with *and* and a coordinate finite verb.

Try to come if it is at all possible. [*Rather than:* Try and come if it is at all possible.]

5.   "NEITHER . . . NOR"

Neither should be paralleled with *nor* and *either* with *or.*

I have neither the inclination nor the time. [*Not:* I have neither the inclination or the time.]

I do not own either a car or a bicycle. [*Not:* I do not own either a car nor a bicycle.]

6. "NO ... NOR" OR "OR"

If an additional item merely adds or qualifies a previous negative, *or* is correct. If a second item offers a definite alternative, then *nor* is correct.

No man or woman would think of such a thing. [*Woman* is merely an addition to or a qualification of *man*; hence, *or* rather than *nor* is correct.]
I have no inclination for such an undertaking, nor the time. [*Time* is a definite alternative; hence, *nor* rather than *or* is correct.]
I have no inclination for such an undertaking, nor do I have the time.

7. "AS ... AS," "NOT SO ... AS"

Some authorities still rule that the correlatives *as ... as* should be used for affirmative statements and *not so ... as* for negative statements. But actual usage today makes little distinction between them, *as ... as* actually being more common than *not so ... as* for negative statements.

It is as cold as it was yesterday.
It is not as cold as it was yesterday. [*Or*] It is not so cold as it was yesterday.

8. "REASON ... IS BECAUSE"

The subordinating conjunction *because* is normally used to introduce adverbial clauses. Inasmuch as the construction involves bad logic, most careful writers avoid using *because* to introduce a noun clause functioning as the equivalent of *reason*.

The reason I failed to meet you is that (*or* the fact that) I missed my bus. [*Not:* The reason I failed to meet you is because I missed my bus.]
That (*or* the fact that) her boy friend was five minutes late is no reason for Emily's getting so angry. [*Not:* Because her boy friend was five minutes late is no reason for Emily's getting so angry.]

NOTE.   Similar bad logic is sometimes seen in the use of *where, when, as,* or *how* to introduce a noun clause functioning as a complement.

Did you see in the papers that income taxes are to be lowered next year? [*Not:* Did you see in the papers where income taxes are to be lowered next year?]

I don't know that I can go. [*Not:* I don't know as (*or,* as how) I can go.]

9.   "IF" AND "WHETHER"

The most common use of *if* is as a conjunction introducing an adverbial clause of condition.

If we grant your major premise, your conclusion follows.

Both *if* and *whether* introduce noun clauses. A distinction formerly advocated, that *if* introduces clauses expressing doubt or uncertainty and that *whether* introduces indirect questions, is rarely followed nowadays. But when the alternate . . . *or not* is added, and especially when the clause functions as the subject, *whether* is generally used.

I doubt if [*or* whether] I can keep the appointment.
I do not know whether [*or* if] I can attend.
Whether you attend or not is no concern of mine.
Whether or not he accepts is unimportant.

10.   "LEST"

Lest means "that not." Hence, *lest* should not be used with another negative in the statement.

Take care lest you be deceived. [That is, "Take care that you not be deceived." *Not:* Take care lest you not be deceived.]

11.   "AND SO"

And so, rather than *so* alone, is preferred to introduce a clause of result. (*So,* of course, is a transitional adverb; see p. 105.)[4]

---

[4] *So* is so greatly overworked as a transitional adverb indicating result that a writer will usually find it desirable to consider such transitional adverbs as *hence, therefore,* and *consequently* as possibilities.

I could not get anybody to go with me; and so (or hence, therefore, consequently) I went by myself. [*Rather than:* I could not get anybody to go with me; so I went by myself.]

12. "THAT" UNDERSTOOD

The subordinating conjunction *that* introducing a noun clause (see p. 162) is very frequently omitted by ellipsis (see p. 154). This omission is especially common in indirect discourse. But this *that* has to be supplied in grammatical analysis to make evident the subordinate character of the clause that it introduces.

I think I shall go to the movie tonight. [That is, "I think that I shall go to the movie tonight."]

13. "THAN"

Than is a conjunction, not a preposition. Hence the situation may demand either a nominative or an objective after *than*, depending on the construction of the substantive in its own clause (see p. 154).

John likes Mary better than me. [That is, "John likes Mary better than he likes me." *Than* is a conjunction introducing the subordinate clause *he likes me*.]

John likes Mary better than I. [That is, "John likes Mary better than I like Mary." *Than* is a conjunction introducing the subordinate clause *I like Mary*.]

NOTE.   *Than whom*, although ungrammatical, is an accepted idiom in such sentences as "We shall next discuss Kipling, than whom there is no greater master of the modern short story." But, acceptable as it is, *than whom* is at best an ungraceful locution.

14. "PREFER . . . RATHER THAN"

"Prefer . . . than" should not be substituted for *prefer . . . rather than* if logical consistency is to be obtained.

She prefers playing bridge to going swimming. [*Or*] She prefers to play bridge rather than to go swimming. [*Not:* She prefers to play bridge than to go swimming. *Not:* She prefers playing bridge than going swimming.]

15. "AS IF" AND "AS THOUGH"

A few authorities insist that *as though* should not be substituted for *as if* when there is no notion of concession. But in present-day practice *as though* and *as if* are used interchangeably.

I feel as if (*or* as though) I were catching cold. [If we fill out the ellipsis involved we shall have "I feel as I should feel if I were catching cold." Thus we can see why there is an objection in logic to the use of *as though*. But not many people are conscious of the ellipsis. Hence, *as though* is generally regarded as just as acceptable as *as if*.]

16. "WHETHER OR NOT (NO)"

Whether may be used correlatively with or followed by *not* or *no* depending on the construction of the element understood to follow *not* or *no*. Often the two constructions may be used interchangeably, the *whether or no* giving a slightly heavier emphasis.

I wonder whether Mr. Kapen has left or not. [That is, "I wonder whether Mr. Kapen has left or has not left." *Rather than:* I wonder whether Mr. Kapen has left or no.]
I have not heard whether we are to have a vacation or not. [That is, "I have not heard whether we are to have a vacation or shall not have a vacation."] [*Or*] I have not heard whether we are to have a vacation or no. [That is, "I have not heard whether we are to have a vacation or are to have no vacation."]

17. "SUPPOSING," "IN CASE," "PROVIDED," "PROVIDING"[5]

Such expressions as *supposing, in case, provided, providing* may be used as subordinating conjunctions introducing adverbial clauses. Like *if*, they introduce clauses expressing some kind of condition on which the idea of the main clause depends.

Supposing he doesn't show up at all, what shall we do then? [That is, "If he doesn't show up at all, what shall we do then?"]

[5] The prejudice against the use of *providing* in this capacity is unfounded; the word is quite generally used by educated speakers and writers.

I can substitute for you in case you are late. [That is, "I can substitute for you if you are late."]

Provided differs slightly from *if* in that the conditional clause it introduces expresses a stipulation or a requirement. Many careful writers do not use *provided* indiscriminately as a synonym for *if*.

You may use my car provided [*or* provided that] you return it by noon. [*Better than:* You may use my car if you return it by noon. (*Provided* may also be regarded as elliptical for "it being provided"; but its treatment as a subordinating conjunction is simpler.)]

18. "DOUBT THAT," "DOUBT WHETHER"

Doubt that is used with negative statements and in questions; *doubt whether* is used with affirmative statements.

I do not doubt that you are right. There is no doubt that you are right. Do I doubt that you are right? Is there any doubt that you are right?

I doubt whether your brother is right. There is doubt whether your brother is right.

NOTE. *Doubt but* and *doubt but that*, although frowned upon, are used increasingly by reputable speakers and writers and may be regarded now as acceptable idioms. But *doubt but what* is not standard.

I do not doubt but (*or* but that) you are right. There is no doubt but (*or* but that) you are right. [*Not:* I do not doubt but what you are right.]

19. "CAN BUT," "CANNOT BUT"

See under Prepositions, Note, pp. 351 f.

20. "FROM" AFTER "DIFFER"

See under Prepositions, p. 350.

21. "WITHOUT," "EXCEPT"

For the misuse of *without* and *except* as conjunctions, see under Prepositions, pp. 350 f.

22. "LIKE"

Like may be an adjective, an adverb, or a preposition (see pp. 119 f.). But present-day practice frowns on its use as a conjunction in serious writing.

> He talked as if he meant what he said. [*Not:* He talked like he meant what he said.]
> It looks as if it might rain. [*Not:* It looks like it might rain.]

NOTE. There is a growing tendency, encouraged somewhat by the latest editions of the dictionaries, to sanction *like* as a conjunction when it indicates resemblance and connects at the same time, as "He looks like his father looked at the same age."

23. "OR"

Or introducing an appositional item may be regarded as an expletive rather than as a conjunction. (See also p. 149.)

> Laissez-faire, or the doctrine of "letting things alone," seems to have gone into an eclipse. [*Or* here functions as an expletive introducing the appositional item *the doctrine of "letting things alone"* rather than as a conjunction.]

24. "THEREFORE," "MOREOVER," "CONSEQUENTLY," AND SIMILAR EXPRESSIONS

Such expressions as *therefore, moreover, consequently, hence, however,* and *nevertheless* are sometimes listed as conjunctions (or "conjunctive adverbs"; see footnote, p. 105). But inasmuch as they effect rhetorical transitions rather than grammatical connections, this book has preferred to call them transitional adverbs (see pp. 105 f.).

25. "BUT"

For *but* used as a preposition (although sometimes interpreted as a conjunction) see p. 351.

CHAPTER 12

Interjections

An interjection is a word used to express strong or sudden emotion. An interjection is not actually a part of speech, although words and even complete statements may function as interjections. In any case interjections are to be regarded, from the point of view of grammatical analysis, as independent or absolute elements — that is, as elements with no actual grammatical function in the sentence in which they appear.

Typical of interjections are such exclamations as *oh, ah, ouch.* But many words recognized as parts of speech may be used as interjections.

Nouns — Goodness! Mercy!
Adjectives — Impossible! Splendid! Excellent! Admirable!
Verbs — Hark! Look! Listen!
Adverbs — Indeed! Certainly!
Pronouns — My! Oh, miserable me! Dear me!

Interjections are often followed by the exclamation mark.

NOTE. Oaths, curses, and various forms of profanity are forms of interjections, from which emotional content has, in many cases, practically disappeared.

USAGES IN "O" AND "OH"

Although O and *oh* are frequently used interchangeably, careful writers seem to prefer to observe the following distinctions.

O is used in direct address. It is always capitalized and is never followed by any mark of punctuation, although the utterance that follows it may be followed by the exclamation mark.

Oh usually indicates pain, surprise, or disappointment. Sometimes it is used as a sort of stammering word, to prepare the way for the coming utterance — "Oh, I don't know." *Oh* is never capitalized, except at the beginning of a sentence (or line in poetry), and is always followed by some form of punctuation, either the comma or the exclamation mark.

O is much commoner in poetry; *oh* is much commoner in prose.

> O Lord, Father of mankind!
> O tempora! O mores!
> Oh, I am sorry you can't go.
> "Oh, oh, oh!" she cried.

APPENDIX

DIAGRAMMING

The Diagram in Grammatical Analysis

When we resolve a sentence into its parts we are describing the function that every expression appearing in the given sentence performs. On the basis of these functions we may classify the expressions as to parts of speech (see pp. 5 ff.). But most of us have difficulty in keeping in mind the whole sentence and the various divisions and subdivisions of our analysis. Hence, we are likely to lose ourselves as we proceed from one part of the sentence to the next. But we may meet this problem by using a simple graph or chart by means of which we can plot out before our eyes these various relationships. Such a graph or chart we may call a diagram.

A diagram for grammatical analysis is, then, nothing more than a map or chart that makes a subject easier to grasp in its entirety. A diagram in grammar bears about the same relationship to grammar that a map bears to geography, that a drawing of a piece of apparatus in a laboratory manual bears to chemistry, that a chart bears to some aspect of economics in a treatise on that subject. A diagram is ever a means of giving pictorial representation to analysis and is never an end in itself. Because it can reveal to the eye in one glance what the process of analysis is discovering, a diagram can have as much usefulness in the study of grammar as in the study of any other subject where analysis plays a leading role. In other words, there is nothing occult or hidden or mysterious about a diagram in grammar. It can be as simple and usable as a set of drawings telling one how to put together the separate parts to make a machine and then how to operate it.

But there are certain conventions that must be understood if a blueprint, a graph, a chart, a map, a diagram is to be interpretable. We could not make much out of a map in geography if we did not understand such conventions of any map as that the top represents the north, that certain markings represent mountains, that certain symbols represent county seats and state capitals and national capitals. In fact, a road map will usually have down at one corner a list of its conventions.

So it is with a simple diagram to represent grammatical relationships of the parts of a sentence; there are certain conventions that must be understood at the start. If we understand these conventions, we shall be able to comprehend the grammatical make-up of a sentence in probably one-fifth the time it would take if we tried to work out all the details in our heads or wrote out all these items in declarative sentences. Hence, a diagram can be an immense saver of precious time.

Below are listed first of all some of these conventions of one system of sentence diagrams. Then follow some typical diagram patterns. With a mastery of these we should be able to interpret from a diagram the grammatical make-up of a sentence; or we may ourselves proceed to make a diagram to show the relationships among the various parts of a sentence, no matter how complicated that sentence may be.

1.   SIMPLE SENTENCE

a. Subject and predicate   (Use a heavy base line for a main clause and a full vertical line to separate subject and predicate.)

Birds fly.

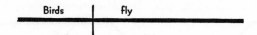

b. *Single word adjectival and adverbial modifiers*   (Place on slant lines attached to the element modified.)

Little birds fly swiftly.

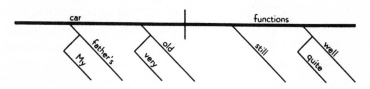

My father's very old car still functions quite well.

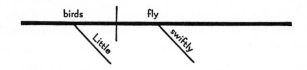

c. *Prepositional phrases as adjectival and adverbial modifiers* (Place the preposition on a slant line that drops slightly below the horizontal line, on which is placed the object of the preposition.)

A gentleman from Indianapolis will speak in the auditorium.

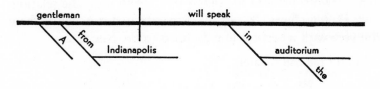

2.   COMPOUND SUBJECTS, VERBS, AND MODIFIERS

a. Subjects and verbs compounded

Jack and Jill came up the hill and went down again.

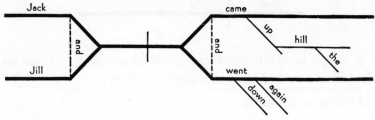

b. Adjectives and adverbs compounded

The shy and timid animal approached the food hesitatingly and even fearfully.

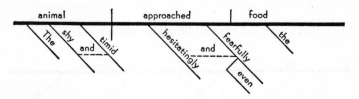

c. Phrases compounded

Jane ran into the house and up the stairs.

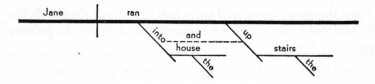

3.   COMPLEMENTS OF TRANSITIVE VERBS

a. Direct object P. 45 ff. (Separate a direct object from the verb with a vertical line dropped to the base line.)

Bill hit the ball squarely.

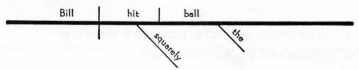

For phrases and clauses used as direct objects see p. 378, p. 380, and p. 398.

b. Indirect object　Pp. 47 f. (Use the same design as for a prepositional phrase.)

James gave me the book.

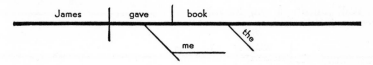

Phrases seldom function as indirect objects. For a noun clause functioning as an indirect object see p. 399.

c. Objective complement　Pp. 49 ff. (Separate an objective complement from a direct object with a line that slants back toward the object and the verb.)

The court declared the law null and void.

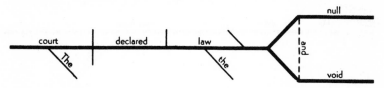

We elected Kenneth secretary-treasurer.

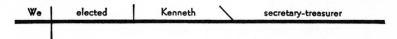

His action renders our protest of no avail. [A prepositional phrase functioning as an objective complement]

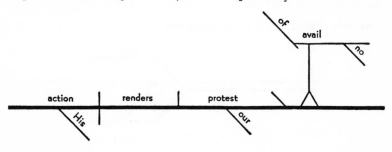

For a clause functioning as an objective complement see under Noun Clauses, p. 400; for an objective complement introduced by the expletive *as* see under Expletives, p. 419.

d. Cognate object   P. 46. (Use the same design as for any other direct object.)

Will you sing a song for us?

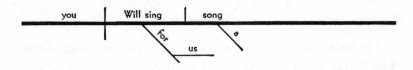

e. Double object   Pp. 48 f. (Separate double objects from the verb with two vertical half-lines.)

He asked me a puzzling question.

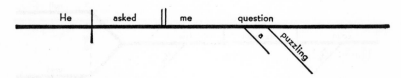

For a clause functioning as one of double objects see under Noun Clauses, p. 401.

4.   COMPLEMENTS OF INTRANSITIVE VERBS

a. Subjective complement   Pp. 5 ff. (Separate a subjective complement from the verb with a line that slants back towards the subject and the verb.)

Mother is gentle and kind. [Adjectives]

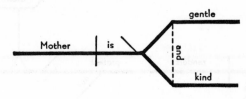

Tennis is my choice. [Noun]

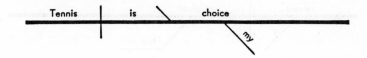

Her gown is of expensive silk. [Prepositional phrase]

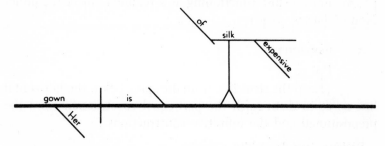

Mr. Smith was appointed manager.

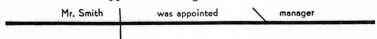

The slate was wiped clean.

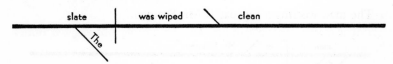

For an infinitive phrase or a noun clause functioning as a subjective complement see p. 380 and p. 400.

b. Retained object Pp. 53 f. (Separate a retained object from the verb with a wave line. Use the same design for a retained indirect object as for a regular indirect object.)

He was given a reward.

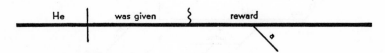

A reward was given him.

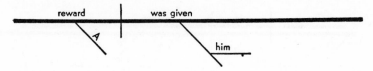

For an infinitive phrase functioning as a retained object see p. 381. For a clause functioning as a retained object see under Noun Clauses, p. 401.

5.   PARTICIPLE

Pp. 59 ff.

(Keep the slant line from dropping below the horizontal line so as to distinguish the participial construction from the prepositional and the infinitive constructions.)

Barking dogs don't bite.

The man wearing a topcoat is Mr. Seaman.

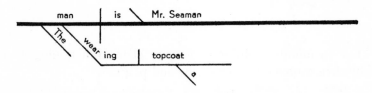

Having told the judge my story, I was released.

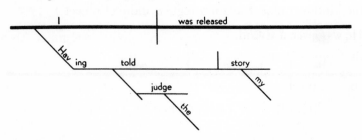

Our team, outweighed and outplayed, lost by a big score.

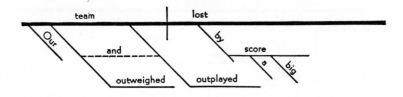

The situation was encouraging. [Participle functioning as a subjective complement]

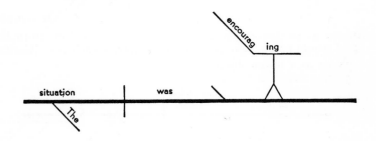

Father found his car gone. [Participle functioning as an objective complement]

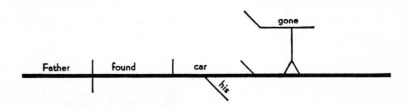

For the participle in a nominative absolute see under Absolute Constructions, p. 412.

6.   GERUND

Pp. 63 ff. (Use a stepped line for a gerund.)

Examining specimens critically requires' a strong magnifying glass. [Gerund phrase as a subject]

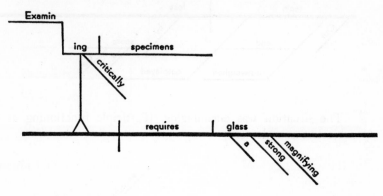

I would enjoy being given a salary increase each year. [Gerund phrase as a direct object]

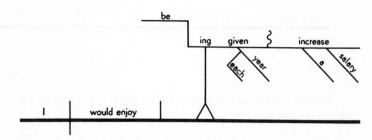

I like teaching grammar to beginners. [Gerund phrase as a direct object]

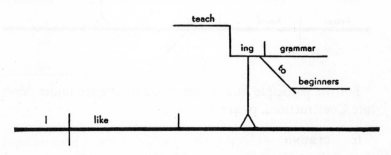

Such becomes merely carrying coals to Newcastle. [Gerund phrase as a subjective complement]

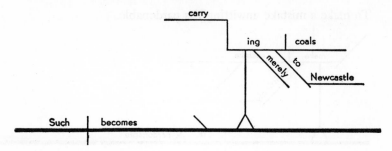

They talked about playing the game at night. [Gerund phrase as the object of a preposition]

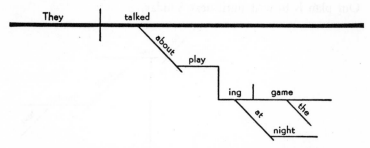

Before calling the portrait a forgery, you must subject it to severe tests. [Gerund phrase as the object of a preposition]

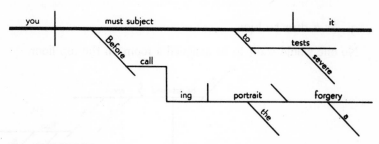

7.   **INFINITIVE**

Pp. 65 ff. (Use the same design as for a prepositional phrase.)

a. Noun use

1. As a subject

To make a mistake unwittingly is pardonable.

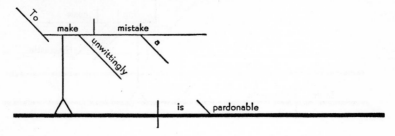

2. As a subjective complement

Our plan is to wait until next Sunday.

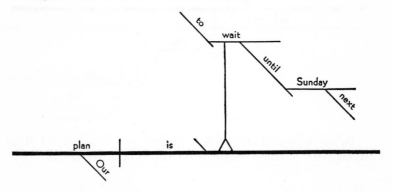

3. As a direct object

No one would want to be assigned a room on the top floor.

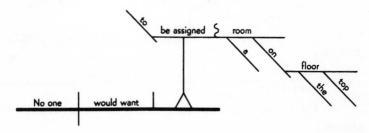

4. As a retained object

The young lady was asked to start the song.

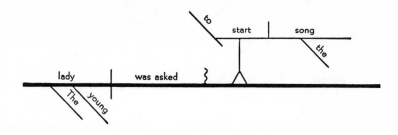

5. As the object of a preposition

I have done everything except use force.

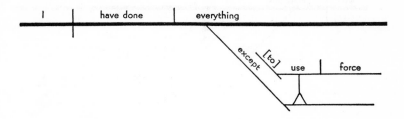

6. Introduced by the relative adverbs *how, where, when,* etc. and by such pronouns as *what, which*

How to raise that much money is the question.

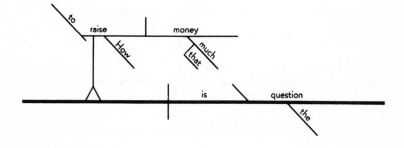

The problem is where to find such leaders.

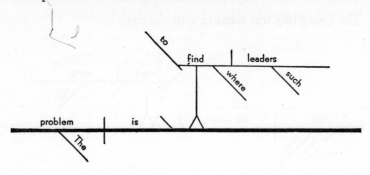

We must talk about when to start the campaign.

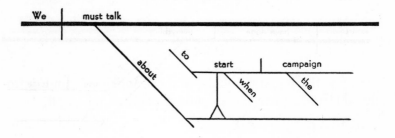

I do not know what to do next. [That is, "I do not know to do what next."]

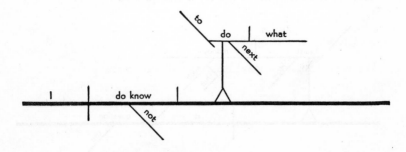

Mother taught me where to find mushrooms. (The infinitive becomes one of double objects after the special verb *teach*.)

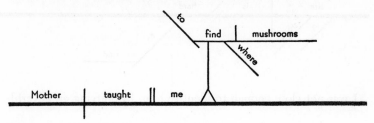

We were never told when to report.

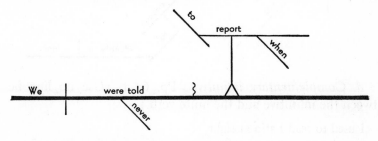

7. For the infinitive phrase and the infinitive clause introduced by the expletive *it see* under Expletives, pp. 415 ff.

b. Adjective use P. 67 f.

You have a task to perform.

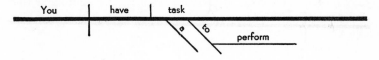

c. Adverb use P. 68 f.

We went to have a good time. [Modifying a verb]

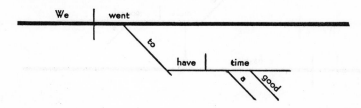

A good tire is hard to find. [Modifying an adjective]

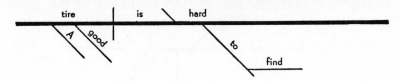

I was not close enough to identify him. [Modifying an adverb]

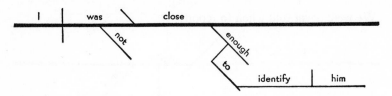

d. Complementary infinitive Pp. 69 f. (Use no line between the infinitive and the finite verb.)

I used to read Latin at sight.

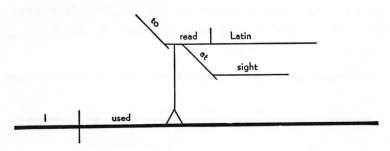

I have to make a speech.

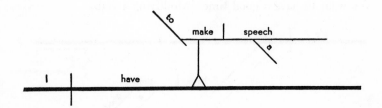

e. *Infinitive clause*   Pp. 70 f. (Place the subject of an in-finitive on a horizontal line attached to the top of the slant line.)

We thought him to be the best player.

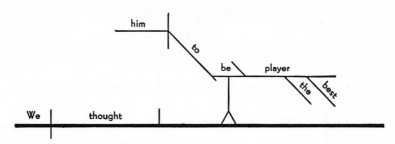

The major ordered the bridge to be taken at any cost.

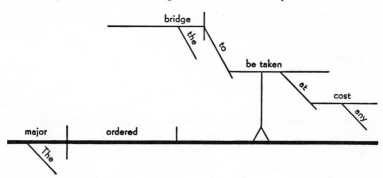

He left too quickly for me to get a good look at him.

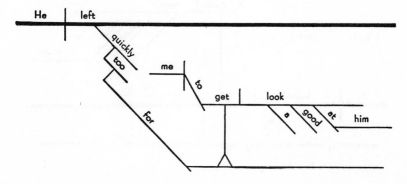

f. Infinitive with "to" omitted

I saw him fall.

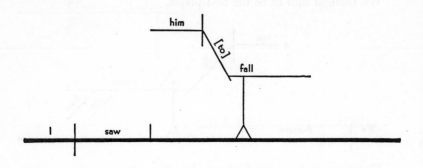

I never heard her make an unkind remark about anybody.

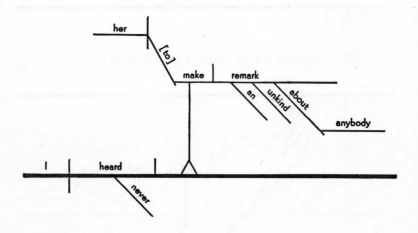

Let me help you change the tire.

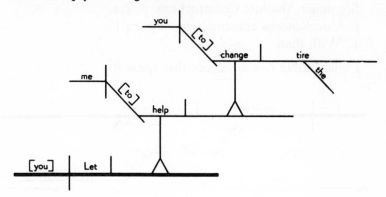

g. *Infinitive clause introduced by the expletive "for"* See under Expletives, pp. 418 f.

h. *Construction with the passive voice* P. 73 f. (The infinitive becomes a retained object.)

I was ordered to report for duty.

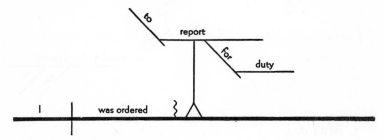

He was thought to be the right man.

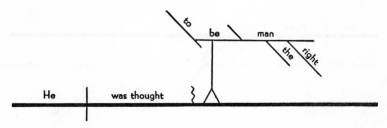

i. Infinitive phrase and infinitive clause used absolutely
See under Absolute Constructions, p. 412.
j. Miscellaneous constructions Pp. 74 f.
1. With *than*

I would rather save my money than spend it.

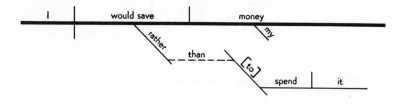

2. After *as* to complete a comparison begun by *so* or *such*

His explanation was such as to amaze the most skeptical.

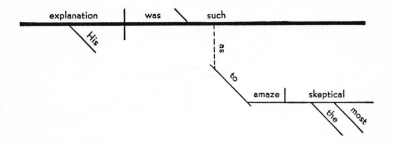

3. After *as if*

He made a motion as if to throw the ball.

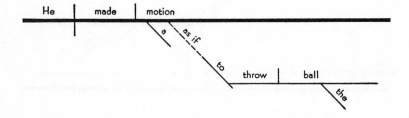

8. **CONNECTIVES BETWEEN COORDINATE ELEMENTS OF A SENTENCE**

Pp. 123 f.

a. Between words

You and I seem to have the same ideas.

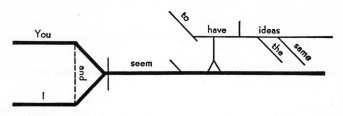

b. Between phrases

It works equally well on alternating current or on direct current.

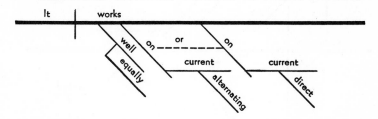

My plan is to graduate in two years and to spend the next year in Europe.

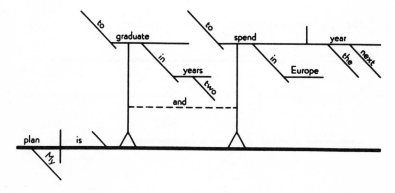

c. Between independent clauses

Man proposes; but God disposes.

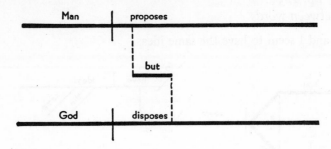

I haven't a cent in cash; hence, I must get a check cashed. (See also p. 105.)

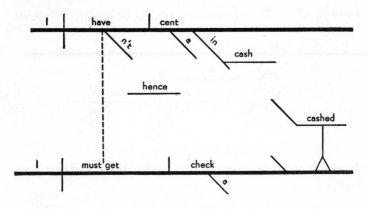

Either we hang together or we hang separately.

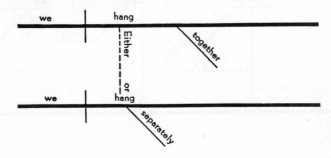

d. *Between dependent clauses*

If it doesn't rain and if it doesn't seem too cold, we can have our picnic on the lawn.

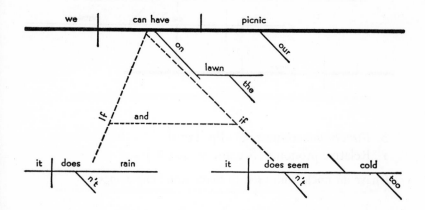

9. CONNECTIVES INTRODUCING SUBORDINATE CLAUSES

Pp. 124 ff. (See also under Noun Clauses, pp. 397 ff.; Adjective Clauses, pp. 402 ff., and Adverbial Clauses, pp. 407 ff.)

a. *Simple subordinating conjunction*

You meet me at six unless I notify you to the contrary. (See also p. 124 f.)

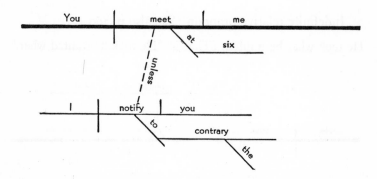

I believe that you are mistaken.

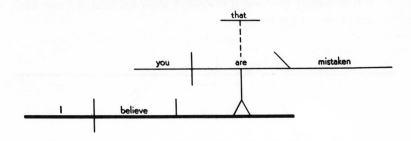

b. Functional connective   Pp. 127 ff.
1. Relative pronoun (See also p. 403 ff.)

I have an uncle who used to make wood engravings.

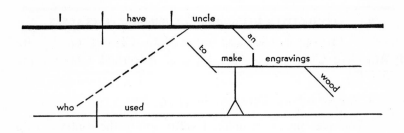

2. Indefinite relative pronoun (See also p. 399.)

He took what he wanted. (That is, "He took he wanted what.")

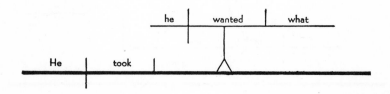

3. Interrogative pronoun (See also p. 401.)

We wish to know who spread the rumor.

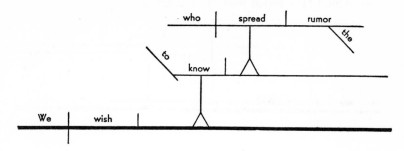

4. Relative adjective (See also p. 406.)

I know a man whose name is Launcelot Smith.

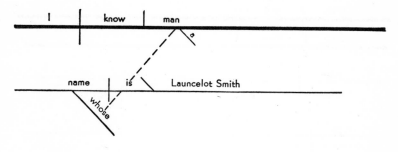

5. Indefinite relative adjective (See also p. 402.)

I shall take whatever wage is offered me.

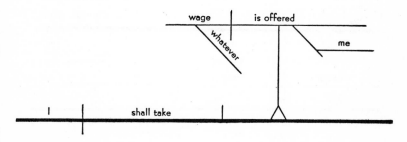

6. Interrogative adjective (See also p. 399.)

We asked which road we should take. (That is, "We asked we should take which road.")

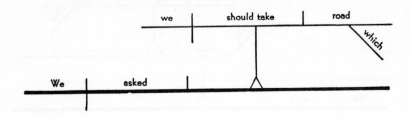

7. Relative adverb (See also p. 407.)

A time will come when you will regret your action.

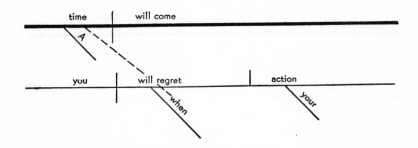

8. Indefinite relative adverb (See also p. 408.)

We played tennis whenever the weather favored it.

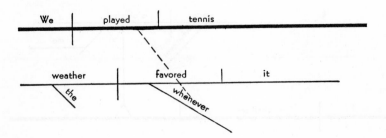

9. Interrogative adverb (See also p. 397.)

You ask where we may find the janitor.

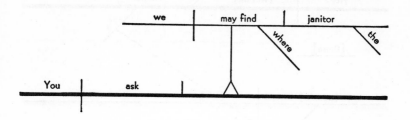

10. Correlative adverbs (See also p. 409.)

He is as old as I am. (That is, "He is as old as I am old.")

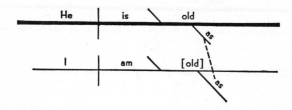

The faster we walk the sooner we shall arrive. [That is, "To which degree we walk faster to that degree we shall arrive sooner."]

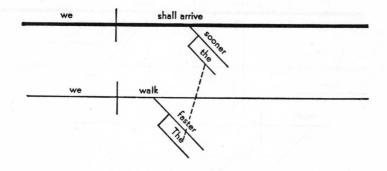

The more the merrier. [That is, "To which degree there are
more people to that degree it will be merrier."]

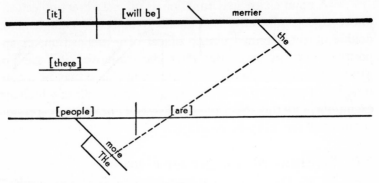

When you signal, then I shall enter.

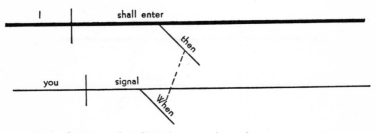

11. Correlative subordinating conjunctions.

Although there is much in his favor, yet I do not feel entirely
certain about him.

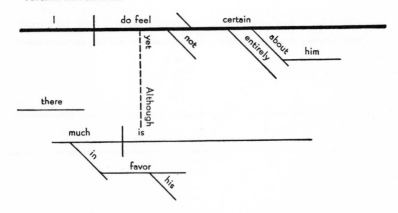

10. NOUN CLAUSES

A noun clause may function as subject, direct object, indirect object, subjective complement, objective complement, double object, retained object, object of a preposition, or appositive. (For noun clauses after the expletive "it," see pp. 416 f.) The word subordinating the noun clause may be a conjunction, a pronoun, an adjective, or an adverb, all of which are exemplified in the following diagrams. (For the unexpressed connective, see Ellipsis, p. 422.)

a. Subject

That we shall have no serious trouble has become evident. [*That* is a conjunction.]

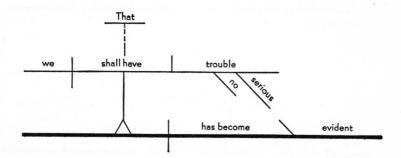

Where we can meet is the next question. [*Where* in an interrogative adverb.]

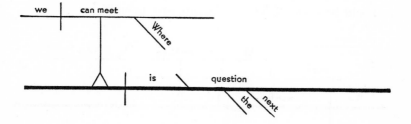

b. Direct object

I heard that Tom had enlisted in the Marine Corps. [*That* is a conjunction.]

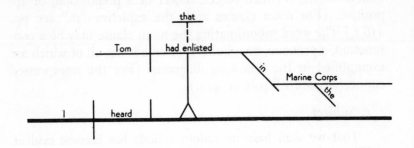

I don't know whether you have grasped my idea. [*Whether* is a conjunction.]

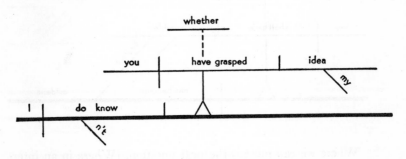

We wondered who he might be. [That is, "We wondered he might be who." *Who* is an interrogative pronoun.]

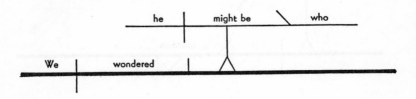

I know where he keeps his scythe. [*Where* is an indefinite relative adverb.]

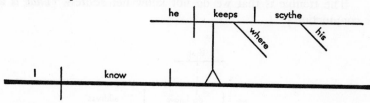

He wanted to know which course he should take and whose textbook he might buy. [That is, "He wanted to know he should take which course and he might buy whose textbook." *Which* and *whose* are interrogative adjectives.]

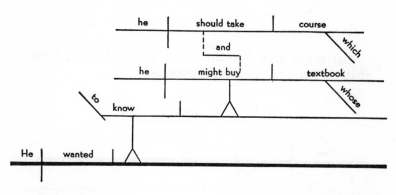

c. Indirect object

We will make whoever asks for it a quotation for the whole job. [*Whoever* is an indefinite relative pronoun.]

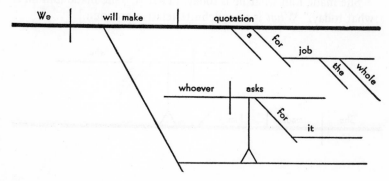

d. Subjective complement

The trouble is that we do not know her address. [*That* is a conjunction.]

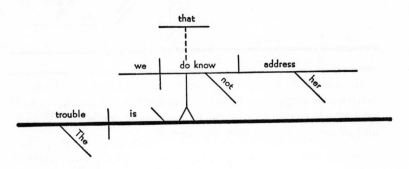

That is not what I meant. [That is, "That is not I meant what." *What* is an indefinite relative pronoun.]

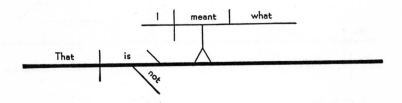

e. Objective complement

She made him what he is today. [That is, "She made him he is what today." *What* is an indefinite relative pronoun.]

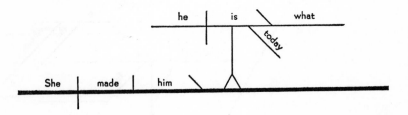

f. Double object

Ask him what his name is. [That is, "Ask him his name is what." *What* is an interrogative pronoun.]

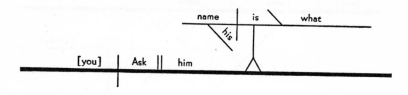

g. Retained object

We were not told which route we should take. [That is, "We were not told we should take which route." *Which* is an indefinite relative adjective.]

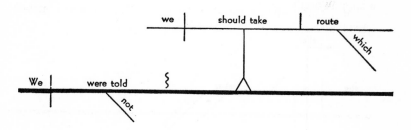

h. Object of a preposition

I know nothing about him except that he is a brilliant conversationalist. [*That* is a conjunction.]

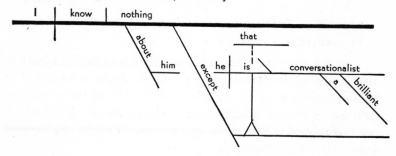

Leave the package at whichever office is handiest. [*Whichever* is an indefinite relative adjective.]

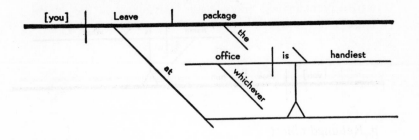

i. Appositive

The fact that she is a pleasing speaker is important. [*That* is a conjunction.]

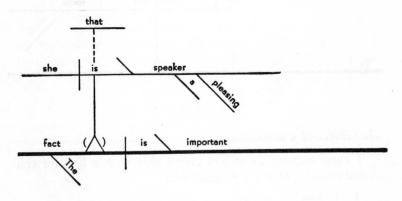

11. ADJECTIVE CLAUSES

An adjective clause may modify a substantive functioning in any of the substantive positions of the sentence. The subordinating word of an adjective clause will be a relative pronoun, a relative adjective, or a relative adverb, all of which are exemplified in the following diagrams. (For the unexpressed connective, see Ellipsis, pp. 421.)

a. Introduced by a relative pronoun

I, who have nothing to gain, will go to see him. [The adjective clause modifies the pronoun *I*, the subject of the main clause. The relative pronoun *who* functions as the subject in the adjective clause.]

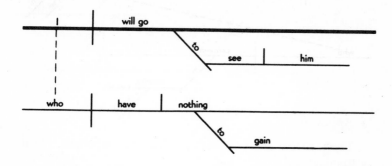

This is the new model that I wanted to show you. [The adjective clause modifies *model*, the subjective complement of the main clause. The relative pronoun *that* functions as the direct object of the infinitive *to show* in the adjective clause.]

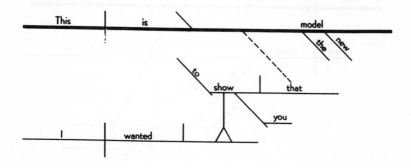

I consider Allen the only candidate who can win in this county. [The adjective clause modifies *candidate*, the objective complement of the main clause. The relative pronoun *who* functions as the subject in the adjective clause.]

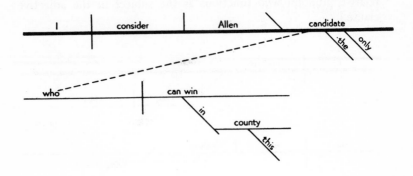

We climbed a tower, from the top of which we could see for many miles. [The adjective clause modifies *tower*, the direct object of the main clause. The relative pronoun *which* functions as the object of the preposition *of* in the adjective clause.]

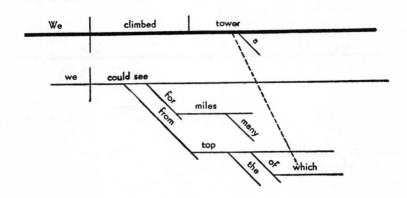

Our club will sponsor any student whom we know to be capable and industrious. [The adjective clause modifies *student*, the direct object of the main clause. The relative pronoun *whom* functions as the subject of the infinitive *to be* in the adjective clause. (*We know* is parenthetical.)]

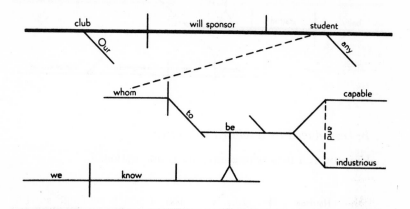

The baby started to whimper, which made Grandmother apprehensive. [The adjective clause has no single-word antecedent. (See p. 174.) The relative pronoun *which* functions as the subject within the adjective clause.]

Either

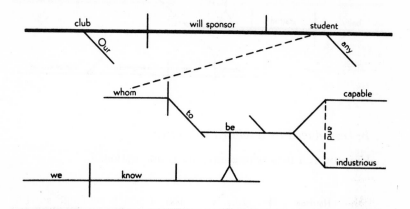

or

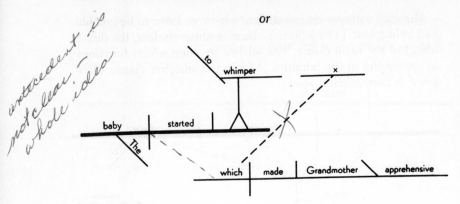

b. Introduced by a relative adjective

Harrison is a man whose integrity is unquestioned.

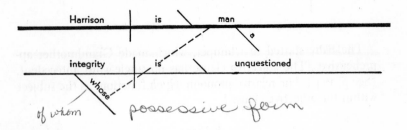

He remained in office until 1962, at which time he retired.

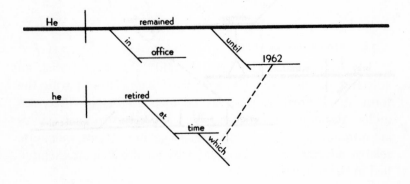

c. *Introduced by a relative adverb*

I know a place where we can have a quiet talk.

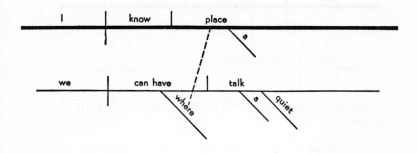

Father became president of the company the year after he joined the firm. (For the adverbial noun, see p. 106.)

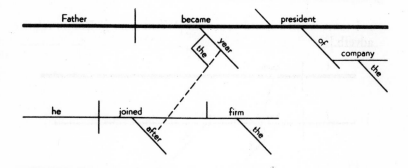

12. ADVERBIAL CLAUSES

An adverbial clause may modify a verb or verbal, an adjective, or an adverb. Certain subordinate clauses having the form of adverbial clauses may be used absolutely. (See also under Absolute Constructions, pp. 412 ff.) Adverbial clauses are introduced by simple subordinating conjunctions, indefinite relative adverbs, or correlative adverbs, all of which are exemplified in the following diagrams.

a. Modifying a verb

Wait until you are summoned. [*Until* is a conjunction.]

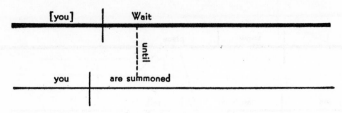

People will not buy goods if prices are too high. [*If* is a conjunction.]

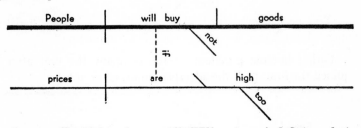

I came when I heard your call. [*When* is an indefinite relative adverb.]

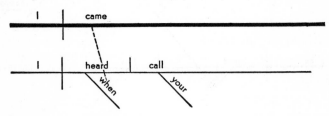

b. Modifying an adjective

She seems confident that she will be chosen. [*That* is a conjunction.]

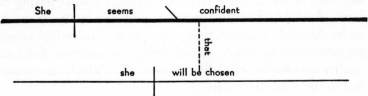

We are sorry that you have to leave. [*That* is a conjunction.]

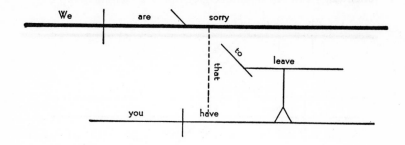

You are younger than I. [That is, "You are younger than I am young." For Ellipsis, see p. 423. *Than* is a conjunction.]

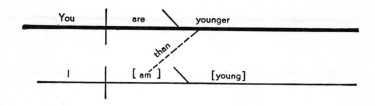

c. *Modifying an adverb*

Grandfather is not so active as he used to be. [*As* is a correlative adverb.]

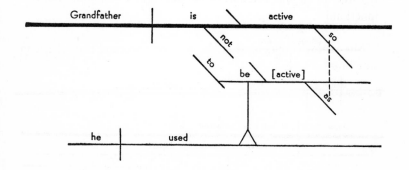

I work so hard that I have no time to play. [*That* is a conjunction.]

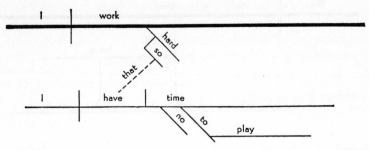

The longer he waits the more he frets. [That is, "In which degree he waits longer in that degree he frets more." *The* is a correlative adverb.]

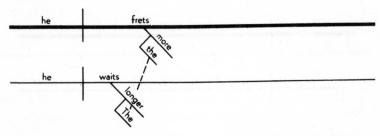

d. Used absolutely   (See also under Absolute Constructions, pp. 412 f.)

Whether we like it or not, Jane has been selected for the leading role. [The unit *whether or not* serves as a subordinating conjunction.]

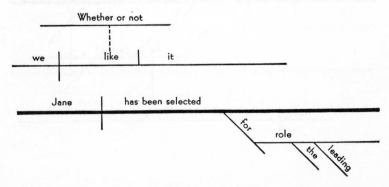

13. SHIFTS

Pp. 134 ff. (Diagram any expression according to its function in the given statement. A noun used as a verb will be diagrammed as a verb; a verb used as a noun will be diagrammed in its noun function; and so on.)

We had to house the stranded passengers for three days. [*House* is here used as a verb.]

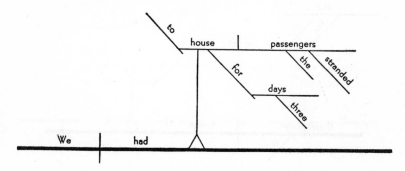

The football team will arrive home next week. [*Football* is here used as an adjective; *home* and *week* are here used as adverbs.]

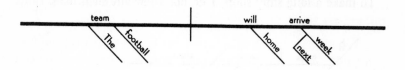

The water is scalding hot. [*Scalding*, a gerund, is here used as an adverbial modifier of the adjective *hot*.]

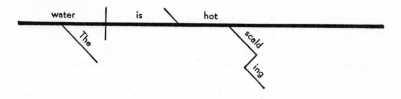

14.   ABSOLUTE CONSTRUCTIONS

Pp. 138 ff. (Diagram any absolute construction for what it is; but show its absolute character by leaving it unattached in any way to the rest of the sentence.)

a. Nominative absolute

The sun having set, the thermometer began to fall.

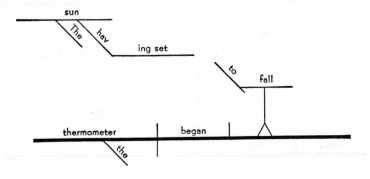

b. Infinitive phrase and infinitive clause

To make a long story short, I do not know any such man.

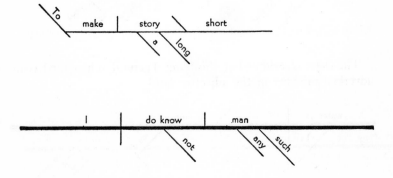

The judges have already departed, their decision to be announced tomorrow.

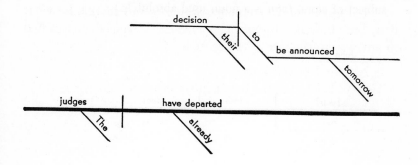

c. Clauses — subordinate and main

As I said before, he is certainly not a handsome dog.

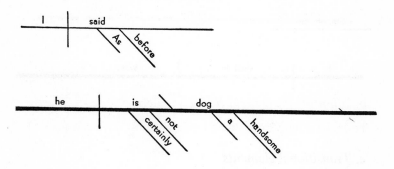

Mary will, I feel confident, prove herself a competent secretary.

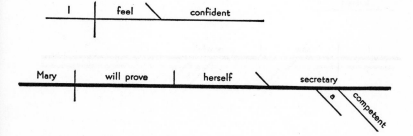

d. Exclamations, interjections, nouns in direct address

John, close the door. [*You* understood, and not *John*, is the true subject of *close*. *John* is a noun used absolutely.]

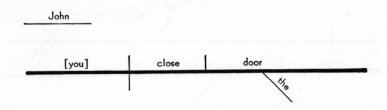

Oh, oh, oh, what shall I do? [That is, "I shall do what?"]

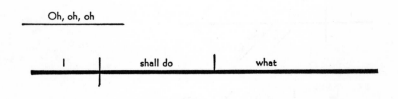

e. Transitional elements

Indeed, I never saw such a snowfall.

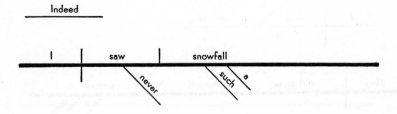

There was a heavy frost last night; hence, we have no flowers this morning. [For the expletive *there* see pp. 417 f.]

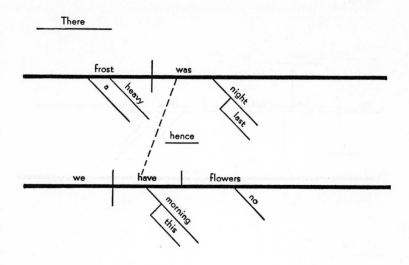

15. EXPLETIVES

Pp. 144 ff.
a. "It" as an expletive

It is hard to understand Mac's reasoning. [That is, "To understand Mac's reasoning is hard."]

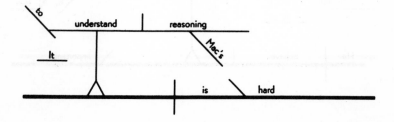

It seems to me that you have overlooked one important item.
[That is, "That you have overlooked one important item seems
to me."]

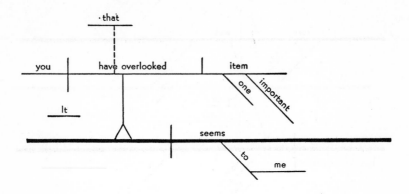

He believes it important to be able to put two and two together.
[That is, "He believes to be able to put two and two together
important."]

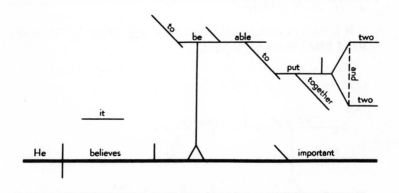

I have it in mind to build a two-car garage. [That is, "I have in mind to build a two-car garage."]

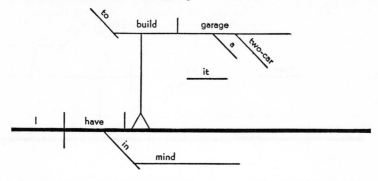

I think it unlikely that he will confess. [That is, "I think that he will confess unlikely."]

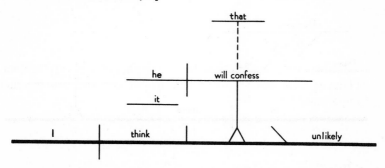

b. *"There" as an expletive*

There is always one right way of doing a thing. [That is, "One right way of doing a thing always is."]

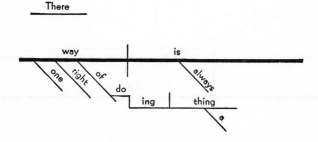

I believe there is to be an excursion. [That is, "I believe that an excursion is to be."]

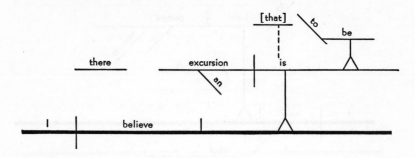

There being no objection, we stand adjourned. [That is, "No objection being, we stand adjourned."]

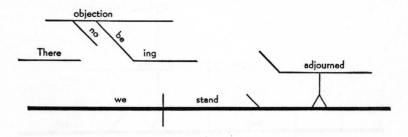

c. "For" as an expletive

For me to go now is impossible.

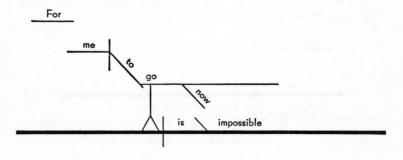

It is difficult for us to trust his word. [That is, "For us to trust his word is difficult."]

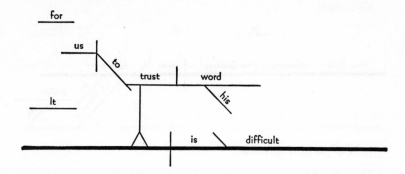

The best plan is for me to go to the mayor.

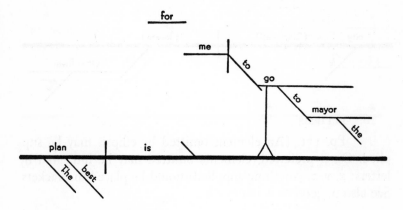

d. "As" as an expletive

We chose Edward as our leader.

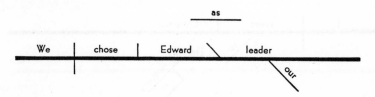

e. "Or" as an expletive

New York, or Bagdad-on-the-Subway, was O. Henry's locale for his stories.

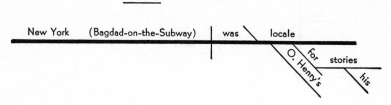

f. "Of" as an expletive

The city of Cincinnati is located on the Ohio River.

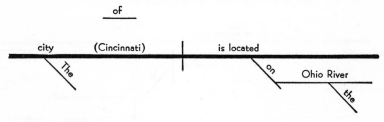

16. ELLIPSIS

Pp. 151. (An element omitted by ellipsis may be supplied. Or, if preferred, elements omitted may be indicated by letters: *x, y, z.* Anything supplied should be placed in brackets. See also p. 409.)

I spent Christmas at my mother's. [That is, "I spent Christmas at my mother's house."]

Either

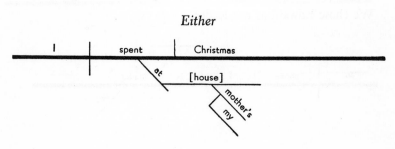

or

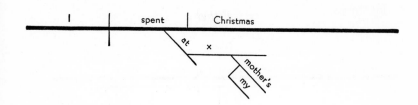

He is the kind of boy a father can be proud of. [That is, "He is the kind of boy whom a father can be proud of."]

Either

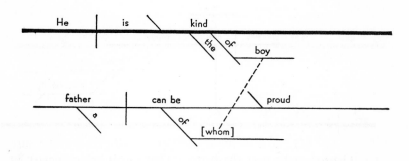

or

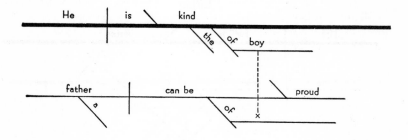

I see you are ready to come to terms. [That is, "I see that you are ready to come to terms."]

Either

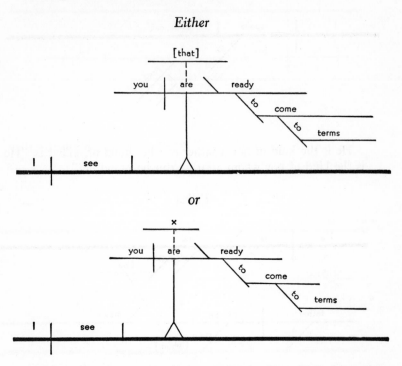

or

The sooner he goes the better. [That is, "In which degree he goes sooner in that degree it will be better." For the adverbial clause see p. 407; for the correlatives *the . . . the* see p. 395 f.]

Either

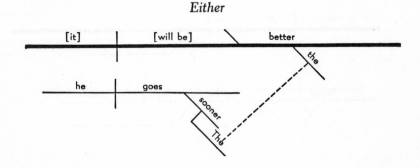

or

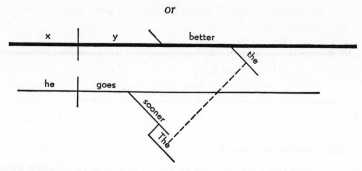

He likes her better than me. [That is, "He likes her better than he likes me."]

Either

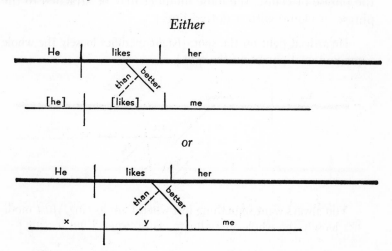

or

He likes her better than I. [That is, "He likes her better than I like her."]

Either

or

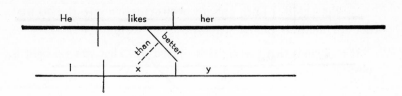

17. LOOSE MODIFIER

(In the case of a modifier that seems to modify loosely a whole phrase or clause rather than any particular word in the phrase or clause, the loose modifier may be attached to the phrase or clause with a dotted line.)

He arrived right on the spot. [*Right* modifies loosely the whole prepositional phrase *on the spot.*]

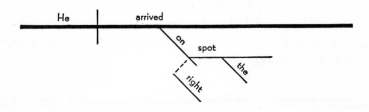

You always want something just when I am leaving. [*Just* modifies loosely the whole subordinate clause *when I am leaving.*]

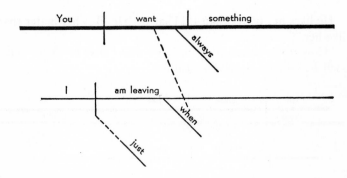

18. INVERTED ORDER

Pp. 156 ff. (Turn any inverted sentence into the normal order for analysis before attempting to diagram it.)

It is obvious that you are right. [That is, "That you are right is obvious."]

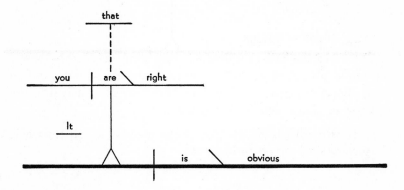

A whole pie he devoured at one sitting. [That is, "He devoured a whole pie at one sitting."]

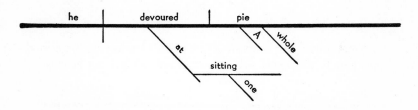

How many tickets did your club sell? [That is, "Your club did sell how many tickets?"]

Whom do you wish to speak to? [That is, "You do wish to speak to whom?"]

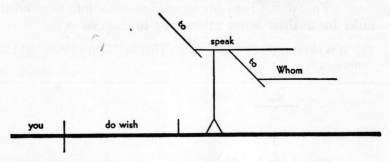

Index

A (*an*), article, 6, 200 footnote, 324 f.
A (=*on*), as a preposition, 61 footnote, 314, 325, 352
About, before an infinitive, 69, 277
Abridged adverbial clause, 189
Absolute constructions, 138 ff.
  adverb, 105
  adverbial clause, 183
  diagrams, 412 ff.
  exclamations, interjections, 141
  exercises, 143 f.
  gerund, 64 f.
  infinitive phrase or clause, 74, 139 f.
  main and subordinate clauses, 140 f.
  nominative absolute, 61 ff., 139
  noun in direct address, 34, 141, 257 Note
  parenthetical element, 142
  participle, 308 Note 2
  prepositional phrase, 118
  transitional element, 141 f.
Abstract and concrete nouns, 200
Accidence, 3
Active voice, 42 f., 247 f.
Additive and restrictive clauses, 175 ff.
Adjectival clauses, 87 ff., 169 ff.
  attribute and appositive, 175 ff.
  connective unexpressed, 171 f.
  diagrams, 402 ff.
  exercises, 177 ff.
  functional connectives introducing, 170 ff.
  functions of, 173 f.
  noun *vs.* adjective clause, 167 f. Note, 174 f.
  punctuation of, 176 footnote
  relative adjective introducing, 172
  relative adverb introducing, 172 f.
  relative pronoun introducing, 170 ff.
  that, introducing, 171 Note
Adjectival phrase, 88
Adjectives, 6, 87 ff., 322 ff.
  adverb as, 95, 109
  appositive, 90 f.
  articles, 6, 200 footnote, 324 f.
  as other parts of speech, 95 f., 135 f.
  attributive, 89 f.
  classes, 322 ff.
  comparison of, 327 ff.
  coordinate and cumulative, 93 f.
  definitive, 323 f.
  demonstrative, 230 f., 323, 326
  descriptive, 322
  ending in *ly,* 339
  exercises, 96 ff.
  indefinite, 323
  indefinite relative, 130
  infinitive as, 88, 323
  interrogative, 130 f., 326
  link verb with, 330 ff.
  noun as, 94, 135 f., 325 f.
  numerals, 323
  objective complement, 92 f., 333 f.
  other parts of speech as, 36, 94 f., 109, 120, 135 f., 325 ff.
  participle as, 60 f., 88
  possessive, 34, 324
  predicate, 88 footnote
  preposition as, 120
  prepositional phrase as, 88
  pronoun as, 221 f., 226, 228 ff., 326 f.

Adjectives (*continued*)
  proper, 322
  relation to noun, 89 ff.
  relative, 130, 326
  s added to form plural nouns, 96, 207
  subjective complement, 92 f., 330 ff.
  the before to form nouns, 95, 207, 324
  usages in, 330 ff.
  verb as, 95
  whatever, which, whichever, used as, 228
  whose, used as, 226
Adverbial clauses, 98 ff., 179 ff.
  abridged, 189
  absolute use of, 140 f., 183
  diagrams, 407 ff.
  exercises, 190 f.
  functional and simple connectives, introducing, 179 ff.
  functions of, 182 f.
  meanings of, 183 ff.
Adverbial objective, 106 footnote
Adverbial phrase, 98 f., 117 f.
Adverbs, 6, 98 ff., 337 ff.
  absolute use of, 104 f., 141 f.
  affirmation, adverb of, 104
  as other parts of speech, 95, 108 f., 114, 118 f., 136
  comparison of, 340 f.
  correlatives, 102 ff., 126 f., 181 f., 356
  exercises, 109 f.
  forms, 339 ff.
  indefinite relative, 131, 180
  independent, 104 ff., 141 f.
  infinitive as, 99
  interrogative, 101 f., 131 f., 165
  kinds, 337
  meanings, 337 ff.
  modifier of phrase or clause, 101, 115
  noun as, 95, 106 f., 136; noun in plural as, 107 Note
  objective complement as, 55 footnote
  other parts of speech as, 106 f., 136
  prepositional phrase as, 99
  relative, 102, 131, 172 f.
  transitional, 105, 141 f.
  usages in, 342 f.
  verb combined with, 55
  vs. prepositions, 108, 118 f.
Affirmation, adverb of, 104
After, introducing adjectival clause, 172 f.; introducing adverbial clause, 184
Agenda, number of, 253 f. Note
Agreement
  of pronoun with antecedent, 220 Note, 234 ff.
  of verb with subject, 250 ff.
  with expletive *there,* 148
All, number of, 254
All, both, 335
Almost, most, 343
Although, 127, 179, 187 f., 189
Although . . . yet (*still*), 126
Among, between, 352
And so, 360 f.
And, at beginning of sentence, 106 footnote; subjects joined by, 251
And who, 358
Anglicized plurals, 211 f.

Answers, omission in, 152 f.
Antecedent expressed and unexpressed, 163 Note, 234 ff.; contained in pronoun, 163 Note, 165 footnote
Any, as adjective, 233, 336
Any, each, some, 233
Any, either, neither, number of, 336
Anybody else's, anyone else's, 232 f., 335
Apostrophe, spelling with, 214 ff.
Appear, link verb, 330 f.
Appositive, 34, 90 f.
 adjective, 90 f.
 clause as, 167
 of phrase, 346
Articles, 6, 323 ff.
As
 before infinitive, 75
 expletive, 51, 149
 introducing adjectival clause, 170 f.
 introducing adverbial clause, 184 f., 188
 relative adverb, 181 f.
 relative pronoun, 170 f., 223 f., 226 f.
As . . . as, not so . . . as, 102 ff., 126, 181, 185 f., 359
As if, as though, 127, 185, 260, 362; before infinitive, 75
As well as, case of pronoun following, 241 f.
At any rate, 141
Attracted sequence, 274 f.
Attribute adjective, 89 f.
Attribute and appositive clauses, 175 f.
Auxiliaries, 39 f., 273, 275 ff.
 be, 40, 275 f., 300 f.
 can, may, could, might, 277 ff.
 dare, 278 f.
 do, 40, 275 f., 302
 have, 40, 275 f.
 infinitive with, 265, 276 ff., 317 f.
 must, 278
 need, 278 f.
 ought, 278, 280
 shall, will, 279, 281 ff.
 should, would, 283 f.
 usages in, 279 ff.

Bad, with link verb, 332 f.
Be
 auxiliary, 40, 275 f., 300 f.
 conjugation of, 295 ff.
 forms of, 249
 link verb, 43 ff., 330 f.
 notional verb, 40, 276
 omission of parts of, 153
Because, 127, 179, 188, 359
Because of, 349 f.
Become, link verb, 43 ff., 330 f.
Before, introducing adjectival clause, 172 f.; introducing adverbial clause, 184
Between, among, 352
Both, all, 335
Both . . . and, 126, 355
But
 as preposition, 351 f.
 as relative pronoun, 227
 at beginning of sentence, 106 footnote, 124 Note

Can, may, could, might, 277 ff.
Can but, cannot but, cannot help, 351 f. Note
Cardinal numerals, 323

Case
 after *as well as*, 241 f.
 complements, 239 ff.
 interrogative pronouns, 244 ff.
 in inverted order, 157 f.
 nominative, 213
 nouns, 213 ff.
 objective, 213 f.
 personal pronouns, 240 ff.
 possessive, 214 ff.
 pronoun after *than*, 361
 relative pronouns, 242 ff.
 subjective complement, 240 f.
Causative verb, 57
Cause (or reason), clauses of, 188
Certain, confident, sure, adverbial clauses modifying, 180 footnote
Clauses
 absolute use of, 140 f.
 additive and restrictive, 175 ff.
 adjectival, 88, 169 ff.
 adverbial, 99 f., 179 ff.
 dependent, 13 f., 160 ff.
 independent, 13 f.
 infinitive, 70 f.
 it, referring to, 220
 main, 13 f.
 noun (substantive), 161 ff.
 subordinate, 13 f., 160 ff.
 which, referring to, 227 f.
Clause *vs.* phrase, 12 f.; exercises, 26 ff.
Cognate object, 35
Cognate verb, 57
Collective noun, 200 f., 253 f.
Come, link verb, 330 f.
Common gender, 201
Common noun, 199 f.
Comparative degree, 327 ff., 340 f.
Comparison
 adjectives, 327 ff.
 adverbs, 370 f.
 clauses of, 185 footnote
 omission in, 154
Complementary infinitive, 69 f.
Complements, 9, 35 f., 45 f.
 case of, 239 ff.
 diagrams, 372 ff.
 exercises, 77 ff.
 intransitive verbs, complements of, 51 ff.
 inverted order, 157
 transitive verbs, complements of, 45 ff.
Complete and incomplete predication, verbs of, 41 f.
Complete predicate, 11 f.
Complete subject, 11 f.
Complex-compound sentence, 18 Note
Complex sentence, 18
Compound expressions, 14 ff.
 diagrams, 371 f.
 exercises, 28
Compound personal pronoun, 222 f.
Compound sentence, 16 f.
Compounds, plural of, 208 f.
Concession, clauses of, 187 f.
Concrete and abstract nouns, 200
Condition, clauses of, 186 f.
Conjugation
 emphatic, 302
 progressive, 301 f.
 simple, 295 ff.

Conjunctions, 7, 123 ff., 161 ff., 354 ff.
  coordinating, 7, 123 f., 354 f.
  correlative, 126 f., 355
  diagrams, 389 ff.
  exercises, 132 f.
  for, 123 footnote
  functional, 124 f., 128 ff., 162 ff., 354 f.
  ideas expressed by, 356 f.
  meanings, 357
  misplaced, 357 f.
  omission of, 154, 162 Note, 358
  phrasal, 356
  subordinating, 7, 124 ff., 127 f., 161 ff.
  usages in, 357 ff.
  See also Adjectival clauses, Adverbial clauses, and Noun clauses
Conjunctive adverb, 105 footnote
Connectives. *See* Conjunctions
Consequently, transitional adverb, 105
Coordinate and cumulative adjectives, 93 f.
Coordinating conjunctions, 7, 123 f., 354 f.; at beginning of sentence, 106 footnote, 124 Note
Copula, copulative verb, 45 ff., 330 ff.
Correlative adverbs, 102 ff., 126 f., 181 f., 356
Correlative conjunctions, 126 f., 355; misplaced, 357 f.

Dangling constructions
  abridged adverbial clause, 189 Note
  gerund, 310 f.
  infinitive, 318 f.
  participle, 306 ff.
Dare, as auxiliary, 278 f.
Data, number of, 253 f. Note
Declarative sentence, 19
Declension, of nouns, 201 ff.; of pronouns, 218 ff.
Defective verb, 58
Definite relatives and indefinite relatives, distinguished, 129 Note, 163 Note
Definite article, *the,* 6, 323 f.
Definitive adjectives, 323 ff.
Degree, adverb of, 338; clause of, 185 f.
Degrees of comparison, of adjectives, 337 f.; of adverbs, 340 f.
Demonstrative adjectives, 230 f., 323
Demonstrative pronouns, 230 f., 236, 326; *so, such* as demonstratives, 230; *that,* subject of *is,* 231
Dependent clause, 13 f., 160 ff.
Descriptive adjectives, 322
Diagrams, 369 ff.
  absolute constructions, 412 ff.
  adjectival clauses, 402 ff.
  adverbial clauses, 407 ff.
  appositional items, 402
  complements, 372 ff.
  compound elements, 371 f.
  connectives (conjunctions), 387 ff.
  correlative adverbs, 395 f.
  ellipsis, 420 ff.
  expletives, 415 ff.
  gerund, 377 ff.
  infinitive, 379 ff.
  inverted order, 425 f.
  loose modifiers, 424
  nominative absolute, 412
  noun clauses, 397 ff.
  participle, 376 f.

Diagrams (*continued*)
  prepositional phrases, 371
  shifts, 411
  simple sentence, 370 ff.
  verbals, 376 ff.
Diagrams in grammatical analysis, 369 f.
Different than, 350
Direct address, 34, 141
Direct discourse, 274 footnote
Direct object, 35, 45 f.; clause as, 166
Direct question, 163 ff.
Discourse, written *vs.* spoken, 246 Note
Do
  auxiliary, 40, 275 f., 302
  forms of, 249
  notional verb, 275 f.
Double genitive. *See* Double possessive
Double object, 35, 48 f.; clause as, 167
Double possessive, 113 Note, 345 f.
Doubt that, doubt whether, 363
Due to, owing to, 349

Each
  as adjective, 233, 336
  number of, 238 f.
  pronoun in reference, 238 f.
Each, every, 336
Each other, 232 f.
Either, neither, any, 336
Either . . . or, 126, 358 f.
Ellipsis, 151 ff.
  adverbial clause abridged, 153, 189 f.
  be, omission of forms of, 153
  comparisons, omissions in, 154
  connectives, omission of, 154, 171 f., 361
  diagrams, 420 ff.
  exercises, 155 f.
  noun, omission of, 153
  object of preposition, omission of, 115
  parallel construction, omissions in, 154
  preposition, omission of, 348
  questions, omissions in, 152 f.
  relative pronoun, omission of, 153, 171 f.
  subject, omission of, 152
  verb, omission of, 152 f.
Else, else's, 232 f., 335
Emphatic conjugation, 302
Emphatic use of compound personal pronoun, 223
en, plurals ending in, 205
Equivalent names for grammatical terms, 20 ff.
Essential subject and predicate, 11 f.
Even if, 187 f.
Every, pronoun in reference, 238 f.
Except, without, 350 f.
Exclamations, interjections, nouns in direct address, used absolutely, 141
Exercises
  absolute constructions, 143 f.
  adjectival clauses, 177 ff.
  adjectives, 96 ff.
  adverbial clauses, 190 f.
  adverbs, 109 ff.
  clauses and phrases, 26 ff.
  complements. 77 ff.
  compound expressions, 28
  conjunctions, 132 f.
  ellipsis, 155 f.
  expletives, 150 f.
  gerunds, 81 f.

Exercises (*continued*)
  infinitives, 82 f.
  inverted order, 158 f.
  main and subordinate clauses, 28 ff.
  modifiers, 25 f.
  noun clauses, 168 f.
  nouns and pronouns, 38 f.
  participles, 80 f.
  prepositions, 122 f.
  sentences and fragments, 22 ff.
  sentences, simple, compound, complex, 30 ff., 191 ff.
  shifts, 137 f.
  subject and predicate, 24 f.
  verbals, 80 ff.
  verbs, 76 ff.
Expletives, 43 f., 67, 144 ff., 166
  as, 51, 149
  diagrams, 415 ff.
  exercises, 150 f.
  for, 51, 72 f., 148 f.
  in inverted order, 156
  it, 67, 145 f., 166, 220 f.
  of, 149
  or, 149, 364
  there, 43 f., 146 f.
  with finite verb, 145 f.
  with infinitive, 67
  with participle, 147

f, fe, plural of nouns ending in, 204 f.
Factitive verb, 49 footnote
Feel, link verb, 331 f.; *of*, used with, 349 Note
Feminine gender, 201 ff.
Few, little, 334
Finite verb, 40 f.
  expletive with, 145 f.
  subject of, 34
For
  at beginning of sentence, 106 footnote, 124 Note
  coordinating conjunction, 123 footnote
  expletive, 51, 72 f., 148 f.
  introducing infinitive clause, 72 f.
  preposition, 73 Note
Foreign terms, plurals of, 210 ff.
From after *different*, 350
Functional connectives, 124 ff., 128 ff., 162 ff., 170 ff., 179 ff.
  introducing adjectival clauses, 170 ff.
  introducing adverbial clauses, 179 ff.
  introducing noun clauses, 162 ff.
Functions of parts of speech, 33 ff.
Functions of subordinate clauses
  adjectival, 173 f.
  adverbial, 182 f.
  noun, 166 ff.
Further, 141
Future perfect tense, 266 f.
Future tense, 265, 281 ff.
Futurity, verb methods of suggesting, 265, 277 ff.

Gender, of nouns, 201 ff.; of pronouns, 203 Note, 237 ff.
Genitive case, 214 footnote
Gerund, 40 f., 63 ff., 309 ff.
  a (=*on*), 61 footnote, 314, 352
  absolute use of, 64 f.

Gerund (*continued*)
  adjective, used as, 94, 315
  adverb, used as, 314
  dangling, 310 f.
  diagrams, 377 ff.
  exercises, 81 ff.
  forms of, 268
  object of preposition, 114
  phrase, 12 f., 63
  subjective complement with, 312
  tense of, 268 ff.
  usages in, 310 ff.
  uses of, 309 f.
  vs. noun, 310
  vs. participial construction, 312 ff.
Get, link verb, 331; to form passive voice, 248
Go, link verb, 330 f.
Going, before infinitive, 227
Good, with link verb, 332 f.
Grammar, definition of, 3
Grammar of subordinate clauses, 160 ff.
Grammatical terms sometimes confused, 20 ff.
Grammatical types of sentences, 16 ff.
  complex, 18
  complex-compound, 18 Note
  compound, 16 f.
  simple, 16
Grow, link verb, 330 f.

Had, in clause of condition, 187
Had ought, 280 f.
Half, number of, 254; as adjective, 335
Hard, hardly, 340
Hardly, scarcely, 343
Have
  as auxiliary, 40, 275 f.
  as notional verb, 40, 275 f.
  forms of, 249
He, used indefinitely, 233 f.
Hence, transitional adverb, 105, 141
Historical present, 263
How, adverb, 101 f.
  introducing infinitive phrase, 66 f.
  introducing noun clause, 164 f.
However, transitional adverb, 105

Idiom, preposition demanded by, 346 f.
If, 127, 161 f., 179, 186 f., 189
If . . . then, 126
If, whether, 360
Ill, with link verb, 332 f.
Imperative mood, 256 f.
Imperative sentence, 19 Note, 256 f.
Impersonal *it*, 58, 219 ff.
Impersonal verb, 58
Inasmuch as, 188
In back of, in front of, 348
In case, 187, 362 f.
Incomplete predication, verb of, 41 f.
Indeed, 141
Indefinite adjective, 323
Indefinite article, 324 f.
Indefinite *it*, 219 ff.
Indefinite pronoun, 231 ff., 236 ff., 252
Indefinite relative adjective, 130, 164
Indefinite relative adverb, 131, 164 f., 180 f.
Indefinite relative pronoun, 128 f., 162 f.
Indefinite relatives and definite relatives, distinction, 129 Note, 163 Note

Indefinite relatives and interrogatives, distinction, 129 Note
Independent adverb, 104
Independent clause, 13 f.
Indicative mood, 256
Indirect discourse, 274 footnote
Indirect object, 35, 47 f.; clause as, 166; retained, 36, 53 f.
Indirect question, 163 ff.
In fact, 141
Infinitives, 40 f., 65 ff., 315 ff.
  absolute use of, 74, 139 f.
  adjectival, 67 f., 88
  adverbial, 68 f., 99
  as, preceding, 75
  as if, preceding, 75
  auxiliaries with, 317 f.
  clause, 70 ff.
  complementary, 69 f.
  dangling, 318 f.
  diagrams, 379 ff.
  exercises, 82 ff.
  for, introducing, 72 f.
  forms of, 268 f.
  how, when, where, which, what, whom, introducing, 66 f.
  in inverted order, 157
  it, with, 67
  miscellaneous constructions, 74 f.
  noun, 65 ff.
  object of preposition, 316 f.
  passive voice with, 73 f.
  phrase, 12 f., 65
  simple, 72, 315 ff.
  split, 320 f.
  subject of, 70 ff., 240 ff.
  subjective complement with, 240 ff., 319 f.
  tense of, 268 ff.
  than, preceding, 74 f.
  to, sign of, 70
  usages in, 318 ff.
  uses of, 317 f.
Inflections
  nouns, 201 ff.
  pronouns, 218 ff.
  verbs, 247 ff., 284 ff.
In order that, 127, 179, 188 f.
Inserted expression, *they thought,* etc., 244 ff.
Intensive use of compound personal pronoun, 223
Interjections, 7, 141, 257, 365 f.
Interrogative adjective, 130 f., 164, 326
Interrogative adverb, 101 f., 131 f., 165
Interrogative pronoun, 129 f., 163 f., 228 ff., 235 f., 244 ff.
  agreement 237
  as adjective, 229
  case of, 244 ff.
  introducing noun clause, 163 f.
Interrogative sentence, 19 f.
Interrogatives and indefinite relatives, distinction, 129 f. Note
Intransitive verb, 42; complements of, 51 ff.
Inverted order, 156 ff.
  complements, 157
  diagrams, 425 f.
  exercises, 158 f.
  expletives, 156

Inverted order (*continued*)
  infinitive and prepositional phrases, 157
  questions, 157 f.
  subordinate clauses, 157 f.
Irregular and regular verbs, 285 ff.
Irregular comparison of adjectives, 330; of adverbs, 341
It, 67, 145 f., 219 ff.
  expletive, 67, 145 f., 220 f.
  indefinite, 219 ff.
  infinitive with, 67
  personal pronoun, 219 f.
  referring to phrase or clause, 220
Its, possessive pronoun, 221

Iust as, 184

Latin comparative, *inferior to,* etc., 330
Lay, lie, 294
Least, less, in comparison of adjectives, 329 f.; of adverbs, 340 ff.
Lest (=*that not*), 188 f., 360
Like, as preposition, 119 f.; as conjunction, 364
Link verb, 45 ff.; with adjective, 330 ff.
Little, few, 334
Look, link verb, 331 f.
Loose modifiers, 104 f., 141 f., 183; diagrams, 424

Main and subordinate clauses, 13 f.
  absolute use of, 140 f., 183
  exercises, 28 ff.
Manner, adverb of, 338; clause of, 185
Many a, such a, what a, 324 f.
Masculine gender, 201 ff.
May, can, usages in, 279 f.
May, might, as auxiliaries, 277 f.
May, might, shall, should, will, would, used in place of subjunctive, 260 f.
Me, myself, 223
Mine, yours, 221 f.
Misplaced connective, 357 f.
Mode. *See* Mood
Modifiers, 10
  exercises, 25 f.
  of clauses and phrases, 101
Modify, meaning of, 6 Note
Mood, 256 ff.
  imperative, 256 f.
  indicative, 256
  subjunctive, 257 ff.
More, most, in comparison of adjectives, 329 f.; of adverbs, 340 f.
Moreover, transitional adverb, 105
Most, almost, 343
Must, 273 Note, 278

Name, personified, 199
Names, proper, plurals of, 209; possessives of, 216
Names for grammatical constructions often confused, 20 ff.
Natural sequence, 273 f.
Near, as preposition, 119 f.
Near, nearly, 342
Need, as auxiliary, 278 f.
Negation, adverb of, 104

Neither, either, any, 336
Neither . . . nor, 126, 358 f.
Neuter gender, 201
Nevertheless, transitional adverb, 105, 141
No, as an adverb, 104
No . . . nor or *or*, 359
Nobody else's, no one else's, 215 f., 232 f.
Nominative absolute, 34, 61 ff., 139
Nominative case, 213, 239 ff.
Nominative or objective, *whose* as, 246
Nominative, predicate, 51 footnote
None, number of, 252
Nonfinite verbs (verbals), 40 f., 58 ff., 303 ff.
Nonrestrictive (additive) and restrictive clauses, 175 ff.
Nor, at beginning of sentence, 106 footnote, 124 Note; joining subjects, 251
Notional verb, 39 f.; *be, do, have*, as, 40, 275 f.
Not only . . . but also, 126
Not so . . . as, as . . . as, 102 f., 126, 181 f., 185 f., 356
Notwithstanding, as subordinating conjunction and as transitional adverb, 125 Note
Noun (substantive) clauses, 37 f., 161 ff.
  adjectival *vs.* noun, 167 Note, 174 f.
  diagrams, 397 ff.
  exercises, 168 f.
  functional connectives introducing, 162 ff.
  functions of, 166 ff.
  simple subordinating conjunction introducing, 161 f.
Noun phrase, 37
Nouns, 5, 34 ff., 199 ff.
  adjunct, 326 footnote
  absolute use of, 34, 61 f., 141
  abstract and concrete, 200
  adjectival use, 36, 94, 135 f., 325 f.
  adverbial use, 36, 95, 136
  case, 213 ff.
  collective, 200 f.
  common and proper, 199 f.
  compounded with pronoun, 241
  direct address, 34, 141
  exercises, 38 f.
  functions of, 34 ff.
  gender, 201 ff.
  infinitive as, 65 ff.
  inflections, 201 ff.
  number, 203 ff.
  object of preposition, 34
  omission of, 153
  other parts of speech as, 36, 95 f., 108 f., 135 f.
  participle as, 306
  plurals of, 203 ff.
  possessives of, 214 ff., 325
  prepositional phrase as, 118
  properties of, 201 ff.
  relation to adjective, 89 ff.
  verb and noun, 36, 135
Now, 104
Number, gender, person, agreement of pronouns in, 237 ff., 249
Number, singular and plural, 254 f.
Number of
  nouns, 203 ff.
  pronouns, 237 ff.
  verbs, 248 ff.

Numbers, letters, symbols, plural of, 210
Numerals, 323

o, plural of nouns ending in, 204
O and *oh*, 365 f.
Object
  cognate, 35, 46 Note
  direct, 35, 45 f.
  double, 35, 48 f.
  indirect, 35, 47 f.
  objective complement, 35, 49 ff.
  of a preposition, 34, 113 ff., 243 f., 245, 345 f.
  retained, 36, 53 f.
  understood, 115, 153
Objective case, 213 f., 239 ff.
Objective complement, 35, 49 ff.
  adjective as, 92 f., 333 f.
  adverb as, 55 footnote
  as, for, introducing, 51
  clause as, 93 Note, 167
  participle as, 61
  prepositional phrase as, 116
  retained, 53 footnote
Object of preposition, 34, 113 f., 243 f., 245, 345 f.
  clause as, 167
  position of, 114 f.
  prepositional phrase, 111 f.
  understood, 115, 153
Of
  as expletive, 149
  superfluous use of, 349 Note
  with possessive, 345 f.
Of-phrase used as appositive, 346
Omission of conjunction in a comparison, 358
Omissions. *See* Ellipsis
Omitted preposition, 348
One, problem of reference, 239
One's, other's, 232
One's self, oneself, 232
One another, 233
One, other, as indefinite pronouns, 232, 239
Only, 339
Or
  as expletive, 149, 364
  at beginning of sentence, 106 footnote, 124 Note
  joining subjects, 251
Ordinal numbers, 323
Other parts of speech as
  adjectives, 94 f., 120, 325 ff.
  adverbs, 106 f.
  nouns, 36, 95 f., 108
  prepositions, 118 f.
  See also Shifts
Ought, 273 Note, 278, 280
Owing to, due to, 349

Parallel construction, omission in, 154
Parenthetical element, 142
Participial phrase, 88
Participle *vs.* gerund construction, 312 ff.
Participles, 12 f., 40 f., 59 ff., 303 ff.
  absolute use of, 61 ff., 139, 308 Note 2
  as adjective, 60 f., 304
  as noun, 306
  as preposition, 121, 306

Participles (*continued*)
  dangling, 306 ff.
  diagrams, 376 f.
  exercises, 80 ff.
  expletive with, 147
  forms of, 267 f.
  subjective complement with, 308
  tense of, 267 ff.
  usages in, 306 ff.
  uses of, 303 ff.
  very, used with, 308 f.
  vs. gerund, 312 ff.
Parts of speech, 5 ff., 33 ff.
Passive verb, infinitive with, 73 f.; subjective complement after, 52 f.
Passive voice, 42 f., 73 f., 247 f., 300 f.
Past participle, used as adjective, 268 footnote, 285 ff.
Past perfect tense, 266
Past tense, 264
Person, of pronouns, 237 ff.; of verbs, 248
Personal pronouns, 218 ff.
  case, 218 f., 240 ff.
  compound, 222 f.
  forms of, 218 f.
  possessive of, 221 f.
  prospective reference with, 222
Phrasal conjunction, 356
Phrasal preposition, 112 f., 344 f.
Phrase
  adjectival, 59 ff., 67 f., 88
  adverbial, 67, 99
  gerund, 12 f., 63 ff.
  infinitive, 12 f., 67 ff., 88, 99
  it, referring to, 220
  noun (substantive), 63 f., 65 ff.
  participial, 12 f., 59 ff., 88
  prepositional, 12 f., 88, 99
Phrase and clause, 12 f.; exercises, 26 ff.
Place, adverb of, 337 f.; adverbial clause of, 187 f.
Pluperfect tense, 261
Plurals of
  foreign terms, 210 ff.
  letters, numbers, symbols, words, 210
  nouns, 203 ff.
  proper names, 209
  titles, 209 f.
Position of object of preposition, 114 f.
Positive degree, of adjectives, 327 ff.; of adverbs, 340 f.
Possessive
  as adjectival modifier, 34, 221 f.
  as noun, 35, 217, 221 f.
  case, 214 ff.
  object of preposition, 113 f., 345 f.
  personal pronoun, spelling of, 221
  pronoun, 221 f., 326
  relative pronoun, 224, 226
  whose used as, 226
Potential mood, 256 footnote
Predicate, 8 ff.
  adjective, 92 f.
  complete, 11
  essential, 11
  nominative, 51 footnote
  simple, 11
  subject and, 8 ff.

Predication, verbs of complete and incomplete, 41 f.
Prefer . . . rather than, 361
Prepositional phrases, 12 f., 88, 99, 111 ff.
  absolute use of, 118
  as adjectival modifier, 88, 116
  as adverbial modifier, 99, 117
  as noun (substantive), 118
  as objective complement, 116
  as subjective complement, 116
  diagrams, 371
  exercises, 122 f.
  functions of, 116 f.
  inverted order, 157
  modified by adverb, 115
  object of preposition, 113 ff.
Prepositions, 7, 111 ff., 344 ff.
  adjective as object, 114
  adverb as object, 114
  and adverbs, 108, 118 f.
  and other parts of speech, 118 ff.
  as adjective, 120
  at end of statement, 352 f.
  but as, 351 f.
  clause as object, 114, 167
  exercises, 122 f.
  for, 73 Note
  gerund as object, 114
  idiom demanded, 346 f.
  infinitive as object, 114
  in inverted order, 157
  kinds, 344 f.
  object of, 34, 113 ff., 243 ff., 345
  object of, understood, 115
  omitted, 348
  other parts of speech as, 118 ff.
  participle as, 121
  phrasal, 112 f., 344 f.
  position of object, 114 f.
  possessive as object, 113 f.
  prepositional phrase as object, 114
  retained, 121
  superfluous, 348 f.
  suspended constructions, 348
  usages in, 345 ff.
  verb combined with, 55 f.
Present perfect tense, 265 f.
Present tense, 261 ff.
Preterit, 261
Principal clause, 13 f.
Principal parts of verb, 285 ff.
Progressive conjugation, 301 f.
Pronominal adjective, 228, 230 f., 326 f.
Pronouns, 6, 33 ff., 218 ff.
  agreement, 234 ff.
  as adjective, 228 ff., 326 f.
  case, 239 ff.
  classes of, 218 ff.
  compounded with substantive, case of, 241
  compound personal, 222 f.
  compound relative, 224
  declension, 218 ff.
  demonstrative, 230 f., 236, 326
  emphatic, 223
  exercises, 38 f.
  gender, 237 ff.
  indefinite, 231 ff., 236 ff.
  indefinite relative, 128 f., 162 f.
  inflections, 218 ff.

Pronouns (*continued*)
  intensive, 223
  interrogative, 129 f., 163 f., 228 ff., 235 f., 244 ff.
  number, 237 ff.
  person, 237 ff.
  personal, 218 ff., 240 ff.
  possessive, 218 f., 221 f.
  reference, 234 ff.
  reflexive, 222 f.
  relative, 128, 170 ff., 223 ff., 234 f., 237, 242 ff.
  than, preceding, 361
  usages in, 219 ff.
Proper adjective, 322
Proper and common nouns, 199 f.
Proper names, plurals of, 209; possessives of, 216
Properties, of nouns, 201 ff.; of pronouns, 237 ff.; of verbs, 247 ff.
Prospective reference with pronouns, 222
Prove, link verb, 331
Provided, as conjunction, 187, 362 f.
Providing, as conjunction, 362 f.
Punctuation, 91 Note, 105 Note 1, 176 footnote
Purpose, clause of, 188 f.

Quaker usage, *thee*, etc., 218 footnote
Question, direct and indirect, 129 f., 235 f.
Questions, omissions in, 152 f.; inverted order, 157 f.

Raise, rise, 294 f.
Reason, clause of, 188
Reason is because, 359
Reciprocal pronouns, 232 f.
Redundant verb, 58
Reference, with pronouns, 219 ff., 225, 234 ff.; to phrase or clause, 220, 227
Reflexive pronoun, 222 f.
Regular and irregular verbs, 285 ff.
Relative adjective, 130, 172; *whose, which*, used as, 172
Relative adverb, 102, 131, 172 f.
Relative pronoun, 128, 170 ff., 223 ff., 326
  agreement, 237, 252 f.
  as, used as, 170, 226 f.
  but, used as, 227
  case, 242 ff.
  forms, 224
  indefinite relative, distinction, 129 Note, 163 Note
  omitted by ellipsis, 153, 224 f.
  possessive of, 224, 226
  that, adverbial use in adjective clause, 225 Note
  that, who, which, distinctions, 225
  usages, 224 ff.
  without antecedent, 226 ff.
Relative time of verbals, 269 ff.
Remain, link verb, 331
Restrictive and additive clauses, 175 ff.
Result, clause of, 189
Retained constructions
  clause as, 167
  object, direct and indirect, 36, 53 f.
  objective complement, 53 footnote
  preposition, 121

Rhetorical types of sentences, 19 f.
  declarative, 19
  imperative, 19 Note, 256 f.
  interrogative, 19 f.

s, added to adjective to form plural noun, 96
Same, as following, 226 f.
Scarcely, hardly, 343
See, conjugation of, 298 ff.
Seem, link verb, 330 f.
Semicolon, use of, 105 Note 1
Sentence, 3 f., 8 ff.
  complex, 18
  complex-compound, 18 Note
  compound, 16 f.
  exercises, 30 ff.
  grammatical types of, 16 ff.
  rhetorical types of, 19 f.
  simple, 16
Sentences and fragments, 4 footnote; exercises, 22 ff.
Sequence of tenses, 273 ff.
Set, sit, 295
Shall, will, should, would, usages, 281 ff.; used in place of subjunctive, 260 f.
Shifts, 8, 134 ff.; diagrams, 411; exercises, 137 f.
Shortened adverb, 339 f.
Should, in clause of condition, 187
Should, would, 283 f.
Simple conjugation, 295 ff.
Simple infinitive, 72
Simple predicate, 11
Simple sentence, 16; diagrams, 370 ff.
Simple subject, 11 f.
Simple subordinating conjunctions, 124 f., 161 f., 179 f., 355
  introducing adverbial clauses, 179 f.
  introducing noun clauses, 161 f.
Simple verb, 11 f., 39
Since, 127, 184, 188
Since . . . therefore, 126
Singular number. *See* Number
Slow, slowly, 339 f.
Smell, link verb, 331 f.; *of* used with, 349 Note
So, 230, 360 footnote
So . . . as, 102 f., 126, 181, 356
So that, 127, 179, 188 f.
Some, any, each, 233
Sound, link verb, 331 f.
Speech, parts of, 5 ff., 33 ff.
Spelling plural, 203 ff.; possessive, 214 ff.
Split infinitive, 320 f.
Spoken discourse *vs.* written discourse, 246 Note
Stay, link verb, 331
Strong and weak verbs, 285 footnote
Subject
  clause as, 166
  of finite verb, 34
  of infinitive, 34, 241, 243
  omitted, 152
Subject and predicate, 8 ff.; exercises, 24 f.
Subject and subjective complement, agreement, 250
Subjective complement, 36, 51 ff., 92 f.
  adjective as, 92 f.
  after passive verb, 52 f., 333

Subjective complement (*continued*)
case of, 240 f.
clause as, 93 Note, 166 f.
gerund with, 312
infinitive with, 240 f., 242 f.
participle as, 61
participle with, 308
prepositional phrase as, 53, 116
test for case of pronoun, 241 Note
Subjunctive mood, 257 ff.
Subordinate clauses, 13 f., 160 ff.
adjectival, 88, 169 ff.
adverbial, 99 f., 179 ff.
inverted order, 157 f.
noun (substantive), 37 f., 161 ff.
omission of verb in, 153
Subordinate and main clauses used absolutely, 140 f.
Subordinating conjunction, 124 ff., 161 f., 179 ff.
functional, 124 f., 162 ff., 180 ff.
introducing adjectival clause, 170 ff.
introducing adverbial clause, 179 ff.
introducing noun clause, 161 ff.
simple, 124 f., 161 f., 179 f.
Subordinating correlatives, 355
Substantive. *See* Noun; *see* Pronoun
Substantive clause. *See* Noun clause
Such, 226, 230
Such a, many a, what a, 324 f.
Such as, ellipsis with, 154 f., 242
Superfluous preposition, 348 f.
Superlative degree, of adjective, 327 ff.; of adverb, 340 f.
Supposing, as conjunction, 187, 362 f.
Sure, adverbial clause modifying, 180 footnote
Suspended prepositional construction, 348
Synopsis of a verb, 300 ff.
Syntax, 3

Taste, link verb, 331 f.; *of* used with, 349 Note
Tenses
auxiliaries, 272 f.
critical writings, usage in, 263
finite verbs, 261 ff.
gerund, 270 f.
historical present, 263
infinitive, 271 f.
participle, 269 f.
sequence, 273 ff.
universal truths, usage in, 263 f.
usages in, 262 ff.
Terms, grammatical, sometimes confused, 20 ff.
Than
after *different,* 350
case of pronoun following, 361
conjunction, 361
infinitive following, 74 f., 317
That
demonstrative, 230 f., 236, 323, 326
introducing adjectival clauses, 170 f.
introducing adverbial clauses, 179 f., 188 f.
introducing noun clauses, 161 f.
referring to persons, 225 footnote
relative pronoun, 128, 170 f., 175, 223 ff., 231
simple subordinating conjunction, 127, 161 f., 175, 179

That is, 231
That not (*lest*), 188 f., 360
That, who, which, distinctions, 225 f.
The
adverb, 103 f., 323 Note 2
article, 6, 323 ff.
capitalization in proper name, 200 Note
The . . . the, 102 ff., 126, 181, 185 f.
Thee, 218 footnote
Their, confused with *there,* 147 Note
There, adverb, 147 Note; expletive, 43 f., 146 ff.
Therefore, 105, 141
They, used indefinitely, 219, 233 f.
This, that, (these, those), demonstratives, 230 f., 236, 323, 326
Though, 127, 187 f.
Though . . . yet (*still*), 162
Time, adverb of, 337; clause of, 184
Title or word of relationship, 199 f.
Titles, plurals of, 209 f.
To, sign of infinitive, 65, 72, 315 ff.
Together with, in addition to, 250
Too, 141
Transitional elements, 105 f., 141 f., 364
Transitive verb, 42
Try and, 358
Turn, link verb, 331

Understood items. *See* Ellipsis
Unless, 127, 179, 187
Unlike, as preposition, 119 f.
Universal truths, tense of, 263 f.
Until, 184
Usages
adjectives, 330 ff.
adverbs, 342 f.
agreement, 234 ff., 250 ff.
auxiliaries, 279 ff.
compound personal pronouns, 222 f.
conjunctions, 357 ff.
demonstrative pronouns, 230 f.
gerunds, 310 ff.
imperative mood, 257
indefinite pronouns, 233 f.
infinitives, 318 ff.
interjections, 365 f.
interrogative pronouns, 229 f.
participles, 306 ff.
personal pronouns, 219 ff.
prepositions, 345 ff.
subjunctive mood, 258 ff.
tense, 262 ff.
Used, before infinitive, 69

Verbals (nonfinite verbs), 40 f., 58 ff., 267 ff., 303 ff.
diagrams, 376 ff.
exercises, 80 ff.
gerund, 40 f., 63 ff., 268 ff., 309 f.
infinitive, 40 f., 65 ff., 268 ff., 315 ff.
participle, 40 f., 59 ff., 267 ff., 303 ff.
tenses of, 267 ff.
uses of, 303 ff.
Verb + adverb combinations, 55
Verb + preposition combinations, 55 f.
Verb phrase, 12 f., 39
Verbs, 6, 9 f., 39 ff., 247 ff.
absolute, 56 f.

436   INDEX

Verbs (*continued*)
agreement, 250 ff.
as adjective, 95, 136
as noun, 135
auxiliaries, 39 f., 275 ff.
causative, 57
cognate, 57
complements of, 9 ff., 45 ff.
complete and incomplete predication, 41 f.
copula, copulative, 43 ff., 330 ff.
defective, 58
exercises, 76 f.
factitive, 49 footnote
finite, 40 f.
impersonal, 58
inflections, 284 ff.
intransitive, 42
link, 45 ff., 330 ff.
mood, 256 ff.
nonfinite (verbals), 40 f., 58 ff., 267 ff., 303 ff.
notional, 39 f.
number, 248 f.
omitted, 152 f.
person, 248
principal parts of, 285 ff.
properties of, 247 ff.
redundant, 58
regular and irregular, 285 ff.
simple, 39
strong and weak, 285 footnote
tense, 261 ff.
transitive, 42
voice, 42 f., 247 f., 333
Very, used with participle, 308 f.
Voice, 42 f., 247 f., 333

We, editorial use, 219; used indefinitely, 219, 233 f.
Weak and strong verbs, 285 footnote
Well, as adjective with link verb, 332 f.; as adverb, 104
What
adjectival use, 228
indefinite relative pronoun, 162 f., 228
interrogative pronoun, 163 f., 228 ff.
introducing infinitive phrase, 66 f.
introducing noun clause, 162 ff.
used with antecedent, 228 Note
Whatever
introducing direct question, 229
introducing noun clause, 130, 162 f.
used as adjective, 228
When
interrogative adverb, 101 f.
introducing adjectival clause, 102, 172 f.
introducing adverbial clause, 102, 180, 184, 189
introducing infinitive phrase, 66 f.
introducing noun clause, 102, 165 f.
When . . . then, 102 f., 126, 181
Whenever, 180, 184
Where
interrogative adverb, 101 f.
introducing adjectival clause, 172 f.
introducing adverbial clause, 180, 184
introducing infinitive phrase, 66 f.

Where (*continued*)
introducing noun clause, 164 f.
Where . . . there, 102 ff., 126, 181
Whereas, as subordinating conjunction and as transitional adverb, 125 Note
Wherever, 180, 184 f., 189
Whether, 161 f.
Whether, if, 360
Whether or not (no), 362
Which
adjectival use, 172, 228
introducing adjectival clause, 170 f.
introducing infinitive phrase, 66 f.
introducing noun clause, 163 f.
referring to phrase or clause, 227 f.
used as interrogative pronoun, 228 f.
used without antecedent, 227 f.
Which, whichever, whatever, used as adjectives, 228
Whichever
adjectival use, 228
indefinite relative pronoun, 162
introducing direct question, 229
While, used in sense of *though,* 187 f.; in abridged clause, 189
Who
introducing adjectival clause, 170 f.
introducing noun clause, 163 f.
used as interrogative pronoun, 163 f., 228 ff.
used without antecedent, 234 f.
Who, which, that, distinctions, 225
Who, which, clauses, punctuation of, 176 f.
Who else's, whose else, 215 f., 232 f.
Whoever
compound relative pronoun, 162 f., 224
introducing direct question, 229
introducing noun clause, 162 f.
used without antecedent, 234 f.
Whom, introducing infinitive phrase, 66 f.
Who's else, 233 Note
Whose
adjectival use, 226, 229
interrogative pronoun, 229
introducing adjectival clause, 172
introducing noun clause, 164
nominative or objective case, 246
possessive, with inanimate objects, 226 Note
Whosoever, introducing noun clause, 162 f.; used without antecedent, 234 f.
Why
absolute use, 104
interrogative adverb, 101 f.
introducing adjectival clause, 102, 172 f.
introducing noun clause, 102, 164 f.
Will, as auxiliary, 276; as notional verb, 276
Will, shall, usages, 281 ff.
Without, except, 350 f.
Worth, 120 Note
Would, should, usages, 283 f.
Written discourse *vs.* spoken discourse, 246 Note

y, plural of nouns ending in, 204
Ye, used for *the,* 323 footnote
Yes, adverb, 104
Yet, as coordinating conjunction, 123 footnote
You, yours, used indefinitely, 219, 233 f.
Yourself, yourselves, 223 Note